D1563366

Tribe, Race, History

The Johns Hopkins University Studies in Historical and Political Science
125th series (2007)

1. A. KATIE HARRIS, *From Muslim to Christian Granada:*
Inventing a City's Past in Early Modern Spain

2. DANIEL R. MANDELL, *Tribe, Race, History:*
Native Americans in Southern New England, 1780–1880

Tribe, Race, History

Native Americans in Southern New England,
1780–1880

DANIEL R. MANDELL

The Johns Hopkins University Press

Baltimore

The Johns Hopkins University Press
2715 North Charles Street
Baltimore, Maryland 21218-4363
www.press.jhu.edu

Library of Congress Cataloging-in-Publication Data
Mandell, Daniel R., 1956–
Tribe, race, history : Native Americans in southern New England, 1780–1880 /
Daniel R. Mandell.
p.   cm. — (The Johns Hopkins University studies in historical and political science)
Includes bibliographical references and index.
ISBN-13: 978-0-8018-8694-2 (hardcover : alk. paper)
ISBN-10: 0-8018-8694-5 (hardcover : alk. paper)
1. Indians of North America—New England—History. 2. Indians of North
America—New England—Ethnic identity. 3. White—Relations with Indians.
4. Blacks—Relations with Indians. 5. New England—History. 6. New England—
Ethnic relations. 7. New England—Race relations. I. Title.
E78.N5M36 2007
974'.03—dc22   2007013961

A catalog record for this book is available from the British Library.

Special discounts are available for bulk purchases of this book. For more information,
please contact Special Sales at 410-516-6936 or specialsales@press.jhu/edu.

For Barbara, finally

Contents

Illustrations and Tables

Acknowledgments

Over the past decade (and more), I have had a great deal of assistance in conceptualizing, researching, and writing this book. It began with a fellowship at Old Sturbridge Village in 1991, during which I first became interested in continuing the study of New England's Natives into the nineteenth century and found more sources that helped me write my first book on the eighteenth century. The first day I walked into Jack Larkin's office at OSV, he showed me a list of "people of color" in nineteenth-century Worcester County, and I recognized to my astonishment many family names from eighteenth-century Indian documents. Then there was the 1995 summer fellowship at the Massachusetts Historical Society, Center for the Study of New England History, during which I got to tell many stories about David, recently born, and enjoyed the weekly Thai lunches as well as the monthly seminars in early American history. One year later, the National Endowment of the Humanities awarded me a year-long research grant; this provided the time and funds that allowed me to gather notes and photocopies of a huge collection of documents from all three state archives and historical societies, to begin writing pieces, and in other ways taking a giant step toward completing the project.

During my first year at Truman State University, I received a faculty research grant that allowed me to return to the region that summer and (finally) plumb the archives on Nantucket and Martha's Vineyard. I was able to stay with friends during part of the trip: the Shermans helped (once again!) with a bed one night, a bike for the entire trip (thanks, Scott!), and a place to park my car while I was on the Vineyard, and David and Jean Betz gave me a room and their good company for two weeks while I traveled to various archives in the Boston area. Mary Beth Norton treated me to a wonderful meal of black sea bass while I was on the Vineyard. In July 2002, a Joyce Tracy Fellowship at the American Antiquarian Society allowed me to go through newspapers, periodicals, town histories, and juvenile literature—and to enjoy a wonderful month in scholarly fellowship at the AAS house. I also benefited from a stay at Schloss Rawson-Wolfe, enjoying the friendship of David Rawson, Susan Wolfe, and their cats. The Social Science Division at Truman State University provided funds for the map and images in the book, in addition to travel to many of the conferences where I presented pieces of this work.

Like other scholars, in researching this work I have depended on the knowledge and cheerful assistance of the staffs at many libraries, including Bruce Stark at the Connecticut State Archives; Barbara Austen at the Connecticut Historical Society; Keith Gorman at the Martha's Vineyard Historical Society; Tina Furado at the New Bedford Public Library; Jane Ward at the Phillips Library at the Peabody Essex Museum, Salem; and Jerry Anderson of the New England Historical Genealogical Society, who not only helped me with their Society for Propagating the Gospel Records but also provided his transcript of Frederick Baylies's 1823 census of Indians on Martha's Vineyard. Bill Keegan of Historical Consultants, LLC, drew Map 2 (several times!). Kelly Drake at Mystic Seaport graciously provided a copy of the Seaport's database of New London Crew Lists Index, 1803–1878. Also supportive were the staffs at Nantucket Historical Society, the Rhode Island State Archives, the Rhode Island Historical Society, and at courthouses in Dukes County, Middlesex County, Nantucket County, and Worcester County. Research librarians at several institutions have provided invaluable assistance over many projects, and I am grateful for these long-term relationships: Peter Drummey and his staff at the Massachusetts Historical Society; Joanne Chaison, Thomas Knoles, and many others at the American Antiquarian Society—and a special thanks to Laura Wascowicz for pointing me to the children's textbooks, which proved significant for chapter 5—and Michael Comeau and Martha Clark at the Massachusetts State Archives.

Writing a book on nineteenth-century New England while living in Missouri presented considerable challenges, many of which were surmounted with the help of others. The outstanding interlibrary loan staff at Truman State University managed to meet nearly every one of my requests for many old, rare, or microfilmed sources. Thank you. Mary Stubbs at the Kirksville Church of Latter-Day Saints helped me obtain microfilmed documents from the Mormon Family Library. Also ready and able to lend a hand from a distance were Cornelia King and James Green at the Library Company of Philadelphia; Rosemary Burns with the Mashpee Historical Society; Richard Ring at the John Carter Library, Brown University; and Barbara DeWolfe, Curator of Manuscripts, Clements Library, University of Michigan. Librarians who helped me obtain reproducible copies of images include Lou Stancari at the National Museum of the American Indian;

Robyn Christensen at the Worcester Historical Museum; Dana Costanza at the Martha's Vineyard Historical Society; and Carolyn Longworth at the Millicent Library, Fairhaven, Massachusetts. A special thanks to Andrew Pierce, genial genealogist, for giving tips about various documents, sending me a copy of the 1792 Mashpee census at Harvard College, and providing access to the massive Segel, Pierce Monterosso collection at Martha's Vineyard Historical Society. Jason Mancini at the Mashantucket Pequot Museum and Research Center provided his analysis of federal census schedule data and Indian overseer reports on the Mashantucket community during the 1830s and 1840s, information on Native and mixed neighborhoods in nearby towns, and access to their repository of local and state documents. My thanks to Doug Winiarski for information on the Society for Propagating the Gospel collections at the Phillips Library, which turned out to be extremely important. Also helpful were colleagues on e-mail listservs who provided important information on various questions ranging from sources to the length of school terms to the identity of E. B. Chace: Norris Burdette, Larry Cebula, Tom Clark, Clayton Cramer, Janet Davis, James Farrell, C. Joseph Genetin-Pilawa, Roland Goodbody, Rae Gould, Leon Jackson, Norman M. M. MacLeod, Pilar Mejia, Joanne Melish, Michael Oberg, Prairie Mary, George Price, Harald Prins, James Roache, John Shy, Eric Slauter, Liz Stevens, James Stewart, James Watkinson, Bridget Williams-Searle, Bob Wilson, and Natalie Zacek, and many others, including colleagues listed below.

I have had many opportunities to discuss sections of the work with colleagues at conferences and to benefit from their comments, ideas, and suggestions. An early version of chapter 3 was presented at the Seventh Annual Conference of the Omohundro Institute of Early American History and Culture, Glasgow, Scotland, 2001; a special thanks to commentator Christopher Tomlins. The arguments in chapter 1 were part of papers that I presented at the International Seminar on the History of the Atlantic World, Harvard University, August 2004; and the conference on "Class and Class Struggles in North America and the Atlantic World, 1500–1800," Montana, September 18, 2003. In both cases, the discussions about my paper and many others pointed to broader theoretical concerns and similar issues in the wider Atlantic world and the Americas—and in some ways the unique situation faced by Indians in southern New England. The participants in these two conferences are too many to name, but I thank them all. An early version of chapter 5 was presented to the Newberry Seminar in Early American History and Culture, February 20, 2003; the comments and questions of Frederick Hoxie, Stephen Foster, Michelle LeMaster, Eric Slauter, Susan Sleeper-Smith, and Alfred Young (among other participants) confirmed many of my ideas about the shifts in images of Indians and led me to reconsider others. Pieces of chapter 4 were presented at the Tenth Annual Omohundro Institute of Early American History and Culture Conference in Northampton, Massachusetts, June 2004; the Conference of the Society for Historians of the Early Republic in Providence, Rhode Island, July 2004; and the annual meeting of the American Society for Ethnohistory, Chicago, October 2004.

An expanded discussion of developments in Mashpee through 1835 (chapter 3) was presented at a conference sponsored by the Colonial Society of Massachusetts at Sturbridge Village in 2002. My thanks to John Tyler at the Society for helping this project along by including me in this outstanding meeting. This paper was published as "'We, as a tribe, will rule ourselves': Mashpee's Struggle for Autonomy, 1745–1840," in *Reinterpreting New England Indians and the Colonial Experience*, ed. Colin Calloway and Neal Salisbury (Boston: Colonial Society of Massachusetts, 2003). An early version of chapter 2 was published as "Shifting Boundaries of Race and Ethnicity: Indian-Black Intermarriage in Southern New England, 1760–1880," *Journal of American History* 85 (1998): 466–501. A revised version of the paper I presented at the Montana conference on class is slated to be published in *Class Matters: Early North America and the Atlantic World*, ed. Simon Middleton and Billy Smith (Philadelphia: University of Pennsylvania Press, 2007). Also, parts of the discussion on race and images of Indians in chapter 5 appeared in "*The Indian's Pedigree* (1794): Indians, Folklore, and Race in Southern New England," *William and Mary Quarterly*, 3rd ser., 61 (2004): 519–36.

Various colleagues have generously helped me in many ways with this project and other work, in addition to that described above, and I have benefited from their criticisms, praise, suggestions, and other assistance. Early versions of chapter 1 were reviewed by Christopher Clark, Larry Goldsmith, Grey Osterud, Jonathan Prude, Alfred Young, and several anonymous reviewers for the *William and Mary Quarterly*. Previous versions of chapter 4 were reviewed by Michael Holt, Daniel Howe, Johann Neem, and Doug Winiarski. Richard Brown, Colin Calloway, and Fred Mautner were kind enough to read and critique the entire draft manuscript. For many years I have benefited from the advice and friendship of John Brooke, Colin Calloway, Peter Hoffer, James and Lois Horton, Jack Larkin, Neal Salisbury, Alden Vaughan, and Laurie Weinstein. Other colleagues who were particularly helpful with aspects of this project included Jack Campisi, Christopher Grasso, Jill Lepore, Gloria Main, Kevin McBride, Mark Nicholas, Mary Beth Norton, Nate Philbrick, Harald Prins, Marcus Rediker, David Silverman, Caroline Sloat, John Wood Sweet, Len Travers, and Laurel Ulrich. Also helpful have been my colleagues at Truman, particularly Marc Becker, Mark

Hanley, Kiril Petkov, and Martha Rose. And because a person's work is inevitably cumulative, I should also thank those who have helped me with other projects: James Axtell, Emerson Baker, Kathleen Bragdon, Constance Crosby, Stephen Innes, Ann Marie Plane, and John Reid.

At Truman I have benefited from many things: research grants, an excellent interlibrary loan department, travel funds, friendly and helpful colleagues, and outstanding students, some of whom have worked for me as research assistants on various pieces of this work. Krista Garcia refined the 1800 Mashpee data and constructed the table on blood quantum in marriages and number of children. Elizabeth Lowe calculated the number and percentage of female-headed households in the Martha's Vineyard censuses from 1792, 1793, 1800, and 1850. Elizabeth Ryan and Matt McDuff searched various microfilm county court records and indices for cases involving Indians and people of color. In addition, these students and Sean Foley, Katie Gehrman, Timothy Ricker, Jason Savage, Jason Turk, Michelle Wright, and Ashley Young transcribed various census schedules. Angela Liquori and Amanda Murphy provided other kinds of assistance.

I began this project in 1992. At the time, this odyssey also involved only Barbara (and two cats). We were renting a small townhouse in Lincoln, Massachusetts, and I had just finished my Ph.D. and was headed for my first temporary teaching job in Indiana. I finish it as an associate professor at a liberal arts college in northeastern Missouri, with Barbara, David (12), Joshua (9), and six (other) cats. These changes make the completion of this project an important milestone and the crest of a difficult climb, and yet somehow somewhat less significant in the larger pattern of life. Barbara and the boys with good grace and spirit (the cats less so), have put up with my absence on research trips and at conferences for weeks or even months every year, and the way I occasionally vanish to jot down some new ideas or to get some writing accomplished. But they also remind me that there are more important things.

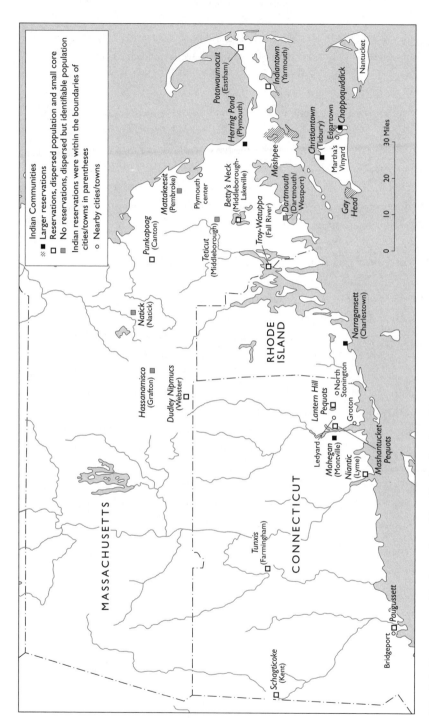

Map 1. Indian communities in southern New England, 1780–1880

Indian Communities
■ Larger reservations
▨ Reservations, dispersed population and small core
□ No reservations, dispersed but identifiable population
▨ Indian reservations were within the boundaries of cities/towns in parentheses
○ Nearby cities/towns

30 Miles

MASSACHUSETTS

Nantucket

Potawaumacut (Eastham)

Indiantown (Yarmouth)

Herring Pond (Plymouth)

Christiantown (Tisbury)

Chappaquiddick

Edgartown

Plymouth center

Mashpee

Dartmouth (Dartmouth/Westport)

Martha's Vineyard

Mattakeesit (Pembroke)

Betty's Neck (Middleborough-Lakeville)

Troy-Watuppa (Fall River)

Gay Head

Punkapoag (Canton)

Teticut (Middleborough)

Natick (Natick)

RHODE ISLAND

Narragansett (Charlestown)

Hassanamisco (Grafton)

Dudley Nipmucs (Webster)

Lantern Hill Pequots

North Stonington

Groton

Mashantucket Pequots

Ledyard

Mohegan (Montville)

Niantic (Lyme)

CONNECTICUT

Tunxis (Farmington)

Bridgeport

Paugussett

Schagticoke (Kent)

Introduction

At the end of the American Revolution, only a few thousand Indians remained in southern New England. Declining in numbers and plagued by alcoholism, poverty, and the contempt of their white neighbors, they seemed to teeter on the brink of extinction. But Indians and their communities did survive, and their story over the subsequent century has great significance for American history. First, the ways in which they struggled to improve themselves, their families, and their communities, as a marginalized yet protected minority, facing the pressures of acculturation and racism, shed light on aboriginal peoples past and present. Natives in southern New England retained some remnants of autonomy, particularly those with sizeable communally held lands reserved under state laws, comparable to modern federally recognized tribes. That status made Indians unique: they were simultaneously within and without the dominant economic, political, and legal systems. Individuals and families moved between their reserves and the outside world—working, selling, living, and often dying outside, but generally planning to return. Wherever they lived, they could not vote, sell communal lands, or be sued for reserved property. Outside, Indians were famous (or notorious) as transient workers: whalers, farm laborers, domestics, herbal doctors, circus performers, basket makers, and peddlers. Once back home, they maintained a culture that reflected aboriginal traditions (such as political and economic rights for women, and disapproval of individual enterprise) even as new bits of outside culture were adopted (such as raising sheep and fencing and inheriting fields).

Second, because many Indians married African Americans or whites, their story illuminates issues of race, ethnicity, and identity in America from an unusual and early vantage point. Relationships between southern New England Indians and African Americans went through three distinct phases: mutual advantage through intermarriage during the eighteenth century; growing opportunities for people of color outside Indian enclaves at the turn of the century; and finally conflict when black men found they had more to gain by ending the legal distinctions that supported Indian boundaries. But intermarriage is also a complex and mysterious picture that confounds historic segmentation, involving whites, Indians, and blacks, and features conflicts that linked race and gender. Scholars have taken two basic approaches to examining the evolution and formation of group identity, whether national (political) or ethnic (primarily cultural). The first is to emphasize internal mechanisms in maintaining core traditions. The second is to emphasize the role of external influences in shaping or reshaping the group. This study shows the interplay of both factors in the struggles of Indians to maintain and reinvigorate their communities.

Third, and perhaps most significantly, the history of Indians during this period provides a unique view of developments in New England between the Revolution and Reconstruction. It highlights the dialectic between race and class in the region's social structure, beginning when poor whites, blacks, and Indians served as servants together and were regulated in similar ways; continuing with the rise of racist segregation and democratic politics following American independence; and ending with the emergence of an abolitionist and civil rights movement in the mid-nineteenth century, which brought together middle-class white reformers and ambitious African Americans–and threatened Indian communities. Within this structure, Indians formed part of a larger transient class that contributed to, but barely benefited from, the rise of industrialization, agrarian improvement, and consumer culture in southern New England, as Indian men worked as whalers or day laborers and women cleaned homes and peddled the baskets, brooms, and mats that helped farmwives keep order.

The Indians' experiences also reveal how evangelical religion in the early republic served to organize and empower the lower classes, and how later religious-driven social reforms among such groups emerged from internal needs and external direction. That direction came from elites associated with the Whig and Republican parties, given in the name of helping Indians, and uncovers significant continuities and changes in the structure and ideology of the region's reform movement, and shifts in how Indians were perceived. Those emerging depictions of Indians at midcentury also show how a distinctive New England identity and history emerged even as the region's intellectuals presented a newly critical view of their past and purpose.

Tribe, Race, History is roughly divided into halves: the first three chapters focus on the first half-century, the last three on the second half. The first three chapters are more thematic than chronological, as Native groups varied widely in their residential patterns, political power, and group cohesion, and these developments moved at different times or rates in different communities. But all these groups and their members shared a similar history, culture, and social structure and were therefore affected in similar ways by the pressures and changes that I discuss. I conclude with an epilogue that looks at the aftermath of termination between 1880 and 1920, and the pan-Indian and tribal revitalization movements that began in the 1920s. I did not include Indians (Montauks and Shinnacocks) on eastern Long Island in this study; while Long Island Indians had social, cultural, and historical connections to Natives in southern New England, they had relatively infrequent interactions during the nineteenth century.

In discussing these groups, their members, and others in the region, I use terms with many meanings. An Indian group with a clearly bounded territory and a distinct system of formal or informal governance falls within the generally accepted definition of tribe. I also refer to such a group as a village, although there might be several discrete settlements with the tribal territory, and occasionally as an enclave—meaning a group or a people in a place with a culture and kinship patterns clearly distinct from the surrounding population. Groups lacking distinct political boundaries and institutions are also enclaves, and I often refer to them as communities, which is a broad but useful term. A group of family networks may sometimes work as a community and at other times may not.

Regarding what term to use for all of these people, Williams Apess wrote in his 1829 autobiography, A Son of the Forest, that Indian "was a word imported for the special purpose of degrading us," and that "the proper term which ought to be applied to our nation, to distinguish it from the rest of the human family, is that of Natives."[1] Then again, other Native writings from this period (and even today) use the general noun Indian rather than Native. I use both terms when not referring to a particular tribe or community. I also use the contemporary Gay Head rather than the earlier or later Aquinnah. I rarely call identifiable Indians "people of color," even though Indian groups during this period, particularly from Martha's Vineyard, often used it for themselves; it seems to deny their essential Native identity, which was and still is contested by whites in the region. More problematic is what to call individuals of African ancestry, particularly since an important element of this study is their frequent intermarriage with Natives and the identity of their children. Neither black, African American, nor "people of color" fits perfectly. I generally use black when discussing individuals who were noted to have partial African ancestry; African American when discussing individuals and groups who identified themselves primarily as African descendants; and Negro when the sources use it. Finally, I refer to individuals of European ancestry who were part of the region's dominant social and cultural structure as either *Anglo-Americans* or as *whites*. All of these terms were, in that time and place, imprecise and malleable.

A significant reason for these often vague or confusing terms relating to Natives, and indeed the greatest difficulty in reconstructing Native history in this region and period, is the nature of the extant sources. Most are writings by Anglo-Americans or appeals by Indians to Anglo-Americans, and are therefore grounded in a racial paradigm that hardened during the early republic. Whites saw Indians as a vanishing people in southern New England and increasingly referred even to those who were obviously still there as "Indians and people of color." The many Indians and their "mixed" descendants who lived in cities or towns outside of tribal reserves were rarely noticed or recorded because they were poor people of color, and when noticed their ethnic identity was almost never recorded–instead their racial category, inevitably black, was assumed by the recorder, particularly if they did not "look" Indian.

In this book, I seek to reconstruct Native communities and their world, even as I follow the path that links the experiences of Indians to those of others in American history. The study explores how Natives lived and their communities developed between the Revolution and the Civil War, and it shows how their experiences in some ways were distinct from and in other ways mirrored those of their non-Indian neighbors. It reveals the complexities of and connections between race and class in that part of the United States in which emancipation and industrialization originated and developed simultaneously, and where (decades later) abolitionism offered both promises and problems for people of color. It demonstrates how Indians remained significant in the region's culture, economy, and politics even though they were a seemingly shrinking marginalized minority. It opens up a rarely-glimpsed world of the rural and urban poor in southern New England, illustrating how they embraced some middle-class reforms and living standards while resisting other aspects that seemed destructive of traditional social networks and norms. This study of Indian groups affected by migration between reserves and cities, exogamous marriages, and outside economic and social pressures on resources, traditions, and political autonomy has relevance for First Peoples today throughout the world. Of course, it is particularly relevant to Indians and others in southern New England as Native groups in the region work for reconstruction, renaissance, and recognition.[2]

Tribe, Race, History

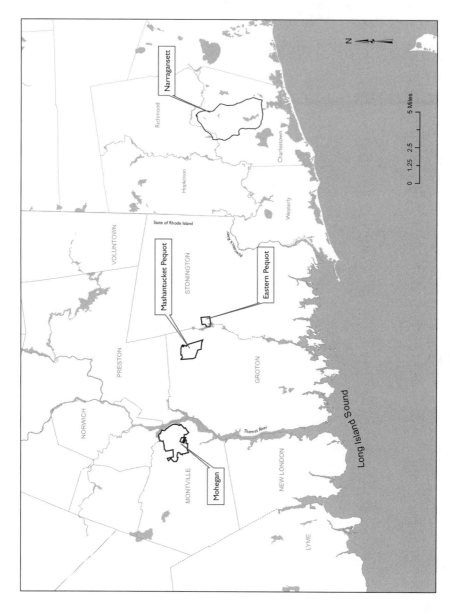

Map 2. Mohegan, Eastern Pequot, Mashantucket Pequot, and Narragansett reserves and environs

CHAPTER ONE

Land and Labor

At the beginning of the nineteenth century, William Tudor of Boston reported that Indians in the region "are a harmless set of beings, and lead a life of hardship, though not of labor." Within their few remaining reserves, "they cannot alienate their lands . . . Each individual has a right to cultivate what piece of land he pleases, and this, as well as the hut he occupies, are his, from a kind of right of occupancy, which is not clearly defined." Many men worked as whalers, sailing out of Nantucket or New Bedford. In addition, "some of the females go into the neighboring towns, as servants, returning home occasionally." Small groups "perambulate the country, offering medicinal herbs, baskets or brooms for sale, almost the only articles they manufacture." Like other Anglo-American observers, the prominent merchant, politician, and founder of the *North American Review* perceived such subsistence, transient workways as "slothful," combining the worst of aboriginal customs and the habits of the early republic's lower sort.[1]

Tudor's description of Native workways, although colored by prejudice, was accurate. In the wake of the American Revolution, the keys to Native identity, persistence, and indeed their *presence* in southern New England were their land and labor. Tribes with substantial reservations were distinguished by informal land-holding, subsistence agriculture, and reliance on fishing and hunting. Traditional crafts also played an important role, as Native women found a growing market among whites for baskets, mats, brooms, and medicine. At the same time, Indians away from their reservations and the survivors of smaller Native groups became part of the region's emerging proletariat. Men went to ports to sign onto whaling vessels; men and women worked in cities and villages as transient laborers and domestics; and children were bound out to work for the "better sort" of white families. But even as Indians developed closer connections to New England's society and economy, political and market forces reshaped both. As a result, the remaining Indian reservations became reservoirs of antimarket traditions that drew poor whites and blacks threatened by an increasingly uncertain, impersonal economy. Thus Indians and their communities shed new light on socioeconomic changes in southern New England during the early republic.

In the century between King Philip's War and the Revolution, Indians in Connecticut, Massachusetts, and Rhode Island were set apart from other peoples in those colonies by law and custom. Their lands were reserved as the result of treaties and provincial laws, so that parts or the whole were not supposed to be sold or alienated without the approval of the provincial assembly—although such laws were occasionally repealed and often flouted. While tribes had varying degrees of autonomy, most had guardians assigned by the provincial legislatures to manage their resources, arrange labor contracts, and prevent illegal acts, liquor consumption, and immorality (see chapter 3). In part to avoid the need to sell land, Indians could not be sued for debts, although adults could be forced into an indenture to fulfill their debts. Natives were not considered citizens and were treated as minors and charity cases by the law; obviously they could not vote. In all three states, these laws survived the Revolution, leaving Indians separate and distinct.[2]

By the outbreak of the Revolution, Indians in southern New England lived in four distinct situations (Table 1). First, tribes with large, legally protected reserves, such as Gay Head and Mashpee, held a high degree of autonomy and had visible political organizations, and some retained substantial resources. Second, smaller groups took the form of either a very small reserve where a small number of families farmed or a neighborhood where a cluster of Indian families lived; in both the core lay within an Anglo-American town that had once been the Native village, and more tribal members lived dispersed in nearby towns. By 1760, many Indian villages had become so small and the land so poor that few members managed to farm there; many members moved to larger tribes or to the cities or remained near the reserve in ancestral territory. Some of these communities (such as the Eastern Pequot or Hassanamisco) often seemed nearly extinct, yet families and individuals frequently and mysteriously reappeared. Third, a few communities existed largely as loose networks of families living near their former reserves. Finally, a growing number of Indians moved to the larger towns, mostly ports, where they were more likely to develop connections to the growing African American neighborhoods. Yet all identified as Indians were still covered by state regulations that limited their liabilities and their rights. All suffered from poverty, disease, and a marginal social status; many men left to fight in the colonial wars and died or stayed away. Most visible Native communities had many more women than men, and many more elderly and children than highly productive adults.[3]

Anglo-American prejudice remained an unavoidable aspect of Indian life. This bigotry drew from a rich mixture of old fears and emerging ideologies—images of marauding savages; notions of unredeemable barbarians; a sense that the region's surviving Natives had lost what few primitive virtues they had possessed; and nascent ideas that humans were divided into biologically distinct groups, with whites inherently superior to people of color. In 1767, David Crosby, an earnest young man who hoped to become a minister for the Indians, ate with "several gentlemen" at an inn in Middletown, Connecticut. He experienced "mortification, & pain" when they told him "they could never respect an Indian, Christian or no Christian so as to put him on a level with white people on account especially to eat at the same Table. No—not with Mr. Ocham himself be he ever so much a Christian or ever so Learned." "Ocham" was Samson Occom, the Mohegan minister who had gained fame in a fundraising trip to England. Just before the start of the war, Occom and his colleagues from tribes in Connecticut, Rhode Island, and Long Island decided on a dramatic solution to their problems: leaving as a group to establish an Indian-only settlement on Oneida land in New York, later named Brothertown.[4]

Regardless of where or how they lived in the region, Indians at the end of the War for Independence were subject (despite their separate legal status) to the economic problems that faced all inhabitants of southern New England. The region was hit hard by a depression, as England barred the new nation from trading with other parts of the empire or charged heavy duties on the imports. Indians, like others, found themselves squeezed by hard times and high taxes. In January 1781, two Punkapoag women, Sarah Berry and Jerusha Hawkins, with six children, asked the legislature for relief. For many years they had gained a "comfortable living," but since the outbreak of the war that living had become increasingly hard. They could no longer support themselves or pay their taxes. Widowhood, as faced by Berry, Hawkins, and so many others (about twenty-five in Mashpee alone), was a terrible economic handicap, in addition to all of its emotional and social problems. Family networks could cushion widowhood, but those who lacked the support of family or community were inevitably left destitute.[5]

Perhaps in response to these wartime problems, many Indians (like whites in the region) sought a better life somewhere else. With the restoration of peace, Occom and other Brothertown organizers renewed their efforts, formally establish-

TABLE 1
Indians in Southern New England: Population and Land, 1780–1865

Tribe (town, state)	ca. 1780		ca. 1800		ca. 1815		ca. 1825		ca. 1835		ca. 1850		ca. 1865	
	Pop.	Acres	Pop.	Acres	Pop.	Acres	Pop.	Acres	Pop.	Acres	Pop.	Acres	Pop.	Acres
Reservations, core villages, large populations														
Narragansett (Charlestown, RI)	528		146		429		300	4,000	199	2,600	150	2,600	302	922
Herring Pond (Plymouth, MA)				3,600	70	3,600	66	3,300	50	3,000	55	2,500	67	3,000
Mashpee (Mashpee, MA)	327		359	13,000		10,500	300	10,000	315		312	13,000	403	16,132
Christiantown (Tisbury, MA)				300	60		51	390	49	390	49	390	53	390
Gay Head (Gay Head, MA)			276	2,400	270	2,400	250	2,400	240	2,400	174	2,400	204	2,400
Chappaquiddick (Chappaquiddick, MA)			77	560	85		99	692	70	692	85	692	74	692
Mohegan (Montville, CT)	346		84	3,000	82	2,400	37	2,600	70	2,700	100	2,300	85	2,300
Reservations, dispersed population or small core														
Eastern Pequot (North Stonington, CT)	237				30		50	300		400	13	400	26	500
Mashantucket Pequot (Ledyard, CT)	186			240	35	900	90			893	31	893	17	180
Niantic (Lyme, CT)	104		60				30		17		10	400	8	5
Golden Hill Paugussett (Bridgeport, CT)	40					112	30	110[?]						
Turkey Hill Paugussett (Orange, CT)							25	12						
Schaghticokes (Kent, CT)	90	1,500	65	1,100	40	400	3[?]	7[?]			54	300	52	300
Potawumacut (Orleans, MA)				1,000			48							
Troy-Watuppa (Fall River, MA)				190			50				37	190	78	190
Yarmouth (Yarmouth, MA)											58	0	126	0
Dudley Nipmucs (Dudley-Webster, MA)	48	200		26			6			0	48	30	94	26
No reservation, dispersed but identifiable population														
Tunxis (Farmington, CT)	46													
Quinnebaug Nipmuc (Windham Co., CT)	120		few											
Hassanamisco (Grafton, MA)							12	0			26	25	73	3
Mattakeesit/Tumtum (Pembroke, MA)							12	12					40	0
Punkapoag (Canton, MA)							12				10	0	117	0
Natick (Natick, MA)	30		30	200		30					few	0	12	0
Betty's Neck (Middleborough, MA)			13				5–18		10	0				0
Total	2,102		1,110		1,061		1,447		1,020		1,212		1,829	

NOTE: Pop. = population. Most of the figures in this table were reported by guardians and other outsiders, and must be assumed to be incomplete and partial estimates. Also, the totals in this table do not include Indians living in towns and cities away from Native communities. 1850 and 1865 figures from Massachusetts include "foreigners."

SOURCES: All Massachusetts tribes, 1850 (population and acreage): Bird 1849. 1865 (population and acreage): Earle 1861.

Narragansett. 1780: 1774 R.I. Indian population in "The Number of Indians in Rhode Island . . . Taken between the 4th of May and the 14th of June, 1774," MHSC, 1st ser., 10 (1809): 119. 1835 and 1850 (population and acreage): Griffin 1858, 4–7 (Griffin listed 121 on or nearby the reservation, noting this was a decline from 109 in 1833) but "the probability is, that the number absent, claiming connection with the tribe, has increased"). 1880 (population and acreage): Adams 1881, 11.

Herring Pond. 1800 (population): Herring Pond tribe to Mass. General Court, 20 Jan. 1804, MUSL no. 3208.

Mashpee. 1825 (population and acreage): Child 1827, 7.

Martha's Vineyard (Christiantown, Chappaquiddick, Gay Head). 1825 (population): Baylies 1823, 1825 (acreage for Christiantown and Chappaquiddick): MIGA, box 3, folder 15. 1825 (population and acreage for Gay Head): Child 1827, 7. 1835 (population): David Wright to Frances Parkman, Boston, 9 April 1839, SPG Papers, box 7, MHS (Gayhead as "over 200" inhabitants, 80 absent "at sea or elsewhere"; Christiantown has 49, 20 absent, Chappaquiddick has "about" 70, 20 absent).

Mohegan. 1800 (population): Abiel Holmes, "Memoir of the Mohegans," *MHSC*, 1st ser., 9 (1804): 79. 1800 (acreage): Conn. assembly committee report, 1 May 1826, CGA1, folder 9; at 1790 allotment of Mohegan reserve, it contained about 3,000 acres. 1815 (acreage): 1814 committee report. 1815 (population): 1817 committee report (about 50 persons met Mohegan rules of inheritance and membership; about 32 claimed a connection with the tribe but had non-Mohegan fathers), in PF Mohegan, 164–65. 1825 (population and acreage): *The Uncas Monument*, 1492–842 (Norwich, Conn.: John G. Cooley, 842), estimating 60–70 individuals and 2,500–3,000 acres. 1850 (population and acreage): John Deforest, *History of the Indians of Connecticut* (Hartford: William Jason Hamersley 851), 487–88, estimating 60 on or near the reserved land and 85 moved away; overseer's accounts for 1855 noted there were 93 in the tribe, CGA, folder 27. 1875 (population): 1870 and 1880 U.S. census schedule from Montville, 59 "on the reservation" and 10 elsewhere in the town, PF Mohegan, 34.

Eastern Pequot. 1780 (population): "Memoir of the Mohegans," *MHSC*, 1st ser., 9 (1804): 79. 1800 (acreage): CAr1, 105–105b. 1815 (population): CAr2, 19. 1825 (population and acreage): Henry Rowe Schoolcraft, *Historical and Statistical Information Respecting the History, Conditions, and Prospects of the Indian Tribes of the United States* (Philadelphia: Lippincott, Grambo, 1851–57) 3:573–76, 583. 1835 (acreage and population): petition signed by ten adults, Pequots to New London County Court, 27 Jan. 1841, NLCC, box 1. 1850 (acreage): North Stonington selectmen to New London County Court, 13 March 1851, NLCC, box 1. 1850 (population): Conn. assembly select committee report, May 1855, CGA1, folder 26. 1868 (population): 26, with several members in other states; overseer's accounts 1868, NLCSC, box 1. 1875 (acreage): overseer's accounts 1881–82, NCLSC, box 5.

Mashantucket Pequot. 1774 (population): "Memoir of the Mohegans," *MHSC*, 1st ser., 9 (1804): 79. 1815 (population): CAr2, cited in U.S. Department of the Interior, Office of Federal Acknowledgment, "Summary under the Criteria and Evidence for Proposed Finding Eastern Pequot Indians of Connecticut" (24 March 2000), 51–52. 1815 (acreage): *Moses Susonun v. John and Ben Packer*, March 1817, NLCSC, box 2. 1825 (population): names of Pequot Indians, March 1825, and Pequot signatories agreeing to appointment of Erastus Williams of Groton as overseer, NLCSC, box 2; these signatories total 44 (I assumed these were adults, and that probably some adults missing, so rounded up to 50 total). 1850 (population): William Morgan, 1857–58 overseers report, NLCSC, box 2. 1850 and 1860–1875 (acreage): Report of committee on sale of Pequot lands, 23 Jan. 1856, NLCSC, box 2, found 892 acres and 26 rods in area laid out; reserved for tribe 179 acres and 34 rods and sold the rest. 1875 (population): 1875–76, Ulysses Avery, overseer's accounts, NLCSC, box 5; 179 acres reserved for tribe, names 17 individual members.

Niantics. 1780 (population): "Memoir of the Mohegans," *MHSC*, 1st Ser., 9 (1804): 79. 1825 (population): "less than thirty" left; Moses Warren, Lyme, to Conn. assembly, 22 March 1824, CGA, folder 4. 1835 (population): petition of 1844 signed by 16 adults; Niantics to New London County Court, 1 January 1844, NLCC, box 4. 1850 (population): nine members identified by C. S. Manwaring, overseer's accounts, Sept. 1855–Aug. 1856, NLCSC, box 4. 1850 (acreage): 400 acres, Act Relating to the Ledyard Pequot Indians, and the Preservation of their Property, 16 June 1855, CGA1, folder 25, and Zacheus Nonesuch, Niantic, to New London County Superior Court, 9 August 861, NLCSC, box 4. 1870 (population): nine of all ages, F. W. Bolles, overseer's report, 13 Sept. 1866, NLCSC, box 4.

Schaghticoke. 1780: 1774 census of Connecticut, 62 Indians in Kent, 90 Indians in all of Litchfield County. 1800 (population): 1799 petition (11 men); Ezra Stiles's 1789 enumeration, 12 men and total population of 67, cited in PF Schaghticoke, 74– 44. 1800 (acreage): Reservation reduced to 400 acres after sale in 1801; PF Schaghticoke, 87, 815; Barzillai Slossom, "Kent" (1812), in *Voices of the New Republic: Connecticut Towns, 1800–1832*, ed. Christopher P. Bickford (New Haven: Conn. Academy of Arts and Sciences, 2002), 1:123–24. 1850 (population): 1859 report from overseer Rufus Fuller, cited in PF Schaghticoke, 93. 1875: 1871 report from overseer Lewis Spooner, PF Schaghticoke, 101.

Dudley Nipmucs: 1780: figures for Woodstock (38) in "Number of Indians in Connecticut, 1774," *MHSC* 10 (1809): n8; for Dudley (10, est.), Ezra Stiles and other sources cited in Daniel Mandell, *Behind the Frontier* (Lincoln: University of Nebraska Press, 1996), 168. 1825 (population): Child 1827, 5.

Nipmucs–Quinnebaugs in Windham County, CT. 1775: data for Windham County except Woodstock in "Number of Indians in Connecticut, 1774," *MHSC* 10 (1809): n8

Natick. 1780 (population): William Biglow, *History of the Town of Natick, Mass.* (Boston: Marsh, Capen, and Lyon, 1830), 43. 1800 (population): Natick Indians (petition signed by 9 adults) to legislature opposing removal of meetinghouse, 1798[?], MUSL no. 2398 / 4. 1800 (acreage): Stephen Badger to Senate, 17 Feb. 1798, MUSL no. 2398 / 13. 1825 (population): Child 1827, 5. 1835 (population): 6–10 residents, increases for "short time by other Indians of a more vagrant character"; G. B. Blanchard, South Natick, to SPG, 4 Dec. 1835, SPG, box 6, MHS. 1835 (acreage): last of the Indian lands sold in 1828; Bird 1849, 45–46.

Punkapoag. 1825 (population and acreage): Child 1827, 5.

Turkey Hill Paugussetts. 1825: about 25 Indians, 15 are resident, the rest wanderers; sold 100 acres, 12 left. Leman Stone to Conn. assembly, 9 May 1825, CGA.

Golden Hill Paugussetts. 1800 (population and acreage): Conn. assembly committee, report, May 1825, CGA, folder 3, noting the population of the tribe in 1818, and the acreage in 1802. 1825: Moses Warren, Niantic overseer, to general assembly, 22 March 1824, CGA, folder 2; the tribe has "less than thirty," and he asks to sell no-acre area belonging to the tribe.

Betty's Neck / Middleborough. 1800 (population): Middleborough Indians to Mass. General Court, 1807, MUSL, no. 3567. 1825 (population): Child 1827, 5.

Potawaumacut. 1800 (population and acreage): Ralph Micah to Mass. General Court, 1799, MUHL no. 4847.

Yarmouth. 1825 (population): 31 Yarmouth adults to Mass. legislature, 1820, MUSL no. 6568.

ing the town in 1795 and attracting a growing number of Narragansetts, Mohegans, and Tunxis—60 households, or about 240 people by 1800. The population
on the Narragansett reserve declined 47 percent between 1774, when a colonial
census found 528 Indians living in Charlestown, and 1782, when a state census
recorded only 280, although it stabilized at the end of the century. Some of those
living in white towns and households moved to the Narragansett reserve, which
held 35.4 percent of all Indians in Rhode Island in 1774 and 53.3 percent in 1782.[6]
Indian communities in Connecticut showed a relatively small decline in numbers
during the war, but a large drop afterward. A census of Mohegans sent to the state
assembly on August 5, 1782, showed 135 persons in 28 households; of those with
children, 11 had only one parent present (eight were widows of Revolutionary soldiers) and 13 had both parents present.[7] Unfortunately, censuses during this period generally combined "Indians and Negroes" into one category, emphasizing
the tendency of Anglo-Americans to see "blacks" instead of "Indians" (see chapter 2).[8] Other problems with data include vague descriptions, such as a 1791 Connecticut report that "a small number" of Paugussetts remained in Milford.[9]

Emigration to Brothertown had significant effects on the tribes in Rhode Island and Connecticut. By 1779, many Narragansetts were leasing land "for a great
number of years" and then moving to Brothertown, "principally those who possess the best farms." In response, the tribe developed a rule that emigrants could
lease their lands "for ten years and a day, and take the rents and go where they
pleased." If they returned within that period, they could renew the lease for the
same period, but very few returned. Brothertown Indians also sought to sell pieces
of lands they or their parents had used or claimed on the tribal reserves. In 1793
and 1801, members of the Tunxis tribe who had emigrated sold pieces of their reserve in Farmington or sought to gain the assembly's approval of previous sales to
white, in part because few members of the tribe remained in Connecticut and in
part because those who had moved need the capital for their new farms. Niantics
asked in 1808 and 1815 to sell tracts from their tribal territory in Lyme, and, in April
1798, Robert Ashbow and other Mohegans asked to sell "sundry tracts " from the
tribal reserve. The assembly was seemingly reluctant to grant permission to sell
land of a tribe with a sizeable population still on and near the reserve; they refused
Ashbow's petition and stalled two petitions in 1822 from Mohegans still in the state
who sought to sell tribal land to meet their personal needs. But in the 1840s both
Connecticut and Rhode Island became far more willing to grant the right of emigrants and their descendants to sell tribal lands.[10]

Few, if any, Massachusetts Indians went to Brothertown, but many moved
within the state, with the similar result that some tribes shrank and even disap-

peared. A few tribes with substantial populations and resources, most notably Mashpee and Gay Head, drew refugees from more vulnerable communities. Gay Head increased from 165 in 1765 to 203 in 1786 and perhaps 276 in 1790, stabilizing at about 270 during the first half of the nineteenth century.[11] To Mashpee, Indians came from Natick, Dudley (Nipmucs), Mohegan, Narragansett, Middleborough, Dartmouth, Nantucket, Martha's Vineyard, Long Island, and Potawamucut (Harwich) on Cape Cod.[12] Nearby villages continued to shrink to the vanishing point, in a continuation of prewar trends. In 1792, Nathaniel Freeman surveyed Indians on Cape Cod outside of Mashpee: Falmouth had about seven, Sandwich about two or three women, Barnstable was empty, Potawamucut had only six or seven, and Truro might still have one. Seven years later, Ralph Micah told the General Court that he was the only man left in Potawamucut. One factor among many was continued problems with epidemics. In 1798, a Yarmouth historian remembered "a small cluster of wigwams" in Indiantown two decades previous, but after a smallpox epidemic, only one wigwam remained, "occupied by a negro and a squaw." No doubt such survivors were likely to seek secure and comfortable homes in larger communities.[13]

In Massachusetts, such relocation was not new but a continuation of a tendency that had developed in the first quarter of the eighteenth century, resulting in a series of subregional clusters of Indian tribes, enclaves, and families behind the frontier of English settlement. Members of Gay Head, Christiantown, Chappaquiddick, and the Deep Bottom neighborhood on the Vineyard often met, sometimes married, and occasionally moved between their communities. The Indian villages on Cape Cod and in Plymouth County were similarly associated by kinship and religious networks, which after the Revolution remained significant between Mashpee and Herring Pond (chapter 3) along with the remaining outlying enclaves and families in non-Indian towns. Similar connections linked Mashpee and the Vineyard Indians. Another social and cultural subregion lay in Bristol County along Buzzard's Bay, consisting of Indians on the Troy-Watuppa reserve and at Betty's Neck (Middleborough), Dartmouth, and along the Westport River.

The situation in Rhode Island and Connecticut was somewhat different although subregional connections and clusters also developed. While many from the tribes in these two states moved out of the region to Brothertown, the proximity of the Mohegan, two Pequot, and Niantic reserves facilitated visits, marriages, and other social connections. Some Tunxis remnants moved southeast to the larger reserves, and members of all of these Connecticut tribes regularly traveled to attend the Narragansett church—while members of that tribe regularly returned the favor. By 1860, most Mohegans had partial Tunxis, Niantic, or Pequot ancestry. Schaghticoke lay at the center of a tribal network that stretched south and north among Mahican villages in the Housatonic Valley and east as far as the Connecticut River. In Windham County in northeastern Connecticut, the southern side of traditional Nipmuc territory, a local writer later remembered that after the war "almost every town had its one Indian family, familiar to all, and regarded as a common charge, while "a few wandering Indians with no fixed home roved about from town to town extorting tribute of food and cider." These families, like Mohegans, Narragansetts, and other Indians, traveled along roads and rivers to visit kinfolk and friends, to trade or to use well-known fishing and hunting places, or to settle in a place where there was better soil and they could find work.[14]

This movement within the region fed an emerging mythology of the vanishing Indian. The myth was encouraged by the terrible Nantucket epidemic in 1763 that took only a few months to kill most of the island's Indians. Crèvecoeur described the incident in his 1782 *Letters of an American Farmer* and opined that the Natives "appear to be a race doomed to recede and disappear before the superior genius of the Europeans." He then remarked how in less than two centuries many New England tribes (which he listed) were gone, "and every memorial of them is lost." The Nantucket story was also recounted in 1789 by an Andrew Oliver letter published in two periodicals, which concluded that the incident was one of the "Arcana of Providence." Various New England clergymen and magistrates noted the decline of the region's Native population and the disappearance of Indian neighborhoods, including a 1792 article that observed how their numbers in the former Plymouth Colony had "much lessened" since 1763, and commented that Natives were "probably extinct" in Bristol County outside of Troy and Dartmouth. Even John Adams remembered, in a June 1812 letter to Thomas Jefferson, that when he was a boy, "there was a numerous Family in [Braintree], whose wigwam was within a Mile of this House . . . But the Girls went out to Service and the Boys to Sea, till not a Soul is left."[15]

Writers frequently linked the Indians' travail to moral decay sometimes abetted by white racism and scorn. Crèvecoeur mused that many had tried to regroup in "their ancient villages" but were soon "surrounded by the improvements of the Europeans, in consequence of which they grew lazy, inactive, unwilling, and unapt to imitate or to follow any of our trades." Yale president and archconservative Timothy Dwight visited Stonington in 1807 and poured his scorn upon the Pequots there. "The former, proud, heroic spirit of the Pequot, terrible even to the other proud heroic spirits around him, is shrunk into the tameness and torpor of reasoning brutism. All the vice of the original is left. All its energy has vanished."

Edward Kendall, an Englishman touring the Northeast in the same year, visited the Mohegans and wrote that, during the past half-century, those Indians "have become dispirited, and have rapidly decayed." Anglo-Americans describing Indian farmers and workers similarly connected their perceived "laziness" to moral and demographic decline. A Windham County antiquarian later remembered that "these various representatives of a fallen dynasty were usually treated with kindness and consideration, strongly seasoned with contempt—the 'Injun' of that date holding much the position of the succeeding 'nigger.'"[16]

For white New England farmers, the early national period was a time of substantial "improvement," as better roads and the growing commercial economy encouraged peddlers to bring books, magazines, and new consumer goods to formerly isolated villages. These same developments, along with rising land prices, meant that a shrinking percentage of New Englanders could farm, but those who remained became more organized and productive, as magazines and village improvement societies spread new scientific ideas about agriculture.[17] Despite the scornful comments of many Anglo-Americans, Indians also made improvements, building English-style framed homes rather than wigwams, for example. In Mashpee, the percentage of homes that were wigwams declined from 90 percent in 1761 to 71 percent in 1767 and 48 percent in 1776. Nathan Birdsey of Stratford, Connecticut, reported in 1761 that within the past fifty years the number of wigwams around his town had gone from about fifty to only a few "scattering." When James Winthrop visited Gay Head in 1791, he found a wigwam very similar to that sketched in 1761 by Ezra Stiles in Niantic, but he noted that Indians "now generally framed their houses in our fashion."[18]

Yet important differences remained. Some Indians still built wigwams in the nineteenth century. Their framed houses were usually described as "huts" or "cabins," with one floor and at best a few rooms, and remained distinct from the larger and more elaborate houses Anglo-American farmers were increasingly constructing. On or off reservations, Indians continued to build on dispersed homesteads that clustered along lines of kinship, probably to take advantage of water, plants, and other natural resources. On tribal reserves, narrow trails connected homesteads; public roads went past, but not through, the area, possibly by choice so Indians could avoid outsiders but in large part because neither whites nor Indians were interested in paying for such infrastructure. There were no village centers or improvement societies, although larger tribes maintained meetinghouses and schools as their community centers.[19]

Within their homes, Indians dressed as their English neighbors and cooked meals that drew from both Native and English traditions. In 1800, Mashpee minister Gideon Hawley boasted that "our Indian females are many of them good spinsters, combers and weavers," although extant accounts show that many if not most Indians purchased finished cloth and clothing, as did their white neighbors. Indians could more easily obtain and prepare food in traditional ways; excavations of Indian housing sites from this period indicate that soups and stews were more common than roasts. These dishes commonly included white-tailed deer, fish, and small mammals—both wild and domestic, including sheep, pigs, raccoons, and even dogs. Shellfish and scaled fish were staples, particularly as the larger Native communities had freshwater ponds and were located along rivers, estuaries, and shorelines. Indians consumed their own crops—maize, oats, peas, potatoes, and probably squash—and less commonly the green vegetables increasingly eaten by whites. They also purchased subsistence and luxury foods, particularly tea and molasses, and rum unfortunately continued to be a problem.[20]

TRIBAL RESERVES

A unique aspect of Indian culture in the region was how the larger tribes continued to manage the land and resources around those homesteads. The Mashpees described their system as one in which "we are tenants in common, all our lands being undivided, but our improvements are in allotments." Those born into the tribe were "proprietors"—the term used among early English colonists for men entitled to pieces of the village commons—who could, like their white counterparts, lay claim to and enclose land for crops and, in what was probably the greatest innovation, pass it to their children. Proprietors could buy, rent, or trade tracts among themselves.[21] But this system also retained aboriginal customs of landholding in common. The lands of deceased proprietors who lacked heirs reverted to the community "as a Common Interest."[22] Most of the salt hay pasture, meadow, and woodlands were managed in common: some was allotted to individuals or families, usually on a yearly basis but occasionally for longer. At any time any resident could cut firewood and building timber from the commons, hunt game, fish in the reserve's rivers and ponds, and take clams along its seashore. Of course, state laws and community norms continued to bar the sale of land to outsiders.[23]

Other tribes in the region with substantial lands held and managed their resources in similar ways. A Connecticut official in 1774 reported that "the matter of Acquiring Lands among [the Mohegans] is for a man to take up as much as he Can Secure and possess it as Long as he Lives and then It Descends to his Children If he has any and If a family is Extinct it is free for any new possessor." When the state made a formal division of the tribe's reserve among Mohegan men in 1790, tribal leaders asked officials to confirm that any surviving family members (and not just the children) could inherit land. Over subsequent decades, those who remained at Mohegan abandoned that particular partition, although individuals and the tribe continued to rent defined tracts of land to whites, and some descendants of those who left for Brothertown later claimed inherited rights to pieces of the 1790 division—particularly those given to Samson Occom. The Narragansetts remembered, generations later, that when their Charlestown reserve was established "it was left for the families to go around as they wanted, where the other members of the tribe hadn't gone. They went around a piece and marked it, and that has been subdivided among their heirs right down." Gay Head held a meeting of proprietors each spring that decided matters such as how many people would plow the fields, which areas would be grazed and when, and how many sheep each proprietor could graze (or "rights" that they could give or sell to others). Christiantown and Chappaquiddick similarly held their land as "joint Tenants," and "when one died the land devolved upon the whole." This system seemed to merge aboriginal and early New England rural landholding.[24]

The blended customs by which Indians came to manage their reserves was symbolized by the way that the Narragansetts assigned portions of land to tribal members. The tribal council grew in power with the decline of their traditional sachem's lineage, the Ninigrets, and in 1792 the state gave it the power to lease tribal lands to whites and to license timber cutting among members of the tribe.[25] The council also exercised the unsanctioned authority, inherited from the sachem's powers, to assign tracts of land to men and women in the tribe.

> A person wishing a tract of land to settle upon, made application to the Indian Council, and, if granted, the Council, with the applicant, went upon the ground and marked trees, or erected bounds around the tract; then, with the applicant standing upon the soil, some member of the Council would remove a piece of the turf from the ground and place it upon the head of the applicant, and place therein a twig; which ceremony was called crowning, and by this act putting them in full possession of the land. Often these ceremonies were attended with joviality, as attested by the broken bottles at some of the prominent bounds.

Rhode Island officials seemed to regard it with bemusement as a vestige of savage custom, but it actually originated in the traditional English land grant ceremony, livery of seisin, which the Narragansetts adopted by the 1770s, even as it died out among their Anglo-American neighbors. Although the ritual had English origins, it reinforced the powers of the tribal council and the group's social boundaries, for individuals seeking land were required to gain the council's approval and to prove membership in the tribe, if necessary by getting the eldest woman in the tribe to attest to their ancestry.[26]

Even with the emergence of allotments, Indians in southern New England continued to resist the acquisitive values embraced by Anglo-Americans. In 1810, visiting minister Curtis Coe commented that each Narragansett "seldom tills more than an acre of land, & may cut a little hay"; even a half-century later, after a wave of social reforms, tribal leaders estimated that their members cultivated only about 60 acres. True, families held larger tracts that they leased to whites or used for timber and grazing, in 1830 totaling about a third of the tribe's 4,000 acres. But even that left most of the land unallotted and open to the entire community. Massachusetts Indian communities divided even smaller proportions of their reservations. In 1822, less than 10 percent of the 2,500-acre Herring Pond reserve was cleared and improved by families, with the rest held in common. Visitors to Gay Head in 1848 reported that about 20 percent of the reserve had been claimed, but that "while one proprietor has but half an acre, and another has over a hundred acres, there is no heart-burning, no feeling that the latter has more than his share."[27]

Although all Indian groups adopted an attenuated form of land holding in severalty, most avoided imposing boundaries within that landscape. Fences were not just a means to keep cattle out of crops; for Native communities they were symbols of troubling transformations. In 1789, a group of Mohegans complained that "all our hunting and fowling and fishing is entirely gone. And we have begun to work our land, keep horses and cattle and hogs; and we build houses and fence in lots." Apparently some Gay Headers and Mashpees did adopt fencing as an aspect of establishing an individual's right to work, hold, and pass land to family members. But most resisted this change; in 1839, a white minister commented that Gay Headers "will not at present" fence their fields, and four years later a legislative committee found few Mashpee families had established clear property markers despite allotments by the tribe in 1834.[28] Similarly, while some Narragansetts fenced their lands, others explicitly rejected the practice.[29] Chappaquiddick refused altogether. In April 1810, when a legislative commission tried to divide and fence much of that tribe's remaining commons and to assign a section to each family for a period of ten years, the Indians protested that it had violated their welfare and traditions. "We further pray your Honours not to permit any fence to be erected on the Indian Lands at present . . . we are apprised of the evil that will follow, it will cause contention & deprive us of the little grazing which we have had, in the usual mode of Tethering" in the commons. Decades later, a visiting minister found that Christiantown had done "commendably" in fencing their fields but that the Chappaquiddicks still "do not fence much" because they lacked materials and money.[30]

On these reserves, men and women pursued a mixed subsistence economy, consisting of small-scale cultivation and livestock, with extensive fishing and hunting, all supplemented by wage labor outside the reserve. This encouraged a life that, to white observers, was unique and backward, implying a persistence of aboriginal ways, although Indian crops and livestock, hunting and fishing, and seasonal wage labor were in many ways similar to the workways of poorer Anglo-American farmers. The largest tribes displayed a mixture of conservative and innovative agriculture. Gay Head's small farms, like those in neighboring towns, produced maize, rye, oats, potatoes, peas, flax, and beans, and they resisted innovations such as vegetable gardens.[31] The reserve was especially famous for its pasture, the finest on the Vineyard, and the Indians raised large numbers of sheep and cattle as well as pigs. Sheep particularly seemed to reflect the Indians' absorption of some elements of Anglo-American farming, as they required careful tending and were highly vulnerable to predators.[32] At Mashpee, Gideon Hawley told a colleague in 1800 that "some few of our middle-aged Indians are considerable good farmers. And many of them plant and sow; and a few of them keep oxen & cows & sheep and horses." Salt hay was one of the reserve's most prized resources, and in 1827 the 80 households held 90 cows, 123 sheep, 5 horses, and 45 hogs (Table 2). At midcentury, most alternated corn on "their little plats of ground" with winter rye every other year.[33]

At the same time, all Indian communities continued to get much of their food by fishing, gathering, and, for some, hunting. A German visitor to Gay Head remarked on that group's dependence on seafood. Mashpee also "derived a considerable proportion of their subsistence" from shellfish along their extensive seashore, particularly the quahog, a large clam, and was well known for the eels, trout, and herring available in its ponds and rivers—which Gay Head lacked. The reserve on Cape Cod also boasted thick woods where deer, otters, raccoons, and fowl thrived; by 1820 it was considered the only place in southeastern New England where one could still hunt deer. Nearby, the Herring Pond Indians "procured their subsistence from the ocean"; although this may have been a reference to whaling (see below), seven years later officials noted that agriculture was not "much attended to," and even in 1848 they held only five cows and six pigs (Table 2).[34]

Whereas Gay Head and, particularly, Mashpee had welcomed immigrants in the last quarter of the eighteenth century, Narragansett, Mohegan, and Tunxis suffered substantial losses from emigration. Those who left for Brothertown were the

TABLE 2
Economic Conditions for Selected Indian Tribes, 1827–1860

	Population	Cows	Pigs	Horses	Sheep
Herring Pond					
1848	55	5	6	2	0
1860	67	5	0	0	0
Christiantown					
1827	45	4	3	0	30
1828	47	6	3	0	32
1848	49	17	11	2	0
1860	53	21	8	1	0
Chappaquiddick					
1827	101	23	15	0	23
1828	110	22	18	0	21
1848	85	31	39	0	12
1860	74	34	11	1	0
Gay Head					
1827	250	61	25	11	73
1848	174	132	57	15	0
1860	204	95	27	21	0
Mashpee					
1827	300	90	45	5	123
1848	305	76	43	16	19
1860	403	54	55	8	6
Mohegans					
1850	60	29		2	

SOURCES: Child 1827; Bird 1849; Earle 1861; Deforest, *Indians of Connecticut*, 489 (for Mohegan data).

"successful" (acculturated) farmers, and those who remained on the reserves seemed to maintain a mixed subsistence economy. The wealthiest Mohegan in 1790 was John Cooper, teacher and preacher for the tribe, who owned two cows and a yoke of oxen for plowing and hauling. The Narragansetts had even less: in 1810, the tribe told Coe that they had no oxen to plow their fields or haul manure and held only about four cows; he had already noted that families on the reserve generally farmed only about an acre. This situation apparently improved somewhat over the next two decades. In 1832, the tribal council defended their people by telling the state that "the Greatest part of our tribe live as well as the commontry [*sic*] of people we Raise pork & Beef and poultry &c." But the Narragansetts never depended on agriculture; at midcentury only a few of the 27 families "follow farming exclusively." Mohegans had become more reliant on farming: 10 of 11 households on the reserve worked a total of 460 acres and held a total of 10 oxen, 12 cows, 17 young cattle, and 2 horses.[35]

The Narragansetts and Mohegans, Niantics, and other Indians in Connecticut

were, like their cousins in Massachusetts, heavily dependent on the natural resources on and near their reserves. Fishing was particularly important. The Narragansett reserve was "a great place for lamprey eels," various fresh and saltwater
fish, and shellfish; as a result, tribal members "were not afraid of starving to death."
In the middle lay a cedar swamp, which they used for building and craft materials. In 1820, when the Narragansetts were asked if they wished to move west of the
Mississippi River, they refused because "we have land enough, and wood enough,
and living on the salt water, and having boats of our own, have plenty of fish &c.
&c." While the Mohegans commented less on their reserve, its resources were
significant, and it was located along the Thames River with easy access to Long
Island Sound. In 1800, a Mohegan told a visitor that they "live well enough
here—land enough—and good fishing." Access to "good fishing" and other resources outside the reservation also remained important: in 1819, the Mohegans
and Niantics went to the Connecticut General Assembly to maintain their traditional right to fish at the mouth of the Connecticut River. Some even settled elsewhere in part for better fishing. Tradition holds that, around 1800, a Pequot extended family moved from their Connecticut reserve to the edges of the growing
town of Providence, settling along the Seekonk River and fishing at Narragansett
Bay.[36]

Indian groups were not unique in their dependence on fish and wood from the
commons. White farmers also relied on those communal resources. Towns managed the taking of fish from streams by appointing fish wardens. Colonial governments followed English common law in passing laws that barred dams from
obstructing the passage of migratory fish. Efforts by budding industrialists after the
Revolution to bypass those laws were resisted by farmers who fought to maintain
this important resource. But by the end of the century, political changes and socioeconomic developments resulted in a fundamental shift away from dependence on the commons. Towns initially had the right to remove threatening dams,
but industrialists won exemptions in 1793 that doomed migratory fish. One reason Indian reserves experienced problems with poachers, as described below, may
have been because some Anglo-Americans sought resources that were increasingly in short supply within their own communities.[37]

Thus tribal reserves were increasingly distinguished by informal land holdings,
subsistence agriculture, and reliance on uncultivated resources. This continuity
with aboriginal traditions was also manifested in the manner in which Indian
women claimed and held farmland and played a public role in community politics. After the Revolution, women signed nearly every petition from every Indian
group, and sometimes even made up a majority of the signatories. Elderly Narra-

gansett women served as the tribe's genealogical judges, pointing to a persistence or development of matrilineal authority. Visitors to Massachusetts coastal groups in 1827 were astonished that women claimed and held land and in meetings "vote in like manner as the men." Women may have helped make Indian agriculture seem more "primitive," as they traditionally wielded the hoe rather than the plow. There are few references to women farming: in 1802, someone noted that "several" Mashpee women "cultivate the ground," and, in 1832, the Narragansetts noted that their few remaining huts "are only occupied in the summer by our women for the purpose of tending and taking care of their gardens." At the same time, Indian women seemed to fulfill some Anglo-American gender roles. In 1802, for example, Gideon Hawley proudly wrote that "some" Mashpee women were "very good wives and cloth themselves and their husbands in every-day-homespun, and on the Lords day appear in a very decent and showy dress." Indian women could be both proprietors and goodwives.[38]

But farming, fishing, and hunting were not enough, particularly as Indians (like their white neighbors) became increasingly dependent on manufactured clothing, imported and processed foods, and household consumer goods. Medicine and nursing care also required money. Most men and some women went away to work, for long or short periods, and some made and peddled crafts. Many groups and families also obtained needed capital by leasing land or selling wood, although the poor and rocky soils in most reserves limited the value of land and availability of timber. These transactions were carried on by individuals or families who leased all or part of their claims, by tribal committees or leaders on behalf of the entire community, or by guardians seeking to raise funds to support the indigent, and point to the persistence of differences between Indians and their Anglo-American neighbors. In 1786, for example, Levi Mie claimed a tract of woodland near the ocean; the following winter, he cut and split five cords of wood and shipped it to Nantucket, where he could obtain particularly high prices. The sale allowed him to get "things I needed for my family." Thus far he seemed a normal American entrepreneur. But Mie was a Mashpee Indian and had learned different values. Instead of cutting as much as possible as quickly as possible, which was becoming the norm in the United States, he resolved to "keep it for my children if I did not stand in need of it for it is good to me as the money."[39]

Gay Head's sale of clay from its famous cliffs is an exceptional example of how Indians managed to participate in the market economy without becoming part of it. Around 1805, industries in Salem, Boston, Taunton, and elsewhere began clamoring for the clay to make hearths, moulds, clay pipes, glass, alum, and blue vitriol, and by the early 1820s the community was selling at least 150 tons each year.

They handled this connection to the regional and world economy in a communitarian manner. When a boat arrived to purchase a load of the clay, the Indians spread the word from neighbor to neighbor, "for this clay is regarded as public property, and every inhabitant of Gay Head who is willing to dig and help load the ship receives a part of the profit." A portion was also reserved for the sick and helpless. Through midcentury, despite the great depression of 1837, Gay Head consistently charged $2.75–$3.00 per ton, further emphasizing resistance to the market economy.[40]

Such placid, beneficial commerce was not necessarily the rule. Traditions, politics, and social patterns made lumber sales among the Narragansetts particularly volatile. The tribal council had the sachem's power to grant land to members who in turn could lease to whites. More valuable and provocative was the tribe's timber. Members obtained wooded tracts and cut the timber for market or sold it without written contracts to whites who cut and hauled it, leading to uncertainty over whether the cuttings were legitimate. The council also sold permits to cut in the cedar swamp, and managed it very poorly, generating little income but great destruction and waste. After 1810, suspicion grew that the council was corrupt, buying liquor with tribal funds and giving away land already held by a member of the tribe in exchange for political favors. In 1831, a state commission blamed the controversies on the council's ambiguous authority under the 1792 law that gave it the right to grant land and sell timber permits and on the tribe's tradition of oral (unwritten) land grants that led to overlapping and uncertain claims. Perhaps, although two council members and their chief opponent joined in a remonstrance that emphasized "as to the Bounds[,] we all know them."[41]

An important role for the natural resources on Indian reserves was to support needy members of the community. Wood was sold and lands rented for funds to provide medical support, food, clothing, and other needs. In Massachusetts and Connecticut, guardians were officially in charge of this community function. Gideon Hawley told Massachusetts governor John Hancock in 1791 that he issued "small quantities" daily to many of Mashpee's thirty widows, fatherless children, and aged and infirmed individuals. One of the most frequent complaints of Indian groups against guardians was that they failed to provide adequately for the poor, and Gay Head, which maintained a high level of autonomy, frequently boasted that it took care of its own. In Rhode Island, the Narragansett council was in charge of such needs. When the council complained in 1779 that emigrants were leasing out the best lands on the reserve, they emphasized that this interfered with their ability to lease enough land to support their poor. The tribe maintained this method until about 1820, when lack of land to lease and rising debts threatened more state interference; tribal members then began taking the indigent into their homes and supporting them as members of their households.[42]

But these communal resources were increasingly under siege. Fishing was endangered by competition from Anglo-Americans along the waterways. In January 1762, the Herring Pond Indians had to plead with the General Court to prevent white fishermen from ruining the pond that gave them their name and their sustenance. The Mashpees also complained during this period about the declining catch of alewives (herring) and trout from their rivers. By January 1788, the bitter foes Gideon Hawley and Levi Mie (who disagreed about everything else) agreed that this was due to outsiders "who have crowded upon this territory." Environmental alterations by newly constructed milldams were also a problem. The state recognized both threats, requiring in 1801 that milldams along the brook from Wakeby Pond have a cleared run during the spring for the alewives to migrate and that outsiders ("nonresidents") pay 25 cents (raised to one dollar two years later) for every hundred taken. But the poaching continued, as whites from neighboring towns took alewives and trout from Mashpee waters and quahogs from their shore.[43]

Wood and pasturelands were also vulnerable to poachers. When Potawamucut leader Ralph Micah asked the state to appoint a guardian for the group in 1799, he did so in large part to deal with whites poaching wood from their land. In 1817, the Mashantucket Pequots sued two neighboring whites, John and Ben Packer, for cutting and carrying away 70 walnut trees worth about $580, and 15 years later repeated the exercise against the three Latham brothers, who cut and carried off about 60 trees worth $115. The tribe had already been forced, in 1793, to sell a small piece of their reserve in order to pay the legal costs of fighting trespassers on their lands, and seven years later went to the state assembly to gain mediation with neighboring whites over conflicting land claims. On Chappaquiddick, white proprietors failed to build a fence between their territory and the Indian reserve, despite a law passed requiring this in 1789; as a result, their livestock frequently destroyed Indian crops. Indian groups experienced problems with poachers for many reasons. Anglo-Americans viewed the surviving Indians with racist, often vicious, contempt. Indian reserves were known to have plentiful wood, fish, and game, resources rapidly dwindling in neighboring white towns. And although special regulations and guardians generally protected Indian reservations, communal resources were not given the legal protections provided to private property.[44]

Another threat was the maneuvers of some whites to gain legal rights to Indian resources. In 1798, Ebenezer Crocker, a Barnstable justice of the peace, tried to use a fraudulent will to steal 150 acres of excellent Mashpee land. Gideon Haw-

LAND AND LABOR 19

ley told the legislature that if the courts upheld the will, other claims to Mashpee totaling about 7,000 acres (two-thirds of the reserve) would be pressed. The legislature ultimately rejected Crocker's claim. In 1818, Gay Headers told the legislature that for many years a cabal in neighboring Chilmark had tried to manipulate the law "to get our land or the improvements out of our hands" but that the tribe successfully defended itself. Not all conflicts were due to fraud or cruelty; misunderstandings of the special laws governing Indians and uncertainty over ancient boundaries were also significant factors. In 1805, for example, the Massachusetts legislature revoked all leases and land purchases made from Christiantown; a quarter-century later, whites who thought they had legal deeds were shocked when that property was given to Christiantown families. Some misunderstanding generated brutality. For at least three decades, East Sandwich claimed riparian rights to the Mashpee River and arrested Mashpees who attempted to exercise their fishing rights; in 1818, the town's claims were rejected and the abuses condemned by a state commission.[45]

While Mashpee and Gay Head managed to halt the fraudulent claims, Indians generally found it very difficult to control threats to their resources. The courts were costly (as the Mashantucket Pequots found) and relatively useless on account of the Indians' relative incompetence in the system, their strange legal status, and the fact that those resources were legally owned in common under the auspices of the state government rather than by the tribes. Guardians were often unhappy with their responsibilities, lazy, or involved with the fraud; sometimes they tried but were unable to solve the problem.[46] Legislatures were too unwieldy, lacked enforcement mechanisms, and operated within a system that was not only racist but, even in southern New England, held to the notion of limited state government. Not until the 1840s and 1850s did Massachusetts and Connecticut begin to pass laws regulating fishing or timber cutting in Indian reservations.

Despite these problems, the resource management strategies pursued by tribes allowed for some individual or family initiative while generally ensuring security, preventing community conflicts, and reducing potential threats in a time of rapid change. It also gave women the right to hold land and vote as proprietors, a "principle of natural right" that astonished Anglo-American men. By contrast, the system barred using the land as collateral for loans and discouraged innovations that involved more extensive or intensive farming, specialization, market risks, and profitability. These entrepreneurial aspects of landowning were increasingly important to New England farmers in the early nineteenth century, as population pressures forced them to make more intensive and extensive use of their lands. For Indians with isolated tribal reserves, however, such changes were risky, required scarce capital, and, in many cases, made entrepreneurs selfish violators of community norms, which invited accusations of witchcraft. This was particularly true as the group's land was a manifest symbol of their distinctiveness. The reserve was their primary bond; it represented kinship, culture, and a sacred past. Even the most literate and "developed" tribes did not document community decisions such as land allotments, relying instead on the memory of elders, although some individuals on Martha's Vineyard recorded deeds and transactions with the county. The Narragansett chairman later recalled that "the oldest members in the tribe" served as their records until the state assembly required them in 1849 to keep written accounts. Such habits and restrictions, according to Anglo-American observers, held progress at bay.[47]

These traditions were upheld, ironically, by state laws barring the sale of Indian lands to outsiders without the permission of the legislature, and (except with the Narragansetts) by guardians who were supposed to manage the finances and resources of Indian groups. Guardians who leased "surplus" marsh and pasture to whites tended to limit herds of cattle and sheep, and they often sold timber or other renewable resources to raise more money for the community fund they administered. In Mashpee, when the Indians sold more wood to buy the hay that they formerly obtained from common lands, the guardians began limiting the amount cut for market, demanding 25 percent of the proceeds from the timber sold. The restrictions imposed by this system and the guardians were often frustrating. In June 1791, Levi Mie complained to the legislature that Gideon Hawley had sold 120 cords of wood from the lot Mie had hoped to maintain for future generations and that the guardians refused to give him any of the earnings. Guardians also occasionally sold small pieces of land, although relatively little from these larger communities. Such arrangements provided a source of capital for community needs but also undercut the ability of Indians to expand their farming or other operations.[48]

SMALL COMMUNITIES

Facing very different circumstances were Indian communities with relatively few families and little common land (Table 1). These groups were quickly swamped by whites who took control of community institutions and kept the original inhabitants out of churches and town meetings. Many individuals were forced, or preferred, to make a living elsewhere; some went to other tribes with reserves, but most emigrants moved to nearby towns or the growing cities. Some stayed and were able to maintain farms or enter a trade, while others settled on the socioeconomic and geographic margins of towns that had been established on their ancestral homelands, becoming "wandering" laborers, basket peddlers, or herbal doctors. Their groups generally retained sizeable (if shrinking) accounts, resulting from the sale of community lands, which were meant in part to help those unable to support themselves. There were also a few scattered Indian families, particularly in Bristol and Plymouth counties, to whom the special state Indian laws also applied. The threat to the community of dividing their reserve in severalty increased as Americans came to see the ungoverned ability of individuals to dispose of land as a moral right. In 1811, when Mattakeesit guardian Edward Mitchell tried to enter and inspect property in Bridgewater held by Indian descendant Sarah Dunbar (who was living elsewhere), she sued him and won, even after Mitchell gained the legislature's explicit recognition of the guardians' authority over property held by expatriates. In 1814, a state court ruled that Dunbar, "although an heir of an Indian, was a mulatto, having some negro blood in her"—a ruling that increased the potential threat to the smaller communities with generations of exogamous marriages.[49]

Some of the groups in Massachusetts had embraced landholding in severalty in the second quarter of the eighteenth century, resulting in the rapid sale of lands to outsiders as individuals found it relatively easy to gain permission to sell their lands when faced with debts or other dire needs. Natick was the first, and by mid-century many of its landholders were forced by debt or illness to sell those holdings to white settlers; a growing number left the town. In 1800 only a handful remained, and they found themselves "forced to go from place to place to get our living." Those who left had no reason to return. One woman who had emigrated when young, probably in the 1740s, decided against returning in 1783 when she inherited a farm in the town, though her house in Dudley had just burned down with all of her possessions. The Mattakeesits in Pembroke and Teticuts in Middleborough had also divided nearly all of their lands in the first half of the mid-eighteenth century, and by the Revolution few with little land remained in those communities. Similarly, in 1727 the Hassanamisco Nipmucs had sold most of their village, which became Grafton, and accepted a division of the remainder into freeholds. In the two decades following the Revolution, all but a few members of the tribe sold their farms and moved to other towns, mostly in the surrounding county.[50]

Some of the remaining small groups found their lands sold at the request of the town in which they were located, with the proceeds to be used to support the surviving Indians when they were poor or sick. The Dudley Nipmucs found all but 26 of their 200 acres sold by the state in 1797 to pay their debts and establish a common fund of about $1,600 for the tribe. A decade later, most lived elsewhere, in towns from Grafton to Dartmouth to Mashpee. More surreptitious was the sale by Yarmouth, on Cape Cod, of land that the town had reserved in the southeast corner for the Indians "to live upon . . . forever." By 1820, those Indians had "no where to settle themselves being wholey distitute [sic] of land." They sent their plea for land with a representative (John Brooks) to Boston, who wound up penniless in the capital and was forced to pawn his clothing for board and finally to ask the governor for help to return home. About the same time, on outer Cape Cod, the towns of Harwich, Orleans, and Brewster asked to sell the 1,000 acres remaining of Potawamucut land. The Indians there were now "nearly Extinct," although recently several had returned as paupers and the towns expected more. The legislature gave its approval and told the towns to divide the money and to use it to support the remaining Indians. With Potawamucut and Indiantown at Yarmouth gone, Mashpee remained the only Indian reserve on Cape Cod.[51]

Natives in southern New England were as closely connected to their ancestral lands as tribes elsewhere in North America; like those others, they faced the end of their communities when they lost their lands. Few records exist of those who remained. Scattered evidence, including folklore, points to the persistence of some small Indian neighborhoods in ancestral areas, often on the edges of Anglo-American towns, where wetlands and woodland allowed them to subsist. In 1793, for example, the eight Wampanoag families still living at Betty's Neck along Assawompsett Pond raised corn and rye and "obtained a meagre subsistence by the sale of brooms and baskets which they manufactured." Scattered households and individuals also remained, as in Nipmuc territory where at least one or two families lived in nearly every town. These survivors also worked as laborers and peddlers, and though they did not wear leather, feathers, or paint, their clothing, appearance, and way of life somehow marked them as Indians.[52]

Hassanamisco descriptions and records are unusually detailed. Andrew and Hannah Brown (who "wore her hair long wore a Red Blanket & a man's Hat") supposedly "had no permanent dwelling place" but around 1800 still remained in Nipmuc territory around Grafton. During the winter they lived in Westborough in a hut and during warm seasons in Northborough, apparently in wigwams, selling baskets throughout the area. Harriet Forbes's story of life in Westborough at the turn of the century described various individuals, including Simon Gigger and Bets Hendricks who lived in "a kind of wigwam" on the outskirts of town. During the summer the two would travel through the area, stopping at farms to sell baskets, replace worn woven chair bottoms, or play music. Sarah Boston lived in Grafton on Keith Hill, where she tended a garden with a great cherry tree;

Figure 1. Hepsibeth Hemenway, ca. 1837. From the Collections of the Worcester Historical Museum, Worcester, Mass.

she often worked for farmers in the area, sold baskets, and told fortunes to young people.[53]

Some moved to the closest city to find work, like Moses and Cesear Gimbee who went to Worcester at the turn of the century. While Cesear went to sea and apparently died in Guadalupe in 1805, Moses remained in the city, and his descendants became active members of the African American community. Such movement was not new: Samuel Bowman (also Nipmuc, ca. 1699–1749) left Natick around 1720 for Pakachoag Hill, site of a seventeenth-century Nipmuc village, which quickly became part of Worcester and later the site of Holy Cross College. Bowman's family remained in the town as it grew into a city. His granddaughter, Hepsibeth Hemenway (1761–1848) gained fame as a baker and decorator of wedding cakes for Worcester's finest families, and a proud family tradition is that she roasted the pig for the city's first Fourth of July celebration in 1789. Shortly before her death, she commissioned her portrait, which was unusual for a working-class woman and unique for an Indian (figure 1). There were others who would also be moderately successful within the limited opportunities allowed people of color.[54]

But the majority of the Indians who left their villages found only poverty and isolation. Attithea Johns sold her last property in Grafton in 1796 and then lived with white families in Leicester as a domestic servant before dying nine years later. Her daughter Polly lived with her until about 1810 and next appeared on May 5, 1822, when she was found in a hut by the side of a swamp in Westborough "wholly destitute of any necessaries of support—and unable to help herself." Johns was taken to a nearby house and nursed there (aided by Hassanamisco funds) for two days until her death.[55] Even Hemenway, who was fortunate in marrying an African American carpenter who owned a house on two acres, was forced by circumstances to work as a cook and a laundress, which was exhausting, difficult, and poorly paid. Scattered documents testify to her family's poverty, and her children were hired out to work with white families in the city. Federal censuses between 1790 and 1830 of Worcester County's nonwhite population, which included "mixed" Indian descendants not viewed as members of a recognized tribe (including Hemenway, whose father was mulatto), show that about a third lived as servants or laborers in white households.[56]

Very small tribes with shrinking reserves were also more vulnerable to ecological problems, such as poor soil or exhausted timberlands. By 1823, the 112-acre Turkey Hill Paugussett reserve in Orange, east of Bridgeport and west of New Haven, had become, according to the tribe's overseer, "exceedingly broken, without timber, without fences, and mostly without fertility." He asked the state assembly for the right to sell land because the resident population of the tribe had declined due to "recent deaths," and he faced debts from medical care and funerals. Only eight to fifteen Paugussetts lived on the reserve, although there were also at least ten who were "wanderers at large"—no doubt in part because of the poor conditions of the reserve. It took him several tries to get $801 for 100 acres, leaving the best 12 acres on the reserve for the resident Paugussetts. By 1827, only one family still lived there, and the overseer sold the rest of the reserve except for a single acre for their house lot.[57]

To white observers, the diminishing of a group's fund and resident population meant the extinction of the tribe. In April 1835, William Brigham, a Grafton orator, told his town that about ten years before "the 'last of the Nipmucks' ceased to exist. They received their yearly income from their fund in the month of May, at which time they usually had a joyous holiday. Blankets, psalters and psalm books, were distributed among them, as well as money." Hassanamisco accounts from this period do show individuals coming to Grafton one day a year, usually in May or September, to receive their stipends drawn on the interest from loans made on their tribal fund. Much of this money went to pay white doctors, boardinghouse keepers, storeowners, and innkeepers, many in other towns. This supports the notion that the Hassanamisco tribe largely abandoned Grafton and dissolved as its members scattered to find their futures elsewhere. But though members of this village gradually dispersed, like others without lands, the community itself did not cease to exist, as kinship networks and occasional social gatherings maintained ancestral connections.[58]

Something similar happened to two other inland Indian groups that had been closely connected to Hassanamisco in John Eliot's missionary network in the mid-seventeenth century. Natick, the first "Praying Town," was quite small; by the end of 1835, only six to ten Indians remained in two households, although they retained the right to a special pew in the church Eliot had established. Natick's minister noticed, however, that their population occasionally grew as "other Indians of a more vagrant character" made that neighborhood "a kind of rendezvous in their wanderings."[59] At the same time, according to local traditions, a "few" Nipmucs still lived in Woodstock, Connecticut, very near the Dudley-Nipmuc reserve across the state line. But one by one, members of the Nedson family "succumbed to drink or disaster . . . John, the last survivor, ended his days at the town poorhouse, and the land they had so long occupied was sold by the town authorities." Yet their descendants and others identified as Nipmucs continued to live in the area.[60]

Some families and individuals seemed to lack any home and were susceptible to terrible poverty and illness. In 1785, Plymouth selectmen reported that, three winters earlier, Deborah Caswell, "an Indian woman not an Inhabitant of any town in this Commonwealth," had been found so badly frozen that they had hired a surgeon to amputate her feet. Nine years later, the nearby town of Pembroke reported that an Indian man, Joseph Warrich, had appeared on March 1, 1793, with his dying wife and two small children, "from what Town or where they belong we know not." Warrich stayed a short time and then disappeared, leaving his wife and children; she died five months later, followed within two months by one of the children. Caswell, the Warrichs, and others like them may have actually been long-term residents of the towns that claimed not to know them; during this period, New England towns faced a growing number of individuals and families falling into poverty and, when facing such cases, either "warned out" those they deemed transients or sought assistance from the state. Marginalized Indians were particularly vulnerable.[61]

In Connecticut, a number of such cases at the turn of the century seemed a consequence of the emigration of many Indians to Brothertown, as others were left behind without community support (resulting in the sale of tribal land), or of state laws that provided no clear means of support for the poor and helpless without tribes. In 1789, Haddam and Guildford each told the state assembly that they had supported the indigent Ann Tantspan, a Tunxis, and asked to sell an island that she supposedly owned in the middle of the Connecticut River. Another Tunxis, Polly Mazzen, fell sick in Canaan and died in Cornwall, and in 1802 both towns asked the assembly to sell land she had held in Farmington. The state had no procedure to obtain compensation for helping needy individuals whom they viewed as outside transients—such as the Indians from nearby or more distant tribes. In 1795, Norwich asked the assembly for help after supporting an Eastern Pequot woman, Peggy George; similar petitions were submitted in 1801 by Woodbridge; in 1817 by Newtown, for supporting a "destitute" Golden Hill Paugussett; and in the 1820s by Cornwall, Brooklyn, and Hartford. In October 1818, Montville complained that they were caring for "many needy Mohegans" but lacked the power to tax the tribe's lands within the tribe; they sought and obtained a special measure from the state assembly requiring that their costs of caring for the tribe's poor be chargeable to the tribe.[62]

Smaller groups and isolated individuals also lacked access to the streams, ponds, and woodlands they needed to subsist or to make saleable crafts, particularly as they were increasingly barred from town commons and private property. In 1820, the Yarmouth Indians complained that they were "debarred" by the town from "all privileges such as casketwood [and] broomwood if we presume to make use of such advantages as our fore fathers made use of we are prosecuted and put to Charge," and that the whites were taking firewood and salt from lands once reserved for them. Southern New England generally experienced high population growth, mobility, and more intensive farming during the early national period, filling up formerly unsettled land and endangering informal agreements that may have been reached between colonial proprietors and Indians. Individuals found themselves turned away from woodland or fishing spots where their ancestors had obtained important resources. Natick minister Stephen Badger wrote in 1798 that Indians in the area frequently entered "into the houses of which they seem to think they have some kind of right to enter, as their forefathers were the original proprietors and possessors of the land."[63]

A century later, Anglo-American folklore took a very different view of such encounters. One town history tells "of a squaw securing splints [for baskets] on the land of an old farmer who charged her with theft, and ordered her off. Raising her hatchet she replied: 'My grandpa's land—you go way, or I will make daylight shine through you.' Her argument was final and she was thereafter allowed her basket timber whenever she desired." A very similar story set in a town north of the Mashantucket Pequot reservation, recorded by Frances Caulkins in the mid-nineteenth century, has the woman deny the white man's legal right to the land: "Show me the paper & tell me what you paid for it. It was bought, there ought to be pay—but we never had any pay." But by that time Indians had become safe, romantic remnants rather than threatening symbols of conflicting claims or disorder (chap. 5).[64]

WORK OFF THE RESERVATION

Most Indians at some point traveled and worked among whites and blacks. As before the Revolution, poverty or debts forced children and some adults into indentured servitude. Children became domestics or farm laborers; women did the same and sold crafts on the side; and men were pressed into whaling. Men and women also chose to leave their homes to work on whaling ships or as laborers in port towns, driven by the need to obtain a living and perhaps drawn by the opportunity to see new places and try new things. Some remained closer to home and worked as day laborers on nearby white-owned farms. Women also found a growing market for their traditional skills: Indian basket-and-broom peddlers became a common sight in villages and along rural roads, and a few became recognized as skilled herbal healers with somewhat mystical abilities.[65]

Such work was not new, although it did become more common after the war, particularly among those from larger communities. These occupations seemed to whites somehow particularly suited to Indians. But though these jobs on one level seemed to confirm or reconstruct Indian identity and culture, on another level they broke down many of the social and cultural boundaries that distinguished Natives from others. At the end of the Revolution, Indian laborers retained their distinctive identities even as they dressed and lived as the "lower sort." But their circumstances, the dynamics of the region's increasingly commercialized economy, and emerging "scientific" racism meant that, by 1820, Indians were increasingly viewed by Anglo-Americans as part of the colored underclass.

Servitude with white families and on whaling ships, common before the Revolution, continued after it. Some were men and women convicted of crimes, like "Joseph Jonson Muste & Mary his wife Indian." In September 1785, the two residents of Stonington, probably Eastern Pequots, were fined for fencing stolen property but, unable to pay the fine, were both sentenced to be whipped and then bound for two and a half years to the man who lodged the complaint. In 1794, Gideon Hawley wrote that many Indian whalers and their children "were transferred from one to another master like slaves," the whalers having been required by the ship captains or masters to sign over their children in case they died or ran away.[66]

Indentured servitude remained common for Indian children until the mid-nineteenth century. Timothy Dwight noted that many Pequots placed their children "in English families as servants," and some parents may have indentured their children from desperate necessity or because it seemed the best way for the children to adapt to the new world. But most were bound over by local selectmen. Stonington selectmen in October 1780 bound two "Indian and mulatto" (probably Pequot) siblings, Mary and Peter Dereck, to Alexander Bradford and four months later two other "poor Indian" siblings, Samuel and Mary Primus, to Alpheus Miner. Another indentured Pequot child was William Apess, who was bound out in 1801 at the age of three and would grow up to lead the 1833 Mashpee revolt. Even in 1820, "a large proportion" of Herring Pond children were servants with white families, and six years later a Connecticut assembly special committee urged that Montville officials be given the power bind out Mohegan children "on the same principles as the children of poor Parents are now bound out by Law." The majority of these children probably performed farm and domestic labor for their masters. Although the law allowed the children of the poor to be indentured regardless of color, such servitude marked a widening divide between whites and people of color as this institution rapidly declined among Anglo-Americans.[67]

Some Indian whalers were indentured, but most were free men. Whaling was a significant part of the New England economy during the eighteenth century and boomed after the Revolution. In 1802, even while boasting of Mashpee's farmers, Gideon Hawley bemoaned that "whaling employs numbers of our blacks and it gets them into a distaste for tilling the ground." A few years later, English visitor Edward Kendall found only 15 men and boys in the fields at Gay Head; the others were "at sea, in the fisheries," which was "their favourite employ." In 1818, a state investigator reported that few Indian men on the Vineyard farmed: "Their employment is chiefly in the Fisheries," which "operates as a disqualification to any industry while they are on shore."[68] Observers noted that this close connection between Indians and whaling was the result of forced servitude due to debts, traditional culture (Indian men hunted and fished), and poor opportunities at home. Ship masters perceived Indians as particularly skilled harpooners and steersmen, with an innate sense of how to find and take a whale even in the deep ocean far from home; indeed, a tradition developed that it was good luck to employ a Gay Header as a steerer. The trade would spread to Connecticut, enlisting most Mohegan and many Pequot men, and it continued to play a dominant role in Indian communities through midcentury.[69]

Indian men were not alone in leaving their villages in large numbers at the turn of the century. Throughout southern New England, farm communities, after generations of population growth, faced a shortage of pasture- and cropland. Efforts to clear more land for use led to the highest rate of deforestation in the history of the region, creating a shortage of wood but not necessarily more arable land because of the acidity of the soil. Farmers tried to adjust by adopting new agricultural methods and producing crops for the growing cities or overseas trade—that required good transportation connections, and in that lottery some towns were winners and others losers. Young men all over southern New England facing a poor future abandoned their towns for new opportunities. Some created new settlements in the north, Vermont and Maine, or west in New York or on the Ohio frontier; others moved to the cities, where some became mariners alongside Indians. Although the larger Indian tribes such as Mashpee and Gay Head retained the wild animals, woodlands, and resources that were scarce in other parts of the region, many of the men who became whalers and their families may have faced the same problems as whites, particularly as they could not move to one of the new frontier towns. Entering the maritime work helped keep pressure off tribal resources.[70]

The whaling industry became so large that masters and captains recruited men from many countries and backgrounds. Perhaps this is why Native men seemed to increasingly share aspects of the international maritime plebeian culture, although that behavior when exhibited by Indians was often depicted as part of their "savage" nature. For example, a supposedly Indian characteristic was their improvidence and inability to plan for the future, and indeed many Indian whalers got themselves and their families deeply into debt before leaving on a voyage. But this was generally part of the subculture of whaling, which also involved the Indians' neighbors. Edward Kendall found that many white men on Cape Cod were whalers, that they commonly spent more than their potential wages before leaving on a voyage, and that the resulting debt forced them to go on the next voyage organized by creditors. Anglo-American reformers and Indian leaders were troubled by problems generated by the transient life whalers led, although for different reasons. Reformers were frustrated by how whaling forestalled their vision of proper, civilized life; Natives were concerned about how it harmed the community and families. In 1788, Mashpee elders complained that many young men remained in "foreign parts . . . having no attachments or Interests to call them home." Such deep involvement in the trade also meant that Indian communities were vulnerable to the unpredictable tides of international politics, as during the War of 1812, when American whalers were kept from the high seas.[71]

But the most harmful aspect of the international maritime culture was the heavy drinking and disruptive habits of sailors and their friends onshore. Hawley complained that when whalers returned to Mashpee, "there is little else but drinking whoring fighting etc etc." Some of the drinking establishments were run by Indians; Hawley noted that Joseph Amos's wife and Hannah Babcock operated "tippling houses" in Mashpee with "lewd women." Gay Head leaders asked the state for help, as the tribe's many whalemen on New Bedford ships brought home "ardent spirits . . . in large quantities, [which they] dealt out freely to all their people who desire it," leading to "intoxication and riot." Alcohol abuse was a growing problem in the United States at the turn of the century, so this was not just an issue for sailors and captains. Of course, Indians were notorious for drinking prodigious amounts of rum and erupting into frenzied violence, so such behavior could be depicted as either "traditional" or as part of being a sailor. Regardless, it was clearly a concern for their vulnerable communities and families.[72]

Not all Indians were whalers: like African Americans, Indians of both sexes continued to labor in Anglo-American rural and urban households. In 1800, Hawley noted that many young Mashpee women had left to work "as maids in the neighbouring towns." Several Hassanamiscos were recorded as having worked as servants, including Hepsibeth Hemenway, Attithea Johns, Deborah Brown, and Brown's daughter Hannah. Mashantucket Pequot women were, according to a local historian, "excellent servants in the household, and were more or less frequently employed by families" in Ledyard and Stonington. Young Indian women found this an opportunity to try city life. Hawley complained that "many of our young females go to Boston for months together . . . to the injury of their morals."[73]

Many Indians worked as farm laborers. In 1807, Dwight visited Stonington and found a "considerable number" of Mashantucket Pequots there, about a third of whom "live on the farms of the white inhabitants in houses built purposely for them, and pay their rent by daily labor."[74] Some were women who, like African American women (slave and free), crossed the gender boundaries of the early republic. Sarah Boston, a Hassanamisco, "wandered about the country, in one place helping the farmer with his work, and receiving her pay in cider. In times of extra work she was considered a very desirable 'hand,' and the heaviest work was left for her to do."[75] These workers were seemingly invisible, as few appear in the accounts kept by white farmers.[76]

Indian women may have also traded products of their farms and common lands, including cranberries, wood, butter, and cheese. But they were most noted for their involvement in the basket and broom trade, which helped them support their families while their men disappeared on whaling trips. The trade was not new, but it became more widespread toward the end of the eighteenth century, stimulated by the rising desire for order and cleanliness that was part of the commercial revolution (which was ironic, as whites saw Indians as dirty and disorderly). By 1802, many Mashpee women found it profitable to "make brooms and baskets, and sell them among their white neighbours." Women and children gathered bark (usually ash) and other products from woods and swamps on their reserves or the interstices between towns, and they spent the long winter weaving. In the spring, the women strapped their finished products to their backs and walked from village to village — expected, and even welcomed, by their white customers.[77]

Traveling Indian craftswomen became a part of New England culture. Lydia Sigourney wrote in an 1824 novel about her town of Norwich, Connecticut, set in 1784, that Mohegan women showed "considerable ingenuity" in "the manufacture of brooms, mats, and baskets," which through the use of plants they adorned with many colors. "Bending beneath a load of these fabrics, and often the additional weight of a pappose, or a babe, deposited in a large basket, and fastened around the neck with a leather strap," these craftswomen "might be seen, walking through the streets of the town, after a weary journey from their own settlement . . . clad in insufficient apparel after the American fashion, with a little bonnet of blue cloth, in a shape peculiar to themselves, and somewhat resembling a scallop-shell, and a small blanket thrown over the shoulders, if the season were cold, they would enter every door in search of a market." John Avery of Ledyard recalled the Pequot Anne Wampy who, during the first quarter of the nineteenth century, "carried upon her shoulders a bundle of baskets so large as almost to hide her from view . . . many skillfully ornamented in various colors. Her baskets were so good that she would find customers at almost every house. And after traveling a dozen or twenty miles and spending two or three days in doing it her load would be all gone." The women themselves were not so sanguine about their situations; Wampy told William Apess in the late 1820s that "by me come trouble very much, me very much troubled. Me no like Christians, me hate 'em, hate everybody."[78]

But basket peddling was a matter of survival for Indian women, not just for income but also to mediate relationships with Anglo-Americans. Molly Hatchett, a Paugussett who visited more than a hundred farms every year with beautiful, delicate baskets, often gave babies woven rattles with corn kernels. Craftswomen continued to use traditional designs and colors, and surviving baskets from this period show distinctive tribal patterns east of the Connecticut River and family styles west of the river. Most whites saw the crafts trade as a quaint though useful remnant of aboriginal culture, but more importantly it was a bridge to the evolving New England economy. Basket makers were able to market traditional skills, obtain necessary materials from swamps, meadows, and forests, and rely on an informal network of Indian families for assistance and a place to stay in foul weather or bad times. It is for good reasons that the basket trade symbolized the region's Indians.[79]

Medicine represented a similar connection between Native traditions and New England's economy and culture. Throughout America, folk medicine was as effective and accepted as that offered by college-trained healers, and Indians in New England, like blacks in the South, were perceived as having special skills and knowledge of local herbs. A Bristol County history observed that during the early colonial period, "the Indian 'medicine man' was frequently called upon for relief in sickness." About 1801, when Noyes Holmes was a boy in the north parish of Stonington, near the Eastern Pequot reserve, he had suffered from "humor in my head," which the doctor (with whom he was living) could not cure but which "an old squaw" was able to cure "with a few applications of cat's grease and Indian posey." *Every Man His Own Physician* (1836) observed, "Who, in America, has not known or heard of repeated instances wherein some decrepit, unpretending female Indian, by means of her simple remedies alone, has effected the most rapid and astonishing cures after the whole skill of the common practice has failed?"[80]

Apparently most Native healers were women. Natick's Hannah Dexter (1744–1821) gained such fame for her skills with roots and herbs that the wealthy sick from Boston and Cambridge sent their carriages for the doctresses. Esther Howossowee (b. 1797) and Tamson Weeks (1806–ca. 1890) from Gay Head "were herb doctors of great renown, both on the islands and on the mainland," who jealously guarded their secret herbal medicines.[81] Also of Gay Head was Patience Gashum (or Gershom, b. 1778), an "herb-woman" who gained infamy among her own people as a witch.[82] Rebecca Davis of Punkapoag (b. ca. 1790) moved to Boston but continued to visit her ancestral community every year and earned money "by the sale of a salve, which she prepared from herbs according to the prescription of some ancient medicine man."[83] Some were men: John Konkepot, graduate of the Moravian school in Pennsylvania, traveled around the Northeast and became famous as "Doctor Konkopot" for curing rattlesnake bites and a wide range of diseases with "Indian medicines."[84]

Stereotypes of Indian laborers were also linked to gender in the early republic. Whites saw all Indians as undependable, mercurial, and immoral, inherently unable to save or plan for the future (like whalers). But whereas the men were lazy derelicts, the women seemed colorful and hardworking.[85] These views originated with European perceptions of Eastern Woodland cultures, as visitors to Indian villages usually saw men relaxing like noblemen while women appeared to do all the work; they endured in part because Indian men worked far from the public eye as whalers, even as women continued to make and sell baskets. Yet some men were involved in the crafts trade as well as doctoring. Pequot men carved and peddled wooden trays, bowls, and spoons door-to-door. Narragansett men were highly regarded as masons, building many stone walls in farms around Rhode Island, and working in other crafts: in 1832, the tribal council told the state that their people were "carpenters, coopers, shoe makers, tailors, weavers &c &c." But the overwhelming image was that Indian men were dispirited, alcoholic vagrants. As is common with such insidious paradigms, their victims sometimes embraced the stereotype.[86]

While medicine and crafts incorporated aboriginal traditions, working among Anglo-Americans inevitably reshaped Indian cultures and communities. Gender roles shifted as the absence, or even disappearance, of men on long whaling trips renewed the distinctive political and economic prominence of Indian women in their communities. Since Anglo-Americans believed in corporal punishment, Indians raised in white households may have inflicted that experience on *their* children, which would have been a significant change in Native child rearing. Servitude and labor with whites also played a significant role in the decline of Native languages, as English became the dominant language in coastal Indian groups by the middle of the eighteenth century. The institution also endangered Indian tribes in other ways. In May 1823, Sally Law, a Mohegan woman living in Norwich, asked to sell eighteen acres of Mohegan land; she told the state assembly that she had been "educated entirely in respectable families of white people," had "no attachment to the mode of Life which the natives pursue," and never wanted to return to the tribe. Although the land sale was permanent, and such alienation appears in other records, Law did return to the tribe and its reserve after her husband died two decades later, in part because her son was being barred from Norwich schools and the tribal school (chapter 4) had gained considerable fame.[87] Some of the deeper social and psychological damage may be seen in William

Apess's description of his childhood indenture: though he was taught to read and write, he was also trained to fear and hate Indians. Most recognizable Indians still lived within their ancestral communities. But by serving as bound *and* wage laborers, subsistence *and* market workers, Natives in southern New England represented a bridge between the past and future of labor in America.

Perhaps the most striking characteristic of Indian work in the early republic was its transient nature. Anglo-American observers were unsettled and amused by how Indians were, as Natick's minister Stephen Badger found in 1798, "strangely disposed and addicted to wander from place to place." Two decades later, William Tudor compared his region's Natives to Europe's Gypsies, and many town histories published in the nineteenth century include colorful stories of Indian migrant workers. One might be tempted to see such work as a continuation of the mixed-subsistence economies that distinguished aboriginal societies in southern New England. Certainly Anglo-American elites connected the Indians' seeming preference for temporary, migratory work as part of their tendency to, as Timothy Dwight put it in typically scathing language, "doze away life in uniform sloth and stupidity."[88]

But as Anne Wampy, Polly Johns, and others demonstrate, Indian peddlers, migratory workers, and other transients suffered from inadequate food and clothing, poor living conditions, winter's biting cold, and a profound sense of inadequacy and loneliness. Not unique was Patience Pometick's life: she was born in Barnstable and grew up in Hingham, and beginning at age eighteen (perhaps after fulfilling an indenture with a white family), supposedly "lived a rambling life, and a very intemperate one." She stayed in Sandwich, Halifax, Middleborough, and Kingston, all in southeastern Massachusetts, but seemed to spend most of her time in and around Hingham, living in the woods in a hut or wigwam during the summer and with a white family in the town during the winter. By 1796, she was blind, elderly, and forced to rely on Hingham's charity.[89]

Yet Indians were not alone on southern New England's roads or in the region's woods. By the end of the eighteenth century, a growing number of men, women, and even whole families, of all ethnic and racial backgrounds, had become transients. Many former slaves were forced into homelessness by emancipation, as racism rose and towns refused to accept the freedmen as citizens eligible for community support if they fell into poverty. Many whites, native-born and immigrants, simply could not find steady work in the region's unstable economy. Others could not or did not want to take on the increasingly impersonalized and wage-structured forms of day labor. This tendency increased as New England industrialized. In January 1833, a Massachusetts legislative committee reported that "the number is very large of these wandering poor" and that some towns recorded up to 200 itinerants during the past year. The commissioners also noted that "these unhappy fellow beings often travel with females, sometimes, but not always, their wives; while yet, in the towns in which they take up their temporary abode, they are almost always recognized, and treated, as sustaining this relation." Such informal marriages were also common among Indians and other "lower sorts." Ironically, in this human landscape Indians may have had an advantage with their ability to move quickly and quietly around the region using family connections, multigenerational memories of useful fishing, gathering, or hunting places, and a range of other survival skills taught by grandparents or parents.[90]

The conditions and circumstances faced by Indian laborers highlights how the Anglo-American class system was racialized in the early republic. By the end of the Revolutionary War, Anglo-Americans increasingly viewed the remaining coastal Indians as part of an undifferentiated group of people of color. This was the result of the bichromatic ideology of racism, the high rate of Indian-African American intermarriage, and new notions of the unchangeable nature of a separate Indian race. People of color were also perceived as a permanent socioeconomic class forming the lowest strata in the infant United States, as Americans forged new notions of nation and class as well as race. On the one hand, Democrat-Republicans promised social and political equality for yeoman farmers and artisans, apparently ending class distinctions, but silently denied parity or citizenship to people of color, thereby connecting race and class in America. On the other hand, Federalist writers tended to see people of color as part of the general socioeconomic class structure, rather than a separate racial category, although their protests were more formal and theoretical than substantial.[91]

INDIAN RESERVES AS REFUGES

Indian reserves served as seasonal homes for families and individuals who labored or otherwise sought their subsistence elsewhere during the rest of the year. In 1800, Gideon Hawley told Jedidiah Morse that many Mashpees would "wander" during the summer but returned to the reserve in the wintertime. In 1827, a state commission counted just four to six Indians (Teticuts) who held land in Middleborough but noted that this population occasionally rose to 15 to 20 due to the "temporary residence of other Indians among them." During this period, "some scattering families" returned to the Mohegan reservation each spring, when the fish swam upriver to spawn, fields were planted, and members received their biennial "rations." The Narragansett population similarly fluctuated as many men left for the summer to find employment as masons or laborers. Some stayed away for many years. Tribal chair Gideon Ammons told a state commission in 1880 that members of the tribe living off the reserve would occasionally visit to boast of the "big team they were driving and how much they were making" but sooner or later "they would be sent to us as paupers."[92]

By 1800, a market economy for produce, capital, and labor had matured in southern New England. Within the region, Indian reserves acted as reservoirs of antimarket forces. This enabled Indian communities to rebuild and maintain their sense of being a separate people, including traditions of social good rather than individualism. Some reserves became refuges for poor whites and blacks from an increasingly uncertain, impersonal economy that (particularly for recently freed blacks relegated to lowest socioeconomic status) seemed a threat rather than an opportunity.[93] Neighboring towns feared that the reserves were becoming asylums for miscreants because they seemed to share similar sinful and unhealthy customs with the Indians, such as informal marriages. In 1788, magistrates in towns surrounding Mashpee told the legislature that the reserve threatened to become "a Receptacle of Thieves, vagabonds & Robbers." Twenty-one years later, Curtis Coe, returning from his first visit to the Narragansetts, commented, "It is said the white people, who live among the Natives, are the lowest part of society." In 1833, the *Boston Advocate* opined that Indian villages throughout the region were "so many Alsatias, where the vagrant, the dissipated, and the felonious do congregate." The Mashantucket Pequot guardian wrote that his charges were "extremely hospitable to all vagabonds; receiving, without hesitation, all that come to them, whether white, mulatto, Indian or negro." The 1861 survey of Massachusetts Indians noted that Indian mariners sometimes returned with "foreign" shipmates, including men of European or African descent, who wound up marrying Native women and staying on the reserve.[94] Thus some whites and blacks joined Indians in what today might be called an underclass and found in Native reserves a home.

Dwight and other Anglo-American conservatives criticized the persistence of subsistence ways and communal work among Indians in the region. After complaining at length about the lazy, alcoholic, degraded Pequots (which followed a similar passage about the Mohegans at Montville), he concluded that the only way to get Indians to improve is to replace their "love of glory" with "that which has been substituted in every civilized nation: viz., *the love of property*" (emphasis in original). Certainly Indians did own property, but their subsistence workways and communal-landholding traditions tended to bar the avarice and ambition that Dwight and other Anglo-American elites viewed as civilized if properly harnessed. Dwight also acknowledged in a sideways manner how others were at-tracted to "Indian" values by using the Pequots as an example to attack the ideas of English socialist philosopher William Godwin. But here again, Indians may not have been alone in their resistance to capitalism. Indeed, the continued in-denturing and nonwage employment of Indians after the Revolution may be seen as part of the desire by some New England farmers to keep the parts of the mar-ket economy at bay.[95]

Modern market capitalism emerged as part of the new American nation. This was particularly evident in southern New England, not only because of its ever-deepening involvement in international fishing and commerce but also because formerly discrete markets of trade and labor merged within the region around 1800. Within this regional economy, which was part of a new national core, Indi-ans retained distinctive lifeways and communities even as they participated in that economy as part-time wage workers—a class that usually includes members of scorned ethnic groups who earn few of the rewards of market capitalism. Every occupation that Indians filled outside their community was temporary, as indi-viduals worked in that field for only a short period during their lifetime, and la-borers, whalers, and domestics rarely served the same master for more than a few years, and generally only a season or two. As exemplified by whaling, basket ped-dling, and medicine, such jobs were dictated by Native traditions as well as An-glo-American prejudice.[96]

The communal values generally maintained by Indians may have primed them for their subaltern niche in the regional economy, particularly as individu-als willing and able to accumulate capital are usually winners in such an econ-omy, and those who do not have such skills or inclination usually lose. Indian groups became famous at the outset of European exploration for producing and sharing everything in common. Those that survived behind the frontier of Anglo-American settlement continued to emphasize subsistence, sharing, and main-taining ancestral reserves, and to condemn excess individualistic striving. These socioeconomic standards may have played into Anglo-American prejudice and therefore reinforced barriers that kept individual Indians from improving their lives in the developing economy.[97] But their persistent communal values helped Indians maintain the land base that provided a measure of flexibility and auton-omy from the abrasive regional economy, which was critical for Indian survival during the upheaval of the early republic. Coastal reserves protected by state laws provided important resources, particularly fish, which could be eaten or sold.

The experiences of tribes living within and without the modern capitalist market system are superb examples of discrete social formations stubbornly persisting outside the larger world system.[98] Southern New England Indians were no longer sovereign (even as they maintained a noticeable level of local autonomy), but their efforts to maintain community and identity reflect in some measure the revitalization movements that swept Native groups confronting colonialism in the eighteenth and nineteenth century.[99] Their efforts also point to how "friends of the Indians" in the late nineteenth century were correct in believing that they had "to kill the Indian to save the man": to remove Native children from their families, communities, and cultures in order to teach them the values of competitive market capitalism and survive in the modern world. Those reformers were right, for Native societies and cultures were clearly antithetical to market values, and it was the ability of those communities to maintain different values that made (and continue to make) them so attractive to others.[100] Although they may have lost ground in the shifting economy, these groups managed to maintain their distinct systems, and in the process they attracted new members, whites and particularly blacks, who apparently also disliked the systemic changes.

CHAPTER TWO

Community and Family

At about the time of American Revolution a Narragansett, Alice Prophetess, bought an African American slave and made him her husband. She would later tell their grandson William J. Brown that she did so "in order to change her mode of living." Brown commented that, among her grandmother's people, "it was customary for the woman to do all the drudgery and hard work in-doors and out . . . The Indian women observing the colored men working for their wives, and living after the manner of white people, in comfortable homes, felt anxious to change their position in life." But as more Indian women like Prophetess married African Americans, he noted, Indian men developed a "very bitter feeling" against blacks. These conflicts, which were sometimes expressed in racial terms, developed from the resentment against Indian women for choosing outsiders, the potential that such marriages could endanger communal resources, and the perception that the children and grandchildren of such marriages were more likely to follow a path away from the tribe's culture. Brown was a leader of the African American community of Providence, Rhode Island, and gave no indication in his 1883 autobiography that he retained any sense of Narragansett identity.[1]

The rising tendency of Indian women in southern New England to marry "foreigners & strangers," mostly African American although also white, created a major challenge for Native groups.[2] As they struggled to maintain their communities and lands, they were confronted with the need to define their social boundaries as a growing number of individuals and families moved between, into, and out of surviving enclaves. This human movement reshaped Indian identity and continually tested the ability of groups to assimilate newcomers and resist challengers. Some groups retained the population, cohesion, and resources to assimilate new-

comers and their "mixed" children, using their lands as political and social controls to manage the effects of exogamous marriages. Ironically, in doing so Natives
relied on their legal handicaps, for neither tribes nor individuals could sell Indian
land to outsiders without the permission of the legislature. In addition to concerns
over immigrants' access to resources and power, after 1820 some Indian communities became alarmed at emigrants' efforts to sell tribal lands and, in response,
sought to limit or deny group membership to those who left.

Exogamous marriages and state laws allowed Indian women to hold far more
political and economic power than their white and black contemporaries. Although the largely familial authority of Indian women had roots in aboriginal culture, it was renewed by the extended absences of Indian men and the increasing
"adoption" of black or white husbands who, as outsiders, lacked the status of those
born into the community. Thus women became guardians of their communities
even as their exogamous marriages served as potential conduits of disruptive
changes. The power wielded by Indian women did not go unchallenged, however,
as Indian men sought at the beginning of the nineteenth century to increase their
power and respectability. A different situation faced Indian groups without the advantages of numbers and lands. They were more easily reshaped by regional trends
such as urbanization as, after 1800, members moved to nearby towns or cities
where they lived with and became part of emerging African American enclaves.
Among such families, dual and shifting ethnic identities and affiliations became
quite common.

The persistence, adaptation, and acculturation of particular ethnic groups, and
the assimilation of members of those groups, are not unusual topics of study for
scholars and policy makers. But this aspect of New England Indians in the early
republic is unusual because it took place earlier than such developments and issues are generally studied, and on the side of America's racial line where few studies of ethnicity have gone. Examining relations between Indians and blacks in
southern New England illuminates the fundamental flaws of a bichromatic view
of racial relations in American history and offers new insight into the complexity,
malleability, and uncertainty of ethnic identity and assimilation.

INDIAN NETWORKS IN THE EARLY REPUBLIC

Indians had forged regional networks in the century before the Revolution.
The migration of individuals and families within these networks continued after
the war, encouraged in part by regular religious meetings. An Anglo-American
resident of Dartmouth remembered from his childhood in the 1770s that Indians

from Martha's Vineyard and elsewhere "came once a year" to the home of Ne-
hemiah Abel, an Indian minister in the town, for communion and worship. Religious meetings at Mashpee drew Indians from throughout Plymouth County,
Cape Cod, Martha's Vineyard, and Nantucket. This network remained very important a century later, during a period of revitalization and reform among Indian
groups, bringing William Apess from Mashantucket to Mashpee and Joseph Amos
to the circuit that connected Mashpee to the Vineyard and Nantucket. In fact, after his death on April 17, 1869, Amos of Mashpee was buried in the Indian cemetery on Chappaquiddick.[3]

These religious gatherings also facilitated kinship connections between groups,
forming an important element of Indian identity and community in southern New
England. Particularly prominent in the records were ties of marriage and blood
among Wampanoags in Martha's Vineyard, Mashpee, and in the Dartmouth–
New Bedford area.[4] Such networks were also formed among Connecticut and
Rhode Island tribes, in large part through religious meetings and the Brothertown
movement. On a warm Sunday in August 1811, visiting minister Curtis Coe noted
that many leading Narragansett men and women had gone to the bimonthly meeting at Mashantucket, where they were joined by "people of different nations." One
week later, those who had made the trip told Coe that "brethren" from Long Island and Brothertown had been there. Such visits continued for decades.[5] As with
Wampanoag networks, these religious gatherings had social corollaries. By 1861,
Connecticut investigators reported that many of the 80 Mohegans had Pequot,
Narragansett, Tunxis, or Niantic ancestors. From outside the region, Oneidas
came from New York and returnees from Brothertown (in New York and then Wisconsin), creating or renewing connections.[6]

Social and kinship connections between tribes were spun for many reasons and
could span long distances. A Paugussett moved for a while to Massachusetts,
where he had two children with a woman from a tribe (not named) in that state,
and then returned by 1823 to his ancestral home on the Golden Hill reserve. The
state assembly committee that reported his story also noted they had "considerable difficulty" in determining the tribe's number and names "owing to their connections, by marriage & otherwise, with Indians of other tribes." Mi'kmaq and
Penobscot travelers came south to Boston and other towns to sell crafts or find
work, meeting and staying with Indians in southern New England, creating new
social and kinship networks. John Johnson (b. 1833), an Anglo-American raised by
Mi'kmaqs and Wabanakis in Nova Scotia, traveled with his Native relatives as far
south as Philadelphia and spent considerable time in southern New England selling baskets and medicine and working in Indian circuses. At one point, he and his

fiancée, who was also apparently Indian (tribe unknown), went to stay with her relatives outside Salem, Massachusetts.[7]

This movement widened Indian networks in the early nineteenth century, expanding to the growing cities as men and some women sought work in the maritime economy. In 1802, the Herring Pond guardians paid a Boston family nearly three pounds for nursing a sick member of the tribe. Yet few Indian names appeared in 1800 on the city's "warning out" lists of colored people who were not residents, which indicates that most lived with white families as domestics, came to get a berth on a ship, or managed to fit in while residing among blacks. But they did not remain invisible. Two decades later, Boston officials sought compensation after providing, over many years, nearly $500 in support to Mashpees. The best count comes from Earle's 1861 survey of Massachusetts Indians, the first to include cities; he found 46 in Boston and 16 in adjoining Roxbury, more than in Christiantown (55) and as many as in Chappaquiddick (62). In the early part of the century, the growth of the deep-water whaling trade made New Bedford the main destination for Indians seeking work. Chappaquiddick, Christiantown, and Gay Head accounts from the 1820s and 1830s show many men working on whaling ships operating out of New Bedford: about 65 from Gay Head alone in 1838. Mohegans and Pequots usually sought berths on ships in New London or Stonington.[8]

Studies of the early republic tend to deal with either rural or urban worlds, and the ties between the two remain relatively obscure. But the human links between city and country were an important aspect of the American scene at the turn of the century as the urban population grew rapidly. While many of those coming to the cities were from other countries, growing numbers of poor families and individuals from the New England countryside moved to the port towns and cities to find work. The human traffic went both ways. Indian women traveled from their villages to cities to work as domestics, some returning with new husbands, and Indian men spent long periods in port waiting for whaling voyages. Individuals and families often spent many years, or part of every year, in the city, returning to their ancestral communities to claim rights to resources or to renew their cultural roots and social connections.[9]

MARRIAGES WITH "FOREIGNERS & STRANGERS"

In addition to marriages between members of different tribes or villages, marriages between Indians and non-Indians played a significant role in reshaping Native communities. These relationships developed when Indians were living in cities or towns or when outsiders visited Native groups; therefore, they created kinship connections that were new in terms of place as well as race. In 1802, Hawley remarked that "many of our [Mashpee] women have found negroe husbands, as they were stroling in the country and bro't them home." A half-century later, Earle noted without rancor or disdain the many generations and high rate of intermarriage among Massachusetts Indian groups, for example describing Gay Headers as "a mixture of red, white, and black races, Southerners, Portuguese, Dutch, etc." He carefully noted that this was because "most of the young men go to sea, and many never return, their places taken by other seafaring men who meet Gay Headers at sea, visit, and marry Gay Head women and settle in for life." His census also points to the significance, usually ignored by other observers, of Indian-white intermarriage. The two Hassanamisco men in Boston, for example, were both married to Anglo-American women, and by that time nearly all of the Yarmouth Indians were the offspring of several generations of Indian-white parents. But, for a range of reasons, most mixed marriages brought the descendants of aboriginals and Africans together.[10]

By the end of the eighteenth century, marriages between Indian women and African American men had become common in southern New England, for these individuals were united by their shared demographic, social, and legal condition. Censuses from Massachusetts, Rhode Island, and Connecticut between 1765 and 1774 show at least 50 percent more Indian women than men, as Native men disappeared on whaling voyages or in the colonial militia. Other censuses from the same period show about 50 percent more African American men than women. This complementary demographic imbalance and Anglo-American prejudice meant that Native women were often able to meet their emotional, demographic, economic, and social needs only by marrying African American men—a process that also served to adopt the newcomer into family and community. Indians and blacks were also brought together by Anglo-Americans, who saw both as sources of social disorder and passed laws to enforce their shared servitude and marginal status. Members of both groups lived in widely scattered households in New England villages and cities. They met in the households where they worked, while running errands, in the New Light religious meetings that attracted all races and classes, and in the annual African election festivals that until they ended in the early republic brought together many blacks and Indians.[11]

Other factors encouraged these exogamous marriages. Eastern Woodland peoples often sought to adopt or marry outsiders as way of improving or gaining new and useful connections for the community. Given the changes in their world by the eighteenth century, Indian women like Alice Prophetess may have indeed married a "foreigner" to improve their lives and better provide for their children.

African men in turn gained economic and social benefits from an Indian wife, particularly before slavery ended. As with William Brown's grandfather, enslaved blacks were sometimes purchased by their Indian wives and set free; even if they remained enslaved, their children would be born free. Eleanor Eldridge, one of Providence's most famous black residents in the 1830s, told a biographer that her Narragansett maternal grandmother, Mary Fuller, sold tribal lands to purchase her husband, the African slave Thomas Prophet. A Canton town historian wrote in 1893 that enslaved blacks came to the Indian community of Punkapog "to marry an Indian wife, for then [their] children would be free, as the law in those days was that the children of Indian women were free-born." In addition, the usually penniless man gained access to (though not legal control over) land and other resources open to his wife. He also gained a supportive community, as Native enclaves generally welcomed new relations regardless of skin color.[12]

Exogamous marriage was initially less prevalent on larger Indian communities before the Revolution. A 1774 list of adults labeled as "not Properly Mohegan" by one faction in that quarreling Connecticut tribe, for example, contained only one name, Pompey George, commonly associated with African Americans. Two years later, Gideon Hawley noted only 14 "negroes" among the more than 300 inhabitants of Mashpee. But intermarriage increased in all Indian communities in the wake of the war. More Indian men disappeared in the Revolution, and many of those who remained went whaling on ever-lengthening and more dangerous voyages. Some of these found better homes elsewhere if they survived. The gradual end of slavery in New England was also a factor in the rise of intermarriage. Hawley wrote in 1800 that "the liberation of slaves in this Commonwealth has bro't many to us of African blood." The growing number of free African Americans "left the country towns and resorted to the seaports" where they could leave servitude behind, find work, and gain the companionship of other "people of color." Some moved to a nearby Indian community and married members of the tribe or found other ways to live on the reserve.[13]

Three examples illustrate how the Revolution and the end of slavery helped to create new connections between Indians and African Americans. Sharper Michael was born a slave, the son of Rose, an African in the household of Zacheus Mayhew of Tisbury. In July 1775, Mayhew agreed to emancipate Sharper, and the freedman moved to neighboring Gay Head. He soon married Lucy Peters of Gay Head, and a few months later Lucy bore a daughter, Marcy. Lucy was a proprietor, Sharper was not, so he raised cattle on his wife's land until his death in September 1777 from a British musket ball. Seymour Burr was a slave in Connecticut owned by a brother of Aaron Burr. He tried to escape at the onset of the war.

Caught, he won a promise of freedom from his owner, but only if he agreed to enlist and give his master the bounty money—not an unusual arrangement. Burr
served with distinction, gained his freedom, and in 1790 married Mary Crowd, a
Punkapog woman, and settled in Canton. His grandson, Lemuel Burr, would become a leader of Boston's African American community in its struggle for civil
rights before the Civil War. Finally, Caesar Cobb, born about 1740 and slave of
Captain Cobb on Martha's Vineyard, bought his freedom after the war. He immediately married a Mashpee woman and settled in her community. According
to Hawley in 1793, she "made him a good wife" and he "carries on a great stroke
of business—sows, plants, raises [good crops] and has a good house & barn, and
lodges in a good bed; and can treat any Company handsomely."[14]

Intermarriages also resulted when Indians sought work or peddled crafts outside their enclaves. Some mixed households helped build backwoods villages on
the edges of Anglo-American towns, many of which started as settlements of Indians and African Americans. One of the most memorable was the Lighthouse,
located in a rugged section of northwest Connecticut, founded around 1740 by
Molly Barber of Wethersfield, Connecticut, and James Chaugham, a Narragansett, who supposedly married after Barber decided to spite her father for forbidding a previous suitor. For about a century, 40 families—Indians, blacks, and
whites—lived, married, and raised families in the Lighthouse, identifying themselves as Narragansetts.[15]

Rarely recorded, such backwoods communities existed throughout the region
at the turn of the century. Before his execution in 1786, Johnson Greene reported
living with Indians and African Americans in several outlying settlements in eastern Massachusetts. William Apess was born around 1798 to his part-white, part-
Pequot father and Pequot mother in a camp on the outskirts of Colrain in the
northwestern part of the state; his father frequently traveled between Colrain,
Mashantucket, and Colchester—a town in Connecticut near Mashantucket and
in Mohegan hunting territory, where a backwoods mixed community may have
existed on the suggestively named Wigwam Hill. At the turn of the century, a noticeable number of "colored" and landless white laborers lived in an area, on the
northwest border of the Pequot reserve in Stonington, which became known as
Lake of Isles. Tax, census, and overseer records also reveal clusters of Pequot
households, often with non-Indian spouses, on the northern edge of the Mashantucket Pequot reserve and just south of Groton center along the edges of Poheg-
nut Bay. Families in such situations were sometimes mixed as well as "blended"
from multiple relationships. In the middle of the nineteenth century, the Dudley
Nipmuc woman Lydia Sprague lived in an out-of-the-way neighborhood on the

southern edge of the Sturbridge with Lemuel Henry, an African American, and her seven children: two by Henry, two by an Indian, and three by a white man. Generally, such settlements were outposts of socially marginal families adjoining Anglo-American villages.[16]

Urban and port town neighborhoods, particularly near docks, similarly became places where people of all races lived together. In 1795, Boston minister John Eliot admitted that in some taverns whites and blacks relaxed together, although only (as he put it) "in houses of ill-fame, where some very *depraved white* females get among the blacks." Jeremy Belknap, who gathered the views of Eliot and others in answering a Virginian's query about the effects of abolition in Massachusetts, called white-black intermarriage "very rare," but he acknowledged that it did happen between black men and working-class white women. The common, and relatively comfortable, mixing of peoples in certain neighborhoods is also indicated by a law passed by the Providence city council in June 1822 requiring "all the Coloured people in this Town who are Housekeepers" to report all "transient white persons or colored persons" living within their homes. But as such measures indicate, racial boundaries became increasingly constricted in the 1820s and 1830s. The vicious antiblack riots that that shook Providence, Hartford, New Haven, Boston, and other northern cities in those decades often took place in mixed neighborhoods and may have been intended to raise racial barriers. Eliot also mentioned that the "houses of ill-fame" where "mixing" occurred were sometimes destroyed by angry mobs, and some of the riots three decades later began with similar actions.[17]

These exogamous marriages were, like those between members of an Indian community, usually informal: that is, unrecorded, apparently unritualized, and not legitimized in law. Even Gideon Hawley, who recorded births and deaths in Mashpee, left only one entry (from 1764) on marriages in the tribe. Some historians point to such marriages as continuing aboriginal traditions, whereas others see them as a new development in the mid-eighteenth century. Such unions were referred to as Indian or Negro marriages and may have widened the cultural gap between Anglo-Americans and people of color. They also marked the rising tide of intermarriage between Indians and African Americans and, in a seeming paradox given the growing racial divide, poor whites. European folk traditions of informal marriages remained strong in America, particularly among the poor, and as Indians developed deeper connections with the emerging proletariat in New England, they married in similar ways. In the early republic, as the growth of cities and free labor loosened the old social and moral restrictions of deference and servitude, informal and serial marriages persisted among the "lower sort" of all races.[18]

Marriages between Indian women and non-Native men were reflected in patrilineal naming patterns. For example, most of the surnames in the 1776 Mashpee census had disappeared by 1790, replaced by the names brought by newcomers. There is an occasional glimpse of matrilineal naming patterns. At least
four generations of Hassanamisco women named their daughters Sarah, beginning in the seventeenth century with the mother of Peter Muckamugg's wife,
hinting at the persistence of Nipmuc matrilineage alongside patrilineal Anglo-
American practices. Peter Muckamugg's wife also passed her family name, Rob-
bins, to her daughter, the mother of Sarah Burnee.[19] Similar examples are difficult to find, given the paucity of Indian vital records, and the fact that such records
were kept by Anglo-Americans. And such patterns may point to the survival of this
element of aboriginal culture or may simply show the effects of men disappearing
in the colonial wars or at sea on whaling trips. It is also true that Anglo-American
families often named daughters for mothers or grandmothers, although they never
passed on the mother's maiden name.

Regardless of lineage patterns, women headed a very high percentage of Native households: 9 of 24 (37.5 percent) in Mohegan in 1782, 57 of 96 (59 percent)
in Gay Head in 1792, and 27 of 83 (32.5 percent) in Mashpee one year later, with
the five districts on the reserve ranging from 20 percent to 45 percent. These numbers are somewhat suspect; when Hawley made another survey of Mashpee in
1800, he recorded only 15 percent of the households as headed by women. But
other documents confirm that the number of Indian households without men was
surprisingly high. This situation was created in a large part by circumstances:
many women were widows whose husbands died in the Revolution, and at the
turn of the century more Indian men disappeared for long periods on whaling voyages. In some cases, the mothers also left the scene; for example, William Apess
was left by his parents in the care of his Pequot grandmother. The persistence or
reemergence of matrilineage patterns may have also been a factor: when the Paugussett man left his Indian wife in Massachusetts, she retained their children. Regardless of the reasons, a large percentage of Indian women—mothers, aunts, and
grandmothers—became the primary, if not sole, child rearers.[20]

ANGLO-AMERICAN VIEWS OF INDIAN INTERMARRIAGE

Anglo-American data on marriages and the identity of individuals is somewhat
suspect because of the racial ideology that grew during the early republic. As the
number of intermarriages increased over time, the difficulty that whites had defining and distinguishing "Indians" from "Negroes" increased. Ship captains filing

their crew lists with New London's customs house described various individuals with clear Pequot or Mohegan connections—Joseph Hoscott, Joseph Faggins, Benjamin Uncas, Edward Uncas, and others—as having the complexion "Indian," "black," "yellow," and "dark." In Rhode Island, town officials sometimes recorded the same person on different occasions as a "Negro," "Indian," or "mulatto."[21]

But the figures recorded by Anglo-American men who worked closely with Native communities seem to reflect the reality of the increasing rates of exogamous marriages rather than racist distortions. In 1776, Gideon Hawley indicated that about 85 percent of Mashpees were "full bloods." Twelve years later, in the wake of the Revolution, he noted that about 25 men and 110 women were "original and not mixed"—about the same percentage, considering that he had counted 150 adults just five years after. That census showed the same number of "Negroes" as in 1776 but a more diverse community than a generation earlier: one Englishman, five Germans, two "pretty white" or "partly white," five "mixed" (probably mulattos), three "Indian-African," and one "white-Negro." His more detailed 1800 census showed an apparent increase in African Americans (26) but still a large percentage of Mashpees (142 of 400) with one parent "full blood" and the other "half" or "full" blood." This depicts a gradual and believable change during a generation of upheaval.[22]

Similarly, a comparison of two Gay Head censuses that focused on blood quantum, one in 1792 by a native leader, the other in 1823 by a white teacher and missionary, reveals an accurate portrayal of increasing intermarriage. In 1792, Moses Howwoswee reported that, of 177 members of his community, more than two-thirds were "pure" Indian. Only 19 were part African American—and 12 of these were the children in just two families—whereas 27 were part white. This census seems to have been in part an effort to refute a report by two Vineyard gentry in 1790 that Indians on the island began to marry blacks about 1765 and that the remaining villages were only 20–50 percent "pure." But it was apparently a good reflection of Gay Head's makeup and supports the accuracy of Frederick Baylies's 1823 census.[23]

Baylies lived in Edgartown, began working with Wampanoags around the region in the 1810s, and maintained good relations with Indian communities (see chapter 4). His 1823 figures show a notable rise in exogamous marriages in Gay Head from 1792, including more residents and a much higher percentage of individuals with mixed parentage. The percentage of part-white individuals had dropped by half, and those of tripartite ancestry—Indian, black, and white—had increased from 5 to 38 percent. This was a huge change within the community, and therefore its accuracy might be suspect. But 13 individuals recorded in 1792 survived to the 1823 census: 11 were described in precisely the same way in both records, and the other two showed only a slight variation. The accuracy of Baylies's report is also supported by similar descriptions of other individuals who also appeared on whaling crew lists.[24]

Although details are available from only Mashpee and Gay Head, descriptions of every southern New England Indian community after the Revolution usually stressed the increasing rate of intermarriage. Natick minister Stephen Badger found it "almost impossible to come to any determination" of the number of Indians remaining in his congregation, for they "are intermarried with *blacks*, and some with whites; and the various shades between these, and those that are descended from them." Edward Kendall wrote in 1807 that the Herring Pond community is "said to be *mixed*, that is, to have the children of Europeans and Africans among them; and this is generally true, of all the Indians in Massachusetts, and in some other parts." Throughout Massachusetts, investigators in 1827 reported that only about 10 percent of the 1,000 Indians were "full blooded," and an 1849 report shows fewer than 8 of 847. In Connecticut, Timothy Dwight visited the Eastern Pequots in 1807 and noted "their decrease has been checked by their cohabitation with blacks." Another observer found in 1832 that the Mashantucket Pequot community held 40 Indians who "were considerably mixed with white and negro blood," and the group's overseer noted 17 years later that no "pure blood" Pequots remained. Rhode Island officials reported in 1831 that, of 200 Narragansetts, "only five or six are genuine untainted . . . all the rest are either clear negroes or a mixture of Indian African and European blood." A quarter-century later, another state commission found not one full-blood in the community and only 11 to be half or three-quarter "pure" Narragansett.[25]

These censuses and descriptions demonstrate that while most Indian exogamous relationships were with African Americans, some were with whites. The 1833 Mashantucket Pequot census, for example, showed that one-fourth were "part white" to "most white." Such marriages were officially banned in Massachusetts in June 1786, joining the existing sanctions against black-white intermarriages three years after the state superior court effectively outlawed slavery. Rhode Island passed a similar law about the same time. But antimiscegenation laws were rarely enforced even before they were repealed in the mid-nineteenth century. By the middle of the century, 10 to 20 percent of Massachusetts Indian spouses were white, and nearly every Yarmouth Indian marriage since 1700 had been with a white person. The whites who married Indians may have done so for many of the same reasons as African American men: they lived on the socioeconomic margins of the dominant culture and found a home in the Native village. Some were sailors, such as Thomas McGregor of Manchester, England, who married a Mashpee woman in 1782 and was still there in 1807 when he met Edward Kendall and extolled his life in the Indian community. His neighbors included five or six Hessian (German) soldiers who had been captured with Burgoyne's army at Saratoga and had married Mashpee women. By 1793, noted Hawley, there were about 14 individuals with German ancestry in the community.[26]

Anglo-American writers generally felt that intermarriage was "improving" the Indians. While Hawley fought against intermarriage and the influence of immigrants in Mashpee, he also believed, writing in 1788, that women within the tribe had become "more prolific, and children healthier since their intermarriage with English, Germans, & Negroes." Twelve years later he wrote, "Indians that are half blooded ameliorate the breed." Similarly, in 1790 two whites on Martha's Vineyard reported that, after more than a generation of intermarriage between the island's Natives and African Americans, "the mixed race has increased in numbers and improved in temperance and industry." But Hawley's own detailed census of Mashpee in 1800, unique in listing each member of each household and providing a description of each individual's race or "blood," shows that the opposite may be true. Among the 69 couples, the 26 Native women who married full bloods had *more* children—an average of between 2.0 and 2.5, depending on the woman's ancestry—than those who married whites (2.0), blacks (1.5–2.0), or mixed (0.3–1.3). The exceptions were three mixed women who married blacks and had an average of 3.3 children. Unfortunately, other Indian records are too scattered and incomplete to determine whether women with exogamous spouses generally had more children. Even within this Mashpee census, the lower number of children among mixed families may simply reflect the recent trend toward exogamous marriages, so those women were just beginning their child-bearing years.[27]

Like other observers, Hawley was most interested in the moral and social consequences of mixed marriages. In his 1793 census, he commented that the German men were "very industrious" and "use severity in disciplining their wives, it is said, when they spend their money and time idlely." He also focused on Cesear Cobb's excellent farm. Similarly, both Jeremy Belknap and Isaac Backus praised the effects of intermarriage among Indian groups on Cape Cod and Martha's Vineyard. But stress and conflict could change minds: as Hawley's battles with Mashpee dissidents increased in 1794 (chapter 3), he bemoaned that the community now contained "a motley medley of characters more heterogeneous, if possible, and some of them not less turbulent, than the elements."[28]

Anglo-American concerns about race were often closely connected to their anxieties about a broad range of threats to social stability and order. Hawley's often-contradictory comments about the Mashpees reflect just such an anxiety. In 1788, he justified his effort to gain more control over the Indian community by decrying the harm caused by "the Negroes mulatoes and poor whites who have crowded upon this territory." With his 1800 census, Hawley noted that "we have too many negroes who have mixt with this people," and to counter that trend he and the other overseers had "discouraged the intigration [*sic*] of Negroes, and have got several families away." He could use viciously racist, biting language: in 1803, he bemoaned that the competing Baptist society has been "built up" by "mongrels" from Rhode Island and Bristol County "who appear to be very much influenced by sinister ends." But he could also boast that "our black communicants are as well behaved & as much civilized, as the whites of their rank in life." Significantly, both comments were inspired by Hawley's concerns for proper authority. Such language shows that conservative standards of social class and deference may have been far more significant than emerging scientific ideologies of race in shaping initial descriptions of Indian exogamous marriages and their mixed children.[29]

But positive views of intermarriage declined as the ideology of race developed. Phrenologists became quite popular after 1820. They proclaimed that the study of human skulls showed that "whites were inventive, creative, powerful; blacks were docile and ignorant; Indians were savage and intractable." These characteristics could not be altered; as a result, intermarriage violated natural law and brought out the worst traits of both parents' races. Joseph Thaxter, a lawyer, judge, and guardian of two Indian villages on the Vineyard, told a correspondent in 1823 that the Indians there "by mixture with the Blacks have lost I believe much of the Fox & acquired none of the Bear & Wolf these perhaps have better Capacities for learning. But the misfortune is that most of the blacks that come & marry among them are very dissipated. They are a most improvident gang." Eight years later, a Rhode Island legislative committee reported that the Narragansett "native blood has been rapidly adulterated by almost every heterogeneous progeny. Forty years ago it was a nation of Indians[,] now it is a medley of mongrels in which the African blood predominates." Descriptions of Indians increasingly emphasized that few "real" (pure-blooded) Natives remained, and many characterized the surviving "mixed remnants" in highly pejorative terms. They were particularly harsh about white men who "disgrace[d] the Saxon race" by marrying Indians.[30]

Three Massachusetts court cases highlighted the fluid and often-conflicting notions of race held by Anglo-Americans at the turn of the century and pointed to ways in which these concepts could substantially affect Indians and their communities. The first, *Medway v. Natick* (1810), created a loophole in the 1786 Massachusetts antimiscegenation law by holding that the offspring of a white mother and half-black, half-white father was legally white. The court refused to explicitly throw out the 1786 law, ruling that the proper definition of "mulatto" was "a person begotten between a white and a black"; because the father in question, Cuffee, was a mulatto and not a black, his daughter had to be classified under the law as white. Thus the offspring of mixed marriages could become white (the opposite of contemporary southern legal doctrine). The case concerned the proper legal residence of the transient pauper Rhoda Vickers and her child, who were then living in Medway. The court called her deceased husband, Christopher Vickers, whom she had married in August 1789, "a white person," although records show he was a Natick Indian whose grandfather had moved there from Medway sometime before 1750.[31] This decision seemed to open opportunities for people of color and to break down the barriers between racial categories.

Andover v. Canton (1816) concerned the legal status and residence of the offspring of an enslaved black father and Indian mother. Lewis Elisha was born in 1773, in the area that became Canton, of an African slave father and a Punkapoag mother, Abigail Moho—herself the child of a Punkapoag father and a white mother. Lewis left Canton about 1788 and in 1803 married Hannah Richardson, daughter of a mulatto father and a white mother, and settled in Andover, where she lived. If he had inherited his father's slave status, then the owner's town (Canton) was liable for the son. But the court ruled instead that the child of a slave father and a free mother was free, that Lewis's mother as a Punkapoag had no legal connection to Canton, and that therefore Andover had to support him and his family. The court also noted that he "had a right to leave the tribe, and did leave it and did in fact become a free citizen." This ruling had the potential to strike down the social and political boundaries that both protected and limited Indians in the Commonwealth. But it did not decide whether individuals holding land recognized as part of an Indian community could separate themselves from laws regulating that community, and it did not permit emigrants to sell reserved lands.[32]

A Plymouth County court tried to decide these issues one year later, in the case of *Dunbar v. Mitchell*. In February 1811, Edward Mitchell of Bridgewater was appointed Indian guardian; his duties included regulating the sale or lease of lands in the town owned by the Mattakeesits and their descendants, including those living elsewhere. One of those absentees, Sarah Dunbar, was offended at the guardian's show of authority and filed a suit of ejectment against Mitchell. The resolves appointing Mitchell and confirming his power, the court wrote, "made him guardian only of Indians, and it appeared that the woman bringing the suit, although an heir of an Indian, was a mulatto, having some negro blood in her."[33]

The most obvious effect of this decision, particularly following *Andover v. Canton*, was that the children of intermarriages could escape the legal restrictions that bounded Indian communities, including controls on the sale of land. This posed a threat to Indian groups wishing to maintain the land base that supported the community, although Indian groups or their guardians could theoretically cite this ruling in order to limit the access of mixed offspring to Indian resources. Ultimately, the ruling was not extended. But these cases point to the substantive effects that racial ideology could have on Indians and their communities.

INDIAN VIEWS OF RACE AND INTERMARRIAGE

Such threats to resources and competition for mates would have, one might expect, driven many Indian men to oppose intermarriage and dislike blacks. Indeed, there were conflicts about the influx of foreigners, and in the second half of the eighteenth century some Indians condemned exogamous marriages and used racial epithets in a manner that showed the influence of the dominant culture. Some charged that blacks (and whites and Indians from other tribes) threatened their community and its resources or were taking all their women. Yet only two tribes in the region, Mohegans and Narragansetts, adopted rules that seemed to echo American racism, and those rules were rarely followed or enforced. Instead, race became significant among Indians largely as a useful code for speaking to white men, primarily about a community's internal conflicts over community leadership, immigration, difficult economic circumstances, and gender relationships and roles driven by a shrinking masculine authority. In fact, power related to gender and control of resources, more than race, seem to have been the primary issues surrounding struggles over intermarriage.

The Mohegans and Narragansetts shared one unique characteristic that drove conflicts in both communities: they were the only tribes that retained leaders in the mid-eighteenth century who traced their ancestry to contact-era sachems. In both groups, conflict involving those sachems grew out of struggles over resources and was expressed in racial language. The first recorded battle over race took place among the Mohegans, already torn for decades by political factionalism. During the mid-eighteenth century, a faction led by Samson Occom tried to regain land from Connecticut and in the process challenged the Uncases, their traditional ruling family. On May 12, 1773, that group agreed that any of their daughters who married "strangers" had to leave the tribe, and that the children of those who married "Negroes" would have no rights in Mohegan. Their action seemed driven by a heightened insecurity about the tribe's right to community land in light of the recent final decision against their appeal to the Privy Council. Uncas's former council members denounced the agreement, and (ironically) tried to discredit the signatories (particularly Occom) as "foreign Indians." This conflict also held nascent elements of class, as Occom's followers had created English-style farms by plowing and fencing fields, leading to complaints that "they Take up more Land than they have Right." More restrictive tribal membership rules were put into place, but they seemed to affect Natives from other tribes as much as African Americans or mulattos. Mohegans continued to marry African Americans, despite occasional complaints (the last in 1823) by some about the "corruption of the pure Mohegan blood."[34]

Conflict over resources similarly caused some Narragansetts to try and draw a rigid line between "foreigners" and those born into the tribe. In December 1765, their white schoolmaster, Edward Deake, reported that the tribal council had disowned "a considerable Number of mixtures as melatoes and mustees" who lived among them, as well as "Sundry families of Indians which properly Belongs to other tribes." At the time the tribe was torn between the supporters of the largely discredited sachem, Thomas Ninigret, and those who rejected Ninigret's authority, led by the tribe's minister Samuel Niles. Because both factions were represented on the council that drew up the list of tribal members, they may have found common cause (unlike their Mohegan counterparts) in limiting access to declining tribal resources. But this temporary alliance did not prevent continuing or new conflicts within the tribe—strife that was interpreted at least in part as racial. In 1792, supposedly at the tribe's request to settle "Disputes and Differences," Rhode Island passed a law limiting the vote for the tribal council to "every Male Person of Twenty-one Years, born of an *Indian* Woman, belonging to said Tribe, or begotten by an *Indian* man, belonging thereto, of any other than a Negro woman" (emphasis in original).[35]

The 1792 law may not have actually erected a racial barrier within the tribe. True, it denied political powers to men born of African American women, and assigned them to a lower status in the tribe, but did not bar them from being considered members of the tribe, and may have even represented a broadening of the Narragansetts' social boundaries. The tribal council noted two decades later that "it has been a former Custom by this tribe that when any of the tribe Married any other [woman] that Did not belong to sd Tribe to take their wife away unless the Council pleased to let them stay in the town." In fact, the most significant aspect of the 1792 act was gender, for it barred *any* women from voting for council members. The law may not have even been at the Narragansetts' behest but because, as a tribal council leader charged a century later, Rhode Island slave owners "wanted the benefit of the children"—so the children of a female slave would be the legal property of her owner. The tribe's *lack* of prejudice against blacks can be glimpsed in their willingness in 1811 to allow blacks outside the reserve to attend their school funded by the Society for Propagating the Gospel among the Indians, and Others, in North America (SPG), even as they insisted on barring white children.[36]

William Brown believed that, as more women like his Narragansett grandmother married African Americans toward the end of the eighteenth century, Indian men developed a "very bitter feeling" against blacks. Their concern was not racial purity, however, but threats to the tribe's resources and its integrity. In 1776, 37 Gay Headers complained to the Massachusetts General Court about the "very considerable number of Negros and Mulatto's that have come among us built them Houses and settled amongst us." They were also unhappy about "some of the Indian women" who had "lately returned [to Gay Head] with a very considerable of Mulattos, as they say Children, Grandchildren and even Great Grand-Children." If this was not stopped, they warned, it "will greatly impoverish, if not entirely Root us out." In July 1788, 29 Mashpee men wrote to the legislature about their fear of "Negroes & English, who, unhappily, have planted themselves here, hath managed us, and it is to be feared, that they and their Children, unless they are removed, will get away our Lands & all our Privileges in a short time." In an echo of these troubles, Wampanoag legends tell how the misfortune or evil caused the introduction of "kinky" or "snarly" hair among their people.[37]

The Gay Head and Mashpee censuses make these petitions seem hyperbolic, reflecting conflicts within both communities rather than real dangers; however, Howwoswee and Hawley, the census-takers, may have deliberately excluded many of these newcomers. Certainly, conflicts over exogamous marriages continued in some Indian groups. In 1845, the white guardian of Chappaquiddick and Christiantown remembered that both groups had suffered conflicts "oweing to their Females Marying Negroes whom they did not wish to have any right to their lands" and that Christiantown men filed at least two lawsuits between 1805 and 1811 to stop African American men from marrying into their community.[38] But these petitions seem more reflective of internal political conflicts that were expressed in racial terms. In all of these incidents, the majority of those opposing intermarriage were men and were primarily concerned with the potential loss of their authority and community resources to the newcomers.

Although such anxieties appear more reasonable than racial prejudice, we should not be surprised that the language of race influenced Indians as it became a more significant part of American culture. In 1789, Samson Occom sought to have a mulatto child dropped from the Mohegan tribal register because "if he takes [root] amongst us not only guinny [Guinea] Children, but European Children and some other Children will take also." Such language certainly reflected hostile prejudice and emphasized the deep inroads that American culture had made among Indians in the region. Occom and other Mohegan and Narragansett leaders became sensitive to Anglo-American views on race while attending Eleazar Wheelock's school in Connecticut. Those students also spearheaded the Brothertown settlement, which was to be a purely Indian effort; one of their early ordinances banned marriages with "persons of negro blood."[39]

After 1810, the use of racial language as a weapon in community conflicts, and perhaps as a means of interpreting disputes or other problems, became more common among New England Indians, as well as in the United States generally. In April 1819, the majority of Mohegans told the state that they did not want "mongrells mollattoes Negroes nor Africans to have any of our lands." One year later, 19 members of the tribe complained about "the corruption of the pure Mohegan blood with that of other nations particularly Negros . . . Their manners, habits & feelings are so different that they cannot endure to live together." Mohegan lands were increasingly passing into the hands of "Negroes and mulattoes," and they asked for a law barring "Negros, mulattos or other people of color," including the children of mixed marriages, from any share in tribal lands. In 1823, shortly after the state assembly assigned oversight responsibility to the county courts, the tribe told their new superintendents that they wanted blacks "kept out of our Tribe." A decade later, the Narragansetts told the legislature that some of the "furron Neagros" who married into the community "are lazy and thieveish, also, which makes trouble in the Neighbourhood, & many Complains on that account has ben made by the white people."[40]

Indian use of racist language in tribal conflicts was in part driven by the need to appeal to Anglo-Americans. This is particularly clear with the Narragansetts. In 1821, eight men from the tribe asked the Rhode Island assembly's help in settling "divers Law Suits, Disputes and Controversies" among members of the community. Many of the cases were against the tribal council; one involved Eunice Rogers's complaint that the council gave her house and land to (as she put it) a "foreign" woman with "A Clear Negro for her husband." The disputes continued unresolved, and ten years later, a legislative committee reported that the tribal council had "arrogated to themselves indefinite powers," disposing of the common property and funds of the tribe without any controls. At first the tribal council, led by Tobias Ross, tried to have the state ignore unsanctioned petitions or complaints. But they were spurred to more serious measures by the 1831 report, which called the tribe a group of "mongrels" with primarily "African blood" and an even more scathing report one year later that not only condemned the Narragansetts as "a vagrant race of negro paupers" but also accused the council of having defrauded the tribe of its funds and resources, and of cheating individual members.[41]

Ross and the council initially protested that only a few Africans lived among the tribe, and just ten or fifteen were "groosly Marked with the Affrican stamp." But the 1832 report pushed them into more active measures. In May 1834 they asked for a state law requiring women who married out of the tribe to leave and surrender their property to the council. This was necessary, Ross told the assembly, because the tribe was "Greatly Enroachd upon, by furron Neagros, and others, by their Coming into the town and Marrying our women, and Raveging our lands and tenements and Cuting Down our wood and timber and Selling it . . . Some are lazy and thievish, also, which makes trouble in the Neighbourhood, & many Complaints on that account has ben made by the white people." A year later the council renewed their request, noting that it had asked outside authorities (apparently the selectmen of the surrounding town, Charlestown) to remove the intruders but that "they say they have no Right to because [the newcomers] have married one of the tribe." The conflicts were seemingly resolved without state action, but one wonders about the personal grudges and factionalism that must have lingered.[42]

Conflicts among the Mohegans and Narragansetts may have taken on racial overtones because their traditional sachems and councilors remained powerful into the eighteenth century, and their increasingly fierce battles with opponents were often waged in terms of "foreigners" versus "real" members of the tribe. The Mohegans were also apparently distinctive in having a social structure with at least two tiers: tribal tradition holds that Pequots captured or "adopted" in the wake of the 1637 war continued for generations to retain a separate, lower status. In the mid-nineteenth century, their white neighbors remembered that Zachary Johnson (leader of the "sachem's party" which in the 1770s and 1780s fought Samson Occom and his supporters, often using racial epithets against their opponents) and his wife Martha (Uncas?) saw themselves as "pure Mohegans" and "looked down upon Pequots, Nipmuks, & Nianticks: 'Me no speaket 'em' said Martha, 'me only speaket Mohegans.'"[43] The Narragansett tribe by the mid-eighteenth century may have also had a significant social division, invisible to nonmembers, formed of a Niantic core (headed by Ninigret) that incorporated Narragansett survivors and remnants of other groups decimated by King Philip's War. As a result of these fractures, controversies over "foreigners" may have become more prominent and taken on racial colorings as internal threats and tensions continued or intensified.

Though much of this language seemed patterned after emerging Anglo-American notions of race, New England's Indians were not simply copying or embracing the increasingly rigid perceptions and categories emerging around them. Indians themselves were the targets of racial prejudice—although the subjects of scorn and hatred may, like the Irish in antebellum America, find partial relief in abusing members of a group lower on the racial or social scale. But, with few exceptions, Indians did not seem concerned about drawing racial lines or creating a racial hierarchy that paralleled the surrounding society. The "strangers" in Gay Head, for example, were outsiders who had married into the community—whites and blacks—rather than individuals seen as inferior because of their darker skins. Many of those complaining about intermarriage (such as Samson Occom) were themselves accused by others in the community of being mixed, and Indians from other tribes seemed to generate as much antipathy among *both* Mohegan factions as did African Americans. Behind the racist language, it is clear that most of the hostility toward foreigners rose from deep, long-standing community conflicts rooted in issues of gender and power rather than race or skin color. Not only did the Narragansetts bar women from voting in tribal elections, but Brothertown also forbade women from testifying in the community's courts.[44]

Indian men protested against intermarriage with African American men in large part because they felt powerless on a deeper level. Guardians leased their lands and sold their wood to whites; they were often forced by lawsuits or other circumstances onto long, dangerous whaling voyages; and they were sensitive to the contrast between their own situation and Anglo-American notions of masculinity, which cast men as the source of authority and independence. Much of this racist correspondence may have also been driven by Indians' concern about how white men who held the reins of power perceived their tribe. Intermarriage posed a potential threat to a Native community's resources and power, particularly as the once-fluid Anglo-American attitudes towards race and gender roles hardened into new, more threatening forms. Those who shaped the region's laws drew increasingly rigid lines between racial groups, labeled the offspring of intermarriages as mulattos or blacks, and therefore saw New England's Indians as vanishing. Protests about race formed an important part of efforts by Indian men to impress white men with their community's existence. But the few efforts by Indians to draw racial lines were ignored or dismissed by whites.

Despite occasional racial protests, Indian groups in New England displayed a high degree of tolerance for and acceptance of black and white newcomers, and intermarriage continued to reshape the appearance of all Indian groups. Of course, scattered individuals and families, along with villages and enclaves with shrinking numbers and resources, were more or less forced to embrace the newcomers who enabled family and group to survive. But women and men were rarely ostracized for marrying outsiders, and even large tribes with substantial resources welcomed newcomers regardless of race. Except for the Mohegans and Narragansetts, Indian groups displayed little evidence of racial hierarchies and instead adapted older customs to new circumstances in order to control the potential influence of newcomers *regardless* of race, creating *ethnic* boundaries even as they occasionally expressed their anxieties in racial terms.[45]

INTERMARRIAGE AND ASSIMILATION

As the differences between Native and Anglo-American cultures decreased and intermarriage increased, Indians in southern New England developed shared norms, including knowledge of distinctive folklore; kinship ties; particular social conduct or individual behavior, such as workways; and, most distinctively, communal landholding and management of resources. Although differences and tribal loyalties among Indian groups remained important, these norms, along with intermarriage and social connections between tribes, encouraged an Indian ethnic identity that transcended tribal differences. Not all communities managed to retain every one of these markers or held them to the same level of intensity, and conflicts over their meanings sometimes raged as among the Mohegans and Narragansetts. Human communities are rarely in complete accord on the ideal or practice of their social and cultural distinctions, and ethnic or social boundaries are often contested, particularly when political power or useful resources are the spoils. But by the beginning of the nineteenth century, all Indian groups had developed social, cultural, and political markers that left their communities and families open to the newcomers while maintaining key differences. These boundaries, while flexible and somewhat amorphous, managed concerns about power and resources.[46]

Indian communities had various cultural and social mechanisms to manage newcomers and their mixed children. Indians within and without reserves worked in ways that reflected and amplified traditions; engaging in such trades and not accumulating wealth confirmed that a member of the group was properly Indian.[47] Indian material culture and agriculture similarly remained distinctive, and folklore and legends delineated community values and traditions. Tellings of

Wampanoag legends of the giant Maushop and his family, who created Cape Cod and the islands, demonstrate remarkable consistency between the seventeenth and the late nineteenth century, even as English and African motifs added slight modifications. Traditional powers of medicine and shamanism also remained powerful in individuals such as Patience Gashum and Betsy Dodge (b. May 24, 1786) of Gay Head. Witches like Gashum and Dodge were respected and feared. Indian folklore associated avarice and the desire for wealth with witchcraft, and some stories connected black men with both. As in other witchcraft outbreaks (such as Salem in 1692), such accusations reflect conflicts within a group that cannot be resolved in other ways. Those legends and stories also served as teaching tools for those who told them as well as for those who listened.[48]

The presence and power of state and local authorities helped to reshape and maintain Indian boundaries. Anglo-American prejudice and coercive economic and legal power served as feedback in internal struggles, as described above, and to amplify or prevent those conflicts. More direct and powerful was the role played by the guardians appointed by colonies and states to manage Indian resources, described below. Guardians generated conflicts as they favored certain individuals or families, or made decisions that shaped how resources were to be used or distributed. At the same time, guardians and state assemblies enforced what they saw as their charges' rules of inheritance and membership. In the late 1760s, for example, Joseph Aaron was perceived by the Hassanamisco guardians as the legitimate son of Sarah Muckamugg and therefore eligible for a share of his late mother's property and annual stipend. But such efforts to prevent change were themselves subtle agents of change, as informal customs were replaced by formalized rules enforced by these postcolonial culture brokers. Thus a group's often-reluctant reliance on or recourse to guardians and state legislatures inevitably affected their social dynamics and economic and power structures.[49]

Tribes with communal resources retained the power to demand proper behavior from foreigners. Gay Head's leader in the mid-nineteenth century, Zaccheus Howwoswee, told a state official that his people were "jealous of the influence of foreigners, having had much trouble with some of those who have intermarried with their women and settled amongst them." The community had arranged things to manage the problem. We "conduct our own business seperate from the foreigners & strangers we never have alowd them any pole right on gay-head." By contrast, Indians from other groups were accepted as full members because they were assumed to have been raised correctly. "We do not say any thing against other Indians that come from other tribes or settlements & settle with us."

Indian communities developed this convention in the late eighteenth century as exogamous marriages increased. These social, cultural, legal, and economic systems built high boundaries and clear gates around Indian communities. Non-Indians got in the gates through marriage, but only their children, raised within and socialized by the community, were recognized as fully entitled to communal resources.[50]

Non-Indian newcomers bought new customs and ideas into the community and were therefore potential sources of disruption. But they could also become conservative influences in a community. Hawley's 1776 census showed that Negro husbands of Mashpee women generally lived in wigwams, even as most Indians had cabins. Three decades later, Edward Kendall found that although nearly every Mashpee had a wood cabin, the English sailor McGregor, who was one of the community's wealthier members, continued living in a wigwam, which contained a brick fireplace and "some mixture of European architecture."[51]

The rise in exogamous marriages meant that Native women came to act as the gatekeepers of their tribes. By marrying an outsider, a woman became the household's representative in community matters, able to choose and hold land and to participate in public meetings. Massachusetts legislators in 1827 (and at other times) were surprised that Indian women could vote and speak on community concerns in a manner contrary to American law, although in accord with theories of natural rights. Women usually signed petitions from their community, sometimes in nearly equal numbers to men. Ironically, state laws reserving Indian lands for particular communities, and the Anglo-American guardians who carried out those laws and often managed community resources despite frequent Native opposition, helped retain and reinforce those traditional social boundaries. These standards persisted and became even stronger in the mid-nineteenth century, when Howwoswee emphasized that non-Indian newcomers "have not any in our Land but work on their wifes portion of land . . . when we set of[f] our planting fields we do not set of[f] any to the foreigner but to his wife if she is a proprietor."[52]

In this fashion women also served as the guardians of Indian enclaves. They remained on the reserves; created families and raised the next generation; passed on tribal stories and values; kept farms operating; and joined or spearheaded efforts against white trespass, poaching, and exploitation. This situation made Native women generally conservative forces, as they were elsewhere in North America, whereas the men, already involved in diplomacy, trade, and war, were more comfortable with the market economy and other transformative aspects of relations with Europeans and Americans.[53] But these women (like Alice Prophetess and

Mary Fuller) also served as conduits of change by seeking and marrying non-Native men, who seemingly had more experience with and interest in New England farming and the market economy. Indian women in the early nineteenth century would also be the first to demand schools and then to serve as teachers (chapter 4).[54]

The use of powers gained by women, and the ways folklore reinforced cultural norms, highlighted how tribes with autonomous political institutions and communal resources managed to assimilate newcomers and their mixed children. Assimilation in U.S. history is normally depicted as the effort to absorb immigrants into this country's social, political, and cultural mainstream. But assimilation is a process with many levels, involving complex issues of ethnicity, class, and race. Until recently, in fact, blacks and Indians were barred from joining the dominant American socioeconomic structure. For these two groups, assimilation was a process that took place on a different stage.[55]

But if the cultural and social process of assimilation helped many tribes survive in a changing world, that same process endangered communities that lacked lands or the cultural and political boundaries to enforce social cohesion, such as the Wampanoags along Buzzard's Bay and Nipmucs in central-southern Massachusetts. Many of their members lived in port towns or cities, perhaps driven by the need to find work, perhaps drawn to the kin of African American spouses or grandparents. Migration and intermarriage weakened the ties binding these groups and increased the socioeconomic and ethnic mobility of their descendants. This created obvious communal risks, as individuals faced numerous opportunities and reasons to reduce their participation in tribal activities, or even completely abandon their affiliation to the tribe or to not pass that connection to their children — in a word, assimilation.

At the same time, a group's survival in a multiethnic world might paradoxically be enhanced by more flexible social and cultural boundaries. Individuals of mixed ancestry can cross ethnic boundaries without necessarily surrendering kinship or other ties to either group. Some who "disappear," or their children or grandchildren, could later create or renew ties to their Native communities — if group norms allowed them to reenter. Reduced cohesion requires fewer communal rules governing behavior and affiliation, but it permits more emphasis on symbolic ethnicity — a voluntary identity that consists of symbols of the group's culture that individuals can embrace in varying quantities and intensities. Symbolic identity would allow the children of Afro-Indian marriages to maintain emotional and social ties to both groups.[56]

Such flexibility also creates frustrations for historians wishing to understand personal affiliation, family connections, and the persistence of Indian communities under these circumstances. But one can reconstruct in a few cases how identity and affiliation shifted across several generations. Particularly well documented is the Cuffee family. In the mid-eighteenth century, the freed African Kofi Slocum, his Wampanoag wife Ruth Moses, and their ten children made their home in the growing port town of Dartmouth, deep in traditionally Wampanoag territory. Although they usually lived on the family farm, they occasionally spent time among their Wampanoag relatives on Martha's Vineyard. Kofi's sons took their father's African name but later tried to gain the tax exemption given Indians in Massachusetts. When their petition was denied in 1780, they joined other "negroes and mulattoes" to protest that if they paid taxes they must also be allowed to vote. After a brief spell in jail, the two brothers took different paths. Jonathan followed his mother's roots, marrying into Gay Head; by the end of the century he had enough authority to sign community petitions, and by 1821 he held land in his own right as a full member of the tribe. Paul became a wealthy merchant, a leader of the African American community in the area, and spearheaded the first back-to-Africa movement. Paul's affiliation did not, however, alienate him from his Indian connections, for he married a Pequot woman (who refused to move to Africa) and occasionally assisted his brother's community. Their son, Paul Jr., chose his mother's path and considered himself a Pequot Indian. All of these Cuffees were aware of, and no doubt honored, their Indian and African ancestral connections. At the same time, they made the choice to affiliate primarily with one of those connections.[57]

Similar dynamics, dual identities, and decisions can be seen in the lesser-known Gimbee family of central Massachusetts. Moses and Cesear Jr. were the sons of Patience Lawrence, a Hassanamisco Nipmuc, and Cesear Gimbee, a free African American. The brothers moved to Worcester around 1800. In 1801, they claimed the right to sell their deceased mother's land in Grafton, formerly Hassanamisco, for "they consider themselves as inheriting from their Father, who was not an Indian, all the rights of free Citizens," including the right to sell land without the legislature's approval. Yet they also continued to claim the annual Hassanamisco interest payments that they had inherited from their mother, *the* prime indicator of membership in Hassanamisco.[58] After Cesear's death, Moses stayed in Worcester and in 1817 married Zona Leonard, identified as a "Negro" in the Worcester vital records. Their children seemed even more distant from the Hassanamisco community, never claiming their father's annual interest. One of their sons, Edward, owned a barbershop, a business that was the social center of northern black communities, and in 1862 he organized a freedom festival "to celebrate both West Indian and hoped-for American emancipation." Censuses of the state's

Indians in 1849 and 1859 ignored Edward and other Gimbees. Thus the Gimbees apparently became African American as they (like other Hassanamiscos) moved to the city and for several generations married African Americans.[59]

The dissolution of an enclave does not mean the end of a community or the extinction of a tribe, even under modern federal criteria. As Hassanamiscos began moving apart, they and their descendants spun a network that maintained the tribal identity among a scattered people and brought families together for festivals and religious celebrations.[60] Many mixed children tenaciously upheld their Hassanamisco affiliation. From 1830 to 1860, Moses Gimbee's nephew, John Hector, who also lived in Worcester, not only claimed to be the Hassanamisco sachem but also Moses's sole heir. Others may have retained in a less public manner their Hassanamisco Nipmuc connections even as they became active members of the African American community. Alexander Hemenway, for example, the grandson of Hepsibeth Hemenway, was listed as a Hassanamisco in the 1859 census of Massachusetts Indians, when he was an active member of an African American church and a black Masonic lodge in Worcester. In 1854 he joined in an attack on a U.S. marshal who attempted to apprehend a fugitive slave and in 1863 enlisted in the 54th Massachusetts (Colored) Infantry and survived the company's assault on Fort Wagner made famous by the film *Glory*.[61]

For individuals like Paul Cuffee, Edward Gimbee, and Alexander Hemenway, Indian ancestry did not determine group affiliation or ethnic identity. William Brown, who was quite fond of his Narragansett grandmother, never gave any indication in his autobiography that he was anything but a member of the Providence African American community. Edward Gimbee had precisely as much Indian ancestry as Brown, one maternal grandmother. Like Brown, Edward and the men he hired in his barbershop may not have seen themselves as Indians (Nipmucs) but as African Americans. Although kinship is a fundamental aspect of ethnicity or tribal identity, kinship alone is insufficient to maintain the social and cultural boundaries necessary to keep individuals within a small, scattered group, especially when stronger processes work to assimilate individuals into the larger community where they live.[62] The Hemenway name does not appear in any of the Hassanamisco guardians' records, indicating that Alexander Hemenway thought of himself as an African American with Nipmuc ancestry rather than the other way around. Of course, the flexibility allowed by ethnic affiliation under such circumstances would have allowed his children or grandchildren to reclaim their Hassanamisco "membership." Men such as Cuffee, Brown, Gimbee, and Hemenway illustrate the significance and flexibility of ethnic affiliation, even in the early republic.

With the growth of African American enclaves and institutions, affiliation with African Americans offered people of mixed descent certain clear advantages of the same sort that Africans had sought in Indian enclaves and villages, including mutual aid, employment opportunities, and marriage partners. Like Moses Gimbee, Alexander's father Ebenezer Hemenway married a colored woman, and both of their sons operated barbershops that served as African American social centers in Worcester. As black communities became more organized and confident, they generated, like Indian villages, a range of overt and subtle pressures to assimilate outsiders. But black enclaves and their organizations were, in contrast to Indian groups, entirely urban. Groups of freedmen initially stressed African roots: their organizations, such as Boston's first black church, usually had the descriptor African in their names, and some endorsed African resettlement efforts. This meant that the children of mixed marriages who were active members of the black community also had to commit themselves, publicly and privately, to African organizations.[63]

Yet members of black communities could retain memories of Native roots. For example, by 1800 on Nantucket the survivors of the 1763 epidemic had seemingly been assimilated into the "colored" neighborhood known as New Guinea. But on May 1822, in an effort to obtain assistance for a teacher or minister, the community's leaders wrote to the SPG that "there are among the coloured people of this place remains of the Nantucket Indians, & that nearly every family in our village are partly descended from the original inhabitants of this & neighboring places." The SPG agreed to send Frederick Baylies, and he added the island's black neighborhood to his annual circuit and efforts to build up schools in Indian communities in coastal Massachusetts (see chapter 4). On April 14, 1823, he told his sponsors that he had visited Nantucket, had gained the support of many of the island's white elites for a school, and noted that many in his new congregation "are part Indian."[64]

But by the 1820s, New England black leaders increasingly stressed their people's intimate connection to mainstream American culture and history rather than their Native or African ancestry. Northern blacks celebrated Emancipation Day or Haitian Independence (and tried to participate in Fourth of July parades) instead of Negro Election Day. Churches and schools became increasingly important cornerstones of the community. Most black leaders rejected the notion of leaving for Africa, particularly after southern slave-owners took control of the African Colonization Society, and sought a new name and identity that reflected their home and their hopes for future equality; while no consensus emerged, most began to call themselves Colored Americans, although some favored black Americans or even Afric-American. Beginning in 1830, annual meetings of the American Society of Free Persons of Color brought together delegates from black communities in 11 states to forge a national network and identity. In 1837, the Boston African Baptist Church decided to become the First Independent Baptist Church of People of Color of Boston, "for the very good reason that the name African is ill applied to a church composed of American citizens."[65]

Their new name and identity also signaled the desire to adopt the values and goals of middle-class American society, particularly individualism, industry, education, self-discipline, temperance, and patriarchy in its more softened, sentimental form. Black ministers, businessmen, and writers urged men to work hard to establish their personal and community independence and to protect their women. They told wives to stay at home and become guardians of the family, even though poverty forced women to work. Organizers of the American Society of Free Persons of Color emphasized "the virtues of prudence, frugality, and purity." In July 1838, the first issue of the New York black newspaper *Mirror of Liberty* told readers that "education and morals are the tenets by which Society and the community measure their moral strength and progress." Maria Stewart, the foremost African American female speaker and writer in New England, called for her people to be good businessmen and "promote and patronize each other . . . Possess the spirit of independence." These leaders sought to have their people embrace (and to be seen by others to embrace) bourgeois New England ideals because that seemed best for their community and, perhaps, because they expected that freed blacks would soon be accepted as full members of New England society. Their embrace of these standards could also be seen as part of the process of forming a free but separate community that would be as inclusive as possible, move closer to the constructive and dominant culture, and help black leaders forge beneficial relations with Anglo-American elites.[66]

Such urbane, individualistic, market-oriented, patriotic values were noticeably different from those fostered in Indian enclaves in the region, where community management of resources and social limits on individual accumulation and ambition still exerted tremendous force. Of course, most Indians lived "soberly, righteously, and Godly," and the very force of the jeremiads preached by Maria Stewart and other black ministers show that many African Americans (like whites) did not conform to dominant social standards. But like moral and economic reformers among contemporary whites, black leaders inculcated the values they espoused, particularly as they exerted social and economic pressure to modify behavior perceived as deviant or harmful to the community. Black liberation came to be viewed as not only political rights but also the embrace of American bourgeois ideals. By the 1830s, the marriage of an Indian woman and an African American man represented a potential clash between the father's culture, which emphasized patriarchy and individualism, and the mother's culture, which gave a woman and her community greater power.[67]

As the gap between the communal traditions of Indian villages and the values of the emerging urban, proto-industrial African American enclaves widened, mixed children must have found it harder to move between the two communities. Of course, the evidence for the assimilation of mixed individuals in the African American community is almost entirely circumstantial, as there are no extant letters or publications, aside from Brown's autobiography, by the children or grandchildren of mixed marriages attesting to their affiliation. But studies of Jewish-Christian intermarriages in America, which, like Indian-African American marriages, do not cross racial barriers or wide cultural gaps, show a high likelihood of affiliation with the culturally dominant group. That affiliation usually deepens as one generation replaces another and varies with the intensity of a parent's affiliation. Also important are the social categories created by the dominant culture, for the children of interracial marriages in America are generally taught by their parents to regard themselves as black rather than white. Thus intermarriage joined with social and cultural pressures to encourage the structural assimilation of mixed children into the black neighborhoods where they lived.[68]

Yet some Indian communities, such as the Nipmucs, survived even as families and individuals assimilated into other groups in the region or kept their Native ancestry and affiliation within the family. As long as the group survived in some form, the children or grandchildren of apparently assimilated individuals could rejoin or reconnect with that community. Such mobility is generally known as the principle of third-generation interest—"what the son wishes to forget the grandson wishes to remember"—and is facilitated by symbolic ethnicity. Thus members of families such as the Gimbees and Hemenways could cross and recross ethnic boundaries as different generations followed particular ancestral ties to forge deeper connections to either the Nipmuc or the African American community. Such connections do not require surrendering kinship ties to the other ethnic group, and some individuals managed to keep their connections to both. Still, community institutions and social dynamics usually lead people to embrace one primary nexus or group affiliation.[69]

During the eighteenth century, Indians in southern New England found it necessary to incorporate foreigners, mostly African American men, in order to create families and maintain their communities. By the end of the century, Indian–

African American intermarriage resulted in a substantial and visible mixed population throughout the region. Unfortunately, new problems emerged as the foreigners inevitably reshaped Native groups, and Anglo-Americans increasingly saw blacks, people of color, or mulattoes instead of Indians. Some communities lacking land, such as the Hassanamiscos, seemed to shrink and scatter, while more cohesive tribes, such as Mashpee and the Narragansetts, with prominent political and social boundaries, managed to adjust to many challenges after 1800, including the "liberal values" brought by African American spouses. While conflict was nearly inevitable in such circumstances, the disputes that were sometimes expressed in racial terms generally involved social issues or control of resources or political power. Even among Indian groups that, after 1825, allotted their lands and in other ways forged closer ties to the regional economy, older values of communal resource management remained significant.

Outside Indian villages and enclaves the children of mixed marriages faced a wider range of social pressures: white perceptions, laws, and economic discrimination; African American expectations; their tribe's behavioral and cultural standards; and the sometimes conflicting desires of family and friends. At the same time, such individuals also faced unique choices of identity and affiliation. They lived in African American neighborhoods and were seen by whites and blacks as blacks, but many also maintained kinship, social, and cultural connections with other descendants of their tribe or (now-scattered) village. Some abandoned those connections for years, or even generations, but their children or grandchildren might decide to reclaim their Native heritage and connections. Thus Indian descendants living in the region formed a lively jambalaya: some were clearly Indians, others African Americans, while still others—perhaps the majority—maintained dual identities.

With the growth of African American communities and institutions in New England cities, affiliation with African Americans offered people of mixed descent many social and economic benefits. And the sudden interest of white American elites in civil and social equality offered some African Americans and a few Indians better opportunities outside Indian villages. Indian groups that struggled to maintain their communities were thus threatened not only by the effects of white racism but also by the emergence of African American enclaves and institutions, and by blacks' embrace of liberal values like individualism, privacy, competition, and civil equality. As we shall see, after the Civil War state politicians would apply these values, sometimes with the applause of those who had married into Indian communities, to strip tribes of their autonomy and land. The same gap between Natives and African Americans would reappear a century later, during the

1960s, when blacks fought for civil and economic equality (although a small minority sought a separate nation) even as Indian activists tried to shore up tribal boundaries and their political, cultural, and social separation from America.

The relationships that developed between Indian and others in New England highlight a number of more universal lessons. They show how ethnic identity and group affiliation is sometimes flexible and at other times fiercely contested, and that while an individual may have a multidimensional sense of self and family, those who claim membership in a group must meet the behavioral demands of that community. They demonstrate how political and economic power can reshape subaltern groups, as Indian communities were influenced (deliberately or not) by Anglo-American laws and officials. The evolution of connections and differences between Indian and African American communities reveals the complex relationships and distinctions that existed, and continue to exist, among people of color. Finally, the experience of "mixed bloods" tells us again how sex and procreation influence society and culture. In these ways, the complex, and sometimes contested, nature of marriages and children who crossed between Indians and African Americans foreshadowed current controversies over the adoption of black children by white couples, and over the rigid racial categories in the census and various federal programs that seem increasingly anachronistic. These American issues first emerged among Indians in nineteenth-century southern New England.

CHAPTER THREE

Authority and Autonomy

On April 17, 1776, as war and social upheaval rocked New England, John Adams took a moment from the Continental Congress in Philadelphia to answer his wife Abigail's famous charge to "remember the ladies." Before twitting his wife that the "numerous and powerful" female "tribe" had "grown discontented," he seriously observed, "our Struggle has loosened the bonds of Government everywhere." Among other threats, he noted, "Indians slighted their guardians." He was almost certainly thinking of Mashpee, whose inhabitants had challenged the guardianship imposed by Massachusetts, protested as far as the king's council in London, and had finally won a degree of autonomy in 1763. Indeed, Mashpee's Gideon Hawley found that this Revolutionary virus spread "doctrines of liberty and equality" among the Indians. But Hawley wrote of his alarm in 1795 and was concerned about religion as well as politics. The postwar efforts of the Mashpees and other Indians for liberty, while having roots in pre-Revolutionary needs, was clearly set in the broader world of the early republic, with its decline of deference, rise of evangelical religion, emergence of democratic politics and culture, and struggle between central and local powers.[1]

Most Indian communities in Connecticut and Massachusetts were assigned guardians in the wake of the Revolution. As during the late colonial period, these officials were justices of the peace and lawyers, merchants, or rural gentry. Their powers included handling the community's finances and resources, preventing trespass and poaching, ensuring the support of the sick and elderly, and encouraging proper morality and habits of industry; in Massachusetts, they also managed seamen's contracts and earnings. They were appointed under English common law, which encouraged government to designate officials as surrogate fathers to manage the property owned by orphans or legal incompetents and to supervise their future. States took such measures because of the longstanding belief that Indians (like orphans and other minors) were incapable of dealing with the dominant legal system, and laws in the region for more than two centuries had barred the sale of tribal lands to outsiders without the approval of the legislature.[2] Rhode Island followed a slightly different path, leaving the Narragansetts relative autonomy, except between 1792 and 1818 when the state assembly appointed a treasurer who could veto the decisions of the tribal council.[3] Initially, most tribes accepted, and even welcomed, guardians as the best way to protect their resources and very existence. But after 1790, many began to challenge the appointed officials as burdensome, autocratic, and corrupt, and tribes became increasingly confident of their right and ability to govern themselves.

The Indians' efforts to challenge privileged authority are part of the larger picture of how Americans fought during the early republic to either contain or attain the promise of the Revolution. Their struggles highlight the Revolution as a process that continued into the nineteenth century, including new conflicts that developed when state governments sought more control over distant towns and villages. They show that subaltern peoples were as much a part of the revolutionary process as Anglo-American gentry, artisans, and "middling" farmers. They support the view that religious dissent in the early republic was at the heart of American's true democratic revolution, demonstrating the continued radical nature of Baptists and the attraction that the denomination had for subaltern peoples and communities seeking more local control.[4] The most prominent example was Mashpee's long battle to gain autonomy, beginning with its efforts in the 1790s to use the ideology of the American Revolution and evangelical attachments to free themselves of their guardian-minister Gideon Hawley and ending with their successful revolt in 1833–34, with its connections to radical Methodism and democratic politics. The Mashpees' experiences also show how efforts to increase a community's autonomy in order to protect against outside threats could open it to deeper changes, as those defending their communal lands against exploitation by guardians and other outsiders seemed to join the capitalist revolution in order to gain more independence and better lives. All these factors were part of regional and national political and cultural developments during the early republic, and they highlight the links between Natives and non-Natives even as they sought to defend their separate communities.

The Indians' emerging struggle was, at first glance, about largely practical matters, particularly who would control essential resources. But the language and the issues involved in those battles show that increasingly divergent concepts of proper public power were also part of the conflict. Indians not only contested the guardians' authority and actions but also, after 1800, generally pointed to themselves and their community rather than a few Anglo-American "betters" as the proper source of authority. However, the reaction of state legislators and guardians to the Indians' demands for reforms shows that the eighteenth-century aspirations of hierarchy, deference, and moral order remained strong in the region. Indian communities were themselves often split between individuals and families who favored "independence" and those who saw elite guardians as barriers to external and internal threats. Only after 1810, with the rise of democratic politics and relative stability in state government, would Indian groups find comparative consensus and increased autonomy. Thus the relationships between Indians and their guardians reflected developments within the larger political and cultural milieu of the early republic.

GUARDIANS REAPPOINTED

The Revolutionary War was extraordinarily disruptive for all communities in America, but particularly for the surviving tribes in southern New England. Public authorities who dealt with Indians believed that irregular and lawless conduct was part of their charges' natural behavior and that the war had set back efforts to civilize them. Massachusetts tried appointing guardians in 1778 for Hassanamisco, Punkapoag, Natick, Dudley, Mashpee, and Herring Pond, but those were the only such wartime arrangements.[5] By the end of the conflict, the majority of the guardians had died, moved away, or resigned their posts without replacements. Tribes were very concerned after the war with the large-scale loss of men in the army or navy, the emigration of many to the growing cities in an effort to find work in a depressed economy, and the growing tide of outsiders seeking Indian land or other resources. Indians were sensitive to their disadvantages in the Anglo-American legal system and therefore sought the protection of state authorities against land speculators, trespassers, and poachers. Native groups also needed to ensure the continuation of colonial laws that established Indian reserves, provided a distinct legal status for their inhabitants, and prohibited land sales to outsiders. In this sense, subaltern Indians shared the experiences of the powerful men who directed colleges (such as Dartmouth) and a few other pre-Revolutionary corporations that sought to maintain powers granted under colonial charters. But state authorities would seek to reform, as well as protect, Indian groups.[6]

Massachusetts and Connecticut authorities saw guardians as the best means for securing and improving Native groups. In August 1783, about 30 Herring Pond Indians complained that their lands were being sold from under them and that if the sales were consummated they would be impoverished. Two years later, the Massachusetts House of Representatives passed a bill to appoint three guardians to prosecute trespassers, "superintend the affairs of the said Indians," and ensure "due improvement" of their lands so that they would not become public charges. The bill did not become law, but its goals became policy when Herring Pond and Mashpee were assigned the same guardians in June 1789. The Connecticut legislature gradually assigned this authority to county courts: in May 1791, when the Paugussetts complained about timber poachers, the legislature directed the New Haven County Court to appoint an overseer to prosecute trespassers and manage the tribe's affairs, including leasing unleased land. In all of these states, Indian families and individuals living in Anglo-American towns (often in poverty and apparently isolated from their tribal connections) were subject to the authority of the town selectmen and overseers of the poor, who picked guardians and bound out their children, although Indian-owned land could not be sold without permission of the legislature.[7]

Most of the surviving tribes in Connecticut went to the state for assistance in the wake of the war. In May 1785, the Mashantucket Pequot headmen asked the assembly to confirm their title to their reserve and to appoint two militia officers from Ledyard to prevent "people round about [from] destroying their Timber and Crowding in upon their Lands." Three years later, the Eastern Pequots told the assembly that they had been without overseers for many years and were suffering from "confusion" in their "public affairs." Like their cousin Mashantuckets, they asked for specific men they felt were dependable, as they distrusted the majority of their white neighbors; the assembly agreed to one of their choices but chose someone else in place of the other. Apparently, the individuals appointed by the assembly did little or soon left, as a decade later the community found itself increasingly "intruded on by the White People, and by Negros, and others" and again asked for "the assistance of some Discreet Overseers." The Schaghticokes and Paugussetts in western Connecticut had similar problems reported by sympathetic neighbors who sought firmer legal support for the protection they could offer.[8]

Natives sought state assistance because they felt they had inadequate power to deal with trespass, poaching, and other threats that emerged during the war. Some of the smaller communities, such as Hassanamisco, Natick, and the Paugussetts, needed such support because they lacked the numbers to resist effectively. When Ralph Micah of Potawamucut asked the Massachusetts legislature in 1799 for guardians to protect his people against wood poachers, he justified his request by telling them that he was the only man left in the community and was getting old. Eight years later, the few Indians left in Middleborough asked for replacements for guardians who had died, as they were "deprived of that Protection which is Necessary for the Security of their property." These small, besieged groups used guardians as watchdogs and managers of their lands and communal funds. Various land sales approved by the legislatures during the colonial period had generated monies to support members of the group in time of need. Doctors, nurses, innkeepers, merchants, and even other Indians would get bills or Native promissory notes paid by the guardians. Guardians managed the affairs of poverty-stricken, ill, or infirm individuals and their children, finding families and doctors to care for the sick or helpless, leasing their lands, and arranging for indentures for the children. Such power could easily, however, lend itself to fraud or honest mistakes that would scar a family and community.[9]

Larger tribes were also assigned guardians after the war, although state authorities tended to allow the groups more autonomy. In 1785, a group of Gay Headers asked for guardians because they had heard that the legislature was considering allowing the unregulated purchase of their lands and were afraid that vulnerability to rum and unfamiliarity with the English legal system would cause them to lose their lands. In response, the legislature reappointed a prewar committee of three guardians — two whites and one Indian — the latter being the Gay Head Congregational minister, Zachariah Howwoswee. Nearly four years later, the state drew a clear line on the map between the Chappaquiddicks and whites from Edgartown and similarly re-created a board of overseers with two justices of the peace and one Chappaquiddick to judge disputes.[10]

Longstanding internal struggles over political power also drove the Mohegans and Narragansetts to seek state intervention. In May 1783, tired of the complaints and conflicts among the Mohegans, the Connecticut legislature appointed guardians for the tribe with extensive powers to manage tribal resources and determine membership. A Mohegan council continued to meet, but it had little power aside from persuasion, community consensus, or guardian support. The tribe found the appointed officials useful: in the fall of 1806, their "Committee of old Men" persuaded the state to appoint a new overseer after the old one died. In August 1779, the Narragansett Council led by the preacher Samuel Niles, in another effort to limit their sachem's power, petitioned the Rhode Island assembly to bar members of the tribe from leasing lands to outsiders without the permission of the council and "two substantial honest white People." Although this measure did not pass, by October 1782 the legislature had created a board of overseers to manage the tribe's affairs. Six years later, the dispute between the Niles and Ninigret factions reached the point that both sides asked the state to settle the conflict. In 1792, after extensive hearings, the state passed a law regulating Narragansett membership and setting up a ruling council with five members elected annually by men of the tribe. Though the council retained the power to manage and lease unallotted lands, the legislature also appointed a treasurer who managed the tribal funds and had to approve any leases the council made. [11]

These requests and appointments all provide the appearance that Indians needed and cherished the paternalistic protection of their guardians, that despite their eager participation in the Revolutionary War, they shunned its democratic potential and sought the traditional order of deference to the protective "better sort" and stronger connections with the central state government. But while tribes sought the assistance of those with power against those who would threaten the community, they did so cautiously. After 1800, conflicts would erupt over the guardians' wielding of legal, political, and economic authority. Indian protests tended to emphasize practical concerns, but there were also ideological conflicts that exposed a widening gulf between how elites and the "lower sort," including Indians, perceived the proper sphere of public authority. Tribes also challenged individual guardians or sought to regain autonomy when the outside authorities abused the community or went beyond their desires.

Guardians chosen from the region's elites were generally concerned with maintaining social order in a time of rapid and threatening changes, while Indians increasingly shared the conditions and concerns of the laboring poor. Many men worked as sailors and absorbed the radical political and social ideas spread around the Atlantic world.[12] Conflicts between Indians and their guardians over authority and community first flared in Mashpee. The struggle was about political control but soon moved into the arena of religious dissent, illustrating the connections between politics and religion in the early republic. These ideological links were also apparent in clashes between the gentry and Indians at Pequot, Narragansetts, Christiantown, and Gay Head.

MASHPEE AND GIDEON HAWLEY

In 1763, after almost two decades of fighting the guardianship, Mashpee gained the right to manage common resources and to hold annual meetings to elect officers. The Yale-trained (1749) Gideon Hawley was initially impressed by the results but soon soured on the system; decades later he told friends that it had become "popular & ineffectuous" because "the Indians will never elect the most suitable men." The upheaval of the Revolution further hardened Hawley's belief in the need for hierarchy and deference; in fact, he quietly became a Tory. The Mashpees, on the other hand, showed their eagerness to support the Revolution by flocking to enlist in the continental forces, and those who remained at home began boycotting Hawley's sermons.[13]

The minister's fears grew through the war, and at its end he began a campaign to alert his Boston friends to the threat posed by the growing number of poor whites and blacks who "have encroached upon this territory in the late lawless times." For Hawley, as for other orthodox ministers and gentry, public affairs went from bad to worse as populist politics and religion boiled over in Massachusetts. This crisis had its foundation in New England's troubled economy and in the political system that kept the Boston-centered merchants and lawyers entrenched in power and continued to maintain public funding for churches and Harvard College. In 1786, the agrarian revolt known as Shays's Rebellion evoked the spirit of 1775 for some but drove conservatives into a frenzy of fear. Indeed, the movement for reform was wider and deeper than a group of farmers angered by excessive taxation. Dissenters increased in numbers and influence, and they were joined by some Congregationalists in pushing democratizing measures and an end to the parish taxes (mandated by the 1780 state constitution) that usually went to the town's Congregational Church. The rise of Unitarianism, whose adherents rejected Calvinism, and the resulting split among Congregationalists broadened the antireligious tax campaign. Hawley's neighbors in Sandwich and Barnstable strongly supported the more radical aspects of the Revolution and, in May 1787, demanded a number of far-reaching reforms, including moving the state capital from Boston, reducing government salaries, regulating prices in rural stores, ending state financing of Harvard College, and ending the clergy's tax-exempt status. When the Mashpee minister heard about this measure, he suggested censuring and excommunicating those responsible.[14]

It was in this tumultuous, fearful atmosphere that Hawley in May 1788 asked the state legislature to give him tighter control of Mashpee in order to "withstand the daily encroachments & trespasses, which are committed upon us . . . [by] Poor people, who have no right here."[15] Five years before, a group of 18 Mashpees had protested that their elected officials were giving away or selling wood to outsiders. Now the legislature also received a petition from several whites complaining that few Indians attended Mashpee meetings, that it was common to bribe with liquor those who did attend, and that the Indians who served as overseers had become dictators who forced young men on whaling voyages. In response, the state imposed rule by three appointed guardians, including Hawley and two men from Barnstable, Rueben Fish and Captain John Percival.[16]

The reaction in Mashpee to the new regime was mixed, pointing to conflicts within the community and in nearby towns. In July 1788, Hawley sent to the legislature a petition signed by 29 Mashpee men, about a third of all adult men in the community. They, like Hawley, were concerned about the threats posed by newcomers and corruption but called the new regime "a very disagreeable constitution," writing that it was "mortifying to be under Guardianship and considered minors." Yet they did not seem angry at their minister, asking that, if they must have guardians, those selected be "men of the first characters for religion and learning, abilities integrity & honor" (i.e., like Hawley). The issue of character arose because Percival, a Baptist, had challenged Hawley's authority and supposedly "spoke lightly of the sacred scriptures," so the minister tried to get the captain dismissed. Hawley was supported by the gentry from neighboring towns, who accused Percival of having "no religious principles," while Percival was backed by other whites from the same towns and by a large group of Mashpees who asked him to represent them before the legislature. Shortly thereafter, the minister submitted another Mashpee letter warning of "pretended petitions" from "Negro trespassers" who backed Percival. Among those who signed, most would stand by the minister in subsequent conflicts. Factions were forming in Mashpee, with Hawley representing and fueling the dissension that grew from indigenous concerns but also reflected outside concerns and interests.[17]

In early 1789, after extensive hearings, the legislature agreed to change the law, replacing the three guardians with a five-member board of overseers, empowered to appoint one or more guardians to carry out its policies. Hawley (but not Percival) became one of the five overseers and at the first meeting the board selected two guardians and commissioned Hawley as treasurer. He would serve in that office until forced to resign in 1795, due to his advanced age and incompetence, but he continued to sit on the board of overseers until 1804, just three years before his death, when he engineered the appointment of his son in his place. A few months after the implementation of the new rules, Hawley reported that the regime was generally "very acceptable to these Indians." Hopeful, cheerful words. But though the new measure may have made the minister feel more secure, opposition to him swelled over the next decade, as the minister's dogmatic belief in the need for strong secular and religious authority increasingly clashed with emerging democratic demands in Mashpee and the surrounding region.[18]

The Mashpees' first set of protests featured appeals for "liberty and property."

In November 1789, a group of Mashpees protested to the overseers that they were poor and needed help that Hawley would not provide. A year and a half later, 21 Indians complained to the legislature about Hawley's overbearing behavior and demanded "the old Constitution and our Liberty." Their protest pointed to the connections between social, political, and religious concerns. "We do not want his Conduct in our affairs[,] we wants nothing at all that is his own he has Conducted in such manner that we have left his meeting entirely and never want to hear him preach nor even to see his face in our place any more." Hawley "discourages us" in "spiritual and temporal" affairs, which included the ability to "injoy our property." These Mashpees wanted political and economic liberty, including the right to hold and sell resources. Levi Mie, for example, testified that in 1786 he had obtained the rights to a large wood lot; cut, split, and shipped five cords to Nantucket; and found the venture so profitable that he decided to stop cutting and hold the rest "for my children." But that future was destroyed when Hawley sold 120 cords from the lot and kept the funds for the Mashpee treasury. Not only did Hawley keep their money, doling it out in "small Draughts," but he and other guardians also tried to regulate inheritance patterns, for "if any our near kindred dies they takes their interest and hires it out and the Nearest relation Cannot have it." A delegation of Mashpees, including the sisters Sarah Mie and Hannah Babcock, went to Boston to present their case before the legislature.[19]

Hawley fought back with a series of letters blaming the protests on neighboring whites, such as Percival, who hoped to regain control of Mashpee. The Indians who put their marks to these petitions, he told Governor John Hancock, were illiterates "half intoxicated and acting at the instigation of designing men." In addition, "not more than one half of these blacks [signatories] are Indians and unmixed." He told Robert Treat Paine that he could empathize with Moses, as like the prophet with the Israelites in the wilderness he had been with the Mashpees for nearly 40 years "and they have as often tried my patience." A month later, he wrote to Peter Thacher that only a very few openly opposed him and that his authority was critical to keeping order and saving these irresponsible Indians from their "insidious" natures. Hawley also tried to discredit the complaints by noting that that the leaders—particularly Mie and Babcock—"improve more land than did their parents and frequently draw money for supplies." He meant that they were lying or hypocritical. Perhaps. But another interpretation is that they were entrepreneurs frustrated by the limitations Hawley imposed.[20]

These protests show that the connection between liberty and property was one of the Enlightenment ideals that these Mashpees had made part of their political language, and they highlight how, in the early republic, liberty and rights were gradually redefined from communal to individual. The protest Mie and the other Mashpees made could be read as either individual (*his* right to hold and pass on resources to *his* children) or communal (*their* rights as Indians against the arbitrary authority of an outsider, Hawley). As described in chapter 1, the Mashpees and other Indians in the region had developed a land-management system that combined aboriginal and Anglo-American traditions. They could not legally *sell* land to outsiders without the permission of the legislature, but the sale of *resources* was, without the intervention of an "interfering" Gideon Hawley, quite legal.[21]

This conflict points to a possible division in Mashpee between those who embraced newer notions of liberty and private property and those who held to older values—who may or may not have supported the guardianship. Other Indian communities in midst of comparable cultural and political upheavals, particularly the Cherokees and Creeks at the end of the eighteenth century, and the White Earth Anishnaabe a century later, experienced similar conflicts. In this context, Hawley acted to maintain Mashpee traditions against troublemaking outsiders—traditions that included communal land management and putting the group before individual improvement. This may seem strange, as Hawley was determined to acculturate the Mashpees to Anglo-American ways, but he and other conservatives were deeply concerned about unfettered capitalism and individualism. Of course, the desire to participate in the marketplace is not necessarily a denial of ethnic or communal affiliation, nor does it necessarily prove a desire to reject traditional communal values. But among Indian tribes, such changes certainly created at least debate and often conflict.[22]

When their petitions failed, Hawley's opponents hired Nathaniel Freeman Jr., a lawyer, recent Harvard graduate, and son of the prominent Revolutionary general from Sandwich.[23] The resulting petition of December 1794 featured elegant and sophisticated language that connected their complaints with America's Revolutionary ideals and their own sacrifices during that conflict and called the current regime "an infringement of that freedom to which as men they were justly entitled." As in previous protests, this petition focused on two Mashpee grievances: that they were not allowed "the miserable privilege of choosing our own Masters" and that they "cannot alienate a single inch of our Land, nor indeed enjoy it, as the Government have undertaken to modify, & apportion it as they think proper." This last concern was prominent: they charged "those who forge our shackles" with removing all "incentives to industry or improvement." As in the past, Hawley tried to discredit the petitioners as "ignorant Indians" who "will never arrive to the knowledge of their true interests" and in any case "know not the purpose of petitions or papers." But the legislature took the petition seriously and, on June 11,

1795, appointed an investigating committee to hold extensive hearings at Mash-pee.[24]

The situation at Mashpee became even more volatile as religion joined poli-tics and economics as a source of conflict. By November 1794, Thomas Jeffers (ca. 1742–1818), an ordained Baptist minister of Wampanoag or Massachusett ances-try, had moved to Mashpee and quickly mounted a significant challenge to Haw-ley.[25] Months later, the orthodox minister told his Boston sponsors about Jeffers, scorning the preacher's ignorance and charismatic sermons, but he was clearly concerned about his rival's popularity, given the influence of the growing Baptist and Methodist congregations in surrounding towns.[26] It was during this intensi-fying atmosphere that the legislative committee came to Mashpee. Hawley's tes-timony to the committee emphasized the connections between social order and his religious and political authority. He was particularly concerned with a Barn-stable man, "Deacon Nye," who was going "house to house" among the Indians, "preaching up the doctrines of liberty and equality" and manipulating the Indi-ans "to bring them to his side in Politicks and to the Baptist side in religion." The weary minister concluded by pointing to the lack of order among the Mashpees, suggesting that if their government became "more popular" the consequences would be terrible. "Our election and popular days will be anarchical in a very high degree . . . They need an umpire or Superintendent."[27]

In early January 1796, as the committee began writing its report, the Mashpees quickly put together another short petition, complaining that their oppression had worsened since the committee's visit. They charged the overseers and guardians with corruption and misrule, and told the legislature that "we do not acknowledge the Rev. Mr. Hawley as our Minister, we not chusing his ways of Worship, we do not hear him, we Rather chusing to Worship the devine being in the Bapptist Or-der, we have made choice of a minister" (i.e., Jeffers). Most adult Mashpees signed this petition, which emphasized how Hawley's religious and political rule had be-come quite unpopular. But the committee backed Hawley, echoed his belief that returning to the 1763 regime would allow whites and blacks who had married into the Mashpee community to control the reservation and dispossess its Native pro-prietors. Regarding the religious conflict between Hawley and the Mashpees, the committee members believed that that "these have arisen, principally, on account of their civil affairs."[28]

Hawley viewed this recommendation as a vindication of his rule and a turning point in reinforcing his authority. Six months later, at Hawley's request, the legis-lature passed a resolution that "many vagrant, strolling and poor people, intrude and shelter themselves [in Mashpee] to the injury of the rightful inhabitants" and gave the overseers the power to eject "vagrant poor" whom they felt lacked proper residency. At midsummer, Hawley wrote that all but a few Mashpees had deserted Jeffers, but he was either boasting or willfully blind. In 1798, Jeffers would leave to revive the Baptist congregation at Gay Head, and another part-Indian minister, James Freeman, would take his place. Until the end of his life, on October 3, 1807, Hawley would regularly write letters confidently describing his unchallenged authority over his flock and noting how the Baptist congregation was "coming to nothing." Yet Freeman led another campaign in 1799 to overturn the guardianship, "praying for relief in their civil and religious concerns." That effort also failed, as Hawley's power and connections were sufficient to bar any change.[29]

Mashpees waited two months after Hawley died to mount one more effort against the 1789 regulations. Their petition, signed by about 50 men and women, began by echoing previous declarations of their sacrifices fighting for the Revolution and their disappointed expectations that they would be given their rights after the war. Many Mashpees fought for the Revolution, the petition stressed: half "fell victim in the cause of their Country and of Liberty," including many of the signatories who "can exhibit the traces of wounds." But they were bitterly disappointed that the promises of the Revolution were still unfulfilled. The petitioners, as in past campaigns, compared the 1763 regulations granting self-rule with the 1788 and 1789 laws, noting: "By the former we had the privileges in part of choosing our Masters[.] By the latter even this small portion of Liberty is taken away."[30]

Unlike previous efforts, however, this petition did not to impugn or assail the guardians. Instead, the writers focused on the high costs of the system (fees for five overseers, two guardians, a treasurer, secretary, constable, and timber agent) and the difficulties that members of the tribe often suffered because several of the overseers lived in other counties. Religion was not even mentioned. The prickly, authoritarian Hawley was dead, and his passing seemed to temper much of the bitterness the Mashpees felt toward the guardianship and to cause them to adopt a more practical and less confrontational approach in their efforts to regain autonomy. In addition, Mashpee proprietors and their families did benefit from the guardians' responsibility (and power) to negotiate whaler contracts, ensuring that Mashpee sailors were treated fairly, and to handle the men's pay to guarantee that families obtained the proceeds of a successful voyage.[31]

Once again, neighboring whites were actively involved in the Indians' efforts, including James Freeman, the state senator from Sandwich, who became the Mashpees' patron, and the Sandwich town meeting of December 9, 1807, which urged the legislature to heed the Mashpee petition.[32] In response, the overseers, including Gideon Hawley Jr., quickly maneuvered to forestall changes. In January, they collected 78 Mashpee signatures (both men and women) on a petition supporting the current system and accusing conniving whites from neighboring towns of bribing signatories. It also emphasized the absence of debt, availability of schools, decent medical care, and other benefits of the current regime, claiming that the majority of the community was "contented and happy." The Herring Pond tribe also sent a petition, signed by 38 men and women, opposing changes in the guardianship system, noting that fewer guardians would lessen their confidence in the system and diminish safeguards against fraud and trespass. Although the opposing petitions highlighted conflict among the Indians, perhaps because Hawley could no longer serve as a lightning rod, they were apparently riddled with fraud. Mashpees and neighboring whites testified that the overseers had used pressure and deceit to obtain the signatures. Such evidence and the relatively modest nature of the Mashpees' request were persuasive. In March 1808, the legislature reduced the number of overseers from five to three and allowed them to appoint only one guardian.[33]

Those asking for reforms passed over the issue of religion, but the controversy did retain a religious component that, as in the past, echoed the Mashpees' social and political concerns. The Mashpees who had bitterly opposed Hawley were prominent in the renewed campaign, though the petition against changes included the comment that when Hawley died "we not only lost our religious teacher, but our father and friend, who preached to us by his example as powerfully, as by his exhortation." At their request, the overseers now sought "to supply his loss, by providing for us an exemplary teacher in the principles of Piety, Religion & Morality." That summer, the Boston-based Society for Propagating the Gospel (see below) sent a Congregationalist minister, Elisha Clapp, to preach in Mashpee for several months. After he left, four Mashpees wrote to ask the organization for a settled minister, "lest the Itinerant Preachers of different denominations, who are traveling about in this part of the Country, should distroy our harmony & bring us to nothing." The initial signatory on this petition, Solomon Francis, had been a leader of the effort to garner support for the overseers.[34]

Throughout Hawley's battles, his frequent use of racist language is conspicuous. But the context of his comments within the Mashpee controversies shows that social class and deference were far more significant to him than race. Hawley was utterly convinced of the need to uphold religious and political hierarchy and orthodoxy, notions increasingly under siege in the early republic. He was horrified, for example, in 1796, when he read Thomas Paine's *Age of Reason*. Hawley commented to Jeremy Belknap that Paine's work "is so very agreeable to common readers that it will have a most pernicious effect in a country like ours;" in another letter he called the book poison. Four years later, in midst of the Jeffersonian revolution, he noted that he and his son had voted the Federalist ticket but grumbled that "we had two to one against us . . . Our people in general must be better informed and better principled than they are here to act with judgment." The connections Hawley made between religion and politics can also be seen in how he regarded "the Baptist society" in Mashpee as "founded upon Democratic principles, and lust of power." More explicitly, at the end of a long letter in 1802 describing religious and political conditions in Mashpee, Hawley concluded, "the Law and the Gospel must be joined for effectiveness." This was his epitaph.[35]

THE STANDING ORDER, CLASS, AND INDIANS

Hawley was not an isolated voice. Other clergymen and magistrates saw a connection between Indians and the "lower sort" in New England and viewed both as potential threats to the organic social order. These ecclesiastical and secular authorities, knit together by shared education, values, and, in many cases, kinship, are often called the "Standing Order"; they sought to "tighten the bonds between the churches, the learned vocations, and New England's republican society." Their efforts were aimed at "constructing a righteous community and assessing the cosmic meaning of the American experiment," and toward that end they sought to maintain properly deferential politics and public life. Many of the leading figures in the Standing Order, including Hawley's colleague Jeremy Belknap, were founders in November 1787 of the Society for Propagating the Gospel among the Indians and Others in North America (SPG). They envisioned the SPG as a successor to the colonial-era, London-financed Society for the Propagation of the Gospel (or New England Company), which until the Revolution had assisted Indian and Anglo-American missionaries to Natives, primarily in southern New England. The SPG's initial public presentation to the Massachusetts legislature, which would partially fund the organization, emphasized that the its primary mission was to continue "the one design of our venerable fathers in emigrating to this land . . . to extend the knowledge of our glorious Redeemer among the savage natives." But the organization's charter also empowered them to work "among other people, who through poverty or other circumstances, are destitute of the means of religious instruction."[36]

It was on destitute white settlers that the SGP initially focused, supporting an orthodox itinerant minister in the three most distant counties in Maine (Lincoln, Washington, and Hancock), which had become infamous for agrarian challenges to absentee Boston landlords. Ironically, those squatters sometimes disguised them-

selves as Indians and were known as "white Indians."[37] The first missionary dispatched, Daniel Little, had been rejected by the Penobscots in August 1786, and
the SPG paid him to minister to the white settlers in those counties. In November 1790, Little told Thacher and the SPG that previous itinerants to the area had
been "illiterate" men who "spread a spirit of bigotry and enthusiasm," creating a
climate of hostility to proper religion, but that the group's assistance would encourage "many persons of property . . . [to] remove their interest, and carry their
virtue into the Eastern Territory." Within a few years, the SPG had also raised sufficient funds to support Hawley and Zachariah Mayhew on Martha's Vineyard.
But it also continued to support missionaries to "the vacant towns and plantations"
in Maine, funded in part by an annual grant from the Massachusetts legislature.
In subsequent years, the society's support for ministers to these Maine settlements
often far outweighed the assistance given to Indian missionaries; most of the latter came through a donation given in 1789 specifically "for the benefit of the Indians."[38]

Although Connecticut's orthodox clergy and magistrates were not directly involved in the SPG, they were perhaps even more concerned about threats to
proper authority and social order. Timothy Dwight, Congregational minister and
arch-Federalist, was the unofficial but generally acknowledged head of that state's
Standing Order, particularly after 1795, when he was appointed president of Yale
College. When he visited Stonington in 1807 and poured his scorn upon the Pequots there ("All the vice of the original is left. All its energy has vanished."), he
used his perception of the tribe's condition to attack the ideas of the English
philosopher William Godwin, who saw freedom as the perfection of man.

> Here the human race, as nearly as possible, are without the restraint of law, morals,
> or religion. At the same time they are free in the fullest sense. No private individual
> possesses or exercises any power to control their conduct; and the government of
> Connecticut, either from despair of doing them any good, or from the unwillingness
> of its magistrates to execute law among these people, seems, in a manner which I
> cannot justify, to have resigned them to the dictates of their own passions and ap-
> petites . . . Promiscuous concubinage also, Godwin's great and favorite step toward
> perfection, they practice in the most unlimited manner.

Dwight also connected these horrors to religious dissent, noting that "religion in
Stonington has suffered from its closeness to Rhode Island." The town's six
churches included three Baptist congregations, the ministers of which "were mere
uneducated farmers or mechanics. Public worship, therefore, was either not celebrated at all, or celebrated in a forbidding and vulgar manner."[39]

Two years later, the retired New Hampshire Congregational minister Curtis Coe began a missionary effort to the Narragansetts sponsored by the SPG.[40] During four summers, 1809–1812, the elderly Coe preached in the small coastal hamlets around Buzzard's and Narragansett Bays. In his first frustrating summer, Coe described visiting poverty-ridden, isolated Anglo-American households little different from the Indian communities. He also revealed his elitist leanings by observing that there was no support for religion in the area because the only meetinghouses were Baptist and Quaker, and those seemed in a sad state of repair. Coe decided to focus on gaining the Narragansetts' acceptance and seemed to feel that the tribe desired his attentions, noting that they were "grateful to be visited by ministers." But in his next visit, one year later, the tribe's radically democratic attitude toward religious authority became clear. "They gave me to understand that they did not wish for [me] preaching the whole time, which before had been understood, and they wish males and females to carry on alternatively. But they consented that I should preach to them again. One of them said, they were spiritual, but my preaching was the Letter"—a Baptist insult.[41]

The Narragansetts had not become Christians until the Great Awakening in the 1740s, and then they formed a separate congregation when their neo-antinomian beliefs and preferences angered the white minister. Their Native minister, Samuel Niles, sparred in the 1760s and 1770s with the orthodox missionary Joseph Fish and also led the battle against efforts by the Narragansett sachem, Thomas Ninigret, to sell pieces of the reserve to leading Rhode Island planters.[42] Four decades later, the tribe again refused to give another orthodox minister any more status than an itinerant preacher, and Coe's frustration was clear in his journal: "They are illiterate & easily biased by evil minded persons."[43] In the summer of 1811, apparently at the invitation of the tribal council, he again sought the acceptance of the church elders. On June 22, he sat through what must have been for him an agonizing service. The congregation began by singing one of Watts's hymns.

Wh[ich] was read by a Negro. A Molatto who is a professed preacher made a prayer. Others, also, spoke after him, some the same & others appeared to me different words. They then sung a hymn, commonly used, when they meet, from the penitential cries. 'My soul doth magnify the Lord etc. etc.' . . . After which both men & women told their feelings & generally added 'Shall I go back, no, no, I am determined to go forward.' Exhortations were also, given to one another, in language of this sort: 'Hold on brother J. Hold on Brother G, Hold on Sister S. etc. One & all hold on.' 'Oh be strong, one & all be strong.' Again they sing the same hymn, as last before, took hold of one another's hands & reeled back & forward, in their devotion.

Afterward, Coe stood up and addressed the meeting, mentioning that the tribal council had requested him to come and asking for permission to preach. He was astonished at their reaction: first, every person present (including the women) was called to "give their voice on the subject," and second, they wished to bar him from preaching even when there was no Baptist minister available. "They wanted to hear no preacher that was paid—That my preaching prevented their speaking when they felt the spirit—That I was of a different denomination—That it was dangerous to give way, lest they should lose their government—That their former Elders had charged them not to give up their government. One said he had heard of a tribe which had had in that way lost their home of worship. That their mode was for all to speak." Coe was appalled at the notion. "Indeed, their tumultuous, noisy meetings, & what we call regular, decent worship are inconsistent." But Native traditional hospitality and Coe's ability to bend triumphed: he resumed preaching occasionally and afterward tolerated the discussions and prayers.[44]

Like other ministers in post-Revolutionary America, Coe knew that he had no legal or political power to force people to listen, let alone accept his authority; he could only persuade and compromise. The Narragansetts (and other Indians) continued to hold "noisy meetings," inspired by itinerants as well as by their own preachers, but they seemed less tumultuous and more decent as the norms of Protestant worship shifted among Anglo-Americans in the region.[45] A decade later, the SPG-sponsored missionary teacher Frederick Baylies visited the Narragansett church to propose setting up and funding a school in the community. He observed, "I had generally about 30, or 40 hearers, they are in the habit of speaking in meeting, in their exhortation they generally approved of what I said, none made any objections."[46]

Coe, Dwight, and Hawley were uncomfortable with, if not horrified by, this situation, particularly as they considered the Indians illiterate inferiors and disdained their enthusiastic, democratic religion. In addition, all three ministers depicted whites around these Indian communities as suffering from the same errors. The connections between religious and political democracy also alarmed Indian guardians on Martha's Vineyard. In 1808, Elisha Clapp visited the Vineyard after Mashpee, and when he went to Christiantown "found that the Indians' meeting house had been pulled down many months by order of their overseers, to prevent the evils, as I understand, which they feared from its being used by sectaries & itinerants."[47]

Indian groups not only linked religious and political autonomy but, as seen in Mashpee's problems with Hawley, also connected both to protecting community resources. A prime example is Gay Head's postwar revolt against the New England

Company. Between 1711 and 1728, the community had contested the company's deed to their territory and resorted to force when its commissioners leased hundreds of acres to a colonist, although the controversy subsided when both sides avoided further confrontations. But in 1775, as the Revolution erupted on the mainland, the commissioners gave several hundred acres of Gay Head land known as the Farm to the Reverend Zachariah Mayhew as partial payment for his supervision of Indian churches on the Vineyard. Zachariah, who was the fourth generation of Mayhews to work with Indians on the island, rented some of the land to colonists and worked some himself beginning in 1779. In April 1787, a group of Gay Headers ripped down Mayhew's fence; after he tried to rebuild it, they destroyed it again, prevented him and his tenants from grazing cattle there, and built and occupied an "Indian house"—perhaps a wigwam—on the property.[48]

The action was apparently led or directed by the Reverend Zachariah Howwoswee, Native minister of Gay Head's Congregational church. Howwoswee inherited the pulpit when his father died about 1774, moving home from Chappaquiddick, where he had preached since 1760. Like his father, Howwoswee combined orthodox Calvinism and the Wampanoag language in his sermons, fighting to maintain proper morals in the community. He also sought to inherit his father's political authority, serving as clerk of the annual proprietors' meeting in April 1784, gaining the Indian seat on the board of Gay Head guardians in 1785, and, two years later, heading the effort to reclaim the Farm. The minister cleverly leased some of the disputed territory to nearby gentry, including some "busy lawyers," staking a legal claim to the Farm that would receive the patronage and support of influential and knowledgeable whites. By 1789, the two-pronged Gay Head campaign was successful as Mayhew abandoned his claims to the Farm, perhaps in large part because the Revolution had severed the New England Company's legal and administrative connections to America. The minister was also forever barred by Gay Headers from visiting or preaching in their community, which made their uprising a revolt against the company, the powerful Mayhew family (which had led the missionary effort among Vineyard Indians for four generations), and the new SPG, which gave Zachariah a stipend.[49]

Howwoswee's efforts on behalf of the tribe increased his prestige and authority. But abuse of that power quickly led to his downfall and the decline of the orthodox church at Gay Head. The minister claimed the parsonage and a third of the Farm as due compensation for heading the church and serving as one of the three overseers, and within a year he accelerated the sale of grazing rights to whites and claimed an unusually large share of the proceeds. In a remarkable parallel to the situation in Mashpee, a large Gay Head faction (52 signatories) petitioned the general court to condemn the overseers' abuse of authority, singling out How-woswee for censure (resulting in his removal from the board, along with Simon Mayhew), and abandoned his congregation to join the Baptist church after the arrival of Thomas Jeffers, Hawley's nemesis. Jeffers preached and held prayer services in English and, unlike Howwoswee, encouraged participation throughout the service. In 1808, a visiting Congregational minister noted that "only a few aged Indians, who do not understand English," attended Howwoswee's sermons and that the minister had become an alcoholic.[50] Three years later, Howwoswee tried to regain control by joining with neighboring whites to ask the state to impose a guardianship on Gay Head. Their subsequent letter to the legislature complained, "Negroes and mulattoes have taken our concerns out of our hands"—no doubt a reference to Jeffers.[51]

Most Gay Headers feared the authority wielded by the guardians summoned by Howwoswee. White visitors in 1807 reported that the Indians "shut themselves up in their houses" for dread that the intruders were "engaged in some project for giving them guardians." The community therefore protested loudly and bitterly when they heard that the legislature had voted on June 25, 1811, to impose the guardianship. Their petition to the governor called the affair a plot, noted that they had not been told of the requests for guardians, and bemoaned that those who asked to become guardians were "men whose property would be enlarged if we should be deprived of ours." Over and over, the Indians stressed that "we have acted as republicans . . . as proprietors nearly twenty years successfully, supported our own poor and schools and have not been chargeable to any town." Their petition was organized by Jeffers, who also tried to curry favor with the governor by sending along seven dollars collected for people injured in a major fire in Newburyport. But their efforts were in vain. Four years later, they tried again without success to have the legislature end the guardianship, complaining that the men "in authority over us" were treating them "unconstitutionally, unlawfully, cruelly, and unjustly."[52]

In May 1816, the community once more met and petitioned to have the 1811 law repealed. They charged that the guardians were hurting their efforts to stop poachers and trespassers and had kept income from community resources without paying debts as per the law. In fact, the Indians wrote, the three men "have ceased to act in the capacity of Guardians and have told us to do our own business," but without changes to the 1811 law the community was unable to hold a legal proprietors' meeting or go to court to defend their lands.[53] That October, they sought the assistance of the influential part-Wampanoag, part-African sea captain,

Paul Cuffee, telling him that the guardians were part of "a connected gang which extends throughout the Vineyard whose interest it would be to impoverish us & get our land sold out of our possession."[54] Though the law was not repealed, the state did not appoint new guardians, and that inaction apparently returned sufficient legal authority to the Gay Head community.[55] In 1839, an Anglo-American minister living at Gay Head wrote that the Indians had done well financially since their guardians had been dismissed. At an annual meeting, Gay Head chose a clerk and treasurer from among whites in the neighboring town of Chilmark and often sought the advice of a white lawyer whom they trusted.[56]

GUARDIANS AND TRIBAL CHALLENGES

The struggles of Mashpee and Gay Head heralded a new confidence among Indian communities. Tribes increasingly demanded an end to guardianships or became quite willing to ask the legislature, the source of the guardians' authority, to replace particular guardians with more acceptable men. Their protests became sharper and more insistent in demanding self-rule. This struggle increasingly revealed an ideological contest between the Indians, all but a few of whom displayed dissident, democratic challenges to authority and its distant source, and the conservative guardians and legislators, who shared a similar status and paternalistic attitude toward their charges. Those Indian groups who accepted guardians demonstrated that they viewed the officials at least in part as their agents and felt that because they paid expenses and sometimes salaries, they should be able to oversee the guardians' actions. But state officials continued to believe the Indians incapable of acting in a virtuous, responsible manner. This debate was part of the decline of patrician authority and the emergence of a democratic culture in America and the tug-of-war over power between localities and central governments. In southern New England, the Standing Order began to lose its hegemony as the Federalist Party declined and conflicts developed among the clergy, and autonomous religious and civil associations became an integral part of the region instead of a violation of the commonwealth ideal. The result was not only increased political participation in America but also the emergence of popular-based movements for social improvement, including those among Indians (chapter 4).[57]

The shift can be best seen in Christiantown. Christiantown was not given guardians until March 1805, when the Indians complained about "the Incrochments made on their Lands by White people & Black persons who Come from other parts & bring their wives & Children and Leave them amongst the original Inhabitants," as well as about sea captains forcing men on voyages and leaving their families impoverished. But 12 years later, and a year after Gay Head regained self-rule, Christiantown asked the legislature to abolish their guardianship. The Indians informed the general court that they had lost no land until the guardians were appointed, but since then nearly half of their property had been sold, and the guardians were abusing their powers and refusing to submit accounts. The guardians protested their innocence and were supported by the legislature's investigator, but after they failed to submit accounts to the general court within the required three months, they were dismissed and new ones appointed.[58]

Chappaquiddick went through a similar struggle. On June 1, 1805, the Indians asked the general court either to dismiss their neglectful guardians or to appoint an agent to help them deal with white settlers who refused to keep their cattle from the Indians' fields. The state rejected their plea. At some point, perhaps at this time, the two white guardians delegated their everyday duties to the Indian member of the board, a role that could have made him quite unpopular. In 1807, the Chappaquiddicks bitterly asked the governor to dismiss their "representative," George Johnson, who was "at all times ready to join the white People on the island to injure & oppress us . . . if we must remain in Bondage, we wish for white men to be our task masters"—or (preferably) replace Johnson with a more trusted member of the community, Jason Peters. The governor agreed to the latter. Between 1807 and 1818, at least six different Chappaquiddick representatives—four Johnsons (George, Isaiah, Moses, and Josiah), Jason Peters, and Ebenezer Cuddody—served on the board of guardians. This high turnover points to the unpopularity of the position, the frequent absence of men to go whaling (which is why Josiah Johnson was replaced in 1818), or perhaps the contested election for this office within the community.[59]

The Chappaquiddicks continued to have problems with their guardians leasing land to outsiders and failing to maintain the boundary against their white neighbors. When a special committee investigated their complaints in 1809, it recommended avoiding future conflicts by appointing a special commission to divide the tribe's lands among its members every ten years. The Indians initially agreed to the idea but were soon angered at the commissioners' decisions, as well as the way their guardians were still renting out land to whites, cutting down wood, and plowing and planting fields without their consent or knowledge. The governor refused, however, to replace those officials. In 1824, the Chappaquiddicks again complained that the guardians were not helping with their neighbors who refused to fence in their cattle. When the animals got into the Indians' fields and ate their corn, the owners threatened to sue if the Indians tried (at their guardians' recommendation) to confiscate the animals. Again, the governor's advisers found no evidence of problems.[60]

As might be expected, during this period the Mashpees once again campaigned for self-determination. In June 1817, nine men, including Levi Mie and others who had opposed the late Gideon Hawley, asked on behalf of the tribe to choose their own overseers and to reduce the number to two, essentially going back to the 1763 regulations. They emphasized the increasing amount of meadow leased and wood cut by the three guardians, their rising debt, and the officials' refusal to show their accounts. "We wish to know what becomes of all our money, that we cant have now privilege of that, that is really our own." Their complaint was answered by another memorandum, featuring nearly 80 Mashpee names, that asserted the current system was the best one ever tried, that conniving white neighbors had influenced the protesters "by promises of reward and other improper motives," and that most of the community was "contented and happy."[61]

A joint legislative committee investigated and found a "diversity of opinion" in the community, "a very small part claiming the entire right of self government, — a much more considerable portion wishing to share it with the authority of the Commonwealth, by choosing overseers to be joined with those appointed by the governor and Council; while others not less intelligent, believed no share in selecting their overseers could not safety be rested in the Indians & that the present mode of government ought to be continued." The investigators agreed, not surprisingly, with the last view, lest power fall into "the hands of the worst of all of the community's men, whose objects would be entirely selfish." The commission also rejected Indian complaints that the overseers were too expensive, and told the legislature that the guardians' only failure was to have been "too lax." Yet the legislature did replace the three with two others, meeting part of the complainants' demands. On the other hand, the overseers were also granted the power to bind out anyone who seemed a "habitual drunkard and idle" for up to three years' service, and to give the income to their families. In addition, the officials were also put in charge of regulating how Indians could cut timber, even for their own uses.[62]

Apparently little had changed since the 1790s in the perceptions and attitudes of Anglo-American elites, or in the lack of consensus among Indians about the degree to which they could manage complete autonomy while protecting their lands. The critical issue remained what guardians did with their authority. Were they overbearing? Did they violate significant community social and cultural norms? Did they interfere with Native congregations or other organizations? Most important of all, did their actions endanger the community or interfere with individual or family enterprise by selling or leasing significant resources to outsiders? Not surprisingly, these practical concerns generated battles about authority that veered into democratic ideologies, much as concerns about taxes, debts, and monopolies drove the American Revolutionaries.

The connections between practical and ideological concerns were highlighted among the Mohegans just one year after the Mashpees lost their case. In April 1819, and again a year later, those who remained on their ancestral homelands (now the town of Montville) protested loudly when a new set of overseers distributed funds to the descendants of exogamous marriages living in the area, which broke the tribe's long-standing rule that any men who married out of the tribe had to leave. The overseers were also not keeping whites from trespassing and they lived too far from the community to be effective. The Mohegans demanded the right to nominate their overseers. But a legislative committee ruled in May 1820 that the guardians had acted in the best interests of the Mohegans and "with a parental solicitude, watched over the Education and morals of this tribe." They believed that the Indians' demands were solely at the connivance of unsavory whites, condemned the Mohegans' "peculiarly vicious habits," and recommended that the Indians not handle their tribal resources or affairs.[63]

One year later, the Connecticut assembly passed a law giving the appointment and oversight of guardians to the county courts in which the tribe was located. The state's paternalistic intentions remained quite clear, for the first section told the overseers that they "shall have the care and management of their lands, and shall see that they are husbanded for the best interest of the Indians, and applied to their use and benefit." There were also fines for anyone found selling or giving liquor to Indians and a ban on lawsuits against Indians for debts or broken contracts.[64] In April 1823, after Golden Hill Paugussetts complained about the paternalistic treatment of the overseer appointed by the county court, a general assembly committee endorsed the general policy of doling out tribal rental income to buy food, clothing, medicines, and other things for needy individuals. The committee reported that the overseer had treated the tribe "as members of a family, expending more upon the sick the aged & the infirm, than upon the young, strong and healthy." They rejected the tribe's request to divide the rents equally; the healthy should earn their own livings, and the sick and elderly needed more assistance. Besides, they sniffed, Indians "are an ignorant & unfortunate race of beings, degraded by intemperance & other vices.—Very little, if any, reliance is to be placed upon their representations and complaints, and to trust them with property beyond what their immediate necessities require would prove injurious to themselves & to society."[65]

The change in administration did not alter efforts of some Mohegans to regain the power to choose a different overseer or the efforts of others to defend the current one. That February, 25 members of the tribe asked the New London County Court to remove their overseer, Nathaniel Bradford, charging him with leasing (at low rates) parts of their reserve to relatives who stripped the timber.[66] Four months later, they sent another petition asking for Bradford's removal and the right to nominate his replacement, appealing to the tribe's ancient alliance with Connecticut, their sovereign rights, and "the spirit of Humanity and Justice" in which the court and assembly had acted. "It is in the Parental Character alone, that the Guardianship of the white people is acknowledged . . . We ask for one last favor, that of our choice of masters . . . The people choose their representatives & these their Judges . . . Altho destitute of the forms of society, our personal rights should be sacred." But their plea gained no change, particularly as another Mohegan petition signed by nearly as many members of the tribe opposed Bradford's removal, saying that he "had our lands well rented and our Rents honestly paid."[67]

Bradford continued in office, and apparently did work for the tribe's interest, two years later using the state's regulations regarding Indian land sales to reclaim a valuable tract of land in the center of the Mohegan settlement that the general assembly had sold. But the tribe (and its neighbors) continued to struggle over the right to choose an overseer. In June 1834, some whites in Montville told the court that they feared the Mohegans' new overseer, John Fitch, was inadequate and asked that Robert Comstock be appointed instead; the tribe itself sent a petition supporting Fitch—and were supported by a different group of Montville men. Seventeen months later, 22 Mohegans (mostly from the Cooper family) charged Fitch with nepotism and fraud and asked that he be replaced—but by Ralph Hurlbutt, not Comstock. A year and half after that, another petition from the tribe supported Fitch, telling the court, "we are well satisfied with our overseer." Fitch remained their overseer until the late 1840s. The Mohegan petitions, even those taking opposite sides on Bradford and Fitch, show that members of the tribe thought that their overseer ought to be their agent rather than their ruler.[68]

Similar views were shown by the Mashantucket Pequots, who, like the Mohegans, retained a distinctive tribal government. The community regularly met at a council house and at various times elected two of their own to act as selectmen and representatives to the state legislature—positions that tended to rest with a particular set of families with generations of service to the tribe. By the middle of the century, women were dominating these positions, as men were increasingly gone for months, or even years, at a time on whaling trips. The tribe showed little reluctance to demand the replacement of guardians who abused their powers or failed to carry out the tribe's wishes. In 1804 and 1819 they petitioned the state assembly to replace different sets of overseers. After the assembly handed oversight responsibilities to the county courts, the tribe requested, in February 1848, to review the accounts kept by their overseer, William Morgan, and then, in June and again in February 1849, asked the court (unsuccessfully) to put Luke Gallop in place of Morgan, "who we do not respect nor consider a suitable person to manage our affairs."[69]

Morgan continued in the office until 1854, when Amos Latham replaced him. The following January, six Pequots complained that Latham had been appointed without their knowledge and against their consent, that he had cut and sold many trees from their reserve "at small and ruinous prices," and that he was demanding such high rents of white tenants on reservation land that he threatened this source of their income. Latham was quickly replaced by William Morgan, which resulted in an angry petition from seven Mashantuckets who complained that the court had appointed Morgan despite their opposition and that since resuming the post he had "neglected to exercise the proper care and management of their lands," paying "exorbitant prices for necessaries" and selling their timber "at small and ruinous prices."[70]

As tribes sought greater control over their overseers and guardians, these officials found their positions held few (legal) rewards and left them caught between the strange ways of the Indians and the desires of white neighbors, relatives, and friends. While some became the Indians' friends and allies, many more were baffled or angered by their charges. Some resisted appointment or neglected their duties once appointed. Compensation was always an issue because only a few guardians received even a small salary for their work.[71] The Indians were aware of this problem; the Chappaquiddicks told the governor in October 1811 that the trust reposed in their three guardians "hath been not only neglected but abused, we say not owing to their want of abilities, but little or no prospect of the recompense of reward, for any services, for which there is no funds or means with us to afford." Some guardians instead dipped into their charges' resources, cutting timber, taking fish, or pocketing money from the funds that they administered. The Mohegan and Pequot petitions already cited are just a few of the many charges of impropriety and dishonesty against overseers, by whites as well as by Indians, sometimes clearly inspired by political or personal conflicts but sometimes found by investigators to be accurate. Sometimes guardians also showed an unwillingness or failure to acknowledge Native kinship and culture. They often sold community land or resources to support orphans and widows, or the aged and helpless. In such cases, the Indians accused their guardians of being arbitrary and

high-handed. But the guardians of course saw themselves as the government's representatives and believed that "Better Regulating" the Indians included guiding
Native welfare and morals.[72]

Indian struggles over authority were not limited to battles against overbearing,
neglectful, or fraudulent guardians. Internal conflicts over political and social
power arising from connections with state authority could also erupt, as with Gay
Head and Mashpee, and hinted at with the Mohegans by their competing petitions about Bradford and Fitch. The history of colonialism demonstrates that representatives of outside, sovereign powers often generate conflicts within subaltern
communities. But self-determination does not necessarily lead to consensus, as
the quarrels among the Narragansetts during the two decades following Curtis
Coe's visits illustrate. In October 1812 and January 1813, groups of Narragansetts
(mostly women) sent petitions to the general assembly complaining about the sale
of land by their tribal council, asking that the assembly bar additional sales until
the council accounted for the funds from previous transactions, and charging that
the council had drawn money from the state-appointed treasurer to spend on
liquor. They also asked that the state reduce the council to three members, that
five were too expensive and only three really necessary. The assembly appointed
a committee to investigate, but no changes resulted.[73]

Instead, the annual tribal elections apparently brought the complainants to
power, for two years later the council sought to expel Frederick Bosemedes, a
Swede married to a woman of Narragansett ancestry, who in 1810 and 1811 had
been the council's spokesman welcoming Coe to preach to the community. The
council complained to the assembly that Bosemedes rejected their authority, that
his wife was not Narragansett, and that he had been assigned land by the former
council "Contrary to our Regulations." Other concerns may have played a role in
the new council's action: Bosemedes's public support of the unpopular Coe may
have been an unstated issue and, as a foreigner, the Swede may have been a safe
target for those who loathed the actions of the previous council but wished to avoid
a feud that might involve kin. A state committee reported in June 1816 that the
controversy involved a disputed piece of land that Bosemedes's wife and two other
Narragansetts all claimed as an inheritance. The committee divided this property
between the rival claimants and declared all satisfied.[74]

But the bitterness of this battle pointed to broader concerns about community
political and social boundaries, as well as the proper use of authority within the
tribe. These issues remained very much unsettled, and for the next 15 years a battle raged between the council and many members of the tribe. The conflict became particularly explosive after 1818, for the treasurer quit and the assembly failed

to appoint a new one, leaving the tribal council with unchecked power and no external, imposed authority against which the community might unite. The dissidents accused the council of acting in an "imprudent and improper," if not illegal, manner, and in 1823 a group petitioned the assembly to terminate the council and appoint a guardian. The council in turn sought to have certain individuals declared nonmembers of the tribe; they and their descendants would then be barred from community resources, including land on the reserve. Nearby whites became involved when Narragansetts, or some claiming to be Narragansetts, incurred debts that the tribal council refused to pay.[75]

The conflict became so intense that in 1828 the state created a special committee to hear and resolve all of the controversies and complainants. The committee met with the complainants in January 1829 and settled some of the issues but noted that under state law the Indians could not be sued for debts—and suggested that the assembly might want to do something about that problem. One year later, the assembly appointed another committee to reconsider Narragansett autonomy. Here the politics became quite muddled, for Dan King, the same man who had circulated the 1823 petition asking for the abolition of the tribal council (having witnessed all of the signatures), chaired this committee. King's report condemned the tribal council as having "arrogated to themselves indefinite power," depicted the community as a degenerate "medely [sic] of mongrels in which the African blood predominates," and proposed setting up a guardian over the tribe. This bill did not pass, perhaps because most of the Narragansetts roundly condemned the King report. In fact, the Narragansetts retained their autonomy until 1880.[76]

THE MASHPEE REVOLT

Eighteenth-century paradigms of patrician authority dissolved in the United States in the 1810s and 1820s, as deep demographic and economic changes undermined the social and cultural walls that had kept the common man from an active role in politics. This was also when the Massachusetts paradigm of a cohesive moral commonwealth was finally shattered by the general acceptance of autonomous churches and secular organizations.[77] The final entrance of southern New England Indians into the Age of Jackson is clearest in the encounters of Massachusetts politicians and Indian communities on Martha's Vineyard and Cape Cod between 1827 and 1840. The maturation of Indian democratic ideas and tactics is particularly manifest in the success of the Mashpee revolt of 1833–34. At the same time, elite assumptions about the need to impose proper moral guidance and Indian concerns about the need to maintain their lands and resources against white trespassers both remained significant factors.

The first clear shift appeared in 1827, when three Massachusetts legislators finished reporting on the conditions of Indians in the Commonwealth. Their investigation had been driven by a number of recent concerns, including a request by some of the Chappaquiddicks for a guardian (in order to deal with neighboring whites) and the authority to appoint a pound keeper in order to legally confiscate trespassing cattle. The committee was to report on all Indians, but it focused on the largest remaining groups: those in Mashpee and the three Vineyard villages. The legislators noted that, because many guardians had resigned without replacements, the four groups generally governed themselves, holding meetings (in which women could vote) and choosing officers. But the Indians lacked the legal standing to file charges against trespassers or poachers. The committee also acknowledged (surprisingly) that guardians had exercised a "paternal, and almost despotic will," in direct opposition to " the popular will of the tribe." Although not news to Mashpee or Gay Head, the *acknowledgment* of these characteristics by Anglo-American elites signaled a shift in attitudes.[78]

In response, the committee proposed what they viewed as a compromise between despotism and democracy: allowing the four Indian groups to annually elect their own overseers and other officers, with the power to examine accounts formerly reported only to the governor or court. They also suggested dividing the Vineyard Indian reserves among the families in each community while retaining the bar against selling land to outsiders, thereby limiting the guardians' authority. But the guardians' powers proposed by the committee were actually more despotic than in previous arrangements, for they would have the authority to remove strangers and intruders; bind out for service of up to three years "habitual drunkards, vagabonds, and idlers," their wages to be used for families or the group; and punish various sorts of violations by the Indians on the reserve, from the sale of liquor to "lewdness and lascivious behavior," with punishments including possible solitary confinement.[79]

These proposals demonstrate the influence of budding social reform movements among the region's elites and middle class. The recognition by state legislators that Indians should have some role in their governance also shows that assumptions about the abilities and rightful public role of Indians were changing. More importantly, the three Indian groups on the Vineyard were actually allowed to choose whether they wanted the changes: Christiantown and Chappaquiddick accepted, but Gay Headers refused to accept either guardians or a formal division of their lands. Nor were the powers granted guardians by this act ever exercised, as those subsequently appointed saw the Indians as intelligent clients to advise and assist rather than as wayward children. In 1840, when the Chappaquiddicks' elected overseers opposed a petition from Edgartown whites requesting an end to the "unjust and anti-republican" guardianship, the officials told the legislature that the tribe still needed outside "counsel and assistance," particularly in settling accounts with whaling captains and ship owners after voyages.[80]

But the Mashpee Revolt of 1833 was the clearest sign that Indians no longer accepted subordination. The goals, rhetoric, and actions of those behind this movement demonstrated a continued link between dissident religion and democratic politics and drew a direct connection between Mashpee and the larger issues of the Jacksonian period. New pressures developed in Mashpee in the 1820s as the children of those who had opposed Hawley returned from whaling to stay and raise families. Matthias Amos told a visitor decades later that "when he was a young man he went whaling and obtained thus all the education he ever had, for at that time they had no schools. He also learned by going to sea that there were better ways of living than he had hitherto known, and when he married he settled down at home, and soon, with other young men of his tribe, he became very much dissatisfied with their condition. They were under the control of men appointed as guardians of commissioners, who were citizens of neighboring towns, and who were always rum sellers, and induced the indians to drink as much as possible, and then took every advantage of them in their power." The returnees found the guardians' repressive control irritating and harmful. Daniel Amos, one of the leaders of the revolt and Mashpee selectman for many years afterward, told a legislative committee investigating the revolt that dissatisfaction had grown over the past decade. Their guardians had refused to make any account of their actions, to provide any additional powers for those who wished to combat illiteracy and alcoholism, or to allow additional resources for individuals who tried to improve their economic condition.[81]

The Reverend Phineas Fish (ca. 1784–1854), appointed by Harvard as Gideon Hawley's successor in 1811, was also infuriating, for he was a liberal Congregationalist with heavily rationalist, anti-Calvinist, Unitarian tendencies, whereas the Mashpees had left scholastic strictures behind and embraced an antinomian Baptist faith in the 1790s. The Mashpees went instead to Daniel Amos's brother, Joseph (1806–1869), who began preaching there and at Chappaquiddick and Gay Head around 1825 and received Baptist ordination in 1830. "Blind Joe" Amos became the latest in a series of Indian Baptist ministers, who competed with orthodox ministers. By 1833, Fish's congregation was almost entirely made up of white families living in or near Mashpee, and Amos's congregants were increasingly an-gered that the orthodox minister refused to let them use the meetinghouse and that his salary was paid by the Williams fund for Indian ministers, administered by the heavily Unitarian Harvard College. Matthias Amos later told a reporter that Fish "took no interest in them, beyond preaching to them on Sunday, never vis-ited them, and did them no good. He was a Unitarian, and most of those who cared for religion at all, wanted to be Baptists."[82]

The revolt began with the arrival in Mashpee of the itinerant Pequot Methodist preacher William Apess (1798–1836). Apess was ordained by a group of dissident Methodists in 1829 and in that year violated older norms of authority and privi-leged discourse by publishing his memoirs. His denomination had a particular ap-peal for laborers, blacks, the young, and others denied power and respectability. The Pequot preacher-activist traveled to Mashpee in May 1833; he attended ser-vices at the Indian meetinghouse and was shocked to find only whites in the con-gregation. He became angry when he found Fish not only unconcerned with the situation but also utterly unsympathetic to the notion of granting the Indians more political and economic autonomy. Apess was probably not really surprised, con-sidering his denomination and decades of struggles with white racism. He preached a few days later to his Indian brethren (Joseph Amos was away, proba-bly on the Vineyard) on "the soul harrowing theme of Indian degradation"—aris-ing out of white oppression—triggering a series of community meetings in which the Indians discussed their problems and considered solutions.[83]

On May 21, a large meeting agreed to adopt Apess in order to give him stand-ing to press their case, to petition Massachusetts governor Levi Lincoln for redress of their grievances and to petition Harvard to discharge Fish and instead support the Methodist minister. The memorial to the governor began with the resolution that "we, as a tribe, will rule ourselves, and have a right to do so; for all men are born free and equal, says the Constitution of the country." The Mashpees in-formed Lincoln that on July 1 they would flout the authority of their guardians by preventing white men from cutting or taking wood from Mashpee. The petition to Harvard emphasized their alienation from Fish and that minister's ineffective-ness and ended with the resolution that "we will rule our own tribe and make choice of whom we please for our preacher." On June 25, when they did not get any reply, they held a meeting, elected officers, and agreed to post their May re-solves in the surrounding towns. They also sent notices of dismissal to their guardians, demanding that they surrender all Mashpee funds and accounts, and to Fish, demanding that he leave Mashpee (abandoning his home) and surrender the key to the meetinghouse. Their note to Fish sternly told the minister, "we Desire to be men in this business and not savages."[84]

At this point, Governor Lincoln sent Josiah Fiske to Mashpee to investigate. He arrived on July 1 and found the Indians "in a state of open rebellion against the laws of the Commonwealth" and the surrounding inhabitants on edge about the Indians. The Mashpees had, as promised, stopped a group of whites from removing cut timber previously sold by the guardians and had taken control of the meetinghouse. Fiske called a meeting on July 4 that drew nearly 100 Mashpees, many carrying muskets. With Daniel Amos presiding, the Indians related their grievances, and Apess pressed the commissioner to end the guardianship immediately. When the commissioner was unable to persuade Apess to back down from the resolution, he began to fear future bloodshed and had the minister arrested by the Barnstable sheriff.[85]

Over the next few days, tempers began to cool as Fiske toured the reserve, met many Mashpees, and gained their trust on behalf of the governor. He, in turn, was impressed by the kind and respectful way they treated him while keeping their resolve "that they ought to have the right to rule and govern themselves. They steadily maintained that, by a proper exercise of self-government and the management of their own pecuniary affairs, they had it in their power to elevate themselves much above their present state of degradation." On July 6, the Mashpee council agreed to table their measures until the forthcoming legislative session would allow them to press their demands before the general court. This last, ultimately successful, Mashpee campaign to gain autonomy exhibited similarities to other social reform movements of the 1830s, and like those efforts it was driven by a rising generation. But the Mashpee revolt shows continuity rather than change, for its proponents were the children and grandchildren of those who had fought against Hawley and the guardianship, and their goals remained the same.[86]

Apess and the Mashpees began to gather important allies to help press their case. They enlisted Benjamin Hallett, lawyer and editor of the *Boston Advocate*, at this time leader of the Massachusetts anti-Masonic Party and later of the region's Democratic Party. William Lloyd Garrison also wrote sympathetic articles in the *Liberator*. In mid-January 1834, Daniel Amos, deacon Isaac Coombs, and William Apess traveled to Boston to press their case. The city and its leaders were primed for the Indians, having just celebrated both the visit of a group of Penobscots and Edwin Forrest's renowned performance in *Metamora*, the play that mourned the death of King Philip, disparaged the Puritans who drove him to war, and romanticized the supposed "extinction" of the Indian. The Mashpees saw their petition discussed in the House and marked up for future action. On a Friday night, the three men spoke to that assembly and about a month later testified to the legislative committee set up to reconsider the guardianship. During their stay in Boston, they also gave public speeches to large crowds in Boylston and Tremont Halls and elsewhere, which stressed how the cost and oppression of the guardianship system was "retarding their improvement, and oppressing their spirits" by discouraging industry, entrepreneurship, and moral reforms, including temperance.[87] The Mashpees and Hallett also displayed their political savvy by publishing articles and letters accusing New Englanders of hypocrisy in fighting for Cherokee rights while denying the same to the Mashpees.[88]

The political and cultural shifts in the region and the lack of opposition to the Mashpees' requests made the general court's decision relatively easy. In 1833, Massachusetts had ratified a constitutional amendment that ended tax support for the Congregational Church, finally separating church and state and severing a symbolic link to the Puritan past. That same year, the General Court organized a Legislative Temperance Society, and no doubt its 160 members were quite impressed by the Mashpee Temperance Society organized by Apess, rather than Fish, and heavily publicized by the Indians and their allies. They were also moved by the Indians' emphasis that with more autonomy they could improve their schools. The Mashpees' opponents were few and subdued, and they tended to blame the controversy on Apess. In March 1834, the state legislature abolished Mashpee's guardianship and made it a district with the power to elect selectmen and other town officials. The new law did set up a white commissioner and treasurer to advise the Mashpees and manage their financial affairs, but there was little doubt that the Indians had won their political and economic autonomy.[89]

The battle to oust Fish lasted longer. Already alienated from the minister, the Mashpees were even more angered by his condescending and racist petitions against their effort to gain independence. They viewed the church as their historic community center, resented that non-Indians now dominated worship there, and saw little difference between their political and religious autonomy. A legislative committee reported that "the Indians would more punctually attend public worship, feeling that they had rights which they might exercise without obtrusion by the white inhabitants, who they stated took the lead of singing, and, as one Indian observed, put the Indian singers back, and the Indian wanted to take the lead in his own meeting." In 1836, the Mashpees asked Harvard to give them half of Fish's salary to pay a minister of their choice; Harvard agreed, and the Indians chose E. G. Perry, an ordained Baptist minister, as their missionary and schoolmaster.

Joseph Amos continued to minister to the Indian groups on Martha's Vineyard as well as at Mashpee. One year later, a Mashpee meeting unanimously voted to dismiss Fish, but he still refused to leave or to share the meetinghouse with Perry.[90]

Finally, in July 1840, after the legislature made Mashpee an independent parish, the Baptists went into the church and forced Fish out. He protested to the state and to Harvard but finally accepted the construction of a new meetinghouse (which Mashpee protested) in Cotuit, at Mashpee's southeast corner, where he ministered to the few white families and some still-loyal Mashpees; he also continued to preach on alternate Sundays to the Indians at Herring Pond. Fish also retained his elitist and racist sensibilities. In 1853, one year before his death, he wrote with a sense of sadness to an SPG official that the Indians held "a considerable degree of false ambition of equality with Whites, without proper fitness for it—and it threatens to impair that docile spirit by which alone they can reasonably hope to increase their true respectability."[91]

The nearly continuous efforts of the Mashpees for autonomy, and the somewhat more reluctant strivings of other Indians in the region, seem to fit quite nicely into the liberal metanarrative of American history as an inexorable movement toward increasing individual liberties.[92] But neither the Mashpees nor other tribes wanted full citizenship and, with few exceptions, saw unchecked individual ambition as a threat to their community.[93] Knowing that powerful outside economic interests wanted their resources, they supported state laws banning the sale of reserved lands to non-Indians and saw no benefits in voting in elections.[94] Their ultimate goal was to regain autonomy and defend the tribe's resources and integrity, not to tear down boundaries against the non-Indian world. But they were increasingly confident of their rights and abilities, even as the poorest of "common men," to think and act in a competent manner for themselves and their communities. They did not see any advantage or superiority in the wisdom of the "better sort." If anything, their experiences had taught them to distrust guardians as ignorant and interfering outsiders. Those experiences were shaped and confirmed by the democratic ideology that emerged in the early American republic.

Thus New England Indian communities joined artisans, farmers, and laborers in their challenges to elite authority. Those efforts highlight the region's post-Revolutionary democratic movement and its strong connections between religious and political dissent. Indians not only contested their guardians' use of power but also increasingly pointed to themselves, rather than a few Anglo-American "betters," as the proper source of authority, even when they wanted the protection offered by guardians against threats to the community. The reactions of ministers and officials to the Indians' demands show that eighteenth-century paradigms of hierarchy, deference, and moral order remained strong in the region. But the Mashpees' winning of autonomy in 1834 provides a fairly clear ending date for that paradigm. In this fashion, the relationship between a few surviving Indian communities and their guardians reflected and may have influenced political and cultural developments in New England, even during the early republic and antebellum periods.

CHAPTER FOUR

Reform and Renascence

In late September 1819, after a summer of working with Vineyard Indians, Troy-Watuppa, and Narragansett, Frederick Baylies told the Society for Propagating the Gospel (SPG) that "a new Era appears to be commenced among the Indians in regard to Education, their Schools are in a flourishing state, & under Providence, I think will be the means of great good. Here the tender mind, is early disciplined to order, here they are early taught the excellency of the Christian Religion, & the importance of a regular life." Three decades later, in 1849, a Massachusetts commission reported that the Chappaquiddicks, a generation ago "a degraded people, unchaste, intemperate, and, by consequence, improvident," were now "chaste . . . temperate . . . and comfortable, not inferior, in dress, manners, and intelligence, to their white neighbors." The Indians told the commissioners that the changes were due to the formal division of their lands in 1828 among families on the reserve, which meant that they were no longer "liable to be dispossessed at the pleasure of the guardian," along with other "new incentives to industry and economy." But they did not wish any more changes in the state laws that separated their tribe from the outside world and had no desire to become citizens.[1]

During the early republic, Native ministers and elders in southern New England struggled to maintain tribal churches and schools. After 1820, building on that foundation and the renewed assistance of Anglo-American reformers, Indians began to rebuild their institutions and to improve their social and economic conditions, encouraging men to save their whaling lays for farming and to stop drinking. By 1840, Native leaders were working with the increasingly activist state legislatures and governors to gain support for schools, teachers, and new ways of managing resources, such as tourism and formalized land allotments. Such reforms were intended to revitalize the community and resist further loss of power rather than to achieve an unlikely and largely undesired legal equality with Anglo-Americans. Native renascence and resistance at midcentury can also be seen in the persistence of traditional resource management and other behavioral norms, including gender roles, and the expanded production and sale of Indian crafts and medicine, particularly with the tourist trade and traveling Indian circuses.

These developments reveal the dynamics of the relationship between subaltern minorities and those with power, and the connections between religion, reform, race, and class in the first half of the nineteenth century. The Indians' experiences show how evangelical religion in the early republic served to organize and empower subaltern groups and lower classes, and how religious-driven social reforms among such groups emerged from the relationship between their internal needs and external direction from those with power.

At the beginning of the eighteenth century, in Christian Indian groups in eastern Massachusetts about 30 to 50 percent of adults and 75 percent of children could read. By the 1750s, most tribes in the region had strong schools and churches, generally led by Native teachers and ministers and supported (inadequately) by the London-financed New England Company, even as they maintained many aspects of aboriginal culture. But after midcentury, those institutions suffered as poverty, social instability, and indentured servitude kept many adults and children from Indian communities, and Anglo-American ministers ceased publishing of Algonquian-language works.[2] Increasing contempt and racism toward Indians in the region disheartened those communities and undermined their already low support. The Revolution and its aftermath amplified these problems. The conflict cut off the financial support of the New England Company. The Brothertown movement pulled nearly all Native ministers and teachers from Rhode Island and Connecticut and continued to attract the leaders from their communities; in 1844, the Narragansetts lost their ordained Baptist minister, Moses Stanton, to the new Brothertown settlement in the Wisconsin territory. With the teachers and ministers went those who were becoming more adept at coping with the Anglo-American colonial system.[3]

MAINTAINING INSTITUTIONS

The four decades following the Revolution may have been the lowest point for Indians in southern New England since King Philip's War. They were confronted

by worsening poverty and a fraying social fabric as children continued to be forced
into white households, whalers disappeared for years leaving their families "suffering for the necessaries of Life," and Natives generally gained reputations for
transience and disorder. They were also abused by white neighbors who stole timber and fish and trespassed on tribal reserves. These problems made Indians particularly vulnerable to alcoholism, even as addiction to liquor generally became
a major problem in the United States.[4] In the face of such tribulations, ministers
and other tribal leaders struggled to maintain their communities and the institutions that provided a vital foundation. This period, though poorly documented,
served as a critical underpinning for the subsequent reforms.

Indian groups in Massachusetts were not involved with Brothertown and were
better able to maintain their churches and schools, particularly Mashpee and Gay
Head, the two largest tribes in the state. In 1834, the Mashpees remembered that
the 1789 guardianship act sponsored by Gideon Hawley had prohibited their education "under pain of death" and that he "*did not teach one* Indian to read during his residence among them" (emphasis in original). Neither memory was accurate (section 4 of the 1789 act listed schooling as one of the fiscal responsibilities
of the overseers) although both reflected their bitter memories of the orthodox
minister. In fact, Hawley had worked to maintain several schools, particularly in
the winter. He found summer school impossible because so many Indians "wander," but the same was true in other rural New England towns where boys were
needed in the fields.[5] A visitor shortly after Hawley's death found that "most"
Mashpees could read and wanted more books. A decade later, Phineas Fish reported that although "increased means of instruction would be desirable," nearly
all children were taught to read and write.[6]

Gay Head's long tradition of Native-run schools was hurt by the war, but the
women continued teaching their youngest children basic reading skills, and literacy
rates remained high. In 1792, Gay Head found funds to hire an Anglo-American
schoolmaster to educate 15 older boys in writing and arithmetic for a term, repro-
ducing the two-tiered system common in New England towns: an upper-level
school that taught boys writing, math, and perhaps advanced reading and even
Latin, and a lower-level, more informal school, in which women taught very
young boys and girls basic reading skills. Within a year their money ran out, and
the boy's school closed. In 1801, the wife of Baptist minister Thomas Jeffers was
teaching younger children during the summer, but the community needed more.
By 1807, perhaps using the new income gained from clay sold to Boston and
Taunton industries, Gay Head reestablished in the Baptist church a winter boy's
school taught by the Anglo-American lighthouse keeper. A visitor complimented

the students, noting that some "are remarkably apt; and the rest are not below the ordinary level." Four years later, Gay Head leaders told the legislature that they had, over the past two decades, "supported our own poor and schools."[7]

Probably because New England women had traditionally taught very young children basic reading and writing skills, other Indian villages that lacked schools (such as Chappaquiddick and Christiantown) still educated some children. In 1819, about half of all children in these communities could write and read from the Bible, and a Chappaquiddick woman became the teacher in an SPG-sponsored school. But these communities felt the lack of trained teachers and other resources; in 1809, Chappaquiddick women petitioned the SPG to support a minister and a school for their children. Tribes involved in Brothertown were particularly handicapped. In 1790, the Mohegans still had a schoolhouse and a "religious teacher," John Cooper, but by the 1810s the schoolhouse was gone and Cooper had died, and in 1826 an legislative committee reported that the tribe had no classes for its children and that only a few sent their children to neighboring district schools. Similarly, the Narragansett schoolhouse was gone by 1809, and only a tiny minority had enough money to send their children "to the school of white people." When Curtis Coe opened his first class a year later, the majority of his students were illiterate adults. In the 1820s, about 30 to 40 percent of the tribe's students demonstrated the ability to read and write—rates slightly, but noticeably, lower than other Native groups with schools.[8]

Bad relations with whites hindered Indian literacy. Mashpees believed that, at the instigation of first Hawley and then Fish, their children's indentures *forbade* learning. They were mistaken—Fish reported that the indentures of Mashpee children required them to be taught to read and write—although racism and the desire to exploit cheap labor kept many Indian children poorly educated. More insidiously, Indian perceptions of white racism and bad dealings led many, like those in Natick, to refuse to socialize with whites, which kept them from schools. Chappaquiddicks and Eastern Pequots refused to attend nearby Congregational churches, probably because the Indians were Baptists and also preferred to avoid the disdain of their neighbors. Such hostility went both ways: in 1811, when neighbors wanted to send their children to the Narragansett school, the tribe was "unanimous against the admission of white children"—but willing "that blacks, not of the tribe, should attend." Schaghticokes were barred from New Milford schools in 1786, but a few decades later they were attending schools and churches in nearby towns.[9]

Some tribes had churches that served as social, political, and religious centers and created networks along which kinship, reforms, and other developments could spread. The Narragansett Free Will Baptist church, with the only meet-inghouse in the area, anchored an association of religious meetings that drew to-gether Montauks, Pequots, visitors from Brothertown, and others at least once every two months. Christiantown, on Martha's Vineyard, had a meetinghouse that hosted Baptist and Methodist itinerant preachers, angering the Anglo-American gentry, who destroyed it in 1808. Nearby Gay Head had two churches after 1800, Congregationalist and Baptist, both led by Indian ministers, with the latter (led by Hawley's nemesis Thomas Jeffers) dominating by 1810. In 1809, Chappaquiddick was the center of a Baptist revival despite the lack of a church building. By 1810, every southern New England Indian community had embraced radical wings of the Baptist and Methodist movements, which, although increasingly conservative and bureaucratic, still promised more dignity and democracy to subaltern groups, put far less emphasis on theological details, and scorned "excessive" learning as harmful to humble piety and salvation.[10]

The beliefs and rituals among these Indian congregations reflected the more esoteric dimensions and aspects of New England's radical offshoots of evangelical churches. In 1773, the Narragansett elder Tobe Cowyass told an incredulous Rev. Joseph Fish that he had recently visited heaven and seen God (a "Great Gentle-man"), Jesus (a "handsome man"), and angels ("a Multitude of Folks . . . Resem-bling Butterflies of Many Colours"). Four decades later, Curtis Coe attended a Narragansett prayer meeting where "an old Indian woman gave account of her devotion, in the woods, while young, that she was taken to heaven, while her body lay, like a lump of clay, on the earth—-that her spirit returned to one end of, & it again rose to life. They often talk of things extraordinary, & the most marvellous accounts appear most to please." When the Narragansetts and other tribes met with the Mashantucket Pequots, the outdoor services lasted three days and were led by William Apess's aunt, Sally George (1779–1824), regarded by Indians and whites in the area as a holy woman, a spirited preacher, and a skilled doctor. Such enthusiastic worship in outdoor meetings, with women leaders and connections between spiritual and physical healing, were also part of a visionary culture that involved many ethnic groups and spread between Europe and America.[11]

But such beliefs, rituals, and leadership also had aboriginal roots that remained exposed in Indian communities. Edward Kendall described passing, on his way from Plymouth to Mashpee in 1807, several "masses of stones, standing in differ-ent parts of the woods, on which the Indians, though professing themselves Chris-tians, still make offerings" of oak and pine branches. These piles were reported elsewhere on Cape Cod and Martha's Vineyard and known to local whites as "sac-rifice rocks," although the Indians would say only that their fathers had taught them to place such tokens in those places. Mohegans have similar sites of historic and spiritual importance marked by prominent rocks, at which memory offerings have been offered for generations. Kendall also noted that the Mashpees "are very superstitious, and very fearful of going about in the dark, in which they are constantly apprehensive of being presented with terrifying visions." Stories recorded in the nineteenth and twentieth centuries confirm continued beliefs among Indians in witches, ghosts, "little people," magical treasure, and other spiritual phenomena. Although some of the same elements appear in New England folklore, there were clear differences in Indian beliefs. For example, while many in the northeast during this period sought magic treasure as "quick wealth and a sense of power over the supernatural world," Indians saw such treasure as a threat and the devil's temptation.[12] Of course, by 1800 they did not differentiate between values, beliefs, and rituals that might have had aboriginal roots and those that may have come through European Protestant or pietistic channels. These were all part of their Christian churches and the communities that those institutions helped maintain; there were no apparent divisions in tribes between "pagans" and "Christians."

On the whole, Indian lifeways changed little in southern New England between 1780 and 1820. In some ways, their social and economic circumstances declined markedly, as mariners, widows, and their children became locked into a desperate cycle of debt, poverty, and alcoholism, exacerbated by white racism and rapacity. Ministers and guardians reported cases of the elderly dying alone of starvation or illness. Those Anglo-American elites had their own solutions to these problems: salvation, education, and moral reform. Indians had a slightly different emphasis. In 1829, William Apess pointed to the hypocrisy of New England's whites, including religious and political leaders, and called on *them* to reform as the first necessary step toward improving social and moral conditions among the region's original residents. But both Indians and their white patrons believed that reform was necessary, and during the 1820s and 1830s, they would grope (together and separately) toward that common goal.

INDIANS, THE SOCIETY FOR PROPAGATING THE GOSPEL, AND REFORMS

During the early republic, New England elites drew on a peculiar post-Revolutionary mixture of Puritan and republican ideals to create many organizations dedicated to the religious and secular education of a moral citizenry. In 1787, some of the most prominent laymen and ministers in Boston established the Society for

Propagating the Gospel with two goals: to teach and improve Indians in the region and white settlers in areas without orthodox minister or teachers. But despite a sizeable bequest in 1789 to fund missionaries to Indians in the region, the Society made few efforts toward that goal. Prejudices of class and race led the SPG to ignore existing Indian churches and schools, and it (unlike the New England Company) rarely paid any salaries to Indian ministers or teachers. Not surprisingly, the 1804 annual report apologized that the SPG "cannot say, that *much* good hath resulted from that part of its labors."[13]

Until the 1810s, the SPG provided stipends to Gideon Hawley and Zachariah Mayhew but sponsored no other efforts in southern New England. The Society's first campaign was Coe's outreach beginning in 1809 to the Narragansett Bay area, which, although not directed solely at the Narragansett tribe, soon developed into a special effort toward the Indians. In 1812, the SPG paid for a schoolhouse on the reserve. Between 1813 and 1816, it sponsored Silas Shores "to diffuse useful knowledge among the Indian children and youth, and to promote Christian virtue and piety among the Indians at large": he taught catechism, spelling, and arithmetic and distributed primers, Bibles, and religious tracts to Narragansett families. But the school collapsed when Shores left and the Indians rejected his successor, Stetson Raymond, either because they perceived Raymond as connected to one of the most unpopular families in the community or because he was also supported by a Charlestown benevolent society and the Narragansetts had a long history of bad relations with their white neighbors.[14]

Despite this brief campaign and its failure, Native groups were becoming more willing to work with Anglo-American reformers. There were many reasons. New England's public culture shifted away from Calvinism and toward the Whig view that human nature was malleable and improvable. Education became more important as moral reform and economic improvement became closely linked to self-control and temperance. Tolerance of unorthodox ideas and dissent increased as Congregationalist churches and organizations split between Unitarian and Calvinist wings and Baptists became respectable. The Puritan notion of the social good as a unitary commonwealth guarded by the better sort crumbled as more magistrates and clergymen accepted a universe of voluntary associations working for different reforms. Many of those organizations ignored denominational differences and sought improvement by distributing Bibles and otherwise spreading "useful knowledge." Middle-class women became the foot soldiers of moral reform and replaced male teachers even in many upper-level schools.[15] The threat of removal may have also played an important though hidden role in encouraging reforms. In 1820, when Jedidiah Morse sought information on southern New

England tribes, he also asked whether they would sell their reserves and move west. All refused, but his query must have sensitized them to the threat. Mohegan tradition holds that the Uncas-Tantaquidgeon women worked to build the tribe's church in 1830 in large part to prevent removal.[16]

In September 1808, Edgartown's Rev. John Thaxter urged the SPG to establish a Chappaquiddick school and suggested as a teacher Frederick Baylies, who had preached there and taught in Edgartown. "He is not a man of publick Education, but of Education sufficient for the undertaking. He is a man of serious Piety & exemplary Life firmly attached to the Peace & order of Society." He also turned out to be extremely effective in working with Indian communities. Baylies (1774–1836) was born in Taunton, Massachusetts, moved to Edgartown about 1798, and on his own initiative began preaching and teaching among the nearby Chappaquiddicks.[17] In February 1810, the Chappaquiddicks asked Harvard College and the SPG to provide a stipend for Baylies, who for the past 18 months had "almost constantly been with us on Lord's Day, preached to us and conducted public worship as well as given private instruction." Thaxter and Baylies also continued to lobby the SPG for assistance. Yet the Society refused to grant more than token support for nearly a decade, probably because it preferred to use their resources elsewhere and (as became clear later) its board thought little of Baylies's background and his focus on teaching rather than preaching.[18]

Society officials finally did show a strong interest when Baylies expanded his efforts. He reported on May 5, 1819, that he had distributed religious tracts to every Vineyard Indian community and that the Gay Headers in particular had asked for financial support for their school. Eleven days later he described a promising visit to the Troy-Watuppa Indians. Nine days after that, he detailed his plan to care for various Indian schools during the summer, including the Narragansetts, and asked for an annual salary of $360. On June 21, Baylies returned to Gay Head and told a tribal meeting that the SPG would help. A week later, they opened a school.[19]

A month later, Baylies traveled to Narragansett, where he opened a school on August 2 and taught for three weeks before gaining the services of Martha Clark, daughter of a prominent judge in the area. He then returned to Chappaquiddick where he hired teacher Betsy Carter, one of the women who had signed the 1809 petition asking for a school. Finally, during the first week in September, he started classes at Christiantown and hired an Anglo-American woman to teach for six weeks. In 1825, he also started a school in the New Guinea section of Nantucket, among people who were descendants of Africans and the island's Wampanoags. Until his death, Baylies worked to maintain these five schools, teaching one to four weeks each year at each, paying salaries to the Native, black, or white teachers, providing books and other supplies, and overseeing operations on behalf of the SPG. With his sponsorship, the state paid for schoolhouses to be built at Chappaquiddick in 1820, Gay Head in 1827, and Christiantown in 1830. He also encouraged a women's benevolent society in Fall River to teach a school at Troy, although that met only in 1819 and 1825.[20]

Like his peers, Baylies felt that education necessarily included lessons in religion and proper morality. He regularly attended religious services at the Indian churches, and encouraged them to spurn liquor and take on other social and moral reforms. In 1835, he noted that "intemperance is spoken against" in all of the Indian communities where he worked, and that temperance societies had been established at Narragansett, Christiantown, and Nantucket. Unlike other reformers, he described Indian students and communities in very positive ways, as he did at the beginning of his efforts in 1819. He made a point of attending Sunday services at each tribe's meetinghouse and praised their regular attendance and moral condition. In 1825 he described a Narragansett assembly: "Place before your eyes a collection of fifty Scholars, from the child of three years old to young men and women grown, all under complete but easy government, emulous to do well, and successful in their endeavours, with their parents and the leading men of the Tribe present, almost without exception, clean, and decent, and comfortable in their dress."[21]

These tribes were deeply involved in the administration and operation of their schools. When Baylies told the Gay Head meeting in June 1819 that the SPG would provide financing, they immediately selected a seven-member committee and chose a woman in the community to teach, which showed the effectiveness of their administrative structure. The next year, the tribe decided to extend the school to 27 weeks, agreeing to pay their own teachers an additional 16 weeks as well as some of Baylies's additional boarding expenses. Within a few years, every community but Narragansett had one of its members teaching most of the sessions, and by 1829 one of the Narragansetts taught their summer school. When a group obtained funding to build a school, like the Chappaquiddicks in 1820, they built it themselves. A few Natives were suspicious of, and even hostile to, Baylies; some on the Vineyard who had no children opposed the use of scarce community income for schools, and some parents kept their children from attending. But most were enthusiastic, almost certainly because Baylies worked with them rather than attempting to control their communities.[22]

The Indians' generally eager reception of Baylies' assistance reveals effective educational programs that had recently fallen on hard times. While his initial account of the Gay Head school seemed to show a shockingly low level of literacy—only 4 of 36 could read "but poorly" in the Bible—his subsequent reports point to decent levels of literacy already existing in these communities supposedly long without schools. From 41 to 51 percent of his students could read from the Bible, and an additional 35 to 38 percent could read from a spelling book. Between 47 and 57 percent could write more than their names, and by 1829 this figure rose to 59 percent. An 1835 SPG committee auditing Baylies's work found that about 60 percent of 155 children in the schools could read and write.[23] By 1824, Gay Head had copied the normal educational programs in the region, creating a separate women's school in which knitting, sewing, and "the common branches" were taught. That tribe also preferred to have the SPG support the women's school, while it administered and financed the men's. Fifteen years later, an Anglo-American minister working with the Vineyard Indians found that "about every *native* can read and write" and that those who were still illiterate were mostly blacks from other countries who had married into the communities.[24]

The Indians generally seem to have regarded Baylies (who was apparently quite corpulent) with respect and a wry affection. The usually mistrustful Narragansetts allowed him to preach at their meetinghouse. Eight decades later, a Gay Header noted that "we hear little of his methods and nothing of the books he used. He taught only a short summer term, but the school was well attended. He was considered a good teacher for his time and was strict in his ways . . . Though this pedagogue occupied three chairs and spent much of his time in sleeping, still he managed to draw the money." In 1909, Joseph Mingo recalled a more active Baylies. Beginning the school at the age of four or five, Mingo was reprimanded by Baylies for his "slow progress" at learning the alphabet and then, after repeating the mistake, received "a sharp cuff" that knocked him over. Mingo told a reporter, "The Indian child was good at crawling under desks, and with the schoolmaster after him, the boy led him a merry chase about the school, crawling under a desk when there was any danger of capture."[25]

As the Indians and Baylies forged a working relationship and their schools became solidly established, the SPG took a critical look at Baylies. In May 1835, a committee reviewing the Society's Indian work expressed disappointment that Baylies spent only 16 weeks a year with the Native communities and hired Indian teachers for most of the school year. Their report concluded that he was "sincere" and "useful as a schoolmaster in these settlements" but regretted that he did not have "more zeal" as a preacher among the Indians. The Society then dispatched Frances Parkman to inspect the Indian schools, churches, and communities. Local magistrates and Indians praised the teacher's virtues, efforts, and success. But Parkman found far fewer Indian students and congregants than Baylies reported—apparently in part because many were fearful or hostile to visitors—and so challenged the missionary's reports and effectiveness. Parkman also focused on Baylies's failure to press his religious mission and, like the committee's report in May, urged the SPG to employ an orthodox missionary more likely to have "a more direct spiritual and religious influence on the people." Yet he also realized that in all five communities the people were devoted Baptists or Methodists, "deeply attached" to their "exciting strain of preaching," and he "doubted" any Society missionary could be more effective. One of the Mayhews told him that "Blind Joe" Amos "would be more acceptable than the best taught or ablest missionary our Society would send."[26]

In November the SPG renewed their stipend for Baylies. In April 1836, Baylies sent in his annual report. Because he "considered an education an object of the first importance," he had obtained a $50 grant from the state legislature for the Vineyard Indian schools. Baylies also highlighted his ecumenical approach to working with the tribes and their positive response. At Nantucket, he worshipped at the Baptist "colored" meeting house, which Parkman had ignored, noting with pride that "we had a small but a respectable congregation." At Narragansett he participated in the tribe's Sunday worship, and in his report reminded the SPG that their elder (and lay minister) Moses Stanton was "a friendly man, and a good character." Back on the Vineyard, Baylies told his orthodox supporters, he often attended worship with the Anglo-American Baptist minister Henry Marchant and the two discussed working together. No wonder, as he concluded, "I am treated with kindness by the various tribes." Unfortunately, several months later Baylies died of apoplexy during a trip to New York. With his death, the SPG's efforts declined, as his replacements gained little influence among the Indians and the states began to fund Indian schools.[27]

Baylies had not been involved with Mashpee, the largest tribe in the region, because it already received funding from Harvard College and had an SPG- and Harvard-supported orthodox minister, Phineas Fish.[28] But the Mashpees felt at best neglected and at worst abused by their minister and guardians, and the records seem to support their (more restrained) view. Although Fish told an official in 1820 that Mashpee had schools, a decade later tribal leaders wrote the state legislature that they had more than 60 children who needed education but lacked suitable places; they asked for and received $400 to build two small schoolhouses, one for each section of the reserve. Fish endorsed the request, noting that the overseers lacked the money to build new schools and that the community had "been held back more by a lack of education than by all other causes put together."[29]

Because Baptist congregations acted as social and cultural centers and created subregional networks between tribes, they must have played an important, though hidden, role in revitalizing their communities. In some ways their efforts resemble those of the churches and voluntary associations that multiplied throughout New England at the beginning of the century and replaced the old notion of an organic commonwealth guided by elites with a new democratic paradigm.[30] But only Gay Head had more than one church, and even in that tribe a consensual community remained both principle and practice, as the Baptist congregation led by Jeffers quickly supplanted the Congregational church. Indian ministers, preachers, deacons, and teachers were also political leaders of their tribes and worked to connect communities. The Narragansett church hosted Sabbath and daily schools and may have acted as a conduit for those services to members of the Pequot and Montauk (Long Island) tribes whose parents attended the religious meetings.[31] The Gay Head, Christiantown, and Chappaquiddick meetinghouses built with SPG and state assistance served Baptist congregations and functioned as the tribes' schools, and members of all three groups often traveled to each other's churches for prayer meetings that lasted many days. These connections were facilitated after 1825 by the Baptist minister Joseph Amos, born in Mashpee with deep kinship connections to the other Wampanoag communities at Herring Pond and Nantucket and on the Vineyard.[32]

The connections between religious, political, and economic reforms were particularly apparent in Amos's own Mashpee tribe. The Baptist preacher was barred by the orthodox Fish from using Mashpee's meetinghouse, which led to the bitter irony of most of the Mashpees being forced to worship in private homes and Fish's congregants consisting mostly of whites from surrounding communities. Amos put his immense influence behind the campaign to reclaim Mashpee's autonomy. The new district government's first report to the legislature noted that two schools were in operation, taught by men and women of the tribe as well as a white man. Indians and visitors alike connected their subsequent social, moral, and economic improvements to winning independence from the guardians.[33]

The Mohegans also received inspired outside intervention and funding, although in their case it came not from Baylies but from a cadre of devout young Anglo-American women. Once proffered, the church, school, and reforms were eagerly grasped by tribal elders. In 1827, Sarah Huntington of Norwich, living within a few miles of the reserve and inspired by stories of missionaries in the Pacific and Asia, became "strongly interested" in the Indians. By 1830, working with Samson Occom's sister and her daughters, whom many Mohegans considered the guardians of the tribe's traditions, Huntington and a friend established a Sabbath school for children in the Tantiquigeon home. They soon raised enough money from local congregations to build a church at Mohegan on Fort Hill, where the tribe had for generations celebrated the Green Corn ceremony, reborn by 1842 as the Wigwam Festival and sponsored for generations thereafter by the Mohegan Ladies' Sewing Society. In 1831, Huntington, with the help of her cousin Congressman Jabez Huntington, persuaded the federal War Department to provide $500 from the Civilization fund for a teacher's home and a salary of $400 a year; two Mohegan elders also set aside land for the church and teacher's house. In addition to academic skills, the girls were taught millinery, dressmaking, and tailoring. The tribe also formed a temperance society, and soon "several drunkards were reclaimed." Looking back from 1859, men and women told visitors that their tribe had made substantial economic and moral improvements during the previous two decades and that the young men who had grown up with the school and church were more likely than their fathers to want to stay and farm than to go whaling.[34]

Huntington, Baylies, and Apess (and probably anonymous others) were not only religious reformers. They were also part of a larger development in New England during the antebellum period, connected to the region's shift from Federalist to Whig culture, and in Massachusetts and Connecticut from unitary commonwealths to diverse democracies, as ministers and others organized ordinary men and women to become active citizens in a multitude of social, religious, and political societies. Sociologists note that this movement saw the replacement of vertical social arrangements, featuring an unambiguous hierarchy in tightly knit towns and villages, with horizontal associations that united individuals of similar class, occupation, or interest across wider areas. More conservative New England magistrates and ministers (like Hawley) feared their loss of authority and the threat of social disorder, but more saw great potential in transforming Americans from passive, obedient subjects into informed, active participants in the republic—and in their own Christian salvation. This shift, and the reformers who were part of it, offered new powers and opportunities to Indians and their communities.[35]

Whig reformers were more optimistic than their Federalist predecessors that civic institutions and associations could guide individuals away from the human tendency of sin and selfishness. This optimism was reflected in the spawning of social reform movements during the antebellum period—temperance, public schools, asylums, prisons, abolitionism, women's rights, and other efforts—which were organized and (initially) guided by ministers and magistrates but depended on the energy and creativity of middle-class men and women. Southern New England Indian communities were a special target of the reformers and their agendas, and many Natives became active participants. Indians embraced these movements because they recognized the need for improvements—alcohol, illiteracy, poverty, and prejudice were particular threats—and saw the reformers as eager and able to give them more power and autonomy.

INDIANS, STATE GOVERNMENTS,
AND ECONOMIC ENTERPRISE

During the 1830s, Native groups became increasingly involved in direct relationships with state governments, in large part because reformers played an increasingly significant role in state politics and policies, particularly as the Whig Party coalesced. Special legislative commissions and commissioners visited and reported on the Narragansetts in 1831, 1832, 1843, 1858, and 1879–80; the Mohegans in 1830, 1859, and 1860; the Golden Hill Paugussetts in 1823; the Mashantucket Pequots in 1855; and most Indian groups in Massachusetts in 1827, 1849, and 1861.[36] The last was noteworthy, as John Milton Earle spent more than two years visiting Indian groups and corresponding with their leaders, as well as carrying on extensive correspondence with town clerks, guardians, and others who worked with Indians, creating an extraordinarily detailed survey of Indian groups, families, and individuals in the state.[37] Although state attention would ultimately work to subvert Native communities, for several decades it offered an additional source of funds and other assistance.

These Indian commissions were part of a general trend, as state governments began studying perceived social and moral problems, and then designing policies, programs, and agencies to implement solutions. The reforms that legislatures encouraged and financed among Indians were partly moral and social (particularly schools), but they also focused on economic and legal developments, including the division of reservation lands in severalty, the protection of key resources such as fish and wood, and the development of new enterprises such as tourism. Indian communities were already experienced in dealing with state agents and legislatures and built new relationships with these governments based on the foundation of their SPG connections. While the U.S. Constitution had given the national government control over relations with sovereign Indian tribes, and subsequent Trade and Intercourse Acts put that policy into effect, no state or federal official questioned the paradigm that southern New England Natives had been subjugated during the colonial period. Tribes could also use national and regional politics to their advantage, as exemplified by the Mashpees, who used the opposition by New England politicians and ministers to the 1830 Removal Act as a tool to shame Massachusetts into restoring their autonomy.[38]

In the mid-1830s, southern New England states governments began creating and funding educational systems, and toward the end of the decade replaced the SPG as the source of money for Indian schools and meetinghouses. In 1823, Massachusetts set up a fund to "civilize" the Indians, although the 1827 commission noted that all Indians in the state spoke (and many read and wrote) English and recommended that those funds be used instead to encourage "agricultural improvements." Beginning in 1835, the Mashpees received an annual payment from the Massachusetts educational fund (like other towns in the state) and employed several Indian teachers, men and women, in the two schools. By June 1841, state school funds were also being distributed to Gay Head, Chappaquiddick, and Herring Pond. Connecticut did the same for the Mohegans beginning in 1839, after the tribe's Anglo-American schoolmaster complained that Norwich was counting and being paid for the Indian students even though they attended the tribe's school. Rhode Island began funding a school among the Narragansetts in October 1838, and seven years later the state allocated $100 a year, administered by an official appointed by the governor, for Narragansett school expenses, including books.[39] Unfortunately, the nearby school district in town used this act to justify excluding the children of Narragansetts living outside the reservation.[40] This transition from a system run by religious benevolent societies to one organized and financed by state legislatures and agencies was an important mark of the emergence of Whig culture in the region.

State instead of SPG backing for these tribal institutions had few effects on Indian communities. Schools were still generally taught by male teachers, who earned about $20–$21 each month, about a fourth more than their female counterparts who elsewhere increasingly dominated the teaching profession. Tribal schools also continued to swell and shrink with the season. For example, Mashpee's two schools during 1839 drew an average of 36 students during the summer and 50 during the winter.[41] States did not draw a hard line between schooling and religion in their funding for Indian institutions. In 1838, seven years after Massachusetts officially ended legal and financial support for religious institutions—the last state in the union to do so—the legislature paid for a structure for Herring Pond to use as both a church and a school, after the Indians complained that their white neighbors no longer allowed their "small number of children" to attend the nearby school. In 1850, the state did the same for Gay Head (figure 2), and in 1855 financed repairs and improvements for the Mashpee church and schools.[42]

State officials, as well as ministers, considered public support for education, religion, and welfare to be key aspects of a morally sound society. Temperance was the first and most important issue connecting religion, welfare, and the state. Because Indians were particularly vulnerable to alcohol and its resulting evils, they

Figure 2. Gay Head school, ca. 1860. From *Harper's New Monthly Magazine* 124 (Sept. 1860), 451.

(and their supporters) were also eager to show that they were dealing with their problem. In 1833, leaders of the Mashpee revolt trumpeted their temperance society as evidence of their ability to manage their affairs. Five years later, Gay Head's Baptist minister and other leaders told the legislature that they had formed a temperance society and asked for a law to stop the tribe's many whalemen working out of New Bedford from bringing rum back to the community.[43] Reports and letters after 1845 from guardians, overseers, legislative commissions, and Native leaders usually noted that alcohol abuse had substantially declined over the past two decades, although they also admitted that intemperance was still a problem for some individuals.

Indians discussing their tribe's condition with state officials often pointed out that they took care of their own poor, a concern with two sources: their very recent memories of indentured servitude and the effects that such near-slavery had on family and community, and the interest (if not eagerness) of legislatures in selling reservation lands to ensure proper support of the poor. In 1811, when Gay Head objected to having guardians, they protested that over the past two decades they had "supported our own poor and schools and have not been chargeable to any town." Much of the fierce battle between the Narragansetts and Dan King in 1831 and 1832 was about whether the tribe was properly providing for its poor. King, a physician, state representative from Charlestown, and author of a scathing report on the Narragansetts in 1831, recommended that the state sell most of the tribal reserve to pay debts and finance future needs. The tribe responded indignantly, rejecting his racist denigration and protesting that they took turns taking care of their poor within their households.[44] In 1837, three years after the Mashpee revolt, dissidents attempting to regain the guardianship emphasized that the new government was neglecting their poor.[45] This focus on proper care for the poor was shaped, and perhaps driven, by the shift in southern New England by 1830 away from the old system of households agreeing to care for the town's poor (and warning out others), toward the construction of supposedly less expensive and more moral work farms. In 1863, as New England states pressed Indian groups into closer legal alignment with state laws, Massachusetts empowered tribal guardians to send individuals to state poorhouses "as they may deem the interest of the state and the welfare of said Indians require."[46]

The increasingly active state governments shared most of the SPG's goals, but they were more focused on encouraging economic reforms and enterprise. The states were very involved in supporting and facilitating private enterprise through laws and corporate charters; information from the growing number of state agencies; grants of funds, land, or other property; and court rulings that increasingly favored development over traditional rights and uses of land.[47] Not surprisingly, they continued to promote landholding in severalty and agricultural reforms among Indian groups, with some success after 1825. State governments (like the public generally) also became more concerned about preserving natural resources and wonders, which led to laws limiting timber cutting and fishing on Indian reserves and the development of a tourist trade in Mashpee. States even became involved with the production and sale of traditional Indian crafts, not only indirectly through the development of railroads and tourism (where many baskets were sold) but, in Massachusetts, directly through the incorporation of the Indian-owned Mashpee Manufacturing Company.

Of the three southern New England states, Massachusetts was unique in the manner in which, between 1825 and 1850, with the encouragement and oversight of the legislature, several Indian communities made structural and substantive changes in how they held and managed their lands. In the mid-1820s, the two smaller Vineyard communities sought the state's help to solve a series of new problems. In April 1826, a group of Chappaquiddicks petitioned for "a permanent division of their lands," citing "much disputes and uneasiness" because their growing numbers generated land conflicts and increasing difficulty in caring for "the old Indian poor," and continuing problems with trespass by their white neighbors' cattle. Their request for a permanent division was a noticeable change from 1810, when the group rejected a similar overture from the state. At about the same time, a group of Christiantown families complained of legal problems from emigrants attempting to sell pieces of the reservation and asked the legislature "to consider our condition . . . [and] to put an effectual bar against the further sale of any of our land."[48]

In response, for the first time the legislature created a commission to report on all Indian communities in the state and to recommend legal changes. The commission visited and provided narrative descriptions of (though little data on) Mashpee, Christiantown, Chappaquiddick, and Gay Head and mentioned various smaller groups around the commonwealth, including not only the well-documented communities at Dudley, Grafton, Troy, and Middleborough but also a few families in Mendon, Malden, Holliston, and West Stockbridge for whom no other records exist. They recommended a bill with two parts: the first divided Christiantown and Chappaquiddick lands while maintaining legal protections against alienating the property to outsiders, and the second called for the governor to name a guardian for each with extraordinary legal powers over the Indians' contracts, persons, and property. Gay Head was offered the same arrangement. The legislature approved, but Gay Head did not and spurned the measure that was applied to the two smaller groups on the Vineyard.[49]

One year later, another commission made a formal allotment of land at the two reserves. Five Christiantown households were apportioned between 25 and 48 acres of cropland, with a median of 47 acres, and 5 to 21 acres of woodland, with a median of nine acres; one obtained 73 acres of improved land and no woodland, and one (the only household without a "small dwelling," possibly an absent mariner) received just eight acres of agricultural land and three acres of woodland. About 100 acres were reserved for community needs. Seventeen Chappaquiddick households were allotted between 15 and 38 acres of cropland, with a median of 24 acres, and one to three acres of woodland (one household, with two adult men, obtained 21 acres of woodland). Slightly more than 230 acres were reserved for community purposes, and the reserve retained in common 65 acres of "unimproveable swamps." But these families must have continued to be dependent on other income, given the small size of their lots and the low number of cattle per household (fewer than one cow and six sheep per household in Christiantown, and about 1.5 cows and 1.5 sheep in Chappaquiddick). Likely sources

Figure 3. Solomon Attaquin of Mashpee, 1890. From Simeon L. Deyo, ed., *History of Barnstable County, Massachusetts* (New York: H. W. Blake and Company, 1890).

included whaling lays, baskets and crafts made from materials gathered in the area, and fish and small game; more indications that allotment did not mean an end to old ways of obtaining a living.[50]

Between 1834 and 1850, Mashpee and Herring Pond also divided their lands, but at their own initiative and in a very different fashion from the Vineyard communities. When Mashpee won its freedom from state guardianship, the new district selectmen began dividing pieces of the reserve among tribal proprietors—men, women, and children born to at least one Indian parent—although initially only small allotments were made. Even in 1840, the selectmen assigned allotments of meadow to families with cattle for grazing, and only small areas of the remainder were held in severalty; most cleared land was leased out to white farmers, and the greatest part of the reserve remained woodland held in common. But tensions in Mashpee grew as more mariners returned to stay, for some proprietors were assigned allotments of 60 to 100 acres while the returnees were given just a few acres each. Decades later, Solomon Attaquin (1808–1895, figure 3) remembered that "the young ones thought they had just as much right to the land as the old ones" and took what they were not given, creating conflicts within the community. As a result, the district decided in 1842, with the approval of the legislature, to formally divide most of the reserve in severalty and to give 60 acres to every proprietor.[51]

Similarly, in January 1850, a group of about 20 Herring Pond Indians asked the legislature to allot most of their 2,500 acres. In April, the state authorized an allotment, and in December state surveyors divided two-thirds of the reserve, giving each of 16 households a 15-acre house lot and allotting the rest (1,756 acres) equally among the 36 men and women aged 18 years or older.[52] Unlike Mashpee, there is no evidence of conflict driving the decision by the Herring Pond community to divide their reserve. They may have been influenced by their close kinship and social connections with the Mashpees; in fact, Solomon Attaquin, one of the driving forces behind the 1842 allotment and other changes in Mashpee, had in 1836 married Cynthia Conant (b. 1815), from one of Herring Pond's leading families. And like Mashpee, Herring Pond divided their lands equally and among men and women, unlike the divisions done by state officials at Chappaquiddick and Christiantown, with different amounts and types of lands provided to each household.[53]

As shown by the situation in Mashpee, these innovations could create conflicts. In June 1827, 11 Christiantown Indians, members of the Weeks, James, and Degrasse families, had complained about the proposal to divide the reserve's lands. Shortly after the allotment, five of them complained to the legislature about "the unequal division in quantity and quality," charging that the men had been at sea during the process, and expressed their concern that "they would be unable to rent their lands" while they were on voyages because they lacked a source of water on their new property.[54] In many ways, allotment was not a radical change in these groups; for generations members could leave fenced and farmed land to their descendants. Plots assigned to families in perpetuity could still not be sold to outsiders without the legislature's permission, and important resources such as wood and peat were still managed in common. Women retained their status as proprietors and received allotments—women were about half of all Mashpee proprietors in 1842. Formalized allotments may have made it easier for tribes to defend resources against foreigners, outsiders, and emigrants who sought to sell tribal land. Yet the very formality of recorded divisions would represent a substantive alteration in the way that land was perceived and treated.[55]

Connecticut also considered dramatic tribal land reforms, but in the form of selling the reserves to whites. In May 1826, as more Brothertown emigrants began to ask to sell pieces of the Mohegan reserve and Connecticut's largest tribe seemed to shrink, an assembly committee recommended selling most of the reserve and, as with other tribes, using the proceeds to provide assistance and allowances for Mohegans, with the additional benefit that the land would be purchased by "people of moral Habits" who would pay taxes to the town and state. They were astonished to find "the greater part" of the tribe opposed. A year later, four Mohegan elders submitted testimony that "they have always heard the same tradition" that the state would not sell any of the tribe's reserve without their consent. The entire tribe also proudly reminded the assembly that they were independent and not supported by the town and complained that their white neighbors "are unwilling we should have any part of this earth spared to us, which we may yet call our own and upon which may *tread* and *roam* without any one to forbid us . . . your honors know that *Indians* require more land than the white people." Their appeal to law, tradition, and stereotype worked, as the state temporarily abandoned the idea.[56]

The deep desire of tribes to retain their ancestral land, along with larger economic developments, often frustrated the desire of Connecticut authorities to turn reserved land over to industrious white farmers—and to treat Indians as dependent paupers. In May 1837, the overseer of the Eastern Pequots asked permission to sell most of the remaining reserve to pay medical debts and future needs of tribal members; the assembly approved a law authorizing him to sell all but a hundred acres, but the sudden national depression later that year resulted in no bids for the land. Eighteen years later, an assembly committee reported that members of the tribe continued to "hold to their lands with great tenacity, and manifest an extreme unwillingness to part with any of it." The Pequots told the committee that they knew their timber and other resources were treated as "common plunder" by their neighbors, but that selling their reserve would not solve their problems. More successful was the decision that same year by the assembly, through the county court, to survey, divide, and sell most of the 1,000-acre Mashantucket Pequot reserve, leaving not more than 200 acres for the tribe and using the proceeds to build or repair "suitable houses for said tribe" and to pay their debts. This action may have been triggered in part by a request in May 1850 from 11 Pequots living in Brothertown to sell tribal land (at a time when only about 30 remained in Ledyard), and in part by their overseer's disparaging description of "immoral vagabonds."[57]

Those 11 Pequots were not alone: between 1844 and 1851, emigrants from other tribes sent a small flood of petitions asking to sell pieces of their ancestral reserves. Most were from Mohegans writing to the Connecticut assembly. In 1844, Pually Mossock in Oneida and five others at the newer Brothertown settlement in Wisconsin asked the state to sell their half-interests in the lots allotted in 1790 to their ancestor Samson Occom; the assembly approved their request and told the county court to auction the land if necessary. Over the following seven years, the assembly received many land sale requests from Mohegans, some in Wisconsin and others hoping to emigrate.[58] In May 1850, the tribe finally complained that the requests had "caus[ed] much trouble and disturbance" and that those who had sold land had returned to the tribe "after squandering the proceeds of the lands." They asked for an investigation and a ban on land sales for at least five years. The assembly refused, and instead authorized county courts to handle all land sale petitions from Indians seeking to leave or living outside Connecticut and to allow the sale if it was beneficial to the claimant, not injurious to the tribe, and only to the tribe or its members. Two years later, the law was expanded, allowing county courts to approve *any* land sale request, although a tribe's overseer was given the right to first buy the land for the community.[59]

Anglo-Americans expected that these land reforms would result in economic and moral progress, although they did not make a fetish of individual enterprise as they would later in the century. Indians held different views on this ideal: many Mohegans agreed, but the Christiantown families who objected to the proposed division in 1827 charged that the change would be "useless as we shall not improve [land] any more pro[fitab]ly than we do now." Two decades after the 1827 allotment, a Massachusetts legislature committee investigated "the numbers and conditions of the several tribes of Indians" in the Commonwealth, providing the first data on whether allotment had its desired effects. The 1849 report shows that while

Christiantown's population had stagnated and Chappaquiddick's had actually decreased, the number of cows and pigs in both communities had noticeably increased (Table 2). The committee praised the "comfortable houses" at Christiantown and described how Chappaquiddick families generally "lived in good framed houses, most of them comfortably furnished, and many of them with their 'spare room' handsomely carpeted, and adorned with pictures and curiosities collected in the eastern and southern seas." The legislators were particularly taken with Chappaquiddick, describing it as "far in advance of any other tribe in the State" in both industry and morals, and noted that the Indians attributed their improvement in large part to the 1828 division.[60]

Although the 1848 committee was delighted at how the adoption of landholding in severalty inspired improvements, the whole picture was far more complicated. Mashpee despite its land reforms showed little improvement, and some decline, since 1827. The population remained about the same, their heads of sheep declined drastically (from 123 to 19), and their cows and pigs decreased. The commission characterized the Mashpees as "behind" the three Vineyard communities in "the social arts and domestic comforts" and "chastity and temperance," although "there have been very great improvements during the last 15 or 20 years." The situation in Mashpee may have been a result of its generally poor soil and problems with allotments and overcutting timber (described below), which would have driven more men to work longer as whalers.[61]

Also, though Gay Head had rejected allotment, farmers there did better than those in tribes that had allotted their reserves. A decade before, David Wright, an Anglo-American orthodox minister sponsored by the SPG and initially welcomed by the Vineyard Indians, found that at Gay Head "they have a general pasture; and general planting fields are fenced from it each year as they in their town meeting appoint. In the pasture each turn all beasts he has, whether many or few. In the planting fields each *native* of Gayhead [emphasis in original] has a right assigned by lots . . . From the public lands, any proprietor may enclose and subdue as much as he pleases for a home lot or farm; and then he makes it his own, and his children's after him, yet inalienable from the tribe in any way whatsoever. Nearly every family keeps a cow; and some of them two or three cows, a yoke of oxen, several young cattle, and a horse." Gay Headers also continued to refuse to fence individual allotments. Yet the Bird commission in 1848 found Gay Headers had more cows per person (about 0.75) than any other tribe that they visited (Table 2). They also found more harmony there, commenting that although some held just a few acres and others had over a hundred, "there is no heart burning, no feeling that the latter has more than his share."[62]

The conservative inclinations of Gay Head Indians were also reflected in other aspects of their material culture. Wright noticed that women in the tribe dressed distinctively: in particular wearing "a handkerchief or small blanket on the head" instead of a bonnet, which he supposed was due to their isolation from white settlements. Despite such resistance, whites often depicted the tribe as morally and socially progressive. In 1835, one of the most prominent men on the Vineyard told Frances Parkman that over the past three decades he had seen "great improvement" at Gay Head—"that they were more industrious & temperate in their beliefs"—which he ascribed to Frederick Baylies's influence. The tribe was not adverse to useful change. Wright found that all three Vineyard tribes had abandoned wigwams and lived in "frame houses, generally comfortable, and some quite elegant within by paint and paper and decent furniture"—although two Gay Head families had built wigwams next to the Chilmark meetinghouse, and a few homes were dug into hillsides with an underground room, which may or may not have reflected aboriginal traditions.[63]

Evidence from the other two states also shows no direct connection between formal allotments and social or economic reforms. In the early 1830s, several Rhode Island legislative committees blamed conflicts over Narragansett land claims on their use of "the short-lived . . . recollections" of the tribal council and urged that allotments be carefully recorded. Tribal leaders angrily replied, "as to the Bounds we all know them," and refused formal allotments. Three decades later, the state-appointed commissioner described the tribe's "improvement" in housing, clothes, education, and temperance, even though "few are disposed to cultivate much land" and those who did held their land "by tradition alone." He noted that "the more industrious and enterprising work at stone masonry" while others went fishing "in its season," and many tribal members made baskets during the winter to sell in the spring. Reforms clearly had limits.[64]

The Mohegans similarly demonstrated "improvements" at midcentury without formal allotments. In 1848, 23-year-old Ezekiel M. Cooper sold 28 acres in order to buy a share in a small coasting ship, the Uncas, after seven years in the trade, including experience as a pilot. In 1857, William Wallace Uncas sold his ancestral share in the tribal reserve after living in Philadelphia for many years: he had dropped the family name, had "a good moral and business" reputation there, and planned to never return. Both sales were made within the framework of the Mohegans' tradition of informal landholding, a tradition twisted by the state to facilitate the land sales. While authorities sometimes justified selling tribal lands as a means of encouraging individual farmers, neither of these transactions could have such a benefit. In fact, Cooper told the assembly that he was "ignorant of the business of husbandry" and therefore the land would do him no good. The ten Mohegan families who *did* farm in 1850 had substantial operations, holding 10 oxen and 29 other cattle and working 460 acres; they lived in "framed buildings, most lathed and plastered, generally decent and comfortable." Still their perception, or at least their testimony to the 1859 commission, was that they could do better with allotment.[65]

Affairs in Indian groups were dictated as much by soil and subregional economic conditions as by whether a tribe had made formal allotments of their reserve. Observers noted that the soil in both Herring Pond and Mashpee was "thin and sandy" and therefore poor for agriculture. In 1861, John Milton Earle noted that the land at Christiantown was better than at Chappaquiddick but had been worn out from efforts to get "a present crop at the least expense," that in all Vineyard Indian communities young men went to sea to obtain the necessary capital to build a house and farm, and that older men had to occasionally work other jobs to augment farm income.[66] The 1828 commission found more sheep than any other animal in all three Vineyard Indian communities and many in Mashpee. Twenty years later, the 1848 commission recorded only 12 sheep in Chappaquiddick, none in the other two groups, and an 85 percent decline in Mashpee (Table 2). This relatively rapid shift highlights how the economic connections between Indians and the rest of the region went far beyond whaling or clay, as during the 1830s sheep raising moved from southern New England into the hills of Vermont, western New York, and the Ohio Valley.[67]

In addition, Indians had their own reasons for adopting landholding in severalty that did not include the desire for economic or cultural change. The Chappaquiddicks told the 1848 commission that the change in landholding had helped because each family held their land in fee simple and therefore were "not liable to be dispossessed at the pleasure of the guardian, as under the old law." The Mohegans opposed land sales in 1850, and their strong support of allotment in 1859 may have been shaped, at least in part, as a defense against the state's threat to sell the reserve. Decades later, Mashpee leaders told visitors that getting rid of their guardianship, rather than allotting their lands, was the most important source of all subsequent reforms in the community. Finally, community traditions of property management remained strong. The 1848 commission noted the continued powers held by women in every Native community and found that although the state had not established rules for inheritance or additional divisions among Christiantown or Chappaquiddick heirs, such issues had been settled without rancor, "owing to the unselfish disposition of the Indians."[68]

Gay Head rejected the 1828 law and landholding in severalty, but at midcentury community leaders became very concerned about foreigners and emigrants and sought state intervention to augment the tribe's power to defend its territory. In August 1859, Baptist minister and headman Zaccheus Howwoswee asked state investigator John Milton Earle "to have our business meetings legalized," their individual holdings "confirmed" (formalized by law), and to have a law passed limiting the time within which emigrants could still claim rights to land in the community. Four months later, Howwoswee asked on behalf of "the proprietors on gayhead . . . to conduct our own business seperate from the foreigners & strangers . . . we do not wish for the foreigner to vote." Earle found 49 Indians who had left and still claimed tribal membership but were "not recognized by those residing there, as having retained any rights." He recommended new laws to provide more formal authority to the tribe's government.[69]

Natural resources on Indian reserves continued to play a critical role in a tribe's economy and culture. For centuries, the sale of wood and fish provided an important source of capital as well as sustenance for many Indian communities, and this continued into the antebellum period. Guardians in Massachusetts were charged with preventing whites from poaching Indian resources and heavily regulated Native cutting and sale of wood, and after 1834 the Connecticut legislature gave Indian overseers more powers to enforce such laws.[70] Before Mashpee gained its autonomy, guardians taxed individuals for wood they took to market, each year sold timber-cutting licenses to neighboring whites without consulting the Indians, and put the proceeds into the community fund they controlled. While highly unpopular, their actions prevented overcutting the coastal ecosystem and allowed the Mashpees to make a small income for decades. Similarly, between 1805 and 1822, Herring Pond Indians gradually cut about half of their 2,000-acre woodland in a manner that seemed sustainable, and in 1822 a proposed ironworks in the area promised a market for the remaining timber farther from shore. The ironworks did not materialize, but the Indians continued to cut timber and sell it at public auction in the woods, retaining part of the income and putting the rest into their common treasury. The 1848 commission reported that the fund replenished by timber sales had continued to grow.[71]

Tribes did not actually need guardians to limit the use of resources as long as their governments and customary limitations retained sufficient authority. The end of Herring Pond's guardianship (along with Mashpee) in 1834 did not noticeably change their pattern of wood cutting. But weak tribal governments or deep internal conflicts could endanger key resources. The Narragansett reserve's 700-acre cedar swamp provided tribal members with materials for fencing, shingles, baskets, brooms, and other needs. In the wake of the threatening 1832 King report, the tribal council accused "furron Negroes and others" with cutting and selling wood from the swamp, and a legislative committee reported "a great deal of imposition" from outsiders taking timber, apparently because rules on group membership were not clear. By 1849, the tribe was complaining that the new commissioner refused to allow the cutting of timber without his permission, and in October the state gave that the tribal council the power to grant timber-cutting permits and to lease or allot lands to members "according to their old usages and customs." One year later, the tribe wrote a constitution formalizing their council and giving it the power to sell timber-cutting permits each year and to determine rights to tribal membership and resources.[72]

The state Narragansett commissioner complained eight years later that the new system had become very destructive and that only a few had benefited, particularly council members and their relatives or friends. Extant Narragansett records (1850–55 and 1860–62) do show that 28 of 70 timber permits (40 percent) were granted to council members, and two to a male family member. But the majority of permits (40) were given to other Narragansetts, and half of those were given to women, only one of whom (Sally Watson) had the same surname as a council member (Gideon), which hints that timber permits may have been used in part to support needy women, much as tavern permits had been used by colonial American towns in the previous century. Timber permits were fairly evenly distributed during the seven years: of the 24 men who served as councilmen and/or received permits, fifteen (62.5 percent) received two or fewer permits, seven received three to four, and two received six. Of the two, one (Benjamin Thomas) was a prominent council member, serving each year between 1852 and 1855, and the other (Luke Hopkins) never served on the council. Four council members never obtained a permit.[73]

The abrupt end of outside authority could similarly leave a vacuum that new institutions could not quite fill, particularly when accompanied by other social pressures and the siren song of nearby markets, which were particularly seductive after generations of poverty. At least some Mashpees, as well as their supporters, were inspired by ideological opposition to communal resource management. William Apess wrote in 1833 that his brethren were mired in poverty in part because "they are made to believe they are minors and have not the abilities given them from God to take care of themselves . . . Their land is in common stock, and they have nothing to make them enterprising."[74] One unfortunate result of the Mashpees' successful revolt was their swift denuding of the trees on the reserve, due in part to their immediate needs and sudden release from the chafing restrictions of the guardianship, and in part from instability in the community, as

whalemen and others who had left suddenly returned and demanded a share of
the new income. In the flush of their new freedom from immediate tyranny,
Mashpee men turned their energies to cutting timber for market.

In the fall of 1837, to carry that timber to Nantucket, some Mashpees with the
assistance of Barnstable whites built a sloop, the *Native of Marshpee*, out of wood
from the district. They chose as its captain Solomon Attaquin, who had left the
tribe at age 14 to go whaling and, like so many others, returned when he heard
that his tribe had gained autonomy. He and his compatriots, Attaquin later recalled, were angered when the Mashpee selectmen would not give them allotments as they returned, so "they commenced upon the coast and cut the wood,
and [the selectmen] prosecuted them, and it created dissatisfaction." The ability
of the Mashpees to wield political and economic influence was reflected in the
selection of Attaquin to captain the ship, although (unfortunately) there are no
details on precisely how the ship was funded or managed, who manned the ship
besides Attaquin (did he command a mixed crew?), or what happened to the ship
when the supply of timber ended. Attaquin would become Mashpee's most prominent citizen.[75]

Far more beneficial for Mashpee in the long run was the tribe's ability to har-
ness its famous fishing to the tourist trade and to gain state protection for that resource. The tourist trade had its birth in New England during the antebellum period, and Mashpee became a major draw for sport fishermen from northeastern
cities. In 1840, Attaquin built the Hotel Attaquin on the reserve near "the best of
fishing"; within a few years it had become a famous resort, attracting luminaries
like Daniel Webster and Henry David Thoreau. But the 1848 legislative commission found that the Mashpees continued to suffer from poaching, as few whites
bothered to buy permits from the district selectmen before taking trout from Mashpee streams. In January 1849, Mashpee selectmen sought state protection for trout
in the Mashpee River and for the right to lease fishing privileges for one or more
years. The measure was endorsed by the *Sandwich Observer*, which opined, "one
of the finest streams for trout in the world . . . has been abominably abused—in
fact, *fished to death*," particularly by men selling the fish to Boston and New York
hotels, and advocated that the "Indian owners" should profit from it.[76]

The legislature quickly responded by banning trout fishing in the river between
September 15 and March 1, allowing the district to lease fishing rights at other
times of the year and requiring the use of hook and line and a permit from the
state-appointed district treasurer during the fishing season. By the end of the year,
the Mashpees had collected $90 in fishing fees. The following year, after build-
ing "a comfortable shell . . . for the accommodation of sportsman," the district

gained $140 from the trout fishery. In subsequent years, the state extended this regulation by permitting the tribe to regulate the taking of pickerel and perch, including the leasing of fishing rights for up to one year; extended the off-season to March 20 and allowed the Mashpees to lease trout and herring fishing rights throughout the district for up to 20 years; gave the Indians the right to regulate the fishery in any manner "not repugnant" with state laws; and added trout fishing on the Quashnet River to the existing regulations. The tribe wrote special regulations governing pickerel, trout, and herring fishing on the reserve, and appointed agents beginning in 1853 to enforce those measures. By 1860, the tribe sold trout fishing permits for five dollars a day, and averaged about $150–$300 per year from the licenses, allowing the tribe to avoid taxing itself. Into the twentieth century, the Indian reserve retained its reputation as a haven for fish and deer, and wealthy anglers and hunters hired Mashpee guides in addition to buying licenses.[77]

State efforts to prevent the destruction of Indian resources were not completely new; guardians had always regulated wood, fish, and land, and Massachusetts laws in 1801 and 1803 required dam owners to provide passage for spring spawning from Wakepee Pond and fined those who took fish without a permit. But the new laws showed the legislature's willingness to give Indian communities the power to shape, enforce, and benefit from such measures and fit into a pattern of wider regulation and economic promotion by the activist state governments. In 1813, the legislature had balked at a request by Mashpee's guardians for a law to prevent the "entire extinction" of quahogs (a large clam) in the reserve. But by April 1854, the state was ready to give Herring Pond its support for "their ancient way" of fishing along the west bank of the Herring River and to require their white neighbors in Sandwich to provide two barrels of fish annually for each Indian family. In 1867, the tribe sought protection for its kelp and seaweed, and the legislature quickly passed a law allowing the tribe's treasurer to claim and sell the stuff on behalf of the community, although this generated limited revenue.[78]

Between 1820 and 1860, nearly every tribe in southern New England worked with Anglo-American reformers and state governments to solve threatening social and economic problems. The positive results were undeniable: schools met regularly and for longer sessions, gained state funds, and were taught by members of the tribe; alcoholism decreased; men became more likely to stay within the community and to tend farms; and families and communities became more stable and comfortable. The 1848 Massachusetts commission described many reforms. The Chappaquiddicks were "chaste . . . temperate . . . and comfortable, not inferior, in dress, manners, and intelligence, to their white neighbors"—which the Indians supposedly attributed to their land division two decades before. Most Gay

Headers worked farms, and sailors returned to settle down after following the sea for a few years. Mashpee seemed poorer than the three Vineyard communities, although the commission noted that conditions had improved since the Indians overthrew their guardianship. Observers reported similar progress among the Narragansetts and Mohegans. But this narrative of whiggish acculturation is simplistic and incomplete.[79]

RENASCENCE AND RESISTANCE

Woven into this tapestry of reform were strong threads of Native renascence (the renewal and revitalizing of tribal and Indian cultures and institutions) and resistance (to dependency and assimilation). These threads could be imbedded in Indian schools, churches, and temperance societies; displayed openly in an effort to use the state's legal and political structure to reclaim or protect land; hidden as folklore and oral history usually kept within the community; woven into livelihoods, including the production of "traditional" crafts and medicine increasingly cherished by whites; or revealed in behavior perceived by Anglo-Americans as arising from differences in class or just plain bad manners. The connections between culture, politics, and economics (including workways) were clear. Many Indians at mid-century explicitly supported the system that protected their lands from the market economy even as it denied them the vote for which they found little use.[80]

The social and moral reform measures contained varying degrees of renascence and resistance. SPG and state support for schools, churches, and the protection of resources were provided at the request of Native leaders who wished primarily to strengthen their distinctive communities and institutions, and to help individuals and families cope with the changing world. The way in which Indians perceived their distinctive identity as rooted in culture and politics was perhaps clearest in the Mashpees' efforts to regain their meetinghouse. This was an important goal in their 1833 revolt—the one they did not immediately win—and might be interpreted as a purely religious concern that they shared with other Baptists faced with orthodox power rather than as part of a program for more *tribal* autonomy. But when a commission visited their worship (in one of the schoolhouses built by the state nine years before), the legislators reported that the Natives complained how whites attending services intruded by dominating the singing and that "the Indian wanted to take the lead in his own meeting." Rev. E. G. Perry told them that "the Indians should have control of the meetings, and that they should not be outnumbered by the whites."[81] The uniquely Indian (even tribal) and more universal Free Will Baptist aspects of this and other Native churches, like the connections between church and community, could not be separated by their members and should not be split by modern scholars.

In Massachusetts, some of the many remnant groups sought to reclaim lands taken by whites during the eighteenth century. Their efforts were probably triggered in part by the prominence of state commissions investigating Indians, particularly the 1848 commission, as so many petitions were filed in the mid-1850s. Their efforts were generally unsuccessful, and those who did gain satisfaction had substantial connections to other groups with more power. The state's willingness to consider such claims may be comparable to the U.S. Court of Indian Claims in the mid-twentieth century, set up to extinguish legal claims by Indian tribes so the tribes could be terminated and their lands privatized. It was during the 1850s that Massachusetts began seriously considering ending the separate legal existence of tribes (see chapter 6).

The first such claim came in 1819 from an enclave in Yarmouth, complaining that the town had sold their land, and that "a great number [of] young heirs have arrived to the age of maturity and [had] no where to settle themselves being wholey distitute [sic] of land." The 1848 legislative commission found 58 members of the tribe still living in Yarmouth and claiming that their reserve had been sold illegally, without the consent of the legislature. The legislators did not investigate their claim and instead emphasized, "These Indians have generally intermarried with the whites . . . most of them gain, by their own industry, an honest and comfortable living. Practically, they are a part of the general community." A decade later, Earle included great details on families in Yarmouth but did not mention their claim, so their efforts were apparently in vain.[82]

The Punkapoags' effort in the late 1850s to reclaim land met a similar fate. In 1854, 12 Punkapoags (seven men and five women) consulted with several lawyers and then petitioned the legislature that they had "good reason to believe" they still held communal rights to land in Stoughton and Canton, that recently "their rights in said respects have been invaded & they have been wrongfully & unjustly deprived" of using the land. A committee held hearings but in the end did nothing. Five years later, during John Earle's visit, a committee approached him to press a claim to a valuable cranberry meadow. The people who lived on the property told Earle they had held the land for a century and that if the Indians' case was just, their guardians would have pressed the claim; the Indians in turn told the investigator that the hundred-year lease on the land was about to expire. In his report Earle suggested a hearing, but again nothing happened. The commissioner did not mention a letter from the Punkapoags' guardian noting that local residents held "a very violent presumption against the right of the Indians to the territory."[83]

Between 1855 and 1857, three other groups of Indians pressed claims to lands they felt had been taken unfairly or illegally. In May 1855, Jemima Easton and some relatives petitioned to regain Deep Bottom, between Edgartown and Gay Head. After investigating, the legislature returned some of the land to Easton and the others in fee simple ownership (rather than as a communal reserve). Their victory was hollow: a few years later, the Indians told Earle that the former owners had cut and sold all of the wood, leaving their land worthless, and that some nearby land should also be theirs.[84] In 1856, Herring Pond families led by Thomas Fletcher asked the legislature to investigate their right to lands in Plymouth County their ancestors had never sold. A legislative commission met, searched, surveyed, and found lots of 12 and 30 acres to which a few might have legitimate claims and recommended that the state require current owners to pay restitution.[85] Finally, in 1859, the Wainer family and others of Wampanoag ancestry in Westport laid claim to large tracts in that town and Dartmouth. Earle chaired a hearing in New Bedford during which several elderly witnesses testified to visiting Indian villages along the Westport River when they were young. The Indians continued to press their claims, which apparently remained unmet, although in 1864 the state gave the petitioners $98 for expenses and provided welfare for some.[86]

Ironically, Indian claims to aboriginal rights were not pressed against only whites. In 1857, Zurviah Mitchell (1808–1898) launched a campaign to win ancestral rights to land in the Troy-Watuppa Pond reserve. The Troy Indians fought her efforts to settle on the reserve, smashing her cabin's windows, harassing her family, and enlisting their guardian to intervene with the legislature, which supported her claim but took no action. A year later, she tried to win the support of the Governor's Council, which ruled against her. In January 1860, after the death of her Cherokee husband, Thomas Mitchell, she again sought the council's assistance, which then passed the issue to the attorney general. Nearly a decade after the state ended the special legal status of tribes and protections of reserves, she published her genealogy to prove her descent from Massasoit and her claim to land and resources at Troy, and for visual proof included extraordinary woodcut prints of two daughters wearing traditional Wampanoag dress (figure 4). Mitchell died in 1898, having gained popular recognition of her "royal descent" but not Troy-Watuppa's recognition of her claims to tribal membership.[87]

These efforts to reclaim lands seemed to unite Indian communities, and in-

MELINDA MITCHELL.
(Indian name, TEWEELEMA.)

Figure 4. Melinda Mitchell, "Princess Teeweeleema," 1878. Courtesy American Antiquarian Society.

deed that goal may have been as important as the need to regain lost resources. The Punkapoags and Westport Wampanoags were described as living in secluded households rather than nucleated settlements, and only one or two families lived on the Troy reserve. Yet the first two groups came together in various forums over an extended period to press their claims before local and state authorities, and the latter seemed to grow and become stronger as they united against Mitchell and her family's claims. Similarly, in 1859, Zaccheus Howwoswee sought state laws that would provide more power for Gay Head proprietors to regulate and limit access to community lands and resources and to prevent efforts by emigrants and their descendants to claim and sell land. These episodes show how by the mid-nineteenth century, Indian groups were willing and able to stake land claims and to use state administrative structures to reify or recreate community social and political boundaries. Their efforts emerged alongside the simultaneous movement among Anglo-American elites to end the legal and separate corporate existence of Indian groups in the region (chapter 6).[88]

Though the threat of land sales did emerge by midcentury, Gay Head retained the necessary power and consensus to maintain absolute control of their reserve, including its cliffs and clay, which was probably the most valuable Indian resource in southern New England. The 1848 commission reported, "They will allow no white man to obtain foothold upon their territory" and refused to allow a factory to be built on their territory to process the clay, "though tempting pecuniary advantages have been held out to induce them to make only some temporary arrangement." Their successful *political* resistance was grounded in *cultural* resistance to capitalist values even though they participated in the marketplace, as the Indians continued to manage and share in common the proceeds from clay, cranberry bogs, and grazing lands—described by the commission as "almost realizing the wildest dreams of the communists."[89] By the 1860s, their clay was being undersold by that from nearby Chilmark, but the tribe continued to sell large amounts through the 1870s and to also make substantial annual income from pasture (about $225) and cranberries ($100–$300), which helped to pay poor relief and support schools. The tribe also guarded the buffer of its system of communal land management and informal individual holdings; in 1861, John Earle reported that this was their "traditional law" and that "they adhere to it with great tenacity, and are fearful of any innovations."[90]

By the 1840s, the tribe benefited from the innovation of tourism, as its famous multicolored cliffs became an attraction to scientists and spectators. In late July 1844, German scientist Albert Koch came to see the cliffs as part of his American trip. He stayed several nights at the home "of an old Indian" (probably Thomas

Cooper) and described his room as furnished "in the customary manner"—with a double bed, wallpaper, and painted floors—and his food and drink as better than he expected. In addition to recording fossils, details of the cliffs, and a ship taking on clay, he noted that the governor of Massachusetts came with a large party to see the cliffs and that tourists visited the community "almost daily." A visitor in 1848 published a narrative of his trip, including a description of Cooper's home as "very comfortable, and so much better than we expected . . . although the charges [the next morning] were somewhat extortionate."[91]

A decade later, a correspondent in the *Atlantic Monthly* wrote, "How many have seen Gay Head and the Gay-Head Indians? Not many, truly; and yet the island is well worth a visit, and will repay the tourist better for his time and labor than any jaded, glaring, seaside watering- place, with its barrack of white hotel, and its crowd of idle people." By the 1870s, the reserve also followed the example of Mashpee by drawing sport fishermen seeking striped bass and other ocean game. Gay Headers sold baskets and other crafts ("shell ornaments") to the visitors and provided services ranging from housing and food to fishing guides and assistants. Tourism also provided a political benefit by building stronger connections with the state government and public.[92]

As highlighted by Gay Head's management of its resources, Indian cultures and societies continued to be shaped, reinforced, and expressed by how individuals, families, and communities made their livings. Whether living in small enclaves and among scattered families or in large tribes like Mashpee and Narragansett, Indians found a growing interest in crafts and skills that whites perceived as unique to Native cultures. Indians gradually responded by marketing the image as well as the item in demand. They expanded their crafts trade, cured the sick with herbal medicine, predicted the fortunes of young white men and women, and, by the 1830s, operated circuses to sell all of the above plus "traditional" dances and animal-handling skills. Their marketing of this supposed Native knowledge ironically tied them to the region's market economy, just as poorer rural and urban whites found themselves, regardless of their desires, drawn into the burgeoning industrial economy of antebellum New England. That economy included a widening gap between rich and poor, increasing numbers of homeless or transient workers, the deskilling of formerly independent craftsmen, the swelling immigration of unskilled Irish, and the growth of cities with mixed-race, proletariat cores.

The persistence of aboriginal gender roles and the few opportunities given Indians in the region meant that many young Native men continued to go whaling even as the industry declined in New England. During the mid-1830s, many

Mashpee men worked as whalers, and two decades later the Mashpee commissioner told Earle, "Young men as a general thing go to sea—no mechanics." In 1842, a Norwich newspaper account of the Mohegan wigwam festival noted that "every mother's son of them [was] out on a whaling expedition from New London." John Avery of Ledyard later recalled that several Pequots whom he knew "became boat steerers and harpooners on whale ships, and as such their services were highly prized by their employers." And over a decade after the division of their lands, the Chappaquiddick overseers, both Indians, told the legislature that "most of our Young men are employed in the Whale fishing"; similar observations were made of Christiantown in 1835 and Gay Head in 1839, and Gay Head men continued to go whaling from California at the end of the century. A Wampanoag from New Bedford, Amos Haskins, even commanded the whaling ship *Massasoit* in the early 1850s. While growing racism in northern seaports after 1840 led to a decline in the opportunities aboard ships for African Americans, Indians were apparently not affected.[93]

Indians also continued to gain an income from aspects of their traditional culture. Indian baskets and other crafts grew in popularity, although by the 1840s these were changing in response to the demands of the marketplace. Artisans developed or purchased new tools to increase the quantity and quality of their products and switched from plant dyes to longer-lasting commercial colors. Men became more active in the business, not only preparing materials but also becoming specialists in weaving heavy utilitarian "Yankee" baskets. The trade grew more lucrative, too, which is probably why men became involved; compare Avery's pathetic depiction of Anne Wampy in the 1820s with John Johnson's description of how he made over $500 in the summer of 1846 by selling baskets in Boston, New Bedford, New York City, and Philadelphia. Some men combined whaling and the crafts trade, carving whalebone and other articles for sale after their return. The masculinization and commercialization of the crafts trade is best illustrated by the Mashpee men, led by Solomon Attaquin and Matthias Amos, who incorporated the Mashpee Manufacturing Company in February 1867 "for the purpose of manufacturing baskets, brooms, wooden ware and other like articles" and to "promote industry and furnish employment" in the tribe.[94]

Indian men and women continued to market themselves as primitive folk healers. For some it was a useful construct that concealed wider medical knowledge. John Johnson worked for many traveling Indian herbal doctors in southern New England, including his wife, Susan Newell. He also worked for two with offices in Boston: Peters, who rented space at the American House, and Peal, a graduate of Hanover College, who owned many medical texts and a human skeleton that he kept in a special walnut case. Peal and other Indian healers apparently knew as much about human physiology and healing as Anglo-American doctors. At the same time, they were aware that an image of Native folk wisdom with herbs and roots helped their practice and may have been more important to (and healthy for) their patients than the antebellum skills and knowledge that lay behind that image.[95]

Circuses formed another connection between Indians and popular culture in America. Frank "Chief Big Thunder" Loring of Penobscot began his career in the 1830s, traveling around the Northeast with his family, initially selling baskets but soon performing Indian dances and other "curiosities" for urban and rural residents starved for entertainment. Over the years, Loring put together various circuses employing Indians from New England and the Canadian maritimes. Loring's troupe was even employed for eight months by P. T. Barnum in his famous Manhattan museum. John Johnson joined the Loring circus in the fall of 1847, taking charge of two young bears and traveling widely to perform various acts including a drama of Captain John Smith's rescue by Pocahontas. When the circus failed after just a few months, Johnson sold the two bears in place of his salary and joined another "Indian Company" that traveled throughout northern New England. After leaving that group, he and his Penobscot in-laws continued to put on exhibitions as they traveled to sell medicine and baskets. Also involved in circus work were Zurviah Mitchell's three daughters, each of whom had Wampanoag names and apparel. A local writer noted, decades later, "At least one of these girls became a well-known sharpshooter, and one or more of them wove very beautiful baskets for sale." These circuses anticipated many of the acts and images made famous by Buffalo Bill Cody's Wild West Show at the close of the century, from the display of Indian dances and other aspects of Native culture as relics of American past to the gender-bending skilled shooting of Annie Oakley.[96]

Indian crafts, doctoring, and circuses fulfilled economic, cultural, and political needs by creating and symbolizing resistance and renascence. Baskets and medicine became a potent means of accommodation *and* opposition to the dominant economic and cultural system in the region, demonstrating to all that Natives survived in the region even as differences among tribal designs disappeared.[97] They served as public performances and artifacts of *Indianness*, and those functions grew in importance with the tourist industry. Mi'kmaq and Penobscot bands regularly traveled south, setting up camps in cities like Salem and towns like Sandwich, probably in the process renewing or forging new connections with Indians in the area.[98] Crafts could even serve an overtly political function: Mashpee women peddled brooms and baskets to help pay the expenses of delegations and lawyers sent to Boston to regain their autonomy and church.[99] Circuses were not invented by Indians, but they did find the traveling shows a useful forum to sell their crafts and make money from the image of Natives emerging in American culture. Indian traveling shows provided various ways to make a living, from dancing to selling crafts to practicing medicine, all of which drew from tribal traditions and the popular images Americans had of Native Americans. Of course, popular images exploited Indians even as such notions offered opportunities to make money. The increasing dominance of the image of Mississippi Valley and Plains tribes as *real* Indians also posed an increasing threat to Indians in southern New England who hardly resembled buffalo hunters.

Another form of Indian resistance could be glimpsed in the persistence of customs and behaviors generally criticized by Anglo-Americans. Studies of class conflict in the nineteenth-century North show how excessive drinking, informal marriages, and other coarse forms of public behavior served as a means for urban laborers (especially Irish and African Americans) to challenge middle-class values and authority.[100] In all Indian communities, informal marriages remained relatively common and traditional learning and folklore continued to be important.[101] But some smaller, more marginalized groups such as the Dudley Nipmucs and Troy-Watuppas were depicted by Anglo-American officials in terms of plebian behavior, in noticeable contrast to their positive reports of reforms in groups such as Christiantown or Gay Head. Part of this had to do with the social connections forged working as itinerant laborers and peddlers; in 1849, for example, the Mashantucket Pequot guardian wrote that his charges were "extremely hospitable to all vagabonds; receiving, without hesitation, all that come to them, whether white, mulatto, Indian or negro." About the same time, the isolated Dudley reserve in the new factory town of Webster, Massachusetts, near the border with Connecticut, developed a reputation as "a resort for the idle and dissolute of the county about, to the great detriment of morals and annoyance of the sober and orderly portion of the community."[102]

The Dudleys became a special target. In 1857, their guardian told the governor that six of eight families on the 26-acre reserve were unable to support themselves. "There is only one small dwelling-house in any way fit to live in: the others are worse than hovels . . . Nearly all the Indians of the whole blood are infirm, some blind, some crazy, and some decrepit . . . They are all a rum-drinking, worthless set, thriftless and quarrelsome." In particular, "something ought to be done with the minor children, who are growing up in complete ignorance, without a knowledge of handicraft of any kind but begging and fishing." In response, the legislature purchased an acre about a half-mile from center of Webster village and a quar-

ter-mile from the former reserve and allotted $3,000 to build tenements and a pub-
lic road for them. Their guardian was directed to send to the state almshouse those
Indians who led "an idle, vicious, and dissolute life" and "to endeavor to inculcate
and promote habits of industry and good morals" among the rest. Two years later,
John Earle found that "the experiment has been measurably successful"—perhaps because the characteristics described in 1857 were Anglo-American perceptions or aspects of Indian resistance, or both.[103]

   After decades of struggling to maintain their communities and institutions, Native leaders gained relief when they developed new relationships with Anglo-
Americans, beginning with the SPG and continuing with state legislatures. Indians worked with reformers to establish, expand, and improve their schools and
churches, form temperance societies, and in other ways improve social and economic conditions in their communities. Some managed to regain land, obtain
new protections for important resources, and even become part of the tourist
trade. They continued to work as whalers and domestics but also began to improve
their farms and live in more comfortable circumstances; a few groups even allotted their lands. By the beginning of the Civil War, these New Englanders were
brought into closer alignment with the region's bourgeois culture. This process
reveals how subaltern minorities could appeal to leaders of the dominant society
to build bridges and help with sources of power and money yet could still maintain their autonomy. That autonomy meant that surviving Indian reserves continued to support many traditions, from women's roles to basket making, and to
provide crucial subsistence for a still subaltern people. In this way, Indians and
their workways also offer a window into the lives of the region's emerging proletariat who resisted and at the same were part of an increasingly market-oriented
economy. After the Civil War, Anglo-Americans would see Indian reforms *and* resistance as important justifications for eliminating the tribes' legal existence.

CHAPTER FIVE

Reality and Imagery

On February 12, 1822, Mercy Ann Nonesuch (d. 1915, figure 5) was born in a wigwam to the last Indian family on the Niantic reserve. She was bound out to white families until 1846 when she married Henry Matthews, a Mohegan stonemason who held a good-sized farm on the tribal reserve. A reporter who interviewed them around 1870 noted that they lived in "an end-frame house of moderate size, comfortably furnished, scrupulously neat," with a parlor organ, many plants, two Bibles, and a picture of Samson Occom. Mercy and Henry were also traditionalists: she was an authority on spiritual and herbal medicine, and he made baskets for the Wigwam Festival and by 1903 served as the Mohegan chief.[1] The Narragansett Council similarly described New England Indian culture in the mid-nineteenth century as combining "improvements" and traditions. "The Greatest part of our tribe live as well as the commontry [sic] of people we Raise pork & Beef and poultry &c." While some of the men were away at sea, many others in the tribe were "trades men and women such as carpenters, coopers, shoe makers, tailors, weavers." Their reserve provided land for farming; a swamp "for building Boards Shingles Ceder poles for fencing our Lands etc. [and] the old women get Bark for bottoming chairs, stuff for Baskets Brooms &c."; and ponds and estuaries for "Salt water fish Such as Alewives and white fish and various kinds of fresh water fish." Amid this activity, the tribe's church and school served as cultural and social centers.[2]

Some Anglo-Americans recognized the complexity of contemporary Native life. In 1858, Rhode Island's Narragansett commissioner wrote that the general condition of the tribe had improved over past few years, with "comfortable dwell-

Figure 5. Mercy Ann Nonsuch, Niantic, 1912. Courtesy of the National Museum of the American Indian.

ings" and more temperate habits; some men went to sea and "few" farmed, but many were "masons, stone cutters, and wallers, [who] command good wages for their work." Three years later, John Milton Earle reported that although the material culture and moral condition of Indians in Massachusetts were comparable to whites of similar incomes and social status, they were still "a race naturally inclined to a roving and unsettled life." He noted, "Nearly all of the males, first or last, engage in seafaring as an occupation," and as a result "are often absent for years at a time, frequently without their friends knowing where they are. The women, left behind, seek employment wherever it can be had, usually in the neighboring towns and cities." Earle's report also emphasized the continued importance to Indian communities of their protected reserves and separate legal status.[3]

By the outbreak of the Civil War, Indians were entangled in the region's political and economic structures, even as in many ways they remained separate. Tribes with reserves obtained state funds for schools and were often visited by politicians and intellectuals. Many of their members continued to find work off the reservation; at the same time, more of the men returned in their late 20s to establish farms and families. State officials described nearly all tribes as more stable and better off, and statistics show increasing average ages and sexual balances, although some smaller groups and individual survivors seemed noticeably poorer and more prone to the socioeconomic and moral problems associated by officials with transient peoples. Families and individuals residing in towns and cities lived and worked alongside blacks or whites, even as many maintained their tribal identities and connections. Indians also continued to favor evangelical churches and to have a reputation for informal and multiple marriages and a tendency toward alcohol abuse—although these characteristics were also linked to New England's plebian class. Thus, Indians continued to maintain their unique identities while illuminating often-cloaked aspects of class and race in the region.

From the beginning of colonization, Natives were forced to find new ways of meeting the perceptions and expectations of the newcomers. This aspect of Indian-white relationships remained significant in the middle of the nineteenth century even as Anglo-American perceptions of Indians in the region shifted noticeably. The New England intellectuals and magistrates involved in the interconnected movements of social reform and sentimentalism forged a new vision of their region's history, which served as the foundation of an emerging sense of unique culture and identity. A rising tide of popular literature featured a startlingly revisionist and romantic depiction of New England's original inhabitants as Noble Savages wronged by dour Puritan colonists. Such literature was produced largely by social reformers linked to the Whig Party as it emerged in opposition to the Jacksonian Democrats during the Cherokee removal controversy, and their perceptions, along with their goals, became part of the books used by the New England public school systems created in the 1830s.

This may have seemed an encouraging development, but it was also a threat because Natives who remained in the region did not look like *real* Indians to whites, especially given strengthening racial perceptions. Francis Willard Bird, chair of the 1848 Massachusetts commission, wrote that in about 500 Indian homes, "we have found but three of pure Indian blood. There are not probably half a dozen in the State . . . The red man is gone, and has left only the most vicious of his characteristics . . . [I]t is sad, very sad, to be reminded, as we are at every step, that the descendants of the Samosets and Massasoits and Philips, have exchanged the savage virtues of the forest for only the lowest form of civilization." A reporter called Mercy Nonesuch "the last of the Niantics" (even though other Niantics, including some from the Nonesuch family, remained in the area) and connected her to the "last Indian" paradigm.[4] Alongside the Noble Savage, older, darker images of degenerate Native remnants remained a significant part of New England literature. Both paradigms were embedded in Anglo-American anxiety about race; both emphasized that Indians were rapidly vanishing from the region; and both posed a new threat to separate legal status that protected and handicapped nearly all of the surviving Indian groups in southern New England.

INDIANS AT MIDCENTURY

In the middle of the nineteenth century, Indian tribes exhibited noticeable variations in demographics, social characteristics, political organization, and economic patterns. Despite significant emigration, exogamous marriages, and reforms, these communities generally remained in the same category (according to population, size of reserve, and degree of political organization) they had been at the outbreak of the Revolution. But there were also important similarities among these groups and most of their members. In some aspects — demographic changes, for instance — they became more like their non-Indian neighbors. In other aspects, such as residence, workways, and property ownership, they remained quite different. One of the most striking confirmations of Indian survival in southern New England is that federal census takers did not count "Indians not taxed," and until termination they did not record Indian communities in the region.

After 1820, the demographic structure of Massachusetts coastal tribes shifted to become more like that of their white neighbors. Between 1823 and 1848, their median and average ages increased noticeably (Table 3). The particularly dramatic change among Native men supports the observation of ministers and magistrates that sailors were now more likely to return and settle down after following the sea for a few years. David Wright noted in April 1839 that "several young men" at Gay Head "have selected sites for building houses as soon as they are able," and that whalers who "obtained several hundred dollars by a good voyage, lay out their money in erecting houses for themselves and families: for they generally choose to marry." Apparently their number swelled during the 1840s. This tendency might have been a result of the social reforms celebrated by Anglo-Americans or of regional economic trends, as the Vineyard, Cape Cod, and New Bedford whaling fleets all declined in the mid-1840s. Over the subsequent decade, the returning mariners and their wives began having more children, making their communities even more like neighboring towns (Tables 4 and 5). The trends in the smaller coastal tribes were more ambiguous, an indication that the larger tribes were gaining in ways not shared by the others. All of these tribes continued to show the effects of living within a regional economy as men and women moved elsewhere to find work. Earle noted that "nearly all of the males" and many women left at some point during their lives to work in port cities and on ships, and "frequently remove from place to place," rarely communicating with relatives back home, until "all trace of them is lost."[5]

Although data on the tribes in Rhode Island and Connecticut are very scarce and do not permit an analysis over time, large percentages of their members lived away from the reserve, working part of the year elsewhere or living permanently in other towns. A January 1858 report on the Narragansetts found that the tribe's population had dramatically declined in the past quarter-century to 122 but that "the probability is, that the number absent, claiming connection with the tribe, has increased." In 1877, a Charlestown resident told the SPG that there were 200 living on the reservation but that many more "living round about"—mostly working as farm laborers, domestics, and craftsmen—returned in winter, nearly doubling the county's Narragansett population. Three years later, a state commission reported more than twice as many members of the tribe (300), but even fewer (103) in or near the reservation, with 73 in neighboring towns and 47 (nearly a fourth) in the more distant city of Providence, where they worked in the maritime industry. In 1857, of 22 Mashantucket Pequots listed by their guardian, twelve lived on or near the 180-acre reserve, four lived elsewhere in the state, four had left New England, and two were at sea. In 1860, the Mohegans had about 100 members, almost half of whom lived elsewhere.[6]

Indians living on tribal reserves in the two states were seemingly much older than in Massachusetts (Table 3). These high ages resulted at least in part because the financial and family support offered by the tribe became critical for individuals as they became infirmed or suffered illness. In 1880, Narragansett tribal chairman Gideon Ammons told state commissioners that those who lived on the reserve were angered by those who visited to show off their jobs or quality animals

TABLE 3
Average and Median Ages by Sex for Massachusetts Tribes, 1823–1860

	Total			Male			Female			M/F ratio
	N	Mean age	Median age	N	Mean age	Median age	N	Mean age	Median age	
Christiantown										
1823	51	20.1	16.0	28	18.5	13.5	23	22.3	20.0	1.22
1848	48	25.8	25.5	26	27.6	26.0	22	24.7	25.0	1.18
1860	53	25.7	21.0	23	25.5	20.5	30	26.0	23.0	0.77
Change 1823–1848	−3	5.7	9.5	−2	9.1	12.5	−1	2.4	5.0	
Change 1848–1860	5	−0.1	−4.5	−3	−2.1	−5.5	8	1.3	−2.0	
Change 1823–1860	7	5.6	5.0	−4	7.0	7.0	11	3.7	3.0	
Gay Head										
1823	250	24.8	21.0	113	23.5	21.0	137	26.0	20.0	0.82
1848	174	25.7	24.0	81	28.7	28.0	90	24.2	24.0	0.90
1860 on reserve	204	27.4	21.0	106	27.8	22.0	98	27.1	20.0	
1860 off reserve	49	20.9	15.0	22	21.5	28.0	27	20.4	14.5	
1860 total	253	26.2	19.8	128	26.8	23.0	121	25.6	18.8	1.06
Change 1823–1848	−76	0.9	3.0	−32	5.2	7.0	−47	−1.8	4.0	
Change 1823–1860	3	1.3	−1.2	15	3.3	2.0	−16	−0.3	−1.2	
Change 1848–1860	79	0.4	−4.2	47	−1.9	−5.0	31	1.5	−5.2	
Chappaquiddick										
1823	99	21.2	16.0	50	18.5	15.0	49	24.0	21.0	1.02
1848	85	28.5	25.0	43	29.6	29.0	42	27.2	23.0	1.02
1860	74	32.0	31.5	36	32.3	35.0	38	31.7	27.0	0.95
Change 1823–1848	−14	7.3	9.0	−7	11.1	14.0	−7.0	3.2	2.0	
Change 1823–1860	−25	10.8	15.5	−14	13.8	20.0	−11	7.7	6.0	
Change 1848–1860	−11	3.5	6.5	−7	2.7	6.0	−4.0	4.5	4.0	

Mashpee										
1848	305	28.9	25.0	154	29.7	26.5	151	28.2	24.0	1.02
1860	403	26.6	21.0	186	23.9	18.0	216	25.6	19.0	0.86
Change 1848–1860		−2.3	−4.0	32	−5.8	−8.5	65	−2.6	−5.0	
Herring Pond										
1848	55	26.4	18.0	28	25.8	21.5	27	27.1	21.5	1.04
1860	67	25.8	23.0	31	28.6	29.0	36	23.2	22.0	0.86
Change 1848–1860	9	−0.6	5.0	3	2.8	7.5	9	−3.9	0.5	
Watuppa-Troy										
1848	37	36.9	39.0	17	29.1	23.0	20	41.5	42.2	0.85
1860	78	27.4	23.0	41	27.0	23.5	37	27.9	22.5	1.11
Change 1848–1860	41	−9.5	−16.0	24	−2.1	0.5	13.6	−13.6	−19.7	
Dudley										
1848	48	25.3	22.0	24	19.2	15.0	22	31.9	30.0	1.09
1860	94	25.1	20.0	41	27.3	22.0	51	27.9	22.5	0.80
Change 1848–1860	46	−0.2	−2.0	14	8.1	7.0	29	−4.0	−7.5	
Hassanamisco										
1848	26	26.5	25.5	12	25.5	24.0	14	27.5	29.0	0.86
1860	90	25.4	24.0	41	25.7	25.0	49	25.3	23.5	0.84
Change 1848–1860	64	−1.1	−1.5	29	0.2	1.0	35	−2.3	−5.5	

NOTE: Mean and median ages are calculated for those whose sex and age are both indicated in the census.
SOURCES: Baylies 1823; Bird 1849; Earle 1861.

TABLE 4

Shifting Age Characteristics for Massachusetts Tribes, 1848-1860

Total N with age shown	No. aged 0-3	No. aged 4-6	No. aged 7-13	No. aged 14-18	No. aged 0-13	Children/adults ratio
Chappaquiddick						
1848 85	10	2	5	10	17	20.0%
1860 74	2	1	13	3	16	21.6%
Change 1848-1860 -11	-8	-1	8	-7	-1	
	-80.0%	-50.0%	160.0%	-70.0%	-5.9%	
Gay Head						
1848 174	12	21	25	9	58	33.3%
1860 253	24	14	48	33	86	34.0%
Change 1848-1860 79	12	-7	23	24	28	
	100.0%	-33.3%	92.0%	266.7%	48.3%	
Christiantown						
1848 49	3	4	8	2	15	30.6%
1860 53	6	2	6	3	14	26.4%
Change 1848-1860 4	6	-2	-2	1	1	
	100.0%	-50%	-25.0%	50.0%	-6.7%	
Mashpee						
1848 305	32	28	38	24	98	32.1%
1860 403	43	20	73	46	136	33.7%
Change 1848-1860 98	11	-8	35	22	38	
	34.4%	-28.6%	92.1%	91.7%	38.8%	

Herring Pond						
1848	55	1	6	12	9	19	34.5%
1860	67	8	4	4	8	16	23.9%
Change 1848–1860	12	7	−2	−8	−1	−3	
		700%	−33.3%	−66.7%	−11.1%	−15.8%	
Fall River						
1848	37	1	0	3	3	4	10.8%
1860	78	5	4	12	8	21	26.9%
Change 1848–1860	41	4	4	9	5	17	
		400%	400%	300%	166.7%	425%	
Dudley						
1848	48	3	3	8	4	14	29.2%
1860	94	15	5	16	7	36	38.3%
Change 1848–1860	46	12	2	8	3	22	
		400%	66.7%	100%	75.0%	157.1%	
Hassanamisco						
1848	26	3	1	2	3	6	23.1%
1860	73	12	3	8	3	23	25.6%
Change 1848–1860	47	−9	−2	−6	−0	17	
		300%	200%	300%	91.7%	40.8%	

SOURCES: Bird 1849; Earle 1861.

TABLE 5
Ages of Indians and Neighbors, 1848–1881

	N	Mean	Median
Charlestown, RI, 1860	986	28.25	23
Narragansetts, 1858	122	37.00	32
Narragansetts, 1881	319	25.90	21
Narragansetts in Charlestown, 1881	103	28.00	19
Edgartown, MA, 1850	1,998	27.70	24
Tisbury, MA, 1850	1,804	29.00	25
Chappaquiddick, 1848	85	28.50	25
Sandwich, MA, 1860*	2,151	44.21	23
Mashpee, 1860	403	26.60	21
Lyme, CT, 1860	1,246	28.08	23
North Stonington, CT, 1860	1,906	28.00	24
Montville, CT, 1860	2,152	46.60	24
Lantern Hill Pequots, 1870	26	25.60	20
Ledyard, CT, 1860	480	27.03	22
Mashantucket Pequots, 1857	22	39.05	36

*data only partially complete
SOURCES: U.S. Department of Commerce, Federal Census of 1860, ms. schedules for Charlestown, R.I. (including Narragansetts in Charlestown); Sandwich, Mass.; North Stonington, Conn.; Lyme, Conn.; Montville, Conn.; Ledyard, Conn.; U.S. Department of Commerce, Federal Census of 1850, ms. schedules for Edgartown, Mass., and Tisbury, Mass., transcribed in Chris Baer, "Historical Records of Dukes County, Massachusetts," http://history.vineyard.net/edgcen50.htm (accessed 13 May 2005). *Narragansetts:* Griffin 1858; Adams 1881. *Chappaquiddick:* Bird 1849. *Mashpee:* Earle 1861, appendix. *Lantern Hill Pequots:* Pequot Indian Papers, 1868–1875, CSA. *Mashantucket Pequots:* Ledyard (Mashantucket) Pequot overseer's report, 1857, CSA.

but who refused to help when the council fought an issue in the state legislature or who would only return (or were sent by their town) when they fell on hard times and required the tribe's support.[7]

Members of smaller communities in all three states that retained tiny or no reserves were even more dispersed. The 1848 commission reported that a few Indians still lived in Natick; others were scattered around the state, but "practically, the tribe is extinct." The same report shows 48 Dudley Nipmucs, half of whom lived away from the small reservation; Earle's more exhaustive survey a decade later listed 82 in the tribe, but only 13 in the recently acquired tribal tenement in Webster, 19 in neighboring towns, and the remaining 50 scattered far and wide. Earle managed to locate 117 Punkapoags and their descendants, far more than the 1848 commission had, but just 31 lived near the tribe's reserve; most had gone to Boston or other cities. Similarly, of 78 Troy-Watuppa Indians, only 21 in six households remained on the group's 190-acre reserve—which lay just five miles from the center of Fall River, near New Bedford and Dartmouth, where most of the tribe's members lived. The situation in Connecticut was similar among the two Pequot groups and the Schaghticokes. In Massachusetts, the average and median ages in the smaller Native communities were in the early to mid-20s, reflecting their high degree of economic, cultural, and social integration into the general population.[8]

Many individuals and families also had historical connections to Indian communities that lacked reserved lands and, as a result, had dissolved into informal kinship and social networks. Earle found about 111 Wampanoag descendants still living along the Westport River although "a number of families" from the eighteenth-century Dartmouth tribe had left for more distant places including western New York and California. This group had no common lands, funds, or clear political leadership, but it had enough organization to press claims to large tracts of land in Westport and Dartmouth. Similar groups had historic connections with other eighteenth-century Indian villages in Massachusetts, including Natick, Mattakee-set, and Tumpum—the last two within the boundaries of Pembroke—but lived scattered in many towns and, in some cases, participated in local schools, churches, and other institutions.[9]

Some Native families or tribes also remained in places they had supposedly left. Absent from state and local records, and therefore nearly invisible, some still left clear evidence of their lives and distinctive cultures. Indians living near Hartford between 1840 and 1870, where none appear in the state or local records, made and sold a large number of unique baskets that combined craft traditions of the Tunxis and Mohegan tribes. In October 1858, on the western edge of Massachusetts, a Berkshire County fair awarded prizes ranging from 50 cents to a dollar to many women for their handmade household goods. The only anonymous winner was "an Indian woman" who received 50 cents for her beadwork basket, yet supposedly every Indian in the county had left for New Stockbridge, New York, by 1800. Town histories and other records tell of Indian families in the nineteenth century who continued to travel between homes and work within tribal territories, such as small bands of Nipmucs along the area bordering Massachusetts, Connecticut, and Rhode Island. Natives of mysterious origins continued to suddenly appear, such as Henry Harris (figure 6), who came from somewhere in central Connecticut (perhaps Stratford, perhaps Milford) to become one of the more prominent Schaghticokes at the end of the nineteenth century.[10]

Regardless of a particular tribe's demographics or stability, all continued to suffer their ancestors' vulnerability to the diseases and alcohol brought by Europeans. Earle noted that liquor continued to be a problem even though he and others felt that temperance had increased among the Indians. He also reported that disease and illness claimed 27 to 30 percent of those recorded by the 1848 commission for Christiantown, Chappaquiddick, Mashpee, and Herring Pond. These figures

HENRY HARRIS, LAST OF THE SCATACOOKS.

Figure 6. Henry Harris of Schaghticoke, weaving a basket, ca. 1880. From Francis Atwater, *History of Kent, Connecticut* (Meriden, Conn.: Journal Publishing Company, 1897), 72.

meant an annual average of one death for every 28 persons, about double that for rural towns in Massachusetts. He puzzled over the reasons for this high mortality rate, rejecting the idea that Indians had "some inherent physiological defect" making them impossible to civilize and doomed to extinction, and found more likely causes in their "sudden change" to civilized ways, old habits of intemperance and licentiousness, and simple but terrible poverty—and thus felt optimistic about their future. Guardians and ministers of most tribes at midcentury noted that abuse of liquor had declined over the past two decades, but they agreed it was still a problem.[11]

There was a similarly mixed picture of household structures and moral standards at midcentury. Earle praised the family stability and sexual practices of most tribes in the state, noting that illegitimacy had declined, and his census shows a decrease since 1800 in woman-headed households in the Vineyard communities. But other records paint a different picture of Indian women continuing to enter informal marriages with multiple partners. At midcentury, the Mashantucket Pequot's overseer wrote that "there is no such thing as regular marriage among them," and all eight Eastern Pequot children lived in three female-headed households. In 1861, many Mohegan women had "several sorts of children," which "added greatly to their embarrassment"—although the embarrassment was more probably the commissioners' than the women's. Even Earle condemned one tribe, writing that at Troy-Watuppa "intemperance and unchastity are but too prevalent," and, off the reserve, 12 children had been born to unmarried women in two families, with the paternity divided equally between men from all three races. But he, like many others, saw such morals, whether admirable or unfortunate, as more a matter of culture and class than race, comparing the behavior and culture of Indians to "others of their class" in the region.[12]

EMPLOYMENT AND WORKWAYS

The need or tendency of Indian men to leave their communities for extended periods in order to find work as whalers or laborers was an important element in this pattern of informal marriages and female-headed households. Earle's 1860 census shows that nearly three-quarters of Massachusetts Indian men with identifiable occupations continued to work as mariners or laborers (Table 6). Within this larger, salient pattern, different occupations and workways distinguished those from the smaller inland Native communities, nearly all of whom lived in cities or towns rather than on the reserves, with their cousins from the larger coastal tribes. Nearly half the Punkapoag, Hassanamisco, Dudley, and "Miscellaneous" men

TABLE 6

Occupations and Median Ages for Men in Massachusetts Tribes, 1860

	Total		Farmers		Mariners		Laborers and Jobbers		Skilled		Semiskilled		Unskilled	
	N	Median age	N	Median age	N	Median age	N	Median age	N	Median age	N	Median age	N	Median age
Miscellaneous	10	39.5	0		0		7	49.0	0		3	32.0	0	
Punkapoag	17	34.0	1	65.0	2	22.0	7	34.0	0		7	35.0	0	
Hassanamisco	17	34.0	1	65.0	0		7	42.0	0		6	31.2	3	34.0
Dudley-Nipmuc	13	37.0	0		1	28.0	7	55.0	1	43.0	3	30.0	1	20.0
Total, inland communities	57	35.6	2	65.0	3	23.7	28	45.0	1	43.0	19	32.3	4.	30.5
Dartmouth/Watuppa-Troy	25	35.0	6	51.0	4	22.0	10	37.0	4	29.0	1	30.0	0	
Herring Pond	13	29.0	2	49.5	7	29.0	1	37.0	1	49.0	2	28.0	0	
Mashpee	67	39.0	17	58.0	40	32.0	6	32.0	0		4	41.3	0	
Yarmouth	12	25.0	0		12	25.0	0		0		0		0	
Chappaquiddick	13	39.0	3	52.0	10	34.5	0		0		0		0	
Gay Head	42	41.5	18	49.5	21	33.0	0		2	45.0	0		1	19.0
Christiantown	12	34.0	8	39.5	4	26.0	0		0		0		0	
Total, coastal communities	184	37.1	54	51.0	98	30.7	17	34.9	7	36.4	7	35.9	1	19.0
Total	241	36.7	56	51.5	101	30.5	45	41.2	8	37.3	26	33.3	5	28.2
% of Total			23.2%		41.9%		18.7%		3.3%		10.8%		2.1%	

NOTE: *Skilled* includes plumber, carpenter, daguerreotypist, sailmaker, ship keeper, trader.
Semiskilled includes barber, cordwainer, caterer, railroad firefighter, cook, shoe/bootmaker, miner, preacher.
Unskilled includes baggage handler, porter, railroad fireman, servant.
SOURCE: Earle 1861, appendix.

worked as laborers, probably for farmers in villages between Boston, Worcester, and Providence. This is about the same percentage as for all men of color in 1850 in Worcester County, which included Grafton (Hassanamisco) and Webster (Dudley), highlighting the deep connections that developed between Indian and African descendants in the inland areas, and the prejudice that both faced in the early nineteenth century. A similar pattern appeared in the 1860 U.S. census from towns around the Schaghticoke reserve in northwest Connecticut. Listings there indicate Indian or mulatto individuals and households—who in other records are identified as Schaghticokes—working as laborers, basket makers, servants, and a washer woman.[13]

The terse data cloaks family stories like that of the Esaus of Warren, Massachusetts. Earle's census showed that Elizabeth Esau, aged 34, a Dudley Nipmuc Indian, was married to Luke Esau, a colored man, aged 50, who worked as a laborer; the two had seven children. The source for these facts was a letter from the town clerk, who told Earle that the two were "very poor, have no property, depend on their daily labor for support. Mrs. Esau goes out washing and etc."—very much like Hepsibeth Hemenway two generations earlier. Her husband was a laborer who "works at farming, sawing wood, or anything he can get to do."[14] Earle listed only one woman with an occupation—Amy Robinson, an Indian doctress—but clearly many Indian women like their African American counterparts worked as domestics or washerwomen. Twelve were barbers (five among the Punkapoags), a relatively stable, entrepreneurial trade that was particularly important for black men in cities. As many worked as shoemakers (five) as mariners and farmers combined. This pattern reflects their sale and loss of reserved land during the eighteenth century, as well as their residence generally in cities like Worcester or Boston with strong links to black communities.[15]

Nearly 80 percent of Indian men in Massachusetts coastal tribes worked as mariners (usually whaling) or farmers. Many of the mariners were married, which seems to challenge the view that Indian men were returning to establish households. D. H. Strother, visiting Gay Head in 1860, wrote that that most men were still whalers, and that "the few poor garden patches that we observed were doubtless cultivated by the women and children, after the Indian fashion." But Earle's data also shows that almost all of the farmers in these tribes were married men, and they were substantially older than mariners and older than the median age of working men in every Indian community. The Christiantown and Chappaquiddick guardian explained that the young men "go to sea & generally earn enough to build a decent little house; & then fish and farm it—in fact do what they can for a living," a development that David Wright had first observed in 1839. Farm-

ing their lands "run down by constant cultivation" did not provide enough, noted
the guardian, "& if they should depend upon agriculture solely for a living, I know
not what would become of them." Earle observed that the frame or stone houses
built within last ten to twenty years were financed with whaling lays. Of course,
he did not record *women's* occupations, and many, if not most, Indian women did
indeed (as Strother noted) continue to farm as well as to make and sell crafts
whether or not they headed their households.[16]

Although Connecticut and Rhode Island officials recorded impressions rather
than data, their accounts show Indian workways similar to those in Massachusetts.
Mohegan men, up the Thames River from the port town of New London, generally shifted from whaling to farming between 1840 and 1860. Pequot men, living
within the inland area of New London County, worked as laborers for neighboring white farmers like their counterparts in inland Massachusetts. The Narragansett reserve lay very near the coast, with access to a bountiful estuary but without a nearby port town. State officials reported in 1858 and 1862 that few men of
the tribe farmed, most young men worked as laborers during the summer on a
monthly basis for white farmers, some fished "in its season" (probably during the
spring), and only a few left to become mariners. During the winter, both men and
women wove baskets to sell.[17]

But some developed reputations for craftsmanship and hard work. In 1839, four
carpenters from Gay Head and one from Christiantown worked on ships and
houses for whites as well as for their own tribe. Schaghticoke Jerry Cogswell was
a respected cooper in Cornwall in the early nineteenth century, and his son
Nathan was highly regarded as a stonemason and farmhand. Nathan married a
white woman, and their two sons served in the Civil War. The eldest, William,
was a popular and successful athlete who rose in the ranks to second lieutenant
before dying of battle wounds; the town erected a red sandstone monument to
him. Rufus Bunker, a contemporary of Jerry Cogswell, was known as a hardworking farmer who "bought a rough farm of fifty acres, cleared it, fenced the
fields with stone walls and built a comfortable framed house for his family." At the
end of the nineteenth century, another Schaghticoke, Henry Harris, was highly
regarded as a skilled tinsmith, basket maker, and farmworker. Earle found at least
a few craftsmen in every Massachusetts Indian community. But some tribes were
particularly well known for skilled work. Narragansett men by midcentury were
sought after for their skill in stonemasonry and commanded good wages in building many of the walls and fences for farmers in the region.[18]

Larger occupational differences between Indian communities were a result of
the three distinctive ecological subregions that shaped different socioeconomic

structures in southern New England—inland (upland), riverine, and coastal—*before* English colonization.[19] Although the routines and technologies of particular jobs resulted from the economic and cultural developments since English colonization, the subregional distinctions within New England were shaped by ecological conditions and also appear in non-Indian towns. In Charlestown, Rhode Island, along an estuary but not a port, a third of the men in 1860 were farmers, a third were laborers, and fewer than 5 percent were fisherman or mariners—a pattern that echoes the 1858 occupational pattern of Narragansett men on the reserve. Montville, alongside the river port of New London, had a similar percentage of farmers (32.5), but a lower percentage of laborers (25) and higher percentages of seamen (8.1) and factory hands (17.6). While no Mohegans were factory hands, tribal leaders testified in 1859 that a growing number of young men were farming rather than leaving for sea, which does reflect the occupational tendencies in Montville. In 1850, in the Vineyard towns of Edgartown and Tisbury, the majority of men were mariners; 16 to 19 percent were farmers, and only about 6.5 percent were laborers, numbers comparable to those in the Vineyard Indian tribes ten years later.[20] Thus the percentages of farmers, laborers, and mariners varied in a consistent pattern between coastal, inland, and riverine towns, and that pattern was relatively similar between Indian and non-Indian communities by 1860 (Table 7).

The striking relationship between age, occupation, and class was another similarity between Indians and their neighbors at midcentury. Mariners were always substantially younger and farmers older than the median age for men with listed occupations, regardless of ethnicity or location; among Indians, 20 years separated the median ages for mariners (30) and farmers (50). Laborers in the Indian communities also tended to be older than the median for all workers in inland communities; in white towns, by contrast, laborers were close to the median ages of all men with occupations and somewhat older than mariners. Seemingly, all younger men, Indian and non-Indian, were more likely to work as mariners, and they shifted to other occupations such as farming or labor—skilled if possible, unskilled if not—as they reached their 30s (Table 6). Indeed, the return of Indian whalers to settle on farms may be more of a reflection of a larger tendency (new or not) within the region than a result of socioeconomic reforms within the tribe. Age seems to have been the primary determinant of occupation, much as it was a determinant of status in colonial New England towns. The relationship between occupation and class was clearer as the data from Indian and non-Indian villages show that farmers regardless of age or ethnicity held more land and personal property than did mariners or laborers within the same community (Table 7).[21]

TABLE 7
Occupations for Men in Southern New England Tribes and Neighboring Towns

	N	%	Median age	Average acres	Median real estate	Mean real estate	Median personal estate	Mean personal estate
*Miscellaneous, 1860	10		40	0.0	$0	$0	n/a	n/a
Barber	2	20.0%	25	0.0	$0	$0	n/a	n/a
Laborer	7	70.0%	49	0.0	$0	$0	n/a	n/a
Cook	1	10.0%	46	0.0	$0	$0	n/a	n/a
*Precise tribal connection not clear; most claim Punkapoag, Natick, or Narragansett								
Punkapoag, 1860	17		34		n/a	n/a	n/a	n/a
Farmer	1	5.9%	65	45.0	n/a	n/a	n/a	n/a
Laborer	7	41.2%	34	0.0	n/a	n/a	n/a	n/a
Mariner	2	11.8%	22	0.0	n/a	n/a	n/a	n/a
Barber	5	29.4%	34	0.0	n/a	n/a	n/a	n/a
Shoe/bootmaker	2	11.8%	36	5.0	n/a	n/a	n/a	n/a
Hassanamisco, 1860	17		35	n/a	n/a	n/a	n/a	n/a
Laborer	7	41.2%	42	n/a	n/a	n/a	n/a	n/a
Farmer	1	5.9%	65	n/a	n/a	n/a	n/a	n/a
Shoemaker	2	11.8%	20	n/a	n/a	n/a	n/a	n/a
Barber	4	23.5%	37	n/a	n/a	n/a	n/a	n/a
Unskilled RR worker*	3	17.6%	34	n/a	n/a	n/a	n/a	n/a
*Porter, baggage handler, RR fireman								
Dudley-Nipmuc, 1860	13		37	n/a	n/a	n/a	n/a	n/a
Servant	1	7.7%	20	n/a	n/a	n/a	n/a	n/a
Laborer	7	53.8%	55	n/a	n/a	n/a	n/a	n/a
Mariner	1	7.7%	28	n/a	n/a	n/a	n/a	n/a
Semiskilled*	3	23.1%	30	n/a	n/a	n/a	n/a	n/a
Plumber	1	7.7%	43	n/a	n/a	n/a	n/a	n/a
*Shoemaker, barber, miner								
Bristol County (Dartmouth and Watuppa-Troy), 1860	25		35	n/a	n/a	n/a	n/a	n/a
Mariner	4	16.0%	22	0.0	n/a	n/a	n/a	n/a
Farmer	6	24.0%	51	21.7	n/a	n/a	n/a	n/a

Laborer	10	40.0%	37	0.0	n/a	n/a	n/a	n/a
Miner (in Australia)	1	4.0%	30	0.0	n/a	n/a	n/a	n/a
Skilled*	4	16.0%	29	0.0	n/a	n/a	n/a	n/a
*Daguerretypist, sailmaker, ship keeper, trader								
Herring Pond, 1860	13		29	64.5	$445	n/a	n/a	n/a
Cordwainer, barber (in CA)	2	15.4%	28	26.9	$84	n/a	n/a	n/a
Carpenter	1	7.7%	49	152.0	$950	n/a	n/a	n/a
Laborer	1	7.7%	37	110.8	$1,175	n/a	n/a	n/a
Mariner	7	53.8%	29	50.6	$331	n/a	n/a	n/a
Farmer	2	15.4%	50	83.9	$588	n/a	n/a	n/a
Mashpee, 1860	67		39	81.2	$0	$495	$0	$26
Mariner*	40	59.7%	32	63.1	$0	$394	$0	$15
Farmer	17	25.4%	58	124.2	$820	$899	$0	$80
Laborer/jobber	6	9.0%	32	76.2	$0	$168	$0	$0
Barber (in Boston)	1	1.5%	21	0.0	$0	$0	$0	$0
Miner (in California)	2	3.0%	47	90.0	$0	$0	$0	$0
Preacher (Joe Amos)	1	1.5%	51	150.0	$1,200	$1,200	$0	$0
*Includes one steamboat hand								
Sandwich, 1860 (some cases missing)	607		35	n/a	$0	$835	$50	$475
Worker in Glass Industry	155	25.5%	31	n/a	$0	$613	$50	$258
Worker not in glass industry	452	74.5%	35	n/a	$0	$911	$50	$549
Mariner	48	7.9%	27	n/a	$0	$123	$0	$229
Farmer	55	9.1%	54	n/a	$1,200	$2,039	$275	$1,179
Laborer	86	14.2%	35	n/a	$0	$135	$0	$76
Edgartown, 1850	733		31	n/a	$0	$825	n/a	n/a
Seaman	387	52.8%	28	n/a	$0	$350	n/a	n/a
Mariner	1	0.1%	41	n/a	$2,900	$2,900	n/a	n/a
Farmer	120	16.4%	45	n/a	$500	$825	n/a	n/a
Laborer	50	6.8%	27	n/a	$0	$151	n/a	n/a
Tisbury, 1850	581		35	n/a	$0	$582	n/a	n/a
Mariner	306	52.7%	33	n/a	$0	$521	n/a	n/a
Farmer	112	19.3%	47	n/a	$900	$1,078	n/a	n/a
Laborer	38	6.5%	34	n/a	$0	$163	n/a	n/a

(continued)

TABLE 7
Continued

	N	%	Median age	Average acres	Median real estate	Mean real estate	Median personal estate	Mean personal estate
Chappaquiddick, 1860^	13		39	9.4	n/a	n/a	n/a	n/a
Mariner	10	76.9%	35	4.8	n/a	n/a	n/a	n/a
Farmer	3	23.1%	52	25.0	n/a	n/a	n/a	n/a
Gay Head, 1860^	42		42	6.5	n/a	n/a	n/a	n/a
Mariner	21	50.0%	33	1.9	n/a	n/a	n/a	n/a
Farmer*	18	42.9%	50	12.0	n/a	n/a	n/a	n/a
Carpenter	2	4.8%	45	15.0	n/a	n/a	n/a	n/a
Servant	1	2.4%	19	0.0	n/a	n/a	n/a	n/a
*Two listed as "farmer/mariner"								
Christiantown, 1860^	12		34	18.0	n/a	n/a	n/a	n/a
Mariner	4	33.3%	26	4.0	n/a	n/a	n/a	n/a
Farmer*	8	66.7%	40	25.0	n/a	n/a	n/a	n/a
*One listed as "farmer/wheelright"								
Lyme, CT, 1860	334		40	n/a	$200	$1,042	$75	$585
Farm laborer	51	15.3%	32	n/a	$0	$62	$0	$32
Laborer	4	1.2%	48	n/a	$0	$13	$0	$8
Sailor	26	7.8%	24	n/a	$0	$108	$0	$269
Fisherman	35	10.5%	33	n/a	$0	$119	$0	$84
Farmer	142	42.5%	48	n/a	$1,700	$2,052	$600	$1,021

Montville, CT, 1860	631		35	n/a	$2,000	$2,648	$400	$1,028
Factory hand/paper mill	111	17.6%	26	n/a	$450	$633	$100	$292
Farm help/laborer	77	12.2%	23	n/a	$188	$221	$200	$416
Day laborer/help	82	13.0%	35	n/a	$500	$528	$100	$165
Seaman	51	8.1%	26	n/a	$1,000	$1,277	$500	$898
Fisherman	1	0.2%	25	n/a	$1,200	$1,200	$1,000	$1,000
Farmer	205	32.5%	50	n/a	$2,000	$2,854	$600	$1,124
North Stonington, CT, 1860	535		37	n/a		$1,025	$100	$589
Farm laborer	80	15.0%	22	n/a	$0	$17	$0	$25
Laborer	44	8.2%	29	n/a	$0	$23	$0	$40
Sailor	4	0.7%	32	n/a	$0	$50	$0	$13
Farmer	291	54.4%	45	n/a	$900	$1,686	$500	$865
Charlestown, RI, 1860	319		36	n/a		$761	$200	$436
Day laborer	6	1.9%	42	n/a	$0	$0	$125	$258
Farm laborer	111	34.8%	25	n/a	$0	$60	$0	$119
Farmer	99	31.0%	50	n/a	$1,500	$1,891	$500	$861
Fisherman	10	3.1%	33	n/a	$0	$110	$450	$400
Seaman	5	1.6%	34	n/a	$0	$1,080	$0	$720

a Counted Indians living in this community regardless of origin and those originally from this tribe but living in a non-Indian town; did not count foreigners.

NOTE: Dollar figures are rounded to the nearest whole figure.

SOURCES: Earle 1861, appendix for Indian tribes; U.S. Department of Commerce, Federal Census of 1860, ms. schedules for Charlestown, R.I.; Sandwich, Mass.; North Stonington, Conn.; Lyme, Conn.; Montville, Conn.; Ledyard, Conn.; U.S. Department of Commerce, Federal Census of 1850, ms. schedules for Edgartown, Mass., and Tisbury, Mass., transcribed in Chris Baer, "Historical Records of Dukes County, Massachusetts," http://history.vineyard.net/edgcen50.htm (accessed 13 May 2005). .vineyard.net/edgcen50.htm (accessed 13 May 2005).

But the distinctions between ages and subregional economies do not fully account for the stark differences between Indians and their neighbors in occupations and wealth. Men in non-Indian towns regardless of size had a great variety of occupations, representing the wide range of socioeconomic conditions and skill levels typical of a community in an industrialized, mature economy. By comparison, men in Indian communities had a very narrow range of occupations, regardless of where they were located. Those inland were more likely to have a larger variety because their members lived in cities or towns with commercial development, but even they had a much lower range than their white neighbors. Indian mariners also generally remained in that occupation longer than their non-Indian counterparts. The median age of mariners in the three Vineyard Indian communities was 32.6, and in Mashpee 32, whereas in Sandwich it was 27 and in Edgartown 28; only in Tisbury was the median age of mariners comparable to that among Indians (Table 7).

The constricted range of listed Indian occupations and the older median age of Indian mariners in part reflected the racial prejudices that barred them from serving in most skilled positions and or commanding whaling ships. Massachusetts investigators visiting Christiantown in 1848 found a young sailor, "one of the best seamen who sailed from the South Shore" but now "discouraged, disheartened, with ambition quenched." He spurned their urgings to try harder. "The prejudice against our color keeps us down," he told them. "I may be a first rate navigator, and as good a seaman as ever walked a deck . . . but I am doomed to live and die before the mast." Even as second mate, he was sent to eat with the lower ranks when a visitor boarded the ship.[22] There were some exceptions. In 1847, Amos Jeffers Jr., of Gay Head, served as first mate on the whaling bark *Mary* of New Bedford and was due to sail as master on her next voyage, but in early July he was lost at sea on a swordfishing expedition to Norman's Land (an island near the Vineyard) with his friend Meremiah Weeks. Three years later, Amos Haskins, also of Gay Head, was given command of the New Bedford whaling ship *Massasoit*; unfortunately, *Massasoit* disappeared on his first voyage as her captain.[23]

The occupational listings in the censuses are inevitably incomplete. For example, teenagers and young men who remained dependents of their farmer fathers were usually not identified as having an occupation even though they may have worked full time in the fields. Such shortcomings are particularly true for Indians living on or near large or small tribal reserves or the ocean, who used the land and water in ways that combined old and new methods. Households grew small crops of maize, rye, oats, potatoes, peas, beans, and other crops; raised pigs; and grazed a few head of cattle and sheep. Most grew their crops on small plots they or their parents had claimed and perhaps fenced (although Gay Headers continued to work some areas communally), and they grazed their animals on the commons or in pastures assigned on a yearly basis. They continued to obtain wood and fish from the remaining forests, rivers, and ponds, despite competition and poaching by white neighbors. From smaller segments of the varied patchwork ecology, often on lands formally owned by Anglo-Americans, as well as in areas still held by Indians, they gathered wild-plant and tree products for medicines, food, and crafts. Non-Indian farmers and laborers similarly found other ways to supplement their meager incomes by fishing in the spring and summer and taking on part-time piecework during the winter. But Indians with tribal reserves had resources that heavily privatized white towns lacked, and they had deeper traditions of gaining their subsistence in this fashion, supplemented by occasional labor for white farmers—which state and local officials viewed as laziness.[24]

When done for the marketplace, some of this work was also invisible in the records. Many Gay Head men listed as seamen or farmers by Earle appeared in an 1870 census of the tribe as both seamen *and* farmers. In 1839, only a few members of the tribe owned boats and fished near shore, but, by the mid-nineteenth century, urbanization and other factors drove a commercial market for fish in New England, which offered new opportunities to former whalers and others in Native maritime tribes, and Gay Head's location at the edge of the Elizabeth Islands and prime fishing grounds gave them an advantage in the trade. Decades later, Mary Vanderkoop wrote that young men of the tribe went whaling to earn enough money to furnish a house and buy a boat so he could stay at home "and follow ordinary fishing, clay carrying, or some other local industry." Gay Head families could earn $150–$300 in a season fishing for alewives and cod or other deep-sea fish off nearby islands, about the same each year gathering and selling cranberries, and about the same for clay. Members of the tribe involved in supplying and guiding tourists, as in Mashpee, did not have those occupations listed in either the Earle or the federal censuses.[25]

This movement between different types of work was quite common among poorer Americans during the antebellum period, regardless of race or ethnicity. New England Indians did have a unique niche in the market for traditional crafts, particularly baskets and brooms, which provided an important source of income for men as well as women—highlighted by the establishment of the Mashpee Manufacturing Company in 1867. Unfortunately, the informal and volatile nature of the crafts trade did not lend itself to organized manufacturing, so two years later the company turned to cranberry cultivation and sales and became so successful that within a decade neighboring whites took over the company, although the new owners continued employing Mashpees to raise the fruit. By 1889, more cranberries were produced in Mashpee than any other town on Cape Cod.[26]

Only a few Indians were listed as servants in state reports by midcentury, yet indenture remained a threat, as indeed it was for all poor people. State governments considered poverty both a symptom and a cause of social disorder and empowered town officials and Indian guardians to bind out disruptive adults or children from poor families. In 1872, for example, Connecticut passed a measure confirming the right of tribal overseers to take children from Indian parents if the father allowed them to "live in idleness" or if the family did not "provide competently" for them. The overseers were empowered to indenture the children to a good white family, the boys to serve until age 18, the girls until age 16. This act was passed after another law that allowed selectmen to intervene in any household that neglected the education of children; if the problem continued and the children grew "rude, stubborn, and unruly," the selectmen were to indenture them to a "proper master, or to any suitable charitable institution or society," boys until age 21 and girls until age 18. So the measure directed at Indians was meant to deal with their unique legal situation. But by midcentury such laws were rarely used, judging by the data from state officials and the absence of complaints by tribal leaders.[27]

Household and residential stability may have increased by midcentury, but Indian communities continued to face considerable social and economic problems, particularly those with very small reserves and few resources, and were challenged by the need of members to find opportunities elsewhere. In the Earle census, 16.6 percent of all Indians with known residences (1,574) lived more than two towns away from the tribe of their origin, many in Boston (39), Providence (14), Worcester (59), New Bedford (88), and some even in California (12); 26.6 percent lived in neighboring towns. In 1881, of 319 on the final Narragansett list, only 103 lived in Charlestown; many lived in neighboring towns like Carolina, Kingstown, and North Kingstown, but many lived farther: for example, 48 lived in Providence, and some lived in Boston or Worcester. This scattering was not new, but it marked the continued existence and renewal of regional networks of tribal and kinfolk.[28]

The individual and family dynamics of this movement can be glimpsed in the life and family of Alice Chace, a Troy-Watuppa woman born in 1802. Her father, Joseph Chace, lived all of his 70 years on the tribe's reserve and drowned in Watuppa Pond in 1816. Around 1829, Alice met and married Cato Northrup, a "colored foreigner." Together they moved to Providence, Rhode Island, where he worked as a porter (one of the better-paid jobs open to African Americans) in a wholesale store and she had at least six children over the subsequent 15 years. The family lived comfortably on his salary and other income that she may have earned. About 1855, when the last child was 13 years old, the family decided to return to Alice's community and built a house on the Troy-Watuppa reserve. But after only one year they found conditions too difficult and returned to Providence, where they still lived in 1860. From that city their five sons worked, like so many other Indians, as day laborers and occasionally as sailors.[29] Similar stories emerged in the 1881 Narragansett tribal hearings.[30] Clearly some found it best to cut their ties to the past and, like William Wallace Uncas, made a future for themselves elsewhere.

TRIBAL IDENTITY AND POLITICS

Yet Indians who left their reserves often retained a strong tribal identity. Earle's study opened with a description of how he found 150 Indians from many different communities living in New Bedford, with many more at sea. But "few consider themselves permanently located there, but generally, are looking forward to the time, more or less remote, when they shall return to the places of their nativity, finally to mingle their dust with that of their fathers." Edward Cone, a Narragansett, lived in Providence when he heard of a petition to terminate his tribe. "I was one of the first to act, and thought I should inform all of the members, even in the city," and to spur them to defend "our tribal rights." By the 1840s, the Narragansetts and the Mohegans both held annual summer fairs that combined church meetings and tribal celebrations, which served as homecoming celebrations for those who lived elsewhere as well as open houses for curious visitors. The Narragansett council elections every March also drew members of the tribe living elsewhere in what for some seems to have been an annual pilgrimage. Stories of "the last Indian," which became part of the growing genre of New England town histories, often included the caveat that at certain times of the year a noticeable number of Indian relatives would show up for a homecoming.[31]

This human movement in and out of Indian reserves remained important, particularly with the need to find work and visit family members elsewhere. Tribes became increasingly concerned that those who came or went threatened the community, particularly as some who lived elsewhere sought to sell land on the reserve that they or their parents had held. Those who remained perceived those who left, particularly for extended periods or even generations, as nonmembers. At midcentury Gay Head and Chappaquiddick sought new protections against these emigrants. The Narragansetts had the rule, apparently dating from about 1790, that those who left retained rights to tribal resources for a decade, after which they were regarded as having cut all ties with the community. The Troy-Watuppa Indians were quick to defend against Zurviah Mitchell's claims to a piece of the reserve. Guardians could play a significant role in defending tribal resources and social boundaries: Benjamin Winslow helped press the Troy-Watuppa case against Mitchell, and the Mashantucket Pequot overseer resisted claims in 1856 to a portion of the sale of tribal land by a woman in Griswold, and in 1857 to claims by Ledyard for assistance given a Pequot family. But generally those who lived outside the reserve retained many, if not all, rights if they regularly participated in tribal elections and other gatherings.[32]

While all Indian communities could influence their social and economic boundaries, those with political autonomy backed by the state government had structures and systems that could govern access to the community and its resources. The three strongest tribes—Gay Head, Mashpee, and Narragansett—left a scattering of records from the middle of the century that provide a unique glimpse of their decision-making processes and leadership patterns. All tribal council members were men, although women continued to vote in meetings and play a significant role in tribal politics; for example, in 1858 the Narragansett council asked the oldest women to decide whether Aaron Rodman had the requisite ancestry for tribal membership.[33] These formal processes were only part of the tribe's organization, as each of these groups also featured a strong church that exerted considerable influence within and without the community. But these secular and ecclesiastical structures together highlight political, social, and cultural patterns in each tribe and point to some general patterns and concerns.

The Narragansetts elected five members of a governing council each year in a tribal meeting on the last day in March. Even after the state appointed a commissioner beginning in 1840 to supervise the tribe, the council continued to hold extensive powers, including the authority to allot lands to families and individuals; review boundaries of lands left by a deceased member of the tribe and determine inheritance or repossession by the tribe; lease communal lands to outsiders; sell licenses to cut timber on the commons; investigate possible trespass and poaching of tribal resources; approve and oversee the construction of roads through the reserve; and review the tribe's accounts and settle debts or payments due. These powers, formalized by a tribal constitution in 1850, were subject to state laws, legislative review, and Narragansett traditions such as the right of the oldest women to review petitions for tribal membership. Representatives of the council also frequently went to the state capital to represent council and tribal interests to the legislature and governor, often in opposition to proposals to limit the council's power or the tribe's legal existence.[34]

Narragansett council membership showed noticeable persistence in this position of power. Only 11 different men held office between 1850 and 1862. Four men served seven terms: Gideon Ammons, Joshua Nocake (or Noka), Joseph Stanton, and Gideon Watson; one (Samuel Nocake) served five terms; and three (Henry Champlain, Brister Michael, and Benjamin Thomas) each served four terms. Only two men served one term each, Aaron Seketer and Joseph Nocake, and Seketer later became preacher in the tribe's church and served as the tribal meeting moderator—positions that may have made the holder ineligible for council. There were direct benefits to being a member of the council, in addition to the prestige, power, and connections that come with such positions. As already noted, council members often purchased permits to cut and sell timber, and they also received a small stipend for their service. State investigators and white neighbors sometimes complained about the council's autocratic nature and corrupt decisions; certainly its structure and powers could have created such a pattern, although members of the tribe did not complain to the state about such problems. The council charged in turn that the Narragansett commissioner created chaos by ignoring the council's powers and endangered the tribe by leasing reserved lands to outsiders.[35]

Mashpee's organization and leadership patterns were very different from that of the Narragansetts. When the state abolished the tribe's guardianship in March 1834, it made Mashpee a district that, like a town, elected officials and kept records of decisions but, unlike a town, could not elect representatives to the legislature. The Mashpees therefore adopted a New England town structure, electing each year three selectmen and one or more constables, field drivers, pound keepers, and fence viewers, which highlighted how the tribe had also adopted aspects of Anglo-American landholding. These officers had the powers and responsibilities of their white counterparts, including making arrangements for poor relief, overseeing roads, and managing other community needs. The selectmen often acted as the district's school board, monitoring the two schools, hiring teachers, and distributing funds. District meetings also chose a clerk, who kept detailed minutes of town meeting and selectmen's decisions. Other officers were chosen for short-term needs, including assessors and a collector of taxes in 1850. With state authorization, Mashpee wrote special regulations governing pickerel, trout, and herring fishing on the reserve and appointed agents beginning in 1853 to enforce those measures.[36]

Mashpee's new structure provided opportunities for many men to be involved in community office, and patterns of office holding highlight greater democracy and instability. Between 1834 and 1859, 23 different men served as selectmen, the most powerful and responsible position in the district. Solomon Attaquin, who captained the ship that took Mashpee lumber to Nantucket markets, served 17 terms as selectman, far more than any other man, and held every other district office except field driver. Daniel Amos (who led the 1833 revolt) and Oak Coombs were each elected seven times; Ebenezer Attaquin, Moses Pocknett, and Nathan S. Pocknett had six terms; Sampson Avis was elected four times; and three men had three terms. The instability of district politics is shown by the unwillingness of Mashpee voters to reelect all three selectmen: this only happened three times during this period, whereas seven times all three men were replaced, and nine times two of the three were replaced. But while power was widely shared, Mashpee like New England towns generally had a noticeable cohort that filled lower-tier positions like constable and fence viewer. Although selectmen were paid a small stipend each year, many more men earned public money by housing the poor, shoveling snow, building fences, and performing other community labor.[37]

This structure facilitated an active polity. In 1837, Nathan Pocknett and 11 other voters (out of 66 in the district) asked the legislature to investigate the selectmen's corruption and mismanagement. The state refused, and a year later 15 men submitted another petition, which was also rejected. So the town meeting voted out all three selectmen. This upheaval shows young men involved in district politics: Pocknett was 28 in 1837 and would first serve as selectman in 1844. In 1842, young whalemen recently returned persuaded the state to authorize a new allotment, dividing nearly all of the district lands and giving each proprietor (male and female) 60 acres.[38] But there was one group that apparently lost political power in Mashpee: women. While women and men were proprietors in the district, entitled to claim pieces of land and other resources, women never held district offices, and apparently few, if any, were officially allowed to vote in local elections.

The new Mashpee leaders were unhappy about the one outsider with authority in the district: the commissioner, Charles Marston, who was appointed by the governor under the 1834 law to monitor and report on the district's finances. In January 1840, they petitioned for the right to choose their commissioner. The legislature refused, and Marston continued in an apparently amiable relationship with the Mashpees and often commented favorably on the district government's competency. But the district did have problems raising funds to support the aged and helpless; residents refused to pay duties on the wood they cut and sold, and when that source of income was exhausted, many refused to pay the taxes that the selectmen tried to collect in 1843 and 1844. By the mid-1850s, however, new revenue from fishing leases and licenses improved the tribe's situation.[39]

Gay Head polity at midcentury combined many traditions—communal regulation, republican representation, and democratic elections—although its leaders recognized that they needed stronger legal support within the state's administrative system for its decisions. The tribe usually held one or two annual meetings to transact business and choose committees and agents to handle concerns between meetings. By 1860, the meeting was electing three overseers (selectmen), a clerk, a treasurer, a school committee, and a committee on public lands. The same meeting assigned annual individual rights to communal resources, particularly grazing and clay, and tried to regulate the prices charged for sales and leases. In 1859, for example, the tribe decided that each proprietor could dig and sell 30 tons of clay for 12 cents a ton. These limits were dictated by communal, rather than individual, needs: in 1861, the tribe barred the sale of clay by individuals, instead dictating that all sales would be on behalf of the community to raise money for the tribe's needs, probably to support the poor and the schools. One year later, the meeting began appointing a clay agent to negotiate contracts on behalf of the tribe, usually for 100 tons, while allowing individual proprietors to each sell 10 to 15 tons. But the decisions of the meeting and its officers had little legal standing in court cases or financial transactions because the tribe was neither a town nor a district under state law.[40]

There were remarkable differences between the three tribes, resulting in part from state laws and in part from the unique history and conditions of each tribe. The Narragansett council held the cachet of traditional tribal leadership and showed remarkable stability, serving as an anchor in an unstable world; the Mashpee district government was modeled after those of other New England towns, and was larger and more volatile, probably because the tribal leaders were more acculturated; and Gay Head made its decisions in a more informal structure and fashion, leaving few records behind and facilitating communal management and the authority of the elders. But there were also similarities. Councils and committees were chosen by annual tribal meetings, regulated the use of communal resources, and represented the tribe to state legislatures. Narragansett and Mashpee leaders, with more formal tribal administrative structures, used their positions to gain special access to income from community resources and jobs.

Most tribes did not have formal councils; instead they selected (apparently informally) a few spokesmen or women to deal with legislatures and guardians. Tribal guardians continued to be appointed by legislatures in Massachusetts and county courts in Connecticut to manage community funds and to serve as intermediaries between the tribe, non-Indians on the reserve, neighboring towns, and state executive offices. These were many of the same duties exercised by the Mashpee district selectmen and the Narragansett tribal council. Guardians had special

access to community resources, of course, and some tribes continued to have problems with fraud. As Narragansett Tribal Historic Preservation Officer John Brown
observed recently, "The state-appointed guardians used legislative maneuvers and
theft to obtain tribal lands." But the problem seemed rarer than in the previous
century, and neglect seems to have been a more common problem. Perhaps the
Indians had less to steal. Perhaps the stipend that guardians began to receive from
the state helped. But their more limited role may have also been a factor. Guardians no longer sought to reshape their charges in proper patterns of deference and
moral order but instead saw their duties as providing efficient administration of
group assets and assistance to the sick, elderly, and helpless. The Chappaquiddick
and Christiantown guardian never used the 1828 Massachusetts law empowering
him to send "habitual drunkards, vagabonds, or idlers" to sea, or to put disruptive
individuals into solitary confinement for 20 days.[41]

There were exceptions, of course. In 1836, the Mashantucket Pequot guardian
made "great exertions" to remove "a troublesome family" from the reserve, and
two decades later the Massachusetts legislature told the Dudley-Nipmuc guardian
"to inculcate and promote habits of industry and good morals amongst said Indians," and he coordinated their removal from the isolated reserve to a tenement in
the center of town. Guardians could displace Native authority, as the Narragansetts complained in 1851. But tribes, families, or individuals were able to appeal
directly to the governor or legislature, and some went to sympathetic lawyers or
other local elites if they found their guardian obnoxious. In the 1850s, for example, Christiantown and Chappaquiddick generally ignored their guardian, B. C.
Merchant, and instead went to Leavitt Thaxter, a lawyer in Edgartown who also
worked with Gay Head. These alternative channels were useful, although they
could be used to wreak havoc in a tribe. Guardians could also help knit together
more scattered communities and provide important help when the community
requested it, as with the Troy-Watuppa tribe. Unfortunately, such positive relationships were rare.[42]

In most of the Indian communities without evident governing organizations,
members lived scattered around the area, with a few families on the (usually very
small) reserve and others in nearby towns and cities. As a result, white observers
differed in their perceptions of who was a member of a tribe. For example, while
Indians "not taxed" were not supposed to be listed by federal census takers, the
1830 and 1840 census schedules from Ledyard included some Mashantucket Pequot families, and the 1840 census from Webster (but not the 1850 census from the
same town) included the Dudley Nipmucs on their reserve. Lists of tribal members made in different years also varied wildly. A Grafton orator in 1835 told the

town that there were 14 Hassanamiscos, but 13 years later the Bird commission found 26, two-thirds of whom owned a little land and lived as full members of the town; the commissioners predicted that "they will undoubtedly lose their individuality, and become merged in the general community." Earle found even more, 90 individuals in 27 households, scattered far and wide without any collective organization.[43]

The question of who retained that ambiguous tie to an Indian community became more problematic during the first half of the nineteenth century. Indeed, as perceptions of race and of Indians shifted, Anglo-Americans found it increasingly difficult to *see* Indians in southern New England. The image of "the Indian" that developed out of poetry, novels, plays, speeches, and children's schoolbooks emerged as part and parcel of a distinctive New England identity rooted in a unique past. This emphasis on a special past, celebrated or criticized, along with new scientific notions of race and popular images of western Natives, made contemporary Indian descendants in the region seem part of the general population of color rather than the heirs of Massasoit, Uncas, or Metacomet.

IMAGES OF INDIANS

On January 24, 1791, three years after the establishment of the SPG, Jeremy Belknap, powerful minister of Boston's Federal Street Church, called a meeting of friends interested in collecting and preserving historical accounts and documents. Belknap was a member of the American Philosophical Society and the American Academy of Arts and Sciences; his first volume of *The History of New Hampshire* had appeared in 1784 and the second would appear later that year. The meeting agreed to form the Massachusetts Historical Society (MHS), the first such organization in the United States, and pledged to contribute funds and family papers and to seek contributions from prominent men throughout the nation. The MHS had much in common with the SPG: both limited their membership in order to insure that only "the best sort" would be involved, mixed secular and ecclesiastical leadership and purpose, had roots in Puritan culture and concerns, and wished to guide and improve society. As with so many of the organizations created during the Second Great Awakening, the two had overlapping leadership: Belknap himself was a member of the SPG, and two of the four with whom Belknap first discussed creating the MHS were also SPG founders (Rev. John Eliot and Rev. Peter Thacher of Boston); indeed, a historian of the SPG writing in the middle of the twentieth century found that a third of its members had also been members of the MHS.[44]

The MHS was, like the SPG, an organization very interested in New England Indians. One year after its founding, the first volume of its *Collections* featured a previously unpublished 1674 account by Daniel Gookin, the Bay Colony's Indian superintendent who worked alongside John Eliot. Most of the subsequent *Collections* contained past and present accounts of New England Indian groups, including many letters from Gideon Hawley, along with articles on southern and western tribes and general discussions of Native culture. These descriptions reflected not only the New England intellectuals' great interest in Indians and Indian history but also their increasingly prominent perception that Natives in the region had experienced a rapid and inevitable demographic decline over the past century.[45]

During the early republic, Anglo-American perceptions of Native Americans drew from two stereotypes that had originated with European exploration: the Nasty Cannibal, who was Satan's creature, and the Noble Savage living in Edenic innocence. The former was particularly prominent in Puritan accounts of King Philip's War (1675–76) and the captivity narratives that cast Indians as inferior, irrational, bloodthirsty beasts. The latter was prominent in Enlightenment literature that portrayed the American Indian as a model of natural simplicity and order that civilized society had lost in its inevitable, but somewhat regrettable, maturity. The MHS members and their colleagues believed that, regardless of whether New England Indians had originally been savage threats or childlike primitives, they were rapidly approaching extinction.[46] As William Tudor, one of the men who worked with Belknap to found the MHS, wrote in his 1819 account of New England, "Some have described the Indians as possessed of every virtue, while others degrade them below the rank of humanity, as destitute of every good quality, and practicing all the vices, that can come under the heads of dishonesty, perfidy, and ferocity." But while these arguments rage, "the unfortunate race which is the subject of dispute, is mouldering away, and at no remote period will have no existence but in history."[47]

The New England observers who wrote about contemporary Natives agreed that the Indians' dramatic decline was related to their perceived moral decay, with Natives supposedly becoming degenerate as they lost any original savage nobility while failing to gain civilized habits. Some, like Hawley and Stephen Badger, blamed this decline primarily on the greed and prejudice of surrounding whites; others, like Timothy Dwight (another MHS member) and Tudor, saw it as the inevitable fate of Indians exposed to civilization.[48] All tended to view Indians as somehow inherently generous, taking only what they needed or desired immediately from Nature while failing to prepare for the future. Badger noted that the remaining Indians in Natick "by the peculiarity of their natural constitution . . . are addicted to, and actually contract, such habits of indolence and excess, as they cannot, without the greatest efforts, which they seem not much disposed to make, give up, up, if ever they entirely get rid of them."[49] Similarly, Hawley told Governor John Hancock in 1791 that "Indians left to themselves, as appears from their conduct in every instance in such case, will get rid of their lands and spend their capital . . . They cannot look forward to remote consequences."[50]

These early historians did become increasingly sensitive to perceived racial aspects of this "degeneration" as scientific notions of race began to gain credence. They agreed that the few "pure bloods" who remained were but a shadow of their ancestors, and many felt that the one hope for Indians and their descendants was intermarriage with others, particularly blacks.[51] Belknap, in his 1795 letter to Secretary of War Henry Knox, emphasized that white civilization and Indian savagery could not coexist, that the Puritans had tried to convert Natives but had failed, and that Indians had either retired in the face of civilization or were "imperfectly civilized and reduced to a state of dependence." But although they increasingly discussed *race*, their primary concern was with proper hierarchical *order*. Members of the Standing Order viewed the Indians who still survived in the region as sharing many of the characteristics of the lower sort of all races, including indolence, intemperance, and uncontrolled passions.[52]

The tendency of gentry to see Indians in terms of class was not followed by others in New England. The region's urban growth and socioeconomic transformations during the early republic were reflected in a growing gap between elite and popular cultures.[53] That gap was marked in part by divergent images of Indians as stories of inexplicably savage and barbaric warriors in captivity narratives, sermons, and folklore retained their power among farmers and workers. Some town militias at the turn of the century staged mock battles with one of the companies taking on the role of Pequots or Narragansetts. A revealing broadside produced in Boston in 1794 for rural and urban readers, *The Indians' Pedigree*, depicted the region's Indians as the offspring of Satan and a pig. Its pungent prose shows that colonial folklore connecting Indians and the devil remained strong, perhaps in part as a reaction against growing elite sympathy for Indians. It also points to how this folklore was reshaped by new anxieties about race and social disorder into a new trope of Satan copulating with swine to create the Other.[54]

The potency of such perceptions and anxieties can be glimpsed in the 1813 murder of the Penobscot Nicholas Crevay in his wigwam at Spot Pond in Stoneham, about ten miles north of Boston. Crevay and his wife Sally were from St. Francis (Odanak) in Canada, had developed close trading relations with Americans, and at the outbreak of the War of 1812 received a pass to resettle in New England. Late Tuesday evening, November 23, several Anglo-American laborers in a nearby nail factory in Malden took loaded muskets, walked to Spot Pond, and fired into the wigwam, intending to either frighten or murder the sleeping Indians. When the judge condemned two of the men to hang, he noted that Crevay "had excited, in the neighborhood where he had placed his hut, a degree of ill-will, of apprehension and dislike" that was "accompanied with contempt, with a most erroneous prejudice and delusion. It seems to have been an opinion, adopted and talked over there, that Indians were not regarded as human beings; but were exposed as wild beasts or vermin, to be hunted and destroyed." The trial and subsequent testimony show that the Crevays were condemned not as British allies or dangerous Canadian savages but simply as *Indians*.[55]

Anglo-Americans regardless of class shared many perceptions of remnant Indians in southern New England, based in part on increasingly popular racial archetypes and partially on distinctive workways. Indians worked as whalers, herb doctors (or doctresses), domestics, basket makers, woodcarvers, and (in Rhode Island) as stonemasons. Individually or in small groups, Indian tramped around the countryside like gypsies, using knowledge gained from their parents and grandparents to find concealed paths and bypassing more popular byways—Frances Caulkins noted her "great perplexity in following [Mashantucket Pequot] encampments"—seeking shelter and food at farms, peddling, hunting, and fishing in order to scrape their bare subsistence. Tribes held and managed their lands and resources in common, provided more power and authority to women, and were asylums for fugitive slaves and other "lower sorts." Natives were certainly handicapped by these stereotypes and the accompanying white prejudice, but they also found that those images provided some unique sources of survival. At the same time, Indians in the region increasingly seemed unlike the *real* Indians in the Ohio Valley and Great Plains described in contemporary periodicals: *those* Indians were distinctive and noble in appearance and dress, and were brave, tough, hospitable, just, and sincere, like the ancient Romans.[56]

This image of the noble savage, used by some as a symbol of the new American republic, was imbedded in the development of American Romanticism, which after 1820 would be yoked to a more positive vision of New England's Indians, still as vanishing but now as the noble victims of Puritan aggression, their remnants deserving of pity and sublime reflection rather than hostility and contempt. This image was part of a new view of the region's history and a unique New England identity, driven and shaped by a strange mixture of optimism and unease in the early nineteenth century and harnessed to social reform movements. New

Englanders who promoted this new vision generally opposed Democrat Andrew Jackson's removal policies and in the 1830s became Whig Party activists. Yet the regional culture that nurtured the Whig Party transcended politics, even though conflicts that raged between New England Whigs and Democrats over social reforms and national policies were reflected in how they viewed Indians.

The belief of New Englanders that they were unique may have begun with the Puritans' errand into the Wilderness. After 1796, the region's Standing Order defined itself largely in Federalist opposition to southern Jeffersonians and in support of a stable, traditional social order in opposition to anarchy, while public celebrations and sermons reminded residents that their distinctiveness—and American's most noble mission—originated with the arrival of their ancestors.[57] But the New England history that emerged after 1820 was very different. The explosion of adult and juvenile literature often celebrated Metacom and the region's indigenous peoples and sometimes, particularly in light of Jackson's removal policy, presented a critical view of the intolerance of the Puritan founding fathers. While older stereotypes of Indians remained strong, contempt was often replaced by affection and respect, although this new paradigm also viewed New England Indians as a vanishing people.

This transition can be glimpsed in William Tudor's work. His *Letters on the Eastern States* (1819) emphasized the virtuous influence of New England's developing international commerce and rural factories and featured glowing depictions of the exceptional characteristics of the people of his native region. While Tudor's emphasis on social rank and deference echoes the Standing Order, his positive depiction of the virtuous present and future of a commercial and industrial New England marked his writings as Whiggish, particularly when compared with the earlier gloomy, combative writings from Gideon Hawley and Timothy Dwight.[58]

Tudor's *Letters* included an extensive description of Indians in his home region. "They preserve most of the traits of the Indian character," he believed, "though imbedded in civilization, and knowing no language other than English." He compared "the few that remain" with Europe's gypsies in their wandering and peddling, and "while they commonly make use of our roads, they retain a knowledge of its natural topography; and are never afraid of being lost in a forest." While many worked as whalers or domestics they "still are acquainted with all the rivers and ponds, and the most probable places for finding game." The remaining Indian tribes existed "in a state of perpetual pupilage." Race was a particular concern for Tudor, as he scornfully wrote that these Indians "are all of mixed breed, some crosses with the white, and some with the African," and he was "strongly inclined to believe, that the negro is much more susceptible of civilization, and the improvements that follow it, than the Indian."[59]

In the same year, Tudor's *North American Review* reviewed John Heckwelder's *An Account of the History, Manners and Customs of the Indian Nations,* a study of the Lenni-Lenape or Delaware, today considered one of the first serious anthropological studies of Native American tribe. The unsigned review admitted, "How far our ancestors deserve censure for their general treatment of the Indians, is a question which admits of some variety of opinion," although clearly European settlement was the "undeniable" cause of the Indians' "ruin and almost total extinction." Despite that unfortunate result, the founders of the majority of the English colonies in this country, particularly those in New England, were "extremely conscientious and upright in all of their dealing with the natives, and humane in their treatment of them." The Indians' "decay and ruin" was therefore, the reviewer concluded, a result of "their own mode of life, and not to injustice and rapacity in those who knew better than they how to improve the bounties of providence."[60] Such analyses straddled Federalist and Whig views of the past, present, and future of Indians in the region.

But the shift in how Indians and New England's colonial past were viewed was already under way, driven by the blossoming of literature that often included the romantic image of the Noble Indian, which became an archetype in 1826 with James Fenimore Cooper's *Last of the Mohicans.* This paradigm was first applied to a historic Indian by Washington Irving, generally regarded as America's first homegrown literary talent. His "Philip of Pokanoket," published in the *Analectic Magazine* in 1814 and then in the *Sketchbook* collection (1819), recast Metacom as "a true born prince, gallantly fighting . . . to deliver his native land from the oppression of usurping strangers." Philip, even while a warrior involved in "constant warfare," was "alive to the softer feelings of connubial love and paternal tenderness, and to the generous sentiment of friendship." The Native patriot's story, Irving felt, was "worthy of an age of poetry, and fit subjects for local story and romantic fiction."[61]

Others clearly felt the same way. *Yamoyden: A Tale of the War of King Philip,* an ode published by James Eastburn and Robert Charles Sands in 1820, presented not only a startlingly sympathetic depiction of a noble Indian marrying an Anglo-American heroine but also a fiercely revisionist view of King Philip's War, casting the Natives as suffering "foul oppressions" from Puritans who reeked of "soulless bigotry" and "avarice." A few years later, Lydia Maria Francis of Boston read a review of *Yamoyden* and wrote *Hobomok,* which in 1824 became a best seller and launched her literary career—a career that would soon send her, as Lydia Maria

Child, into abolitionist politics. Although her Indians were noble and virtuous, and her (English) heroine's father and friends severe, dour Puritans, Francis refused to denounce their treatment of the Natives. *Hobomok* instead revolves around the marriage of an Indian sachem with a colonial girl and ends—after the sachem leaves the girl to her "proper" English suitor—with the mixed son attending Harvard and forgetting his father's heritage. This ending reflected a common prescription of how to civilize Indians, and the more general Whig willingness to consider racial intermarriage as the best means for their survival.[62]

The emerging mythology of New England's Noble Savage, increasingly represented by descriptions of Philip, inevitably included the older trope of the "vanishing Indian" tragically doomed by a stronger (if not better) civilization. By 1825, this sentimental image was so firmly ensconced that the famed orator Charles Sprague could feature it in his Fourth of July speech in Boston. After an extensive discussion of the need to remember and celebrate American independence, Sprague told his audience that they also needed to remember the Natives who were once here. After describing their wigwams and noble, savage nature, he reflected on how

> Two hundred years have changed the character of a great continent, and blotted forever from its face, a whole, peculiar people . . . Here and there, a stricken few remain, but how unlike their bold, untamed, untamable progenitors. *The Indian*, of falcon glance, and lion bearing, the theme of the touching ballad, the hero of the pathetic tale, is gone! and his degraded offspring crawl upon the soil where he walked in majesty, to remind *us* how miserable is man, when the foot of the conqueror is on his neck. As a race, they have withered from the land . . . their war cry is fast dying away to the untrodden west. Slowly and sadly they climb the distant mountains, and read their doom in the setting sun. They are shrinking before the mighty tide which is pressing them away; they must soon hear the roar of the last wave, which will settle over them forever.[63]

Similarly, Catherine Maria Sedgwick's celebrated romance, *Hope Leslie* (1827), set in New England during the Pequot War, depicted Indians sympathetically but as inevitably doomed and resigned to their fate.[64] This "vanishing Indian" trope would become an integral part of how town histories published in the mid- to late nineteenth century, described below, related the fate of Indians locally and regionally.

Sarah Savage's *Life of Philip* (1827) followed the Noble Savage motif but moved it in an explicitly political direction by using it to condemn the emerging U.S. Indian policy of forcing tribes to move west of the Mississippi River. Her sentimentalist novel, written for children as well as adults, was structured as a discussion between a mother and her son, Charles. When Charles confesses that he had perceived Indians "as a race of cruel, revengeful savages," Mother tells him, "You have not placed yourself in their situation, you have not entered into their feelings, trials, griefs and privations." Mother then goes on to relate the history of the encounters between Puritans and Indians, declaring that Massasoit's welcome of the Pilgrims demonstrated that "hospitality is one of the most prominent Indian characteristics," even as Metacom's attacks on the English showed that Indians lacked the virtues of forgiveness and integrity. Still, Mother celebrates Metacom as "a penetrating statesman, a great warrior, a noble, disinterested, self-denying patriot." While she calls the "revered" Puritans' intentions "just, and even kind," she condemns contemporary U.S. Indian policies, telling her son, "There seems now no possible excuse for advancing upon Indian lands. We are great, powerful, and rich."[65]

Some of the more imaginative reformers even returned to the old idea that Native Americans were the survivors of the Lost Ten Tribes of Israel. Sarah Huntington, who taught and preached among the Mohegans in the 1830s, wrote in her diary that "I felt a strong conviction that the Indians are really Israelites" and that she feared what God would do to America if the Indians being forced west of the Mississippi were in truth the lost tribes of Israel. New England Indians found this conceit appealing, even useful, in their efforts to gain respectability. William Apess wrote, in his 1829 autobiography, *A Son of the Forest*, that his brethren were "none other than the descendants of Jacob and the long lost tribes of Israel." To support his case, Apess described similarities in language, customs, and appearances and cited a range of authorities from William Penn to the Cherokee writer and leader Elias Boudinot. Two years later, he published a sermon that proudly confirmed that his race is "no other than the descendants of the ten lost tribes" but mourned that they were "melting away like dewdrops in the morning's sun."[66]

The state public school systems created in southern New England by the early 1830s provided a rapidly expanding market for children's books on regional and national history and geography, books that featured the new sentimental images of Indians. Samuel Goodrich was among the earliest publishers of public school textbooks, and his first, *The Tales of Peter Palfrey about America* (1827), tells America's history through the eyes of an eponymous character growing up in Boston in the mid-eighteenth century. New England's Natives were his first focus. "When I was a boy," Palfrey begins, "there were a great many [Indians] who lived at no great distance from Boston." He then launches into a long story about how, when he was 12, the Indian chief Wampum, a friend of his father, took him to stay with his family in western Massachusetts. Wampum showed him the Connecticut River and told him wistfully, "That valley, which now belongs to white men, then belonged to the red men. Then the red men were rich and happy; now they are poor and wretched." His grandfather's people welcomed the first white men but then the whites "grew strong, and drove the red men back into the woods. They killed the children of the red men, they shot their wives, they burned their wigwams, and they took away their lands."[67]

These stories were followed by others, often designed for the growing market for children's textbooks and gift books but also intended for adult audiences. In November 1828, four years after *Hobomok*, two years after *Last of the Mohicans*, and a few weeks after Andrew Jackson's election as the seventh U.S. president, the already-famous American actor Edwin Forrest announced that he would give a prize to the best play utilizing a Native American hero. The result, written by John Stone, was *Metamora, or the Last of the Wampanoags*. Beginning with the first performance by Forrest at New York City's Park Theatre on 15 December 1829, *Metamora* became a national passion, as "audiences wept over the hopeless cause of the freedom-loving Philip as he tried in vain to defend his homeland against the hostile New Englanders." Like others, Stone and Forrest made Philip their hero while maintaining the paradigm of the inevitably vanishing Indian.[68]

The emerging image of heroic Indians and intolerant Puritan settlers became a means to criticize Indian removal as New England reformers mobilized newspapers, speakers, and children in opposition to the efforts of Georgia and its southern allies to force the Cherokees to move west. Lydia Marie Child's didactic *First Settlers of New England* (1829) followed Savage's sentimentalist format of a discussion between a mother and child but went further than either Savage's work or her own *Hobomok* in challenging New England mythology. When daughter Elizabeth asks, "Is it not generally believed, mother, that the Indians are a vagrant, idle race, who have no settled place of abode," Mother replies, "The Indians have been strangely misrepresented, either through ignorance or design, or both . . . the first settlers appear to have fostered a moral aversion to the Indians, whom they had barbarously destroyed." After savaging Puritans as intolerant hypocrites, she comments that the marriage of Indians and English would have helped both peoples, with the Indians' "primitive simplicity, hospitality, and generosity" softening the Puritans' "stern and morose feelings" and the former gaining "new light and vigour" from "our arts and sciences." Mother goes on to explain Metacom's nobility before concluding with the trope of the vanishing Indian.[69] In her introduction, Child tells her readers her purpose is to show that this treatment of Indians "has been, and continues to be, in direct violation of [our] religious and civil institutions" and will inevitably doom America "to the calamitous reverses which have fallen on other nations."[70]

Newspapers and writers in New England associated with the Democratic Party vigorously defended President Jackson's policies including Indian removal. In June 1833, the *Barnstable Patriot*, an enthusiastic supporter of Jackson's policies and workingmen's parties, commented that the recent arrival of Pequot (Methodist) preacher William Apess would make the Mashpees "ten times more turbulent[,] uncomfortable, unmanageable and unhappy than they now are . . . if the style of this 'prophets' preaching to the heterogeneous population of Marshpee is what we learn it is, we hope a little of the spirit shown by the authorities of Georgia in a somewhat similar instance will be exercised towards him." The paper also cried betrayal when Benjamin Hallet, leader of the state anti-Masonic party and Democratic activist, represented the Mashpees in their effort to gain autonomy and defended Apess against local charges of disorderly conduct.[71]

But the *Patriot* reflected local prejudices about the Mashpees more than partisan politics, as shown by their support for the Whig governor's effort to settle the Mashpee crisis and their later reporting of the tribe's victory in an objective, dispassionate manner.[72] More generally, Massachusetts Democrats gleefully echoed Apess and Hallet when they accused opponents of Georgia's Cherokee policy of being hypocrites for denying the Mashpees the same autonomy desired for the Cherokees. *The Old Colony Democrat* of Plymouth proclaimed that the Mashpees' "title to independence of the control of this State is far more valid than any ever urged in favor of an independent government of the Southern Indians. We wonder whether those people who strove to induce our Government to uphold the Southern tribes in their attempts to erect independent nations in the heart of other States, despite the solemn pledge of this nation, guaranteeing to those States sole control of all the territory within their limits, will act consistently in this case?"[73]

The Democratic Party was becoming notorious for its racism, and the hints of bigotry in the *Patriot* article about Apess and the Mashpees were more apparent in a few other pieces in that paper. In May 1832, the *Patriot* reported on a verdict by a Massachusetts Supreme Judicial Court, in which seaman Matthias Smith sued Uriah Clark, chief mate of the *Uncas* of Falmouth, for excessive abuse. The report called Clark's actions "an *unjustifiable* abuse . . . not only the filling of [Smith's] mouth with tar and beating him with a rope's end . . . but to order *an Indian* to apply the end of a rope, as Clark did at that time, is beyond endurance."[74] In July 1833, the *Patriot* refused to print the Mashpees' manifesto demanding autonomy and mocked its grammar and spelling, telling the writer, "if

he sends us any 'more hereafter' to send an interpreter with it." The paper continued to attack Apess: seven months later, reporting on the Mashpee delegation
in Boston, it denounced "his ribaldry, misrepresentation and nonsense" and told
its readers that the tribe had been "quiet and peaceable" until "this intruder, this
disturber, this riotous and mischief-making Indian, from the Pequot tribe . . .
[had] stir[red] them up to sedition, riot, *treason!*"[75]

While such language might be viewed as mirroring the prejudice common
among Democratic politicians and voters, the relatively few articles printed in the
Patriot and the *Old Colony Democrat* about New England Indians (the majority
of which were on the Mashpees) were paternalistic rather than vicious. Before
making fun of the Mashpee manifesto, the *Patriot* reported on the recent revolt
and remarked, "If they have been wronged let not justice be longer withheld from
them. They are a jealous people, and all causes of excitement should be cautiously
removed from among them. Many of them are intelligent, and if they are not governed with economy and prudence they can quickly detect such failings." While
denouncing Apess and noting that the tribe had been perfectly happy before the
"wily, unprincipled Indian" had misled them, the paper also told its readers that
the Mashpees were "mentally, morally, and pecuniarily improving."[76] A month
and a half later, the *Patriot* reprinted a joke that was directed more at pompous
authority than Indians.

> John Sequashequash, an Indian of one of the remnants of a tribe, in Connecticut,
> was some years since, brought before a Justice of Peace on some charge or other,
> which we do not now recollect. John happened to be pretty drunk at the time, and
> instead of answering directly to the questions put by the Justice, merely mattered
> out—"Your Honor is very wise—very wise—y-y-your honor is v-very wise." The Jus-
> tice had him locked up for the night until sober, then questioned him again, in-
> forming him that he had been "drunk as a beast" and could only answer that "Your
> Honor's very wise." "Did I call your Honor wise!" said the Indian, with a look of in-
> credulity. "Yes," answered the magistrate. "Then," replied John, "I must have been
> drunk, true enough."[77]

New England Democrats also seemed to share the Whig reformers' new vision
of New England's history with its startlingly revisionist depiction of Indians. The
Old Colony Democrat praising Metacom's "pure and elevated patriotism," mused,
"There is a kind of grandeur in the character of the Indian warrior which fills the
mind of the beholder with admiration. We here see man in his native, untamed,
undegenerate supremacy . . . Such was Philip, the hero of Mt. Hope." This agreement between anti-Jacksonian novelists and Democratic newspapers highlights

how the new view of New England's colonial past had quickly become the dominant paradigm in the region.[78]

The efforts by many New England writers, ministers, and politicians against Jackson's removal policy may have been in vain, but they were important in forging the Whig Party.[79] They also drove a growing interest in New England's Indians and Indian history. A young John W. Deforest published in 1851 a volume completely dedicated to the *History of the Indians of Connecticut*, which not only recounted the colonial conflicts between Pequots, Mohegans, and colonists but also included reports from current guardians on the remaining Native communities. Deforest's *History* features a fairly objective history of Indian groups throughout the state that is still useful to modern scholars but at the same time is deeply immersed in contemporary perceptions of Indians in the region, including the drunken "do-nothing," the savvy woodsmen, the wandering basket peddlers, and the reformed, poor-but-virtuous subsistence farmer or whaler. These images were derived from the two Indian archetypes: the lazy, threatening barbarian and the Noble Savage, both of whom tended to drink too much liquor. These images were among the earliest products of the colonial period, and through the spate of antebellum publications on New England history became deeply woven into the region's mythology even before Francis Parkman's more famous works.[80]

LOCAL HISTORIES

The literary and political discourse over Indians helped New Englanders develop a sense of their region as unique in its history and characteristics. Part of this discourse was an outpouring at midcentury of county and town histories that usually contained folklore and personal reminiscences, descriptions of important families and landmarks, details on commerce and industries, and summaries of local records. In addition to building a regional mythology and identity, such histories were written in large part for the descendants of the original founders and others forced by shifts in the economy to move elsewhere, and who now wanted somehow to renew their spiritual ties with an idealized past. Some of the volumes included stories of the town's "last Indians," which inevitably followed the Vanishing Indian trope.

The origins of the New England town history may lie in Peter Whitney's *History of the County of Worcester* (1793) or A *Gazetteer of the States of Connecticut and Rhode Island* (1819), which may have been inspired by a series of questionnaires sent in 1800 by the Connecticut Academy of Arts and Sciences to towns in that state. While Belknap's *History of New Hampshire* (1784–1793) presented a secular political history of the state, and the third volume included some statistics on towns along with details on flora and fauna, both Whitney's *History* and the *Gazetteer* featured a historical and anecdotal details on individual towns, including colorful descriptions of colonial relations with Indians as well as biographies of local heroes. The authors also briefly depicted the surviving Indian groups—Mohegans, Pequots, and Narragansetts—when covering the town in which their reserves were located.[81]

More evocative and inspirational was Lydia Howard Sigourney's 1824 barely fictional account of Norwich, *Sketch of Connecticut.* Sigourney (1784–1865) operated a highly regarded girl's school that nurtured many prominent reformers including Sarah Huntington. Her *Sketch of Connecticut* is set in 1784 and features her childhood reminisces of the town, including depictions of individuals and circumstances based on documents and oral history, with an extended and sympathetic portrait of the Mohegans. Sigourney begins by describing how the "once powerful tribe" had become "diminished in numbers, and oppressed by a sense of degradation." She depicts the Mohegans as caught between their savage (but noble) nature and the progressive (but aggressive) Anglo-American culture. As a result, "the survivors exhibited the melancholy remnant of a fallen race, like the almost extinguished embers of a flame, once terrible in wildness." Although a few continued to display "gleams of brightness," most were haunted by "intemperance, indolence," and "the contempt of others." She goes on to describe, with substantive detail, Mohegan leaders (all *men*) from Uncas to John Cooper and Zachary Johnson. Cooper was "a patient, and comparatively skilfull agriculturalist," whose "untutored mind also found the connection, which has been thought to exist between agriculture and natural religion." Johnson was "Arrowhamet the warrior . . . Tall, erect and muscular," who had served in both the Seven Years and Revolutionary Wars. The Mohegans still lived in Sigourney's Norwich, and a few were notable for their "wild" virtues, but she clearly felt that the survivors were remnants of a vanishing culture and tribe.[82]

In the wake of the *Gazetteer* and Sigourney's book came a growing tide of articles and books on New England towns and counties, which generally reflected a Whig vision of the region's past and present. For example, John Barber's very popular books on Connecticut and Massachusetts, published in 1836 and 1839 and reprinted many times through the late twentieth century, expanded on the *Gazetteer* when describing the histories and highlights of each town, and provided more of a pastoral vision of the region. His books also added illustrations of steepled churches and neat town greens (products of the early nineteenth century rather than the "messy" colonial period), historic homes (including Samson Occom's), and the orderly farms of middle-class Yankee yeomen. When describing Gay Head, he emphasized that their ministers had recently helped improve the morals and temperance of that community, and on the Mohegans quoted their teacher that "of late there is a change for the better, a number of reformations having taken place." Barber's encyclopedias of towns in the two states were very popular, but his style and viewpoint became part of the more focused town and county histories that often featured narratives of Indians who had lived in the area.[83]

Descriptions of Indians in this regional literature initially tended to highlight their "wretched" living conditions (particularly itinerancy) and "dissolute" habits, including the abuse of alcohol and informal, interracial sex. Such descriptions, as in Joseph Allen's 1827 "Historical Account of Northborough," typically complained that the Indians were "troublesome to their neighbors," much as the judge had observed in the 1813 Stoneham murder trial. In his 1830 *History of the Town of Natick*, William Bigelow noted that Hannah Dexter, the last "real" Indian in John Eliot's first praying town, had died a few years previous, trying to stop a riot in her house instigated by "a set of unwelcome visitants, chiefly of a mixed breed of English, Indian, and African blood"—visitors who included some of her kin. Nine years later, *Niles' National Register*, in reporting the death of the last Montauk sachem and his wife, "burned to death in their wigwam," added that the tribe had "long since dwindled to a few basket making miserable half-breeds." In 1849, activist Frances Caulkins, author of *A History of Norwich* (1845 and 1866) and *A History of New London* (1852 and 1866), who considered writing a history of Indians in the region, contemptuously called the nearby Mashantucket Pequots "stupid, lazy, [and] drunken."[84]

But even descriptions of itinerant, alcoholic, and "mixed" Indians increasingly exhibited the influence of Whiggish sentimentalism and affection for the past, as can be seen in various descriptions of Hannah Shiner (ca. 1738–1820) and Deb Saco (ca. 1759–1839), who were friends and traveled together north of Boston. In 1855, Charles Brooks of Medford wrote that Shiner was the last "full blooded" Indian in town, "kind-hearted, a faithful friend, a sharp enemy, a judge of herbs, a weaver of baskets, and a lover of rum," and that Saco "was another specimen that many remembered." Another historian from neighboring Winchester remembered Shiner living as a "solitary waif" on the edge of a swamp "where she made baskets and 'Indian trinkets' for sale, when not employed among the families in mending chair-bottoms, or other services . . . traveling about with a little dog, which, when she called at a house, she was accustomed to hide under her skirts, in a manner very amusing to the children.[85] A writer from Malden repeated Brooks's description of Shiner, adding details about her death (blown off a bridge in a storm and drowned in Woburn's Abajona River), and also recalled Saco, who died in the town's poorhouse. "Whether she was a negro or an Indian, I cannot say. Those who remember her are divided as to that matter . . . She was a tramp, or, in the speech of that day, a 'walk-about,' ranging the country from Salem to Cambridge. She would disappear for months, returning suddenly, as eager to tell fortunes, as dirty, and as fond of rum as ever."[86]

Farther west, Harriett Merrifield Forbes, in her history of Westborough, Massachusetts, *The Hundredth Town*, described in affectionate detail various Nipmucs who lived around the town around 1800. Typical was her depiction of Simon Gigger and Bets Hendricks, who, despite fearsome quarrels, "used to wander around together, she carrying a load of baskets, which they sold at the farm-houses, he, the violin. They often found work in rebottoming the chair, and when the work was done, and the bread and cider disposed of, Gigger or Bets would delight the children by getting what music they could from the old fiddle."[87] Such depictions painted a portrait of how Indians were compelled by Nature (i.e., race) to revert occasionally to their primitive virtues. A more famous New England historian, Alice Earle, in her *Stage-coach and Tavern Days* (1900) described Deborah Brown in the first half of the century as living a "respectable life all winter, ever ready to help in the kitchen of the tavern" where she lived and worked. "But when early autumn tinged the trees, and on came the hunting season, she tore off her respectable calico gown and apron, kicked off her shoes and stockings, and with black hair hanging wild, donned moccasins and blanket, and literally fled to the woods for a breath of life, for freedom. She took her flitting unseen in the night, but twice was she noted many miles away by folk her knew her. Tramping steadily northward, bearing by a metomp [strap] of bark around her forehead a heavy burden in a blanket."[88]

The stories of the "last Indian" in these town histories generally drew on the archetype of the Noble Savage. In 1835, the orator celebrating the centennial of Grafton, formerly Hassanamisco, described how the "last of the Nipmucks . . . usually had a joyous holiday" when given their annual stipend before the last one (supposedly) died in the 1820s. In nearby Paxton, Aaron Occom was "a temperate and peaceful man and came to be respected and was a frequent visitor during the long winter evenings, at the dwellings of his neighbors, whom, in broken English, he would entertain by his wonderful stories of his ancestors and their exploits." He made and sold brooms and baskets "in which arts he was a master, and his wares found ready sale in the vicinity." Similarly, historians of Derby, Connecticut, remembered (as one of the last Paugussets) Molly Hatchet, who died in January 1829, aged nearly 100. "She was a wanderer upon the earth, but wherever she went she always found a hearty welcome, and was never turned away with an empty basket. She was a favorite among the people, and was looked upon with sad sympathy. The children in the streets flocked to meet her, and the old folks always paid her deference." Perhaps the most famous "last Indian" in New England was Abram Quary of Nantucket, who died in December 1854. A decade later, one writer noted, "Our islanders well remember the spare form and aboriginal features of the last of the red men. Dwelling like a hermit alone at his home, which commanded a full view of the spacious harbor and thriving town, for years he was the solitary relic of a once-powerful people. Those peculiar traits of the sons of the forest, quick observation, strong prejudices, imperturbable secretiveness, were noticeable in Abram Quary's character."[89]

A common element in these stories was the notion of the inevitably vanishing Indian: that, as *Williard's History of Greenfield* (1838) put it, "from the first settlement of the whites among them, [Indians] have constantly been dwindling in numbers . . . the time is now rapidly approaching when the race shall be utterly extinct and annihilated." These narratives depicted an inevitable though (for some) unfortunate conquest of "primitive sons of the forest . . . their posterity forced to recede rapidly before a civilized people."[90] *Nonantum and Natick* (1855), a history of the "Praying Town" that included current information on Indians in the area and a beautiful woodcut of a small band of Indian basket peddlers (figure 7), closed with a maudlin poem:

In the gay and noisy street
Of the great city, which usurps the place
Of the small Indian village, one shall see
Some miserable relic of that race,
Whose sorely-tarnished fortunes we have sung;
Yet how debased and fallen! In his eye
The flame of noble daring is gone out,
And his brave face has lost its martial look.
His eye rests on the earth, as if the grave
Were his sole hope, his last and only home.[91]

Similar sentimental poetry and prose about the poor vanishing Indian appeared in many southern New England town histories.[92] The same image could be used by Indians and state officials: the Mohegans told the general assembly in 1827 that they should be allowed to keep all of their reserve for now because they would soon be extinct anyway, and an assembly committee reported a quarter-century later that the Pequots would soon disappear.[93]

XXII.

TO-DAY.

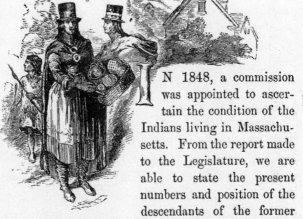

IN 1848, a commission was appointed to ascertain the condition of the Indians living in Massachusetts. From the report made to the Legislature, we are able to state the present numbers and position of the descendants of the former sovereigns of the soil. They may all be counted now, the few in whose veins flows the blood of Samoset and of Massasoit. The whole number, in 1848, was eight hundred and forty-seven; of whom only six or eight, at most, were of pure Indian descent, the red men for several generations having intermarried with the blacks.

The most flourishing community now within our limits,

Figure 7. Indian basket peddlers, in Sarah S. Jacobs, *Nonantum and Natick* (Boston: Massachusetts Sabbath School Society, 1853).

Some saw such sad inevitability as a source of sentimental contemplation. In 1842, for example, *Niles' National Register* depicted the death of "The Last of the Mohegans" (John Uncas) as both inevitable and transcendent in meaning. "The passing away of a whole tribe of men, once the free, dauntless lords of the soil, is certainly well calculated to awaken sensibility; and the contemplation of the oppression and wrongs under which they have dwindled away, and finally perished, naturally excites painful emotions. But their decay is the natural, inevitable result of the progress of society." In his 1855 Dorchester speech, famed orator Edward Everett related a childhood memory "of one poor solitary Indian, who, it was said, occupied a lonely wigwam on Stoughton Pond, and who used to come down, once or twice a year, to the seaside, hovered a day or two around Squantum; caught a few fish at the lower mills; stroll off into the woods, and with plaintive wailings cut away the bushes from an ancient mound, which, as he thought, covered the ashes of his fathers; and then went back, a silent, melancholy man,—the last of a perished race." This vanishing Indian made a superb Noble Savage, with an innate connection to Nature, an impassive appearance, and a childlike innocence, which provided useful moral lessons in the rapidly urbanizing and industrializing culture without threatening Anglo-American security.[94]

These images were not complete fabrications. Like others mired in poverty, unemployment, discrimination, and the disorienting and alienating changes of the early industrial era, many Indians became alcoholics, committed petty crimes, became involved in violence, and traveled the countryside looking for a way to support themselves and their families. As detailed in chapter 4, many Indians used pieces of their past and their present public culture in order to survive: making baskets and other crafts, working as whalers and in circuses, and peddling medicines. Tribes exhibited little entrepreneurial spirit as they maintained their resources in common against outsiders and provided women more power than allowed in the outside world.

But this was not the entire story at midcentury. Mashpees, Gay Headers, and Narragansetts marketed resources and their talents. Indians and their descendants also worked as barbers, boot makers, stonemasons, miners, and in other semi-skilled occupations. One town history called the (supposedly) last Mattakeesit in Scituate "a bright and enterprising man." A Medfield history recorded that the last Indian in the town was Lucy Bran, who "occupied much of her time in weaving homespun cloth; she seems to have supported herself by her own industry, and to have lived a respected life" until she died in 1835. Letters from town clerks and state-appointed guardians described some Indian descendants living in poverty and dissolution and others "industrious and steady in their habits." More amusing to the modern reader is how many Indians described as the last ones in town were also noted as having children and even grandchildren.[95]

Europeans and colonists used Natives to comment on contemporary social issues, and some New Englanders continued this tradition. Henry David Thoreau described Indian survivors in part to censor his neighbors' acquisitive and industrious values. In July 1850, he wrote that in various places could be found "an Indian squaw . . . in some lone house, insulted by school-children, making baskets and picking berries her employment . . . with melancholy face, history, destiny; stepping after her race; who had stayed to tuck them up in their long sleep . . . Not yet absorbed into the elements again; a daughter of the soil; one of the nobility of the land. The white man an imported weed,—burdock and mullein, which displace the ground nut." A few months later, he recorded that "a squaw came to our door to-day with two papooses, and said, 'Me want a pie.' Theirs is not common begging. You are merely the rich Indian who shares his goods with the poor. They merely offer you an opportunity be generous and hospitable." In 1856, he visited Martha Simons near New Bedford, supposedly the "last of her race . . . the solitary specimen of a full-blooded native," who also drew the attention of painter Albert Bierstadt, and noted her "peculiarly vacant expression, perhaps characteristic of the Indian" (figure 8). Such encounters convinced even Thoreau that Indians were "inevitably and resignedly passing away" because of their "fixed habits of stagnation."[96]

The trope of the vanishing Indian, like literary discourse about King Philip, became a tool for New Englanders to revise their history. A Norton (Bristol County) antiquarian mourned in 1859 that many local Indians had ended up as slaves "cruelly deprived of their possessions, and crushed to the dust beneath the avarice of those calling themselves *Christians." Willard's History of Greenfield* (1838) condemned colonists and Natives, for whites committed "fraud and imposition" on the Indians, while the Natives living near whites became "more vicious and corrupt," lost their savage nobility, and would soon be "utterly extinct and annihilated." Some found the increasingly fashionable regret for the Noble Savage absurd. In 1831, a Scituate historian wrote, "It has been very common for people to lament over the fallen fortunes of the Natives of these shores, and to criminate the forefathers for driving them from their wonted forests . . . we believe these to be the cant of very superficial readers and reasoners, and certainly without the least truth or pertinency so far as respects Plymouth Colony"—which included Scituate. Francis Caulkins wrote in 1866 that the Indian who met the colonist "was a heathen of the most untameable species . . . Vagrancy was his nature and his habit, and he was moreover deceitful and thievish beyond remedy." But regardless of whether New Englanders praised the Indians or the colonists, they agreed with the Malden historian who concluded that the Natives "were in the way of civilization, and, opposing it, they were doomed as surely as the wild beasts that infested the forests and have disappeared with them."[97]

What these descriptions of Indians reveal, as starkly as any facts about particular individuals or communities, are the *writers'* concerns and perceptions. Changes and continuities in those descriptions illuminate shifts in the culture of southern New England. Some things remained constant: anxieties about lawlessness, itinerancy, and lack of social controls. Other concerns changed as the Federalist fo-

Figure 8. Albert Bierstadt, "Last of the Narragansetts" [Martha Simons], 1859, Courtesy Millicent Library, Fairhaven, Mass.

cus on hierarchy and Calvinistic acceptance of the inevitability of sin and the folk culture of the lower sort shifted to the Whig and middle-class focus on individual redemption and improvement regardless of social rank. Whig reformers were willing to challenge the past in order to construct a more perfect future even as they celebrated sanctified forefathers. In these ways, the images of surviving Indians in southern New England highlight significant shifts in southern New England's culture by the middle of the nineteenth century.

One striking aspect of these works is that women wrote so many, at a time when American women were just beginning to publish. Some of these individuals were quite prominent during their lifetimes, becoming as well, or better, known for their efforts at social reform—temperance, abolitionism, women's rights—as for literature. Lydia Sigourney, one of the first American women to make a living by writing, was at the center of a large network of New England women who went to her Norwich school and, like Sarah Huntington (who consulted with her while working with the Mohegans), became involved in various reform movements. She wrote novels, poetry, and histories that included descriptions of Indians in the region, past and present—like one of her first students, Francis Caulkins. Sigourney and other prominent women writers, including Catharine Maria Sedgwick, Sarah Savage, and Lydia Maria Child, corresponded and wrote for each other's publications, including the latter's *Juvenile Miscellany*.[98]

The vanishing Indian trope that appeared in so many of these writings rested in large part on hardening notions of race. Anglo-Americans began focusing on race during the early republic, with reports from Hawley, Belknap, Morse, and others emphasizing how Indians were frequently marrying blacks and occasionally whites, and how their descendants were no longer truly Indian. Those concerns hardened and became systematized after 1810 in scientific racism. Reports on Indians during the Whig era often carefully recorded the blood quantum of each adult and almost always emphasized that few real Indians remained. Such concept were reinforced by the growing body of literature in books, magazines, and newspapers, on Natives west of the Ohio and Mississippi Rivers, which described physiques and cultures that were clearly bracingly barbaric, primitive, noble, and quite different from those of the Indians who survived in southern New England.

This increased focus on race in the vanishing Indian paradigm had substantive and harmful results for Native groups after midcentury as state policy makers began calling for an end to discriminatory state laws. In 1869, the governor of Massachusetts called for the state's Indians to be "merged in the general community." Any concerns about the obligations owed those who greeted the English colonists could be dismissed, for they "are not Indians in any sense of the word. It is doubt-ful if there is a pure blooded Indian in the State." Decades later, Mary Vander-hoop, a Gay Head writer, remembered the governor's words and angrily replied that while the descendants of mixed marriages—including herself—may look white or Negro, "the inner self, the ego, the soul, the mind, the living principle, is wholly and always and forever—Indian."[99]

CHAPTER SIX

Citizenship and Termination

On October 9, 1866, the Narragansetts met a joint legislative committee at the Ocean House in Charlestown. Its chairman told the tribe that the state was considering terminating their separate legal status and giving them full citizenship. The nation was moving toward civil equality for all men regardless of race or color, he noted, as exemplified by Congress's recent passage of the Civil Rights Act. In addition, the legislature was concerned that the Narragansetts "should still claim to owe allegiance to their tribe, rather than to the State" and thought that "there ought to be no privileged class" in Rhode Island. The tribe was outraged by the suggestions. Though they had heard much about "negro citizenship and negro equality," they had not found that such equality or rights existed anywhere. "We are not negroes; we are the heirs of Ninigret, and of the great chiefs of and warriors of the Narragansetts," they told the officials, and "we are entitled to the rights and privileges guaranteed by your ancestors to ours by solemn treaty." Now their "grasping neighbors, of a grasping race" were conspiring to take what remained of the tribe's territory. Their individual allotments were mostly held by women, and termination would endanger their estates by forcing them to pay taxes and making them liable for debts. They did not want the right to vote and denied the legislature's right to take "that which never came from you."[1]

Between 1860 and 1880, inspired by a strange mixture of racism and egalitarianism, the three southern New England states ended the special legal status of nearly all Indians.[2] The change developed gradually during the second quarter of the century, as a few groups had their lands allotted and legislatures became increasingly willing to allow emigrants to sell reserved land. But in 1859, Massachusetts pledged to make Indians full citizens, and over the following decade worked to implement that goal, ending in 1870 with complete termination of all tribes and the division of remaining reserves. Connecticut moved during the same decade to terminate the Niantics and the Mohegans—by far the largest tribe in the state—but left the other groups, probably because they were all very small and managed by county courts. Rhode Island did modify the Narragansetts' legal status after the 1866 hearing, turning the tribe into a corporation very much like modern Alaskan Native tribes, while continuing to protect the reserve from sale to outsiders. Fourteen years later, the state took a more dramatic step, quickly terminating the large tribe and auctioning its reservation to the public.

While these laws reflected New England attitudes and state policies, they were also part of the national movement to eliminate Indian tribes and assimilate Native peoples. The shift in how Indians were perceived and treated was reflected in the instructions for the 1870 U.S. census, as census takers were told to include "Indians out of their tribal relations, and exercising the rights of citizens under State or Territorial laws," and if living in a distinct neighborhood to make a special report on the group.[3] The movement climaxed with the 1887 Dawes Act, named for its chief sponsor, Massachusetts senator Henry Dawes, which called for Indian agents to allot tribal lands throughout the nation, assign 160 acres to each adult member of the tribe and 80 to each child, sell the "surplus" at auction, end the legal existence of a tribe when all of its lands were allotted, and after a 25-year trust period end all federal oversight over Indian lands. But the laws passed by southern New England states actually resembled more the federal policy of termination in the 1950s, in which tribes were summarily extinguished and their resources divided or privatized with a minimum future role for government oversight.[4]

When termination and citizenship were suggested to several larger tribes before the Civil War, they were nearly unanimous in their opposition; the occasional lone voice calling for the change was quickly stilled. However, the war and Reconstruction emboldened those who sought change and apparently weakened the ability of elders to control dissent. When state commissions came to the same tribes after the war with the clear intention to end legal distinctions, they were drawn in part by petitions asking for changes and, once there, found a few strong voices speaking for full citizenship, particularly African American men. The Narragansett women who feared for their informal allotments also accused members of their tribal council of involvement in the legislature's initiative, and it was indeed a petition from the tribal council that would trigger termination in 1880. But the elders and most members remained opposed, sometimes unequivocally, other times carefully pleading for more time and assistance in preparing for such a huge change. They expressed little interest in voting or other benefits of citizenship and feared that this alteration in their legal status would result in the rapid loss of their lands along with impoverishment and the destruction of their community and way of life. In some tribes, the threat exposed conflicts between newcomers and native-born, generally expressed in terms of gender and occasionally race. Once the dreaded laws passed, some tribes sought to safeguard their collective history by ensuring that their graveyards or sacred places were set aside and marked. Gay Head and Mashpee were able to retain self-government and autonomy under the new rules, while the Narragansetts and Mohegans managed to maintain strong social networks. But other groups were submerged when they lost their lands and separate legal status.

RACE AND CIVIL RIGHTS

Southern New England tribes faced many threats to their corporate existence from English colonization, beginning with the Pequots officially extinguished by the 1638 Treaty of Hartford. But those that survived King Philip's War retained a diminutive, but still potent, legal status that, while shifting over time and between states, kept their inhabitants separate from the Anglo-American civil and political systems. The emerging crack in this structure, however, was identified in 1815 by a correspondent in the *North American Review* who urged abolishing Mashpee because "it is surely time that the State should cease to maintain a depot for vagabonds of all colours; from all parts of the country; or keep up an establishment for producing every possible variety of *cross*, between Indians and Negroes." New notions of race and the growing tide of racism undermined the ability of Indians to remain apart. In 1820, Jedidiah Morse reported that the Narragansetts and Mashpees rejected the idea of selling their lands and moving west to Indian Territory, and a year later Frederick Baylies told the Society for Propagating the Gospel (SPG) that the Vineyard Indians were also "totally opposed." In 1831, Daniel King's report on the Narragansetts recommended selling most of the reserve and ending the tribe's separate legal status while protecting lands held by individuals against sale to outsiders. Morse and King both focused on how few pure-blood Indians remained in the communities, and both embraced the paradigm that this racial makeup meant that the groups were no longer truly Indian and therefore should no longer be protected or separated by distinct laws.[5]

Some of the actions taken by state governments and Indians after 1825 could be viewed as laying the foundations for termination. The allotment of lands in Chappaquiddick and Christiantown in 1828, by Mashpee in 1834 and 1842, and in

Herring Pond in 1850 happened for many reasons, but one result was at least the *appearance* that capitalist, individualist values and abilities had emerged in these communities. The notable expansion of Indian schools with state financial support was seen by reformers as the best path toward equality and assimilation. As more Indians left the reservation for opportunities elsewhere, they or their children sought to sell land once farmed by the family. State legislatures became far more likely to approve these petitions after 1840—not with the intention of undermining the Indian community but to fulfill the dictates of liberal capitalism and help individuals gain new opportunities or to avoid poverty. This shift also appeared in an 1837 Massachusetts Superior Court decision that individuals from tribes that had divided communal lands could sell their allotments without legislative approval; the decision also laid down the policy that "the Indian right of occupancy"—which could not be alienated to non-Indians without the legislature's approval—"shall be presumed to have been extinguished, unless the contrary is shown."[6]

Tribal leaders became increasingly concerned about the threat to community and resources posed by this development and by individuals who returned years or even generations after leaving and claimed land. Allotment was one response to this threat. But some saw the threat posed by this change in land management and sought other solutions. In 1859, for example, Gay Head proprietors asked the state to set limitations on how long absentees could claim rights in the tribe. Exogamous marriages also played an important role in the erosion of Indian social and political boundaries, particularly with the evolution of distinct African American values. Indian tribes or villages seem to have become less able to assimilate newcomers as their autonomy and cultural distinctions were worn away by reforms driven by internal needs and external demands. This situation pushed some groups toward allotment and others, like Gay Head, to become more insistent about maintaining distinctions in political and economic privileges between foreigners and Indian newcomers from another tribe. These tensions were exacerbated by midcentury as growing numbers of white elites embraced the idea of civil and political equality for people of color, including Indians.[7]

Racism remained a prominent part of American society and culture. Antiblack violence racked New England cities in the 1820s and 1830s, increasing residential segregation and pressures to keep blacks from skilled work and out of public life; particularly vicious were riots in Providence in October 1824 and 1831. In 1831, when Massachusetts considered striking the ban on intermarriage, Boston newspapers decried the change as "attempting to break down the barriers of nature" and endangering the state's "real Anglo-Saxon blood." Also in 1831, New Haven whites ferociously protested abolitionists' efforts to establish a college for blacks in the town. In 1833 and 1834, citizens of 16 towns in Connecticut fought Prudence Crandall's school for black girls in Canterbury, charging that "the negro and 'his kindred' have ever been blots on the fair face of civilized society, and corroding cancers to a free state." In response the state barred teaching blacks who were not legal inhabitants unless permitted by town authorities. Crandall was arrested and convicted after the judge instructed the jury that blacks were not citizens under the constitution; although her appeal was successful, the school and its students were assaulted, and Crandall closed the school in September 1834.[8]

Such prejudice affected Indians as well as blacks because, as the colonial archetypes of Indians as Satan's spawn faded, whites categorized people of Native ancestry as part of the region's people of color. Even individuals who were clearly Indian faced social and political barriers. In 1824 and 1825, the marriage of two deeply acculturated sons of Cherokee chiefs to the daughters of prominent white families in northwestern Connecticut generated a firestorm of outrage, and in 1832 to be flogged by an Indian sailor was considered "beyond endurance." The *Boston Courier*, commenting on the 1849 Bird report on tribes in Massachusetts, noted that Indians in the state "dislike all connection with the town governments in their neighborhood, and the townspeople equally dislike political connection with the Indians" and that any proposal to "absorb them into the community . . . will find a formidable obstacle in the mutual jealousy existing between the Indians and those with whom they are expected to associate." State reports on Indians in or outside reservations often referred to "people of colour, called Indians," a conflation with substantive effects. In December 1859, the town clerk of Carver, Massachusetts, told Earle that a family in town headed by a negro father and an Indian mother did not enjoy full citizenship because "we believe the constitution of our Federal government does not recognize such persons as citizens of the United States." He could have been referring to either the 1857 *Dred Scott* decision, which held that descendants of slaves could never become citizens, or the status of Indians not taxed, or both.[9]

But northern elites became increasingly committed to civil and political racial equality. More blacks in the region were embracing middle-class values, the growing tide of Irish Catholics seemed a much greater threat, and the increasing controversies over slavery (particularly the 1850 Fugitive Slave Act) turned many New Englanders against racial laws. In 1839, more than 1,300 women from four towns petitioned the Massachusetts legislature to repeal the ban on intermarriage, and four years later the state complied. In Rhode Island, blacks won the right to vote in 1842 by building on their regional alliance with Whigs. In the 1850s and 1860s,

New England railroads and schools were desegregated; even Harvard College and Medical School accepted black students. The eruption of the Civil War intensified the belief that discrimination must be abolished.

From the beginning, African Americans were part of this movement for civic equality; most saw it as their best path to America's socioeconomic mainstream, although some thought black-only schools were preferable, and others began to reconsider moving to Africa when confronted by the still-virulent public opposition to integration. Black leaders also became more confident of their ability to mobilize political and economic power and eagerly sought the right for their people to fight for the Union to end slavery and to solidify and extend their political and civil rights. Their efforts seemed rewarded at the end of the war when Massachusetts made it illegal to discriminate against blacks "in any licensed inn, in any public place of amusement, public conveyance, or public meeting" and barred shows that ridiculed any person "on account of race or color."[10]

Like other men, Indians went to fight for the Union and against slavery. A comprehensive survey of these soldiers would be nearly impossible, given the many generations of exogamous marriages and movement to cities, and because states rather than towns formed units in the national army. Not surprisingly, given the ambiguous racial status of Indians in southern New England, some served in colored regiments while others were put into white units. At least three Mashantucket Pequots enlisted in two Connecticut colored regiments. Several men of Hassanamisco ancestry from Worcester, including Alexander Hemenway, enlisted in the famed 54th Massachusetts colored regiment. Five or six Dudley Nipmucs served in the army; two died in Andersonville prison. Coastal tribes sent more to the navy: from Gay Head three joined the infantry and six served in the navy, and from Mashpee two went to the army and seventeen to the navy.[11]

While some Indian men joined the war, some tribal leaders saw the draft as a threat to the remnants of their sovereignty. On July 25, 1863, Mohegan leader Anson Cooper wrote to the War Department to protest Norwich and Montville officials taking men from the tribe to satisfy those towns' requirements under the new federal draft. Cooper told the War Department (which was also in charge of Indian policy) that he and his tribe have never "been reckoned as citizens of any State or citizens of the United States." They had held and lived on their reservation "in a tribal form for time immemorial" and having never been taxed should be considered a sovereign Indian tribe like any other within the United States. Apparently Cooper's letter was ignored. Three years later, the Narragansetts told a Rhode Island commission that "Your imperious draft cannot touch us now; we may volunteer to fight your battles, but now you cannot force us into the ranks of your army to be shot down without our consent."[12]

Indians feared overly intrusive state governments for good reasons. After 1860, tribes in southern New England were endangered by Anglo-American leaders who embraced free-market egalitarianism and bichromatic racial views. Whites who supported equal rights for blacks felt that *all* people of color should be treated the same way. The ban on Indian land sales to outsiders seemed particularly evil and counterproductive. After the war, a Massachusetts legislative committee concluded that, despite more than a generation of reforms and advances, the existing reservation structure meant that "the enterprise which is pushing the outside world ahead is shut out from the Indian 'plantation'; and thus the Indians are shut in to comparative thriftlessness and decay." A noticeable number of African Americans who had married Indians loudly agreed with the need to "make us men," and their testimony encouraged the reformers. The desire for resources or railroad routes was also a motivation for state politicians. Between 1860 and 1880, all but a few tribes would be terminated.[13]

PROPOSING TERMINATION

Toward the middle of the nineteenth century, northern state governments became far more active in flexing and expanding their powers; this was especially true in southern New England. States became deeply involved in economic development, chartering railroad, factory, and other corporations, and facilitated the taking of private lands for those enterprises. But their primary focus was social reform, creating state-directed, tax-funded systems of education, incarceration, medicine, and other needs. Legislative or executive commissions often investigated, collected, and published information about a particular problem and then proposed a bill to (hopefully) provide a rational solution. One result is that state records and reports became far more detailed and thorough, providing more information for historians and other scholars. But state officials also approached their mission with a set of cultural paradigms that shaped their goals, if not their recommendations. They regarded the inhabitants of the reserves as not really (racially) Indians, who would be better off if their legal "disabilities" as tribal members were terminated and their reserves allotted in severalty.

In April 1859, Massachusetts made the first move when the legislature authorized the governor to appoint a commissioner to investigate and provide data that would allow it to decide whether Indians could "compatibly with their own good and that of the other inhabitants of the state" be made full citizens. John Milton Earle's visits and research resulted in a relatively objective analysis of the past, present, and future of Natives in the state, revealing many more than any previous study, including mariners in ports like New Bedford. His report also emphasized that every tribe with a reserve rejected citizenship, fearing that the change would result in the loss of their land, but agreed that the smaller groups in the state had little or no separate property or political structure and were already fairly integrated into local schools and other institutions. In response, on April 30, 1862, the state extended full citizenship to all Indians except for those in Chappaquiddick, Christiantown, Gay Head, Mashpee, Herring Pond, Troy-Watuppa, and Dudley. Members of these tribes living elsewhere in the state could obtain citizenship by applying to the town clerk and paying a poll tax.[14]

The state clearly intended the 1862 act as a partial step along the path to full citizenship for all Indians in the Commonwealth, and within a few years the destruction of slavery and measures to reconstruct the South made that final goal seem easy. Radical Republicans and other reformers wondered why, if they were giving former slaves equal political rights and economic opportunities, Indians should be treated differently. By the end of the decade, Massachusetts leaders were determined to enfranchise Indians. They were encouraged by petitions from Mashpees, one of which asked for an end to restrictions on the sale of Indian lands and the other (from women) that asked that all women in the Commonwealth be given full civil and political rights. In early January 1869, the governor dedicated a sizeable portion of his annual address to Indians of the Commonwealth, and after noting their "partial civil disabilities" called for them to be "merged in the general community, — with all the rights and privileges, and with all the duties and liabilities of citizens." The legislature took up the challenge, appointing a joint committee (including Francis Bird, who had headed the 1848 committee) to examine the proposal and develop a bill to bring the charge to fruition. The *Worcester Daily Spy*, a radical Republican paper formerly edited by Earle, commented, "This suggestion is so manifestly wise and reasonable. That we can only wonder that it was not urged and acted upon long ago."[15]

Rhode Island officials also began to seriously consider termination at midcentury, similarly influenced by the apparent success of moral reform efforts and the strange combination of racialist paradigms and egalitarianism. In 1858, the newly appointed state commissioner for the Narragansetts reported that, of 122 members of the tribe on the reserve, there were no full bloods and only 11 of half blood or more. Moral and material conditions within the tribe had improved over the past few decades, particularly since alcohol abuse had declined. He concluded, "It would, no doubt, be better for the tribe and the town if their conditions were changed, and they were placed on an equal footing with other citizens of the State," a change which "must eventually take place."[16]

Eight years later, as the Civil War ended, the legislature authorized a joint committee to hear the tribe's reaction to a proposal to abolish their separate legal status and sell their land. The October 1866 meeting at the Ocean House in Charlestown followed, during which men and women in the tribe expressed their outrage at the proposal.[17] The legislature decided instead to incorporate the tribe, with its members as shareholders, and to maintain restrictions on land sales to outsiders. The state finally decided on termination in 1879, perhaps because a railroad company wanted to construct a route across the reserve.[18] Five years later, council member Joshua Noka told a gathering that "while we were trying to preserve and quietly maintain our government, some of our white neighbors were running to the General Assembly asking for the abolishment of our tribal authority."[19] In January, someone in the legislature introduced a bill to sell all the tribe's undivided lands and create a fund to support Narragansett paupers.[20] Apparently hearing of this bill, tribal president Gideon Ammons and "other men and women" asked the assembly to investigate encroachments on tribal lands "and whether it was better to continue the tribe as a tribe or enfranchise them, and how it was best to proceed." Another council member, Benjamin Thomas, spearheaded another petition to the assembly that may have raised the issue of citizenship.[21]

Termination in Connecticut was a long process that was different for each tribe, in part because it was often done by the state to facilitate local economic development, and in part because the assembly in 1822 had transferred much of its oversight power to county courts—although it was perfectly willing to step in to sell tribal lands. For example, in 1848 the legislature had required the Mohegan overseer to sell sections of the reservation for a railroad right of way, and three years later it did the same to the Niantics. But as in other states, Connecticut lawmakers had racial and egalitarian motivations for ending Indian tribes, as when they voted in June 1876 to make all Niantics full citizens in the name of equality (as of July 4, 1877) and because so few "true" (full-blood) Indians lived on the reserve.[22]

The state's termination of Mohegan, the tribe with the highest population and largest reserve, began with land sales to outsiders driven by the many petitions from Brothertown emigrants and Mohegan residents in the 1840s. In 1859, after several members of the tribe petitioned to sell land leased to white farmers, the assembly sent a committee to investigate conditions within the tribe.[23] One year later, the legislature directed three commissioners to allot nearly all of the reserve to individuals of the tribe, taking a major step toward reshaping the community.

A year after that, in July 1861, the legislature took back most of the county court's authority over the tribe and authorized the governor to appoint three men each year to manage its resources and affairs.[24]

REJECTING TERMINATION

Termination was not a new threat for Indians in southern New England. The larger tribes had in 1819 rejected Jedidiah Morse's notion that they leave their reserves and go west, and in the 1830s they were well aware of removal and what it was doing to the Cherokees. During the 1840s, many faced the threat of losing their lands and tribal autonomy when emigrants to Brothertown or other tribes petitioned to sell land that their ancestors had held on the reserves. In August 1843, after several Narragansetts petitioned to sell land from the reserve before moving west, a legislative committee visited and urged the entire tribe to leave. The committee chair told them that the land on their reserve was exhausted, that the land in Wisconsin was excellent, and that the state would help those who wished to leave—although it would also continued to "protect" those who stayed. Tribal council members argued against leaving, and few emigrated, even though one who left was their minister, Moses Stanton.

At midcentury, tribal leaders became increasingly concerned about the willingness of state officials to sell their reserves. In October 1852, Mohegan leaders opposing a petition from a Montville white man to sell reservation land told officials that the lands were the tribe's "common" and "sacred" property, protected by state laws, and any sale to outsiders would be "extremely injurious" and "in violation of their rights."[25] In this atmosphere, Indians viewed termination largely as a plot by their white neighbor to eliminate the laws that protected their tribal lands and rights. This was particularly true with the Narragansetts, who had deep conflicts with Charlestown, and accused the town's residents of seeking to "foment our quarrels, trespass upon our inheritance . . . and even desecrate the graves of our kings"—a reference to an incident that April, when a group of whites (led by tribal member Samuel Nocake) dug up one of their graveyards looking for "curious relics."[26] Ironically, this enmity may have helped forestall termination, for Charlestown authorities opposed accepting the Narragansetts as residents.[27]

In Massachusetts, Earle found that every Indian group opposed termination and citizenship. The Chappaquiddick elders (whom Earle called "thoughtful, considerate, and prudent") asked for no change because outsiders would steal their land and resources. The next generation might be ready, they told him, if they were raised with that goal. There were a couple men on the island who hoped that the change would open new opportunities but then went along with all of the others who opposed the idea. Similarly, when the Mashpees met with Earle, a newcomer to the community urged full citizenship "but after a full and free discussion the vote was unanimous in favor of remaining as they are, the individual who had spoken on the other side voting with the rest." Again they emphasized the economic threat: the council wrote to Earle that they were "bitterly opposed" to the change and feared that taxes along with other changes would result in the alienation of tribal land to outsiders. The lawyer who worked with Gay Head told the investigator that only "foreigners" supported allotment and termination, and Earle found during his visit to the tribe that all opposed the changes but a few of "bad character."[28]

Some tribes were willing to have their reserves allotted as long as the land could not be sold to outsiders. Chappaquiddick, Christiantown, and Mashpee had made that change three decades earlier, in part because allotment allowed a measure of protection under state civil laws against the efforts of white to obtain their land and the efforts of some emigrants to sell pieces. The Mohegans told state commissions in 1859 that allotment would help make sure their young would have enough land, perhaps because the current system left members unable to obtain mortgages and created a high degree of economic uncertainty.[29] A year later, after commissioners allotted the reserve with the assistance of Mohegan elder Emma Baker (1830–1916), they reported that most "expressed great satisfaction in the prospect of having a particular piece, or parcel of land assigned them, that they might feel encouraged to make improvements, with a reasonable prospect that if they planted a fruit tree, they or their children should gather the fruit." The commissioners also asked the legislature for a ban on land sales to outsiders.[30] Not all tribes supported allotment at this time. Gay Headers felt that allotment was part of the larger threat of termination and would allow their property to be taken by "shrewder and sharper men." Earle agreed, noting that they were "fortunate" in spurning allotment, as it would have greatly increased inequality and poverty in the community, costing the state money.

Tribes balked at the idea of losing their autonomy and separate legal status. Some maintained their rights to sovereignty imbedded deep in history. In 1859, the Narragansetts angrily reminded Rhode Island of its sixteenth-century treaty obligations when state commissioners first raised the prospect of termination.[31] The same year, Mohegan leader Anson Cooper angrily rejected the idea of citizenship and detribalization, insisting that the tribe's "constitutional" rights to self-government were grounded in their assistance to the English against the Pequots in 1636.[32] Both tribes took the same legal stand in their objections to the draft during the Civil War. Tribal sovereignty also offered psychological and social protection against the racism and contempt of their neighbors. Gay Headers told Earle that the prevalence of "prejudice of color and caste" meant they would not be accepted by the neighboring town of Chilmark. Protection of tribal reserves were, of course, grounded in the same laws that gave tribes a range of powers to govern themselves and regulate their resources including lands.

Few Natives had changed their view of termination when the states became more insistent after the Civil War. In 1869, the joint Massachusetts legislative committee set up to consider Indian citizenship and an end to tribal status traveled to Mashpee to hold hearings. All but two Mashpee speakers opposed mandatory citizenship; although a few were willing to see the change *after* the current generation of schoolchildren became adults, this was probably an effort to delay or avoid change. Several men thought that the end of land sale restrictions would cause them to lose their lands, leave the community, and fall into poverty. Deacon Matthias Amos, one of the two who supported citizenship, denounced neighboring whites for violating his people's treaty rights to fish, hunt, and cut timber in nearby areas. Race and class were issues for many; William Simons argued that the tribe had "prejudice to fight" and that "capital, of course, is against us." Some also insisted that the tribe held rights and status that could not be terminated: Nathan Pocknett reminded the visiting legislative committee that Mashpee held aboriginal rights to the reserve that came from its treaties.[33]

In 1879, the Narragansetts were even more adamant than the Mashpees about their objections to termination and their rights to sovereignty. In July, the legislature sent a committee to the tribe with the intent of gaining their assent to the change. At the hearings, Benjamin Thomas testified that the call for citizenship came from outsiders who wanted to take their remaining commons; Abraham Champlin decried the desire of whites to take their lands, and Henry Champlin noted that regional and national interests who wanted Narragansett resources were behind the idea. Edward Cone told the visitors that he and others were concerned about paying their taxes as citizens and that they feared white prejudice would wreak more harm with the change. "We don't want to do all the drudgery and have no advantages."[34]

The tribe was particularly concerned about racism. Council members Joshua Noka, Brister Michael, and Daniel Sekater each told the Rhode Island legislators that as men of color they would gain nothing from citizenship, that the vote did not mean access to power and the change would impoverish the tribe. Sekater went on to decry racialist notions that his people were no longer truly Indians, for "other classes are mixed up with other nations just as well. There is hardly one that can say, 'I am a clear-blooded Yankee.'" Gideon Ammons, who seemed initially willing to accept citizenship, then bitterly told the commissioners that the state's racist laws made him uncertain about the change, observing that "I don't think that many of these white gentlemen here would like to have any of our nigger tribe hang around your daughters and court them. If we come out as citizens, it would be a name without any gain to it."[35]

The Narragansetts, like the Mashpees, felt that their economic and racial oppression was closely connected. When the legislative committee asked for details about their complaints of "encroachments on their territory," Benjamin Thomas told them that it was an old controversy, still before the state courts, which had (among other things) featured the Anglo-American claimant taking a stick, hitting Edward Cone's father over the head, and driving the tribe's delegation out of the gate. He complained, "We are always beat and expect to be. I have looked on and seen them fix out the judgment of the court before there was a witness called." These conflicts became apparent during the hearings: Charlestown town clerk William Cross accused the Narragansetts generally and council members in particular of thievery, and he in turn was accused by them of stealing their land, building on part and selling part to a third party.[36]

The Narragansett and the Mashpee voices were representative of Native concerns after the war about their legal status and economic condition and their continued rejection of termination and citizenship. A short newspaper account noted that Gay Head leaders—Baptist minister Zaccheus Howwoswee, Deacon Simon Johnson (1794–1875), and Jane Wamsley (b. 1798)—opposed the change. Howwoswee represented the tribe in their dealings with Earle and other state officials; Johnson (figure 9) combined, according to Harper's in 1860, "the character of the Indian chief with that of the New England Deacon"); and Wamsley (figure 10) had, when young, served as a Baptist preacher and continued to be central figure in the tribe. Unfortunately, the only transcripts of Indian discussions of termination proposals are of the hearings in 1859 at Mohegan and Narragansett, in 1869 at Mashpee, and in 1879 at Narragansett.[37]

One tribe did welcome termination: the Niantics, who in 1855 still held a 400-acre reserve in East Lyme. Ten members of the tribe lived on the reserve, only two of whom farmed, using a total of about 15 acres. That June, the assembly whittled the reserve down to a hundred acres, ordering the county court to sell the rest. Ten years later, Zacheus Nonsuch asked the county court to sell the tribe's remaining land, noting that he and other Niantics had moved to Mohegan and that East Lyme was too far. The court either delayed or refused, for a year later he and other Niantics petitioned the assembly to sell or divide their lands; the legislature

Figure 9. Deacon Simon Johnson of Gay Head. Courtesy Martha's Vineyard Historical Society, Edgartown, Mass.

told the county court to investigate; and the court in turn decided to divide and sell the reserve. Tribal members then persuaded the assembly to divide the proceeds among them except for a sum to repair and maintain their burial ground. In 1873, the state told the overseer to give all of the remaining funds to tribal members. The Niantics sought termination but not because they wanted to become citizens; instead, they had already found new tribal communities and seemingly saw their reserve as useless except to supply needed capital. They were unique:

Figure 10. Jane Wamsley of Gay
Head, 1860. From *Harper's New
Monthly* Magazine 124 (Sept.
1860), 451.

other tribes saw their reserves as sacred homelands as well as a dependable and
necessary source for their livelihood.[38]

But a few members of those tribes were more willing to publicly support
changes in their status. At Mashpee, the most prominent supporter of citizenship
was Solomon Attaquin, selectman, former ship captain, and co-founder of the
Mashpee Manufacturing Company. At the February 1869 hearings, Attaquin described how he and other tribal officials had gradually taken on more governing
responsibilities, replacing the state-appointed commissioner and treasurer with
men of their own choice. "I want to see the day that I am a citizen and man, as
well as other men," he told the meeting, and believed that "we are ready for it to-
day." Matthias Amos supported *voluntary* citizenship, largely because he had been
frustrated by his inability to obtain mortgages or otherwise develop his land. Three
months after the Mashpee hearings, eight Gay Headers asked the legislature for
allotment and citizenship. At the hearing that followed, one of the eight, Serena
Randolph (married to a Haitian) bitterly told the meeting that she wished she'd
never returned (although why she did not explain). Among the Narragansetts,
Samuel Congdon told the committee that he was "a black republican and an abolitionist clean to the backbone, every inch of me . . . I want my rights, my privileges, — to act like a man and be as a man." He also complained that council members opposed citizenship largely to maintain their control of the tribe's land and
resources—although when asked, he confessed that he did not know any other
member of the tribe who agreed with him. But even Congdon, like Attaquin and

Amos, seemed skeptical of complete termination—an end to all legal distinctions and protections for the tribe and its lands and annexation to a nearby town—while they were more welcoming of equal political status and participation with others in their state.[39]

Those who supported sweeping changes were foreigners who still held different values from the rest of the community. At Mashpee, three men from the South who had married into the community trumpeted their support for termination and full citizenship. Their testimonies highlight how the embrace by African Americans of patriarchal and liberal capitalist values, along with the dominance of Republican ideals and the rising tide of civil equality in the region, made exogamous marriages a liability instead of a benefit for Indian villages. George Sewell noted that he was from the South, "where men were not allowed to be men," and had been delighted to be treated as a full citizen when he came to New England. But under the current law, "My wife possesses land that *she* holds; if she dies to-morrow I can have no benefit from it, and all my labor and improvements go to somebody else. You can see that is not right . . . not republican." Samuel Godfrey, from Richmond, Virginia, complained that "you can make all the improvements you may choose; when your children come home they can drive you [out], because you are a stranger and they are Indians."[40]

The persistent differences between Indian and mainstream gender roles and privileges were particularly annoying to the newcomers. Young Gouch was born a slave in Missouri, but came to New England and fought in the 54th Massachusetts, married his Mashpee wife in Boston, and then moved to her home. He told the committee, "I wish to be a man, with equal rights with every man . . . if I am capable of paying [my wife's] taxes, I should think I am capable of holding some land." Sewell asked the legislature "to make us men, and give us all the dignity of manhood," and if the Mashpees opposed the change, "I want you to consider your duty to make them men." At the Gay Head hearings, John Anthony (a Portuguese veteran of the Civil War) told the state representative that he "considered himself a man among men, as good as 'any other man,' and wished for a chance to prove it."[41]

Ten years before, at similar meetings, the few in these tribes who had asked Earle to make them citizens had backed down when faced by the opposition of the community and its elders. Now, in the wake of the Civil War, state civil rights laws, and the 14th and 15th Amendments to the U.S. Constitution, some, particularly African American immigrants, were open and insistent about the need for their rights as men to be imposed on the tribe by the state if necessary. Their willingness to defy the tribe's religious and political leaders shows that older lines of authority had weakened under the pressure of the war, Reconstruction, and other developments. Outsiders such as state politicians and the newspaper reporter who concluded (after the Gay Head hearing) that "the sentiment of the people generally" favored termination apparently did not recognize this situation, but if they had, they probably would have applauded.[42]

These termination hearings exposed and exacerbated conflicts within tribes. At Mashpee, Sewall disparaged opponents of citizenship as "Red Jackets"—in reference to the infamous traditionalist Iroquois leader—who "oppose civilization, and don't do what they should for the Christian Gospel." Simons charged that those who put together the petition asking for the change did so in an "underhand" and secretive manner. Pocknett told those who did not like the tribe's traditional system that they could always leave. When the committee took a quick vote at the gathering, the majority opposed removing land restrictions, but half supported and half opposed becoming citizens. While such public quarrels in Mashpee were not new—after all, Hawley and Fish both had their Mashpee defenders—the division was a striking contrast to the unity presented to Earle a decade earlier and undermined the ability of the tribe and the Indians generally to stop the revolution. What was not said—or more importantly, who did not speak—was also significant: at Narragansett and Mashpee, no women presented their views of the change that would undermine, if not destroy, their remaining socioeconomic power in the community.[43]

Termination also raised conflicts about tribal boundaries and membership, which, as earlier in the century, could have racist overtones. This was particularly apparent among the Narragansetts when the tribe argued over who had a proper claim to community resources. Tribal leader Edward Cone found himself left off the list of tribal members. A current council member curtly told him that, because his mother was "a nigger woman," he was ineligible despite his offices. When Cone continued to press his claim, Gideon Ammons curtly told him that "if we can judge anything from color, we should judge that you was an African." Cone shot back "Then I should judge that you were. There is not much difference in our color." In the end, Cone and many of the others rejected by the council were added by the legislative committee to the tribal rolls. Unlike the Mashpees, the Narragansetts had enough concern about race 90 years before to limit membership on racial terms, and now that old issue was resurfacing to trouble the community. But underneath the heated words one can see that, just as in the earlier conflict, racial rhetoric was part of the fight to preserve or renew the community's social and political boundaries and expressed personal and family animosities.[44]

The Narragansetts were not alone after the Civil War in their concerns about race. The commissioners who allotted Mohegan lands made a list of members' blood quantum, based on genealogical data provided by elder Emma Baker, with only four "pure bloods." Although the last Mohegan protest about marriages with blacks came in 1823, antiblack resentment remained, as evidenced by the folk belief that "to dream of negroes is a sign of trouble and disappointment."[45] In 1859, the supposedly last full-blood Schaghticoke, Eunice Mawee "spoke sadly of the decay of her people, and almost contemptuously of those whose blood was mixed with other than that of the Indian race." Mawee told her visitor that "she was the very last of the Pequods whose pedigree was free from the taint of amalgamation."[46]

Concerns about race and ethnicity were certainly part of termination. State leaders saw people of color, rather than Indians, living on the reserves and therefore conceived of no reason not to grant them the same rights that other people of color had recently won. Within the tribes, the majority of the leading voices for change came from blacks who had married Native women but after 1865 saw higher virtues and more economic and political opportunities in the outside world. Their Indian wives could vote in community meetings or claim pieces of communal land; they were denied these rights. But outside the Indian village, men of all colors could vote and own property, and their daughters and wives were subservient. These patriarchal values became the primary threat to the social and cultural constructs tied to communal landholding. Although African American leaders did not comment on this issue, they espoused the values of competitive capitalism and patriarchal families.[47]

COMPELLING TERMINATION

Indian reluctance to and rejection of their proposals did nothing to change the desire of state leaders to terminate tribes. In Massachusetts, the legislative committee that ran the hearing at Mashpee ignored that tribe's concerns and condemned the current system of legal restrictions on land sales and state assistance as degrading and impoverishing the Indians. "We believe that Massachusetts is ready to-day," their report concluded, "to wipe all distinctions of race and caste," with the possible exception of the Dudley Nipmucs and Troy-Watuppa. The committee proposed two bills; both were enacted into law. The first eliminated any special legal status for Indians, authorized county probate judges to divide all common lands and monies belonging to Indian tribes (with the exception of Gay Head and Mashpee, which as districts already held control of those resources), and to sell the Dudley Nipmuc tenement and land. The second made Mashpee a town instead of a reserved district and directed the county probate judge to divide and sell the tribe's remaining lands.[48]

For several weeks the bill lay before the legislature. There was no doubt that the state would enfranchise members of the remaining tribes and end all of their legal distinctions. Initially, the proposal to make Mashpee a separate town was defeated, as its opponents claimed that "the Indians would be colonized practically, and the place degraded into a 'negro town.'" But the alternative, to divide the district among Falmouth, Barnstable, and Sandwich, was rejected by Mashpee and by the surrounding towns — primarily for racist reasons, as they had little desire for more Indians or blacks. On June 11, the initial proposal was added as an amendment to the enfranchisement bill, and on June 23 the "Act to Enfranchise the Indians of Massachusetts" became law. Gay Head and Mashpee were made separate towns, which would help them survive as distinctly *Indian* communities.[49]

Three years later, in May 1872, a number of Mohegans petitioned the assembly for fee-simple ownership of their allotted lands and an end to the state's guardianship.[50] Perhaps inspired by Massachusetts, Connecticut responded quickly. On July 23 the legislature received a bill that proposed detribalizing the Mohegans and giving them full citizenship effective October 9; the bill became law just eight days later. The Mohegans and their reserve would be annexed to the surrounding town of Montville, and the tribe's school would become part of the Montville School District, although the location of the school could not change unless two-thirds of the tribe's men approved. Allotments would become the full property of their holders, who would be taxed as any other citizen of the state, and all remaining lands (except for the church grounds and the tribe's cemetery) would be sold at auction and the proceeds divided among the members of the tribe.[51] A group of Mohegans led by Anson Cooper and Emma Baker protested that they had been "satisfied with our condition and status," that the July act "was entirely without our solicitation or knowledge," and that the taxes they now owed were "burdensome." Their protests were fruitless.[52]

Other tribes in that state experienced a strange and uneven trajectory, escaping absolute legal termination while losing all or most of their reserved land. In December 1802, the state sold the last 20 acres of the Golden Hill Paugussett reserve, in the center of Bridgeport and rapidly increasing in value; the proceeds ($1,576) were given to the overseer of the tribe to support the remaining members who were expected to become "extinct" soon. But the tribe survived as a distinct community, even as a smallpox epidemic in the 1830s killed several families in nearby Derby. In 1841, the state purchased 20 acres in Trumbull for two women who had petitioned for assistance as the only surviving Paugussetts, but that land was sold eight years later after one woman left and the other was jailed for arson. Decades later, in 1876, members of the community (and its overseers) remained, even though they held no land and had no apparent organization. That same year, the state rediscovered a few Tunxis survivors and told the Litchfield County court to appoint an overseer to manage the tribe's property.[53]

The two Pequot tribes and the far northwestern Schaghticokes were unique in surviving as legal entities with reservations. The Eastern Pequots almost lost most of their reserve in 1837 when the legislature gave their overseer permission to sell all but 100 acres, but he decided not to sell when the depression that year made land in the area worthless. In 1879, despite tribal members' protests, the overseer did sell 30 acres, but the community and its reserve survived.[54] The Mashantucket Pequots lost most of their 893-acre reserve in 1855 after the legislature decided that the tribe's needs—only 30 members, with a noticeable number of elderly, large debts, and many living in poverty—could best be met by the sale of all but 180 acres.[55] The Schaghticokes and their reserve seemed to survive this period in the most intact condition. In 1884, their overseer reported that the tribe retained 300 acres of hilly, forested territory that no one else wanted. Six households with about 25 individuals lived on the reserve, although the tribe had at least 65 members scattered around the area.[56] All three tribes remained legal entities into the twentieth century.

In Rhode Island, a local writer noted that nine-tenths of the Narragansetts and most Charlestown whites opposed that tribe's termination but that "the sentiment of the people of the state at large was in favor of removing [the tribe] from the body politic."[57] On December 26, 1881, the assembly's commissioners met with the tribal council and signed an agreement to pay individual Narragansetts a total of $5,000 for the remaining undivided reserve "and all other tribal rights and claims." The legislature quickly passed an act terminating the Narragansett tribe. About two months later the tribe held a general meeting at which the agreement was read, and in the council elections that followed, members again selected those who had signed the deed, indicating their approval of the action. Soon after, a few members voted in state elections.[58]

The new law required the committee to decide who held enough of a connection to the tribe to receive a share of the $5,000. The hearings that followed highlighted many of the interconnected issues faced by Indian groups in southern New England during the nineteenth century. Conflicts erupted between individuals over who had the right to tribal membership and resources, often expressed in racial terms. Participants debated to what degree residence on the reservation determined tribal membership, why individuals left and remained off the reservation, and how emigrants or their children could maintain or renew their tribal connections. Speakers also supported or condemned the land sale and detribalization law in terms of values that seemed to show an ongoing conflict over acculturation. And because only men testified, gender was a significant if somewhat invisible influence on all of the other issues.

The committee first charged the council to list members of the tribe; Gideon Ammons and Benjamin Thomas came up with 99 names, 80 of whom lived on the reserve in Charlestown, but the list did not include men like Edward Cone, who played an active role in the tribe but lived farther away. At the Narragansett meetinghouse on Saturday morning, June 26, the committee began a new set of hearings. They told the large crowd (which included the governor) that every man, woman, and child recognized as a member of the tribe would get one share and asked anyone not on the tribal council's list who thought they belonged to step forward. Another 473 adults and children submitted their names; many were from Providence or Westerly, but some from distant Worcester and Boston. Many had spent little or no time on the reservation for many years, at the most occasionally attending the annual spring tribal elections or August church gathering. Some were non-Indian spouses of tribal members; others had married blacks or whites. The meetings were lively affairs, drawing 200–400 people and lasting for many hours.[59]

Before these hearings, the commissioners had asked the state attorney general how they should judge whether an individual was a legal member of the tribe and therefore entitled to a share of the proceeds from the sale of the reserve. He told them that each case would be different but that evidence that a person had left the tribe included selling lands they had occupied on the reserve, a long absence from the tribe (more than ten years) with the apparent intention of not returning, and purchase of property elsewhere and participation in another community. In his opinion, the 1792 act mandating that the children of an Indian man and a Negro woman could not vote in tribal meetings did not deny them tribal membership, as women and children were also not allowed to vote under the 1792 rules. He also recommended that children and adults be given equal shares. The commission and the state judge who reviewed their findings followed these guidelines. In the end, of 572 listed by the council or pressing claims to tribal membership, 302 men, women, and children were placed by the commission on the tribal rolls, making each entitled to $16.56.[60]

During the 1820s, federal Indian policy swung toward removal, and the 1820 Morse report demonstrated that tribes in southern New England were at the time potential targets of that policy. But Indians in the region were under state rather than federal administration, and many held their reserves under colonial treaties and laws that continued to have strong legal power within the states. When termination came, it arose from shared ideas of race, ideals of civil equality, and desires for Indian resources. But the process varied in noticeable ways because of differences between the governments and the very different situations of Indians in each state. Massachusetts had a long tradition of centralized planning and reforms, directed by the legislature and its appointed administrators, which since 1746 had tried to manage directly the social, economic, and political conditions of every Indian community. Connecticut, by contrast, had assigned oversight of tribes to county courts, and although the legislature occasionally intervened, it was eager to be rid of its dealing with the only sizeable tribe. Rhode Island had a long history of strong local control, and, until ideological and local pressures mounted, had little problem with delegating significant powers to the council that governed the one tribe in the state. State leaders throughout the region saw all but those living in strong tribal organizations as "people of color," but those in Massachusetts tended to be more protective of smaller communities and households, even as they were uncertain whether they really were Indians, in part because of their desire to micromanage socioeconomic improvements and in part because of the state's long and continuous history of caretaker relations with those groups.

The termination process between 1860 and 1880 highlighted the interaction of tribe, race, and history in southern New England: tribal struggles over land, community, and identity; evolving racial perceptions and ideologies; and emerging notions of a unique regional history and culture. Indian groups depended on a synergy between their lands and communities to support their livelihoods, culture, and very existence. Indian leaders were aware of these needs and tried various strategies to maintain their social and political boundaries, including land divisions in severalty and the embrace of racial distinctions. But their efforts were undermined by newer notions of race: whites no longer saw Indians but people of color, and African Americans in the region embraced a similar bichromatic paradigm that viewed Indians (including their recent ancestors) as feathered hunters rather than whalers or laborers. In 1863, an herbal doctor serving with the 20th Connecticut, in a letter to his wife back home, noted that "the Indians, of whom I am in part a descendant, as well as yourself, were warriors or soldiers [with] savage natures."[61] Such characterizations meant that tribes would have little to no support in their struggle to maintain a separate existence.

Finally, termination was grounded in the dominant view of New England's unique history and culture, which depicted Indians as sympathetic but tragic primitives: the savages had helped the civilized English colonists but were soon nearly extinct, either as part of the inevitable triumph of civilization or because of the Puritans' aggressive intolerance. This story also painted slavery as an insignificant part of the region's past, which meant that the few people of color acculturated in the region could and should be granted civil equality, and proved New England's intellectual, moral, and social superiority. Termination was also justified by Americans' notion of history as an inevitable march of progress and civilization over primitive peoples. As *Niles' National Register* saw it, the Indian race "has no active principle of improvement within itself," and therefore Americans were not responsible for its extinction "though we may well blush at the remembrance of the wrong and outrage [Natives] have suffered at our hands."[62]

This vision inspired the growing number of monuments built and commemorations held by local and state historical societies that often included references to vanished Indians. The monument erected by Farmington to the Tunxis featured a poem written by Lydia Sigourney that began "Chieftains of a vanished race" and toward the end mourned, "And your tribes have passed away. But your fate shall cherished be, in the stranger's memory." Sometimes the state's final act of termination was to set aside a cemetery plot or some other memorial to the supposedly extinct tribe. In 1870, the Niantics' overseer reported that he had erected a granite statute in the Niantic cemetery, the last piece of land belonging to the tribe, that read "Niantic Indian Burying ground/Tribe extinct A.D. 1870."[63] In 1883, Rhode Island erected a boulder at Fort Ninigret to commemorate the Narragansetts and installed a fence around it. That same year, the Rhode Island Historical Society dedicated a monument to Canonicus, the Narragansett sachem during the first few decades of the English invasion. While all of the speeches were made by whites, a supposed Narragansett, M. B. Prophet (who did not appear on the 1881 tribal roll), unveiled the monument, and after the former Indian commissioner George Carmichael Jr. gave a short address, Annie A. Thomas (who did appear on the 1881 list, aged five) stepped up and on behalf of the tribe gave him a bouquet of flowers.[64]

Epilogue

About 1900, a young Columbia College student visited Mohegan. Frank Speck quickly developed a friendship with the elderly Fidelia Fielding (1827–1908), the only surviving fluent Mohegan speaker. Over the next few decades, he would publish several important articles about southern New England Indians, documenting their present and past. Yet they did not appreciate all of his work. In late spring 1903, Speck published his first article, "The Mohegan Pequots and Their Language," which he began by observing, "Although these people are really Pequots in language, they nevertheless refer to themselves as Mohegans."[1] Back in Mohegan, Fielding had begun keeping a diary in the native language, perhaps because of Speck's interest. She apparently read or heard about his article, for on May 23, 1903, she angrily wrote (as later translated by Speck) "I am from Mohegan! I am not Pequot! Anyone saying I am Pequot he is a continual liar, that is so! White men think [they] know all things. Half [the things they are] saying not are so. Poor white man . . . These people are many. Good man is not frequent."[2]

The Mohegan elder's fierce insistence on defining her tribe's identity, preserving its culture, and highlighting differences with the white man points to the persistence of southern New England Native life even after tribal termination. Termination certainly aggravated the corrosive demographic, economic, and political pressures experienced by Indian communities during the nineteenth century. But some survived the subsequent ebb tide through the early twentieth century until the emergence of a pan-Indian movement in the 1920s provided a new vehicle for tribal and regional revitalization. In addition, some families lacking the support of a village managed to pass on tribal identities and some aspects of their remembered culture, providing a route for their descendants to reenter revitalized or resurrected tribal communities. Tribes and families that survived the aftermath of termination at the turn of the century, during the height of assimilationist pressures and racism, did so by alternately working with or working against these tendencies. In addition, even though the American desire for a romantic vision of the past (in a time of disconcerting and alienating industrial and urban growth) could be insulting, it was also useful for Indian communities and descendants in southern New England.

In the wake of the Civil War, southern New England again became America's bellwether. Its industries boomed, and became more exploitive of workers and politics; its cities sprawled, became dirtier and more segmented along lines of class, and dominated the region; and the tide of immigration continued to swell but shifted from Ireland and Germany to eastern and southern Europe, bringing many Jews, Eastern Orthodox, Italians, and other peoples to the region for the first time. Confronted by these often-bewildering, alienating changes, New Englanders responded with a reformist, assimilationist social and political program (which included termination of western tribes) and with a romantic desire to resurrect a rose-tinted version of its colonial past — trends that included strong racist elements and caught on throughout much of the nation. In the 1880s, amateur historians and local historical and preservation societies flourished, placing historical markers and putting on elaborate reenactment pageants. Indians figured in both as characters, and sometimes those still living were invited to participate and warmly welcomed. The wilderness craze (the Boy Scouts of America was founded in 1910) and the near worship of handmade crafts were related phenomenon at the turn of the century and provided a larger opening for Natives to reinsert themselves into America's cultural mainstream — and for "vanished" Indians to reappear in southern New England in the 1920s.[3]

Indian tribes that survived the four decades following termination did so by maintaining their communities, identities, and aspects of their traditions while being part of the mainstream society, economy, and culture. The larger tribes in the region — Narragansett, Mohegan, Gay Head, and Mashpee — retained much of their leadership and institutions (churches were particularly important), and the last two had the benefit of their new status as towns. All four retained close connections to their traditional homelands; Mohegans and Narragansetts continued to live on and near their former reserves and sought compensation for other lands taken by the provincial governments in the eighteenth century; and the new towns of Gay Head and Mashpee kept the boundaries that had marked the reserves even though they lost some land within those boundaries. These large tribes, smaller communities (some barely noticeable to outsiders), and families confirmed their authenticity through the creation of traditional crafts and the adoption of symbolic dress, and on occasion by making public declarations of their identity in wearing their regalia in town historic pageants. Individuals played key roles in maintaining tribal cultures and memories and training the next generation. Finally, old regional connections provided critical support networks and became an important foundation for the pan-Indian councils that emerged in the 1920s.

The Narragansetts did not lose their council or their church on its two acres in the 1880 termination act. The church, council, and tribe as a whole continued to meet, with the latter annual gathering sometimes called a powwow. Gideon Ammons continued to lead the tribe until his death in 1898; his son George became council president in 1896 and served in the position until his death in 1923. Until 1934, the church remained the only tribal institution recognized by the state, and its leaders, Daniel Seketer and John Noka, served as unofficial co-chiefs, having inherited at least part of their authority from their fathers. The tribe also continued to press old claims. In the 1880 termination hearings, the first concern of Narragansett leaders was that their tribe was still owed for the huge area set aside by Ninigret in 1709. Rhode Island legislators waved that question aside; they were only concerned with termination and citizenship. But the tribe did not forget. On February 27, 1896, a tribal meeting agreed to sue the state for $4 million for lands taken in the eighteenth century. Two years later the Rhode Island Supreme Court rejected the suit, so tribal leaders sought in 1906 and 1913 to get the federal government to adjudicate the issue, but without success. Members continued to live in Charlestown on family homesteads established before 1880, or in nearby towns in the county (where they established local churches linked to the one in Charlestown), and to gather every August.[4]

The Mohegan experience was remarkably similar. The tribe remained a distinct community on its former reserve in Montville, led by elders of leading families, particularly the Bakers and Fieldings. They continued to own and maintain the cemetery and church although the majority of church members were not Mohegans, many of its officers were whites, and some tribal leaders were not church members. The tribe pressed claims to land in the state, beginning in May 1897 when they elected Emma Baker president of the Mohegan Indian League. Baker was also head of the Mohegan Sewing Circle, which played a leadership role in the church and tribe and inherited the knowledge and status of medicine woman from her grandmother, Martha Uncas, who died in 1859. Uncas had also raised Fidelia Fielding speaking Mohegan, which allowed the "intensely nationalistic" Fielding to publish the language through Frank Speck. Baker and Fielding were guardians of tribal traditions, including religious and herbal lore, and the two trained Gladys Tantaquidgeon (15 June 1899–November 1, 2005) to be their successor; she in turn has carried the tribe's traditions and leadership into the twenty-first century.[5]

Mohegan elders also continued to teach old songs, tribal histories, folklore, and some terms in their language to youngsters. Men made wooden implements to sell (including war clubs!) and men and women both wove and sold splint baskets. While only Fidelia Fielding was still conversant in Mohegan at the turn of the century, all knew some words in the tribe's language; for example, they called their chief, Henry Matthews, *Wigun:* "The Good." The Mohegans also continued their Wigwam Festival, which it had held almost every year in September as early as 1842. It served to bring the tribe together, including members living in other towns, as men worked together to cut and carry the timbers and to build the structure and used a huge ancient wooden mortar to pound the parched corn for the traditional *yokeag;* the women cooked, made crafts for sale, and organized the festivities. The three-day celebration testified to the tribe's endurance and raised money for the Sewing Circle: many visitors paid an admission fee, happily purchased the traditional foods and crafts, and watched the dances.[6] The tribe also confirmed its persistence by participating in outside celebrations. On May 6, 1896, 22 Mohegan men took part in New London's 250th anniversary commemoration, garnering "continuous cheers throughout the afternoon parade." Mohegan leaders and delegations continued to take part in historical pageants and dedications in the early twentieth century.[7]

Gay Head and Mashpee maintained control of their new towns even as the termination laws had an immediate effect on their lands. The change was particularly traumatic for Gay Head, as the 1870 law allowed a small group to force allotment of the commons — which is what happened a few months later despite the opposition of the new town's selectmen and other leaders, opening the threat of land sales to outsiders. Only the cranberry bogs, seashore, and cliffs were left undivided. In 1876, a white man who worked with the tribe wrote, "Their political enfranchisement was an unwelcome event to them, and so far, has not proved a blessing." Taxation rates had hit Gay Head harder than most towns in the state, forcing some residents to sell lands to neighboring whites, most to get into debts, and the community as a whole to become "disheartened, and reckless." But in the long run, potential threats to the tribe were averted in two ways: first, land sales to outsiders were usually to nonresidents, and Gay Head carefully held its meetings when the mainlanders were least likely to visit; second, conservative Gay Headers continued to refuse to build fences or to follow formal legal forms such as wills, and allowed relatives in need to live and work family lands.[8]

Although the Mashpees had already allotted most of their reserve, and were so acculturated that some mortgaged personal property including tools and animals, they still had a small common, which they lost after termination, as commissioners divided it into parcels and auctioned it off. But as in Gay Head, few outsiders lived there, and Indians continued to monopolize town offices; those elected were generally from the largest families and could draw on those clan connections. White men did purchase the Hotel Attaquin and the Mashpee Manufacturing Company by 1890, although both continued to employ Indians, and the hotel remained an important place where community members met outsiders.[9]

Gay Head and Mashpee also had men and women who continued to guide their communities. Until his death, deacon Thomas Jeffers (1828–1916) managed Gay Head's Baptist church, its most important institution; he also served as selectman in the 1860s and in 1871 was elected by the Dukes County (Vineyard) Republican Convention to be one of their special commissioners. Esther Howwoswee continued to be the tribe's medicine woman until her death in 1883, providing medicinal herbs (drawn on inherited knowledge backed up by a book on English herbal medicine) and passing on tribal folklore and Wampanoag phrases. Though some knowledge and traditions may have died with her, into the twentieth century many members of the tribe knew medicinal plant lore, were able to relate old stories of apparitions and important persons in the community and remembered a few words in Wampanoag.[10]

Solomon Attaquin, Matthias Amos, and William Mingo continued to guide Mashpee, and new leaders emerged such as Watson Hammond (b. 1837), who married Joseph Amos's daughter Rebecca and in 1885 became the first Indian to be elected to the Massachusetts House of Representatives. These men had spent their youths at sea, far from the tribe, and upon their return sought to reform the tribe's economy, society, and politics. The majority of second generation of town leaders would be their sons. Mashpee women became less prominent in the town; the 1827 state commission was struck by their role in public meetings, but the shift to district status in 1834 narrowed the list of voting proprietors, and the final change to a town in 1869 ended the right of women to vote. Finally, after 1870, the pulpits in the Mashpee and the Gay Head Baptist churches, which for so long had been at the heart of each community, were held by Anglo-American ministers; they were liked by their Indian parishioners, but they were still outsiders. Joseph Amos, the Wampanoag Baptist minister who for decades formed a human link by preaching at every Indian church in the area, died at Chappaquiddick in 1869.[11]

Traditional workways also helped these tribes survive termination. Gay Head men continued to go whaling, although they had to take the transcontinental railroad to San Francisco in February where they signed onto a ship to the Arctic grounds until November, returning for a few weeks at home. Mashpee men also went to sea. Gay Head still sold clay, as late as 1907 electing one of their men to

handle sales of the resource.[12] Men and women in both tribes continued to provide services for tourists and sports fishermen and to make baskets and other crafts
for sale, although the trade nearly died out in Mashpee after 1900. Cranberries remained an important moneymaker, particularly in Mashpee, where women worked
in the company recently owned by the tribe. Residents in Mashpee also cut timber and made barrels, perhaps for the cranberries, particularly as a new growth of
trees replaced those cut a half-century earlier, and the town kept taxes low by selling fishing permits for pickerel and trout.[13]

Unfortunately, termination was a severe blow for tribes in Massachusetts with
smaller populations and reservations. Without the state's continuing attention,
communal land, or the autonomy of a town or district, the Herring Pond tribe
seemed to disappear, although descendants maintained memories and an informal social network. Some families continued to live on their allotted lands, others sold and moved due to debt or better opportunities elsewhere, and still others
followed their kinship connections to nearby Mashpee. Only Fanny L. Perry's family remained on the Troy-Watuppa reserve in 1907 when the land was taken from
the state by Fall River to protect the city's North Watuppa Pond water supply. Similarly, by 1880 Christiantown and Chappaquiddick Indians were moving to the
new town of Oak Bluffs on Martha's Vineyard, where they could find employment
and a growing black population from the mainland. The last burial at Chappaquiddick was in 1886, and in Christiantown only the Mingo family was left by the
turn of the century. Joseph Mingo died in April 1913, his widow Lydia died 19
months later, and their only remaining son Samuel, the last Christiantown Indian,
moved to Oaks Bluff before his death in 1935.[14]

The smallest Indian communities with dispersed populations faced comparatively fewer changes at the turn of the century. Connecticut maintained the distinctive legal status of Schaghticoke and the two Pequot groups, and county courts
continued to appoint guardians for each, although there were periods when those
offices were apparently vacant due to death or neglect. While the population of
the two Pequot reserves gradually declined as housing became run down and better opportunities drew them elsewhere, both retained a small core that expanded
and shrank with the seasons and community occasions. The Mashantuckets continued whaling and selling baskets, which occasionally provided enough for feasts
and parties, and drew on their tribe's account to pay for medical care, housing,
and funeral expenses. Eastern Pequots farmed and picked berries to sell along with
the baskets they made. Families attended local churches, and their children went
to town schools. The Schaghticoke population remained relatively stable, al-

though, as with the Pequots, most lived in neighboring towns within their traditional tribal territory; they continued to work as farm laborers and basket makers
and grew and gathered much of their food.[15]

Although all Indian communities in Massachusetts were terminated, the
smaller ones that lacked reserves were far less affected by the change. Earle's report detailed how the Punkapoags, Hassanamiscos, Dudley Nipmucs, Naticks,
and Middleborough and Dartmouth Indians were already living and participating in towns rather than in separate enclaves. Later accounts show that they also
maintained kinship networks, and some worked to sustain their tribal identity.
Families and individuals continued to travel through the area to find work, gather
resources, and visit relatives.[16] In some ways, the Hassanamiscos are particularly
well documented. Only one family (the Arnold-Ciscos) remained in Grafton, on
their 2.5-acre farm, but they maintained close connections with other Hassanamisco descendants (like the Hectors) living elsewhere. The smaller Connecticut and Massachusetts tribes may have maintained an informal organiza-
tional and leadership structure. Cisco correspondence in the 1880s referred to
Hassanamisco elections, and the "ardent traditionalist" James L. Cisco (1846–
1931) held the status of chief or sachem until his death. But such evidence offers
only intermittent glimpses rather than a clear view of a continuous community.[17]

Although termination may not have had an immediate effect among these
communities, as described in chapter 6, some were inspired by the prospective
change to protest past wrongs, revealing a strong sense of tribal identity and privileges.[18] Termination did not end the sense of outrage. A decade later, on June 29,
1881, the Dudley Nipmuc Julia Dailey told a historian in the nearby town of Oxford that "her tribe was conscious of great injustice done to them in all their transactions with the English" and that whites "would destroy the graves of our dead
as of no account." Indeed, when Massachusetts sold the remaining 26-acre Dudley reserve in 1885, it included a small cemetery. Various Nipmucs appeared to
claim part of the proceeds, and in the 1890s they also successfully sued the state
for tribal funds amounting to more than $2,000. In 1904, Sarah M. Cisco asked
the Bureau of Indian Affairs (BIA) to investigate Hassanamisco claims in the
Grafton area, but it saw no federal connection to the tribe and rejected her appeal.[19]

In this context, the costumed appearance of local Indians in historical pageants
at the turn of the century carried subversive meanings. The organizers and observers saw the Indian participants as representing a people that inevitably, and
perhaps tragically, vanished or were displaced by a more civilized race. But those
Indians could also use their participation to organize their people, wear traditional

costume to confirm their sense of tribal or ethnic identity, and deliver the political message that "we are still here." Julia Dailey was the guest of honor at an Oxford historical celebration when she bitterly condemned how whites had treated Nipmucs. James Cisco owned a long feather headdress that he wore at pageants at the turn of the century. Although few Punkapoags remained in the Canton neighborhood that had been their reserve, one who did, Mary Chappelle, took part in local historical pageants, wearing costume that she and others considered traditional (figure 11). Zurvia Mitchell and her two daughters wore their Wampanoag regalia as special guests in Rochester's bicentennial celebration in 1879, and until their deaths a half-century later, the two daughters continued to appear in "the costume of [their] forefathers, feathers and beads" for tourists and special events.[20]

Such colorful appearances masked a deep anger. Toward the end of her life, in September 1921, after helping to unveil the Massasoit memorial for the Pilgrim Society, Charlotte Mitchell told a reporter from the *Boston Globe* that the celebrations "were a farce . . . Massasoit, my grandfather, eight times removed, should have killed the so-called Pilgrims instead of helping them. Then my people would not have been killed and have died out, so that now there is but me, the princess of the Wampanoags, to live out my life alone, on the ground hallowed as the living place of my ancestors." She had taken part in the commemoration because some friends had asked her but would have much rather honored Massasoit's son Metacom, King Philip, "a real man," who "did his best to stamp out the white men from these shores."[21]

Members of tribes without reserves found it particularly important to make baskets and other traditional crafts as a means of confirming and demonstrating their identity. James Cisco's mother, Sarah Maria Arnold Cisco, was an expert basket maker who wove ash splints and grasses and made dyes with berries and beet juice; she considered her designs to be traditional Nipmuc. At the turn of the century, the Punkapoags still living in Canton regularly used stone pestles and wooden mortars for corn, like the Mohegans used in their Wigwam Festival, and made baskets and beadwork to earn a living. Zerviah Mitchell and her daughters made and sold large numbers of rye straw and ash splint baskets. In July 1902, Melinda Mitchell told a Boston reporter that she still made baskets "but not as many as I used to. It is not easy to get the material. We used to send 400 or 500 dozen every year to firms in Boston, and seldom were many returned to us." Observers reported that basket making declined among the Schaghticokes and two Pequot bands after 1900, attributing the change to the death of individuals who had maintained the trade, although Mitchell's comments point to restrictions on gathering bark

Figure 11. Mary Chappelle of Punkapoag, ca. 1920; courtesy National Museum of the American Indian.

and grass, probably because of continued population growth and pressures on resources. Other members of these tribes who lived in nearby towns continued the trade in the early twentieth century and would teach it to a new generation in the 1920s.[22]

But the occasional public presence and the continued creation of crafts by some did not prevent the continued hemorrhaging of their communities. The populations of those who lived on the reserves or who clearly identified with their tribe had been declining throughout the nineteenth century, and that trend continued at the turn of the century. Indians throughout southern New England had become heavily acculturated; most observers noted that they lived very much like, or better than, whites or blacks of the same social and economic class. Termination in Massachusetts, Rhode Island, and for the Niantics and Mohegans in Connecticut removed a critical legal and administrative support for those tribes. Many families lost their Native connections while others maintained and passed on their tribal identity, which became more like an ethnic affiliation. Only Gay Head, Mashpee, and the semi-isolated Mohegan neighborhood in Montville maintained a clear social separation in the early twentieth century. For others, the decades straddling the turn of the century became a black hole into which they seemed to disappear, which later would pose the greatest obstacle to gaining federal recognition.

The pan-Indian movement of the 1920s revitalized New England's Indian communities. Over the centuries following King Philip's War, white perceptions, state policies, and Indian social connections reduced the differences between Native cultures within the region. This development reflected larger trends, as New England and the United States as a whole became more connected, cosmopolitan, and industrialized. After 1900, Indians in the region who cherished their identities and traditions were encouraged by Americans' sudden love of Native culture (reflected in the rituals and images adopted by the Boy Scouts) and by the interest of antiquarians and anthropologists in New England tribes. They were impressed by the public tribute given on July 2, 1907, when Buffalo Bill Cody and a hundred Plains Indian in full regalia made a pilgrimage to Uncas's grave at Mohegan, where the visitors "chanted a war song." In response, they sought to revive their communities and to gain greater public recognition and respect by creating the pan-tribal Indian Council of New England in 1923. The council and its efforts were facilitated by the kinship connections that many Indians in the region had to two or more tribes, a trend that would also become a significant trend among western Natives. The Narragansetts, Mashpees, Hassanamiscos, and others began holding annual powwows, adopting elements of Plains costume and culture to demonstrate that they really were Indians. Each year these events drew more celebrants, visitors, and publicity, raising the profile of particular tribes and Indians generally in southern New England.[23]

Natives quickly took the next step of rediscovering and renewing particular tribal traditions, seeking out any and all sources: elders, anthropologists, documents, and knowledge handed down in other tribes, particularly the Mohegans.

The Wigwam Festival blossomed in the mid-1920s, with many more visitors and more Indian participants wearing homemade regalia that reflected their ancestors' culture. In 1931, the Tantaquidgeon family built an Indian museum that became a repository for Mohegan and other Eastern Woodland artifacts and a place where all people could learn of the tribe's past and present. Basket making became an important symbol of this revitalization, and the craft was taught to a new generation in Mashpee, Schaghticoke, and other tribes. Gladys Tantaquidgeon's brother Harold began teaching Boy Scouts to gather, shape, and weave materials "after the Indian fashion." Perhaps the most symbolic event of this period was the "genuine Indian wedding" on January 9, 1927, of Mantaiskaun, the "last of the Mashpee Indian Medicine Men," to the daughter of Mannatana, "Princess Inowanin of the Mashpees."

Pan-Indian connections remained important, as tribes learned from each other and all Indians were invited to participate in any powwow. In 1934, Mohegan medicine woman (and trained anthropologist) Gladys Tantaquidgeon served as the Bureau of Indian Affairs observer attending the Narragansett's reorganization ceremony. These tribal and pan-Indian revivals were encouraged by the decline among American leaders of the paradigm that tribes must be terminated and Indians assimilated, a shift marked by the Indian Reorganization Act of 1934. Part of the process of tribal revitalization was attracting the grandchildren of those who had moved away and assimilated into black or white communities. Ironically, given the dynamics of intermarriage and ethnic identity, described in chapter 2, termination and the loss of reservations may have facilitated this tribal renewal.[24]

Since the mid-1970s, nearly all of the New England tribes that remained in the nineteenth century have sought federal recognition. A few achieved it through special acts of Congress, while others were rewarded or denied (and are still seeking) that status through the Bureau of Indian Affairs's federal acknowledgment process. Even though some groups (Hassanamisco, Mohegan, Narragansett, Schaghticoke, Mashantucket and Eastern Pequots) had state charters or other official status, federal recognition offered emotional and institutional validation and substantial financial assistance. State and local officials generally opposed their efforts, largely because the Indians' success would transfer sovereignty over the tribe's members and lands to the federal government but also because the Indians were deeply assimilated and didn't *look* Indian — echoing nineteenth-century observers. Recognition was also often opposed by some western tribes, in part for racial reasons (the applicants didn't look like Indians and were deeply assimilated) and in part to safeguard their share of federal resources. Since 1987, the ability of federally recognized tribes to build huge, lucrative casinos has increased the in-

terest (and capability) of New England Indians to seek that status—and intensified the opposition of non-Indians fearful of the myriad problems associated with
the casinos.[25]

In the century between the American Revolution and Reconstruction, Indians
in southern New England were deeply affected by the interplay of tribal societies
and cultures, racial stereotypes and perceptions, and new notions of a unique regional history. At the end of the Revolution, Indians lived in four distinct situations: with sizeable reserves and populations, on or around a small reserve, in
more scattered communities dispersed around a small core that marked their traditional territory, and as neighborhoods or isolated households in white towns or
cities. Regardless of their situation, Indians were often linked by kinship and religious networks within and between these groups. Like their non-Indian neighbors,
individuals and families during the early republic left in large numbers to find
work and opportunities on whaling ships and in other towns and cities. Some
moved to larger tribes, where churches served as political, cultural, and social centers for Indians in the area. Rates of exogamous marriages increased both in the
outside world, facilitating the acculturation and assimilation of mixed descendants, and within some tribes, taxing Native societies, politics, and cultures. These
trends challenged tribal boundaries, but those with sizeable reserves were reinforced by a strange combination of traditional communitarianism and state laws
that treated Indians as children.

One result was that, during the period when American concepts of race became more rigid and powerful, the experiences of Indians in the interstices between white and black highlighted the strange elastic-yet-rigid, often contradic-
tory, prejudices of racism. Indian tribes accepted black and white spouses but
sought to protect their cultures and resources by limiting the privileges given newcomers. Because most exogamous marriages involved Indian women and "foreign" men, this gave more power to Native women than they probably had during the seventeenth century. Some Indians adopted the language and imagery of
race, partially in defense of their communities, resources, or particular goals.
There was also the widening gap between Indian and African American cultures,
even as whites were more likely to see both as people of color. Indians in nineteenth-century southern New England also highlight the associations between
race and class. They were linked by whites as a race to certain manners and occupations that they held in common with white and black "lower sorts": mariners,
domestics, farm laborers, dock workers, circus performers. But Indians were also
perceived as having unique characteristics: holding land (which blacks and la-

boring whites lacked) and managing it in common, making baskets and other Native crafts, and traveling without a clear reason through forests their ancestors knew.

While tribal traditions and reserves provided varying degrees of insulation, Indians were deeply influenced by major developments in the region. During the early republic, the stream of men and women traveling between reserves and towns or cities became a river, and tribal churches created new links with radical Baptists and Methodists who were gaining strength among the "lower sort" throughout New England. In the second quarter of the century, Anglo-Americans established new schools and moral reform movements among nearly all of the larger tribes, just as they were doing elsewhere in the region, and pressured Indians to divide their lands and adopt agricultural improvements. In the process, magistrates, ministers, and intellectuals moved from excluding racial minorities to including them in the larger community. At the same time, these influences and alterations were used by Indians to reinforce their political and religious institutions, often against forces that threatened the community.

The most corrosive force threatening Indian survival in the region emerged at midcentury, as New Englanders developed the concept that their past, their identity, and their purpose were unique, meaningful, and at the core of what made America great. That romantic history included a particular image of "the Indian," which served to both redeem those who had resisted the Puritan invaders and to reinforce the racialist notion that few *real* Indians remained. That perception and the movement for equal rights presented termination as a necessary part of the future. After 1870, termination destroyed most of the buffer remaining between Indians and the outside world. White reformers and politicians quickly took the same paradigms and applied them, in the Dawes Act, to the recently conquered Western tribes. Only a few New England tribes remained relatively intact. In the early twentieth century, the pan-Indian movement and rising national sympathy for indigenous cultures spurred a revitalization of those tribes and the rediscovery and revival of other Indian communities in the region. That development not only provided the route for Indians to rediscover and use their history but also helped others perceive deeper truths about America's past.

Abbreviations

AAS	American Antiquarian Society, Worcester, Mass.
CAr1	Connecticut, Indian Archives [to 1815], 1st ser., vol. 2, CSA
CAr2	Connecticut, Indian Archives [to 1815], 2nd ser., vol. 1, CSA
CAr2-2	Connecticut, Indian Archives [to 1815], 2nd ser., vol. 2, CSA
CGA1	Connecticut General Assembly, Indian Papers, box 1, RG 002, CSA
CGA2	Connecticut General Assembly, Indian Papers, Rejected Bills, box 2, RG 002, CSA
CHS	Connecticut Historical Society, Hartford
CPA	*Public Acts of the General Assembly of the State of Connecticut* (Hartford/New Haven, 1839–1876)
CPL	*Public Statute Laws of the State of Connecticut* (Hartford, 1808, 1835)
CPR	*The Public Records of the State of Connecticut*, 15 vols. to date (Hartford, 1894–1991)
CRPA	*Resolutions and Private Acts, Passed by the General Assembly of the State of Connecticut* (Hartford/New Haven, 1844–1870)
CSA	Connecticut State Archives, Hartford
GPO	U.S. Government Printing Office
MACR	Colonial Records, Massachusetts Archives
MAR	*Acts and Resolves Passed by the General Court of the Commonwealth of Massachusetts* (Boston, 1784–1922)
MGCF	Massachusetts, Governor's Council Files, Massachusetts Archives
MHR	Massachusetts Legislative Documents, House of Representatives, *Reports* (Boston, 1802–1882)
MHS	Massachusetts Historical Society, Boston
MHSC	*Collections of the Massachusetts Historical Society* (Boston, 1792–1941)

MIGA	Massachusetts, Indian Guardian Accounts and Correspondence, Massachusetts Archives
MPL	Massachusetts, Documents Relating to Passed Legislation, Massachusetts Archives
MSR	Massachusetts Legislative Documents, Senate, *Reports* (Boston, 1802–1882)
MUHL	Massachusetts, Documents Relating to Unpassed House Legislation, Massachusetts Archives
MUSL	Massachusetts, Documents Relating to Unpassed Senate Legislation, Massachusetts Archives
MVHS	Martha's Vineyard Historical Society, Edgartown, Mass.
NEC	New England Company (Corporation for the Propagation of the Gospel in New England and Parts Adjacent in America)
NEHGS	New England Historical and Genealogical Society, Boston
NLCC	New London County Court, Papers by Subject: Indians, RG 003, Judicial Department, CSA
NLCSC	New London County Superior Court, Papers by Subject: Indians, RG 003, Judicial Department, CSA
NRIA	Narragansett file, Rhode Island State Archives, Providence
PRO	Public Records Office, London, England
RIAR	*Rhode Island Acts and Resolves* (Providence, 1776–)
RICR	*Records of the Colony of Rhode Island and Providence Plantations*, ed. John Bartlett, 10 vols. (Providence: A. C. Greene, 1856–1865)
SPG	Society for Propagating the Gospel among the Indians, and Others, in North America
SPGPE	Papers of the SPG, Ms. 48, Phillips Library, Peabody Essex Museum, Salem, Mass. (used by permission of the Phillips Library at the Peabody Essex Museum)
SPM	Segel, Pierce, Monterosso Collection, MVHS

Adams 1880—Dwight R. Adams, George Carmichael Jr., and George B. Carpenter, *Report of the Committee of Investigation; A Historical Sketch and Evidence Taken, Made to the House of Representatives at Its January Session, A.D. 1880* (Providence, 1880)

Adams 1881—Dwight R. Adams, George Carmichael Jr., and William P. Sheffield, *Report of Commission on the Affairs of the Narragansett Indians, 1881* (Providence, 1881)

Baylies 1823—Frederick Baylies, "Names & Ages of the Indians on Martha's Vineyard, Taken About the 1st of Jan. 1823," uncataloged mss., NEHGS

Bird 1849—F. W. Bird, Whiting Griswold, and Cyrus Weekes, "Report on Condition and Circumstances of Indians Remaining within This Commonwealth," *Massachusetts House Reports*, no. 46 (Boston, 1849)

Child 1827—D. L. Child, H. Stebbins, and D. Fellows Jr., "Report [on the condition of the native Indians and descendants of native Indians, in this Commonwealth]," *Massachusetts House Reports*, no. 68 (Boston, 1827)

Earle 1861—John Milton Earle, "Report to the Governor and Council Concerning the Indians of the Commonwealth under the Act of April 6, 1859," *MSR* 96 (Boston, 1861)

Griffin 1858—Joseph Griffin, *Narragansett Commissioner Report to the General Assembly* (Providence, 1858)

Hawley 1776—"Number of the Indians, mulatoes, and Negroes belonging to Mashpee, June 24th, 1776," Gideon Hawley Papers, MHS

Hawley 1793—Mashpee census of 1793 (filed as "Gideon Hawley"), Autograph File, Houghton Library, Harvard University

Mohegan 1861—*Report of the Commissioners on Distribution of Lands of the Mohegan Indians* (Hartford, Conn., 1861)

PF Mohegan—U.S. Department of the Interior, Office of Federal Acknowledgment, "Summary under the Criteria and Evidence for Proposed Finding against Federal Acknowledgement of the Mohegan Tribe of Indians of the State of Connecticut" (30 Oct. 1999)

PF Narragansett—U.S. Department of the Interior, Bureau of Indian Affairs, "Recommendation and Summary of Evidence for Proposed Finding for Federal Acknowledgement of the Narragansett Indian Tribe of Rhode Island" (29 July 1982)

PF Nipmuc—U.S. Department of the Interior, "Summary under the Criteria and Evidence for Final Determination against Federal Acknowledgement of the Nipmuc Nation" (18 June 2004)

PF Schaghticoke—U.S. Department of the Interior, Office of Federal Acknowledgment, "Summary under the Criteria and Evidence for Proposed Finding Schaghticoke Tribal Nation" (5 Dec. 2002)

PF Webster—U.S. Department of the Interior, Office of Federal Acknowledgment, "Summary under the Criteria and Evidence for Proposed Finding Webster/Dudley Band of Chaubunagungamaug Nipmuck Indians" (25 Sept. 2001)

Notes

INTRODUCTION

1. William Apess, "A Son of the Forest," in *On Our Own Ground: The Complete Writings of William Apess, A Pequot*, ed. Barry O'Connell (Amherst: University of Massachusetts Press, 1992), 10.

2. I became interested in such connections while working on *Behind the Frontier: Indians in Eighteenth-Century Eastern Massachusetts* (Lincoln: University of Nebraska Press, 1996) and was motivated to investigate further when Daniel Vickers noted in a review that the book "has much to teach about poverty," as "the Indians' story is far more closely documented that that of most other marginal peoples of their day." *Journal of Interdisciplinary History* 28 (1997): 138–39. See also James Merrell, "American Nations, Old and New: Reflections on Indians and the Early Republic," in *Native Americans and the Early Republic*, ed. Frederick Hoxie et al. (Charlottesville: University of Virginia Press, 1999), 345–46.

CHAPTER 1: LAND AND LABOR

1. William Tudor, *Letters on the Eastern States*, 2nd ed. (Boston: Wells and Lilly, 1821), 289, 281, 287.

2. Wendy B. St. Jean, "Inventing Guardianship: The Mohegan Indians and Their 'Protectors,'" *New England Quarterly* 72 (1999): 362–87; Daniel Mandell, *Behind the Frontier: Indians in Eighteenth-Century Eastern Massachusetts* (Lincoln: University of Nebraska Press, 1996); Laura E. Conkey, Ethel Boissevain, and Ives Goddard, "Indians of Southern New England and Long Island: Late Period," in *Smithsonian Handbook of North American Indians*, ed. William C. Sturtevant, vol. 15: *Northeast*, ed. Bruce G. Trigger (Washington, D.C.: Smithsonian Institution, 1978), 177–89.

3. Mandell, *Behind the Frontier*, 68–69, 185–86.

4. David Crosby, East Hartford, to Eleazar Wheelock, 4 Nov. 1767, Wheelock Papers, no. 767604.1, Dartmouth College; Alden Vaughan, "From White Man to Redskin: Changing Anglo-American Perceptions of the American Indian, *American Historical Review* 87 (Oct. 1982): 842–949; John W. Sweet, *Bodies Politic: Negotiating Race in the American North, 1730–1830* (Baltimore: Johns Hopkins University Press, 2003), 9–10, 106–8, 272–352.

5. Sarah Berry and Jerusha Hawkins to Mass. legislature, 19 Jan. 1781, Mass. Revolutionary Petitions 187 (1781–82): 11, Mass. Archives; Hawley to Gov. John Hancock, 8 July

1791, Hawley Papers, MHS; Mass., ch. 5, Resolves of 1784, 4 June 1784, MPL; Jemimah Sowomog and Rachel Amos to Mass. legislature, 1785, in SPM, box 1, "Nashawkemmuch Chilmark" folder.

6. William DeLoss Love, *Samson Occom and the Christian Indians of New England* (Boston: Pilgrim Press, 1899), 247–90, 305; *Third Annual Report of Commission on the Affairs of the Narragansett Indians* (Providence, 1883), 12; "The Number of Indians in Rhode Island . . . Taken Between the 4th of May and the 14th of June, 1774," in *MHSC*, 1st ser., 10 (1809): 119; 1782 census in *Records of the State of Rhode Island* (Providence, 1783), 653.

7. Henry A. Baker, *History of Montville, Connecticut, Formerly the North Parish of New London* (Hartford: Case, Lockwood and Brainerd, 1896), 58–61.

8. *MHSC* 10 (1809), 103–4; Abiel Holmes, "Additional Memoirs of the Mohegans," *MHSC* 9 (1804), 79; Timothy Dwight, *Travels in New England and New York* (1821–22; reprint, Cambridge, Mass.: Harvard University Press, 1969), 2:367; Accounts of C. S. Manwaring, Sept. 1855–Aug. 1856, box 3: Niantic, 1855–1877, NLCSC; John Deforest, *History of the Indians of Connecticut, from the Earliest Known Period to 1850* (Hartford: William Jason Hamersley 1851), 387, 416–20.

9. *CPR* 7:261.

10. Samuel Niles, Ephraim Cohis, Jo Cowyons, James Niles, and Daniel Shattuck, Narragansett tribal council, to R.I. legislature, Aug. 1779, Petitions to the General Assembly, vol. 17, 1778–80, no. 79, R.I. Archives, Providence; Elijah Wampy et al., Brothertown, to Conn. assembly, Oct. 1793, CAr2-2, 153–53; James Wakous et al., Brothertown, to assembly, Oct. 1801, CAr2-2, 163–64; Sarah and Aaron Poquiantup, Brothertown, to assembly, Sept. 1808, CAr2, 98–99; Rhoda Charles, Brothertown, to assembly, Oct. 1815, CAr2, 105–6; Robert Ashbow and other Mohegans to assembly, April 1798, CAr2, 45–46; Mohegan petitions, 1822, CGA2, folder 4; on Brothertown Indian land sales in the 1840s, see chapter 4.

11. Ives Goddard and Kathleen Bragdon, *Native Writings in Massachusett* (Philadelphia: American Philosophical Society, 1988), 1:7–8; Josiah H. Benton, *Early Census-Making in Massachusetts, 1643–1765* (Boston: Goodspeed, 1905); Gay Head petition to Mass. legislature, 18 May 1816, in MUHL no. 8029, 1816.

12. Hawley 1793; thanks to Andrew Pierce for bringing this census to my attention and to Houghton Library for making photocopies. Mashpee census 1800, in Hawley to Peter Thacher, Boston, 5 Aug. 1800, Hawley file, SPGPE; my thanks to Doug Winiarski for information on this collection. "A Description of Mashpee, in the County of Barnstable, September 18th, 1802," *MHSC*, 2nd ser., 3 (1815): 8.

13. Nathaniel Freeman to MHS, 23 Sept. 1792, *American Apollo* 5 (1792): 230–32; Ralph Micah to Mass. legislature, 1799, MUHL no. 4847; "Native Indians," *Barnstable Patriot*, 5 April 1815; Timothy Alden Jr., "Memorabilia of Yarmouth," *MHSC*, 1st ser., 5 (1798): 55.

14. Mandell, *Behind the Frontier*, 80–85, 95–96, 164–196; Mohegan 1861, 9–10; Frank G. Speck, "Native Tribes and Dialects of Connecticut, A Mohegan-Pequot Diary," *Bureau of American Ethnology Annual Report, no. 43: 1925–1926* (Washington, D.C.: GPO, 1928), 207–16; Russell G. Handsman and Trudie Lamb Richmond, "Confronting Colonialism: The Mahican and Scahaghticoke Peoples and Us," essay prepared for "Making Alternative Histories," School of American Research, Santa Fe, New Mexico, April 1992; Ellen Douglas Larned, *History of Windham County, Connecticut* (Worcester: C. Hamilton, 1874 and

1880), 2:389–90. The Windham tradition is supported by the 1774 census, which showed 11 to 25 Indians in 7 of county's 12 towns and 38 in Woodstock—the town closest to what in 1730 had been the largest Nipmuc settlement, Grafton in Massachusetts; *CPR* 14: 489.

15. J. Hector St. John de Crèvecoeur, *Letters from an American Farmer* (1782; reprint, New York: Penguin, 1981), 121; Andrew Oliver to Israel Manduit, n.d., reprinted in *American Magazine* 5 (1789): 28, and *Massachusetts Magazine* 7 (1789): 636–37; Freeman to MHS, 23 Sept. 1792; "Native Indians," *Barnstable Patriot*, 5 April 1815; Addendum to "Progress of the Gospel among the Indians at Martha's Vineyard," in *American Apollo* 5 (1792): 201; Adams to Jefferson, 28 June 1812, *The Adams-Jefferson Letters*, ed. Lester J. Cappon (Chapel Hill: University of North Carolina Press, 1959), 2:310.

16. Crèvecoeur, *Letters from an American Farmer*, 122–23, 121; Dwight, *Travels in New England*, 3:14; Edward Kendall, *Travels through the Northern Parts of the United States in the Years 1807 and 1808* (New York: I. Riley, 1809), 1:308; Larned, *History of Windham County*, 2:389–90.

17. Jack Larkin, *The Reshaping of Everyday Life, 1790–1840* (New York: Harper and Row, 1988); David Jaffee, "The Village Enlightenment in New England, 1760–1820," *William and Mary Quarterly*, 3rd ser., 47 (1990): 327–46.

18. Anonymous, "Report of a Committee on the State of the Indians in Mashpee and Parts Adjacent [in 1767]," *MHSC*, 2nd ser., 3 (1815): 14; Hawley to Phillips, Boston, 24 June 1776, SPG Records, box 3, folder 52, NEHGS; Nathan Birdsey to Ezra Stiles, 3 Sept. 1762, *MHSC*, 1st ser., 10 (1809): 111–12; James Winthrop, "Journal of a Survey in 1791, for a Canal across Cape Cod," *Monthly Bulletin of Books Added to the Public Library of the City of Boston*, 6 (1901): 125–26.

19. Baylies 1823; Myron Stachiw, "The Early Architecture of Southeastern New England: Native and Non-Native Building from the Seventeenth Century to the Early Nineteenth Century," presented at the Third Mashantucket Pequot History Conference, Sept. 2003; Curtis Coe, Journals (on Narragansetts), 24 June–17 Oct. 1809 and 7 July–7 Dec. 1810, box 1, folder 21, SPGPE; Earle 1861, 11; Kevin McBride, "Historical Archaeology of the Mashantaucket Pequots, 1637–1900, a Preliminary Analysis," in *The Pequots in Southern New England: The Rise and Fall of an American Indian Nation*, ed. Laurence M. Hauptman and James D. Wherry (Norman: University of Oklahoma Press, 1990), 111–14; Melissa J. Fawcett, *Medicine Trail: The Life and Lessons of Gladys Tantaquidgeon* (Tucson: University of Arizona Press, 2000), 11 and passim. (Mohegans); Mohegan 1861, 3.

20. Hawley to RDS [Rev. D. Strong], Aug. 1802, S. P. Savage Papers, no. 222, MHS; David Silverman, "The Impact of Indentured Servitude on the Society and Culture of Southern New England Indians," *New England Quarterly* 74 (2001): 625–28; Kenneth L. Feder, *A Village of Outcasts: Historical Archaeology and Documentary Research on the Lighthouse Site* (Mountain View, Calif.: Mayfield, 1994), 23–24; Bird 1849, 18–20; John W. Barber, *Historical Collections of Massachusetts* (Worcester: Dorr, Howland, and Co., 1839), 148–50; John Milton Earle Papers, bound vols. 1 and 2 (Hassanamisco guardian accounts), AAS; various accounts in MIGA.

21. Mashpee petition, MUSL no. 1643 (1792).

22. Gideon Hawley, letter, MUSL no. 2397 (1798).

23. Mashpee petition, July 1788, chap. 38, Acts of 1788, MPL; see also Gideon Hawley

deposition, 22 May 1797, MUSL no. 2397 (Feb. 1798); Levi Mie to Mass. legislature, 13 June 1791, MUSL no. 1419a. On aboriginal land use, see Kathleen J. Bragdon, *Native People of Southern New England, 1500–1650* (Norman: University of Oklahoma Press, 1996), 137.

24. General assembly committee report, 3 Sept. 1774, CAr1 (thanks to David Conroy for this reference); Mohegan tribal council to assembly, 14 Dec. 1799, CAr2, 48a–b; Lucy Cooper (Mohegan) to Conn. assembly, Oct. 1806, CAr2, 62–63; Lydia Wyyoug to assembly, 5 May 1832, CGA1, folder 9; Lydia Wyyoug, Parthena Hoscott, and Cynthia Hoscott to assembly, 5 May 1835, CGA1, folder 11; Puolly Mossock, for herself and for Sophronia Gherts, William Crosby, Clark Sumson, Alnzo Samson, and Avery Samson, to assembly, 4 May 1844, CGA1, folder 16; Puolly Mossock et al. to New London County Court, Nov. 1845, NLCC, box 3; Mohegan 1861, 1–2, 7–8; Gideon Ammons, testimony 30 July 1879, in Adams 1880, Appendix B, 31–32; minutes of Gay Head proprietors' meeting, 16 April 1784, Howwowswee Papers, ms. 1784, John Carter Brown Library, Brown University, Providence; Christiantown petition, 1824, MUHL no. 9419; Joseph Thaxter to Mass. legislature, 26 Dec. 1823, ibid.

25. Griffin 1858, 4–5.

26. Adams 1881, 151, 100–101, 109; William Blackstone, *Commentaries on the Laws of England* (1766; reprint, Chicago: University of Chicago Press, 1979), 2:313.

27. Coe, Journal, 7 July–7 Dec. 1810, box 1, folder 21, SPGPE; *Communication from Governor Dyer Accompanying the Report of the Commissioner of the Narragansett Tribe of Indians* (Providence, 1859); report of legislative committee on Narragansetts, Jan. 1830, doc. 80, NRIA; Nymphas Marston and Kilburn Whitman to Mass. legislature, 31 Jan. 1822, in ch. 75, MPL 1822; Bird 1849, 20–21; Earle 1861, 33.

28. CAr1, no. 330; David Silverman, *Faith and Boundaries: Colonists, Christianity, and Community among the Wampanoag Indians of Martha's Vineyard, 1600–1871* (New York: Cambridge University Press, 2005), 247; David Wright to James Walker and Frances Parkman, Boston, 9 April 1839, SPG Papers, box 7, MHS; Mass. Commissioners' "Report" on Mashpee lands, 9 Feb. 1843, MGCF, box 56.

29. A petition from Narragansett leaders, Jan. 1832, noted that the tribe used cedar from their swamp for "fencing stuff"; Narragansett petition to assembly, Jan. 1832, doc. 89, NRIA. But in 1881, tribal council member Joshua Noka testified that he and others did not want to be forced to fence their lands and that some families did not know their boundaries; Adams 1880, 34.

30. Chappaquiddick to Mass. legislature, 24 May 1810, MUSL no. 4093; Wright to Walker and Parkman, 9 April 1839, SPG Papers, box 7, MHS.

31. William Baylies, "Description of Gay Head . . . July 1st, 1786," in American Academy of Arts and Sciences, *Memoir* 2, part 1 (1793), 152 (corn, rye, potatoes, peas, flax, and beans); Bird 1849, 18–20 (corn, rye, oats, and potatoes); Barber, *Historical Collections of Massachusetts*, 148–50.

32. Table 2; see also William Baylies to unknown, Dighton, Mass., 1 July 1786, in vol. 15, Banks Collection, MHS.

33. Hawley to Peter Thatcher, 15 Sept. 1800, box 2, folder 16, SPGPE; Child 1827; Barber, *Historical Collections of Massachusetts*, 47.

34. Albert C. Koch, *Journey through a Part of the United States of North America in the*

Years 1844–1846 (Carbondale: Southern Illinois University Press, 1972), 23; MUSL no. 4678 (1813); Hawley to RDS [Rev. D. Strong], Aug. 1802; Tudor, *Letters on the Eastern States,* 287; Herring Pond overseers to Mass. legislature, 25 Jan. 1814, MUHL no. 7666; Marston and Whitman to Mass. legislature, 31 Jan. 1822, ch. 75, MPL; Bird 1849, 39.

35. Holmes, "Number and Names of the Mohegans," 75; Coe, Journal, 7 July–7 Dec. 1810, and 24 June–17 Oct. 1809, SPGPE; Tobias Ross, Christopher Harry, and Daniel Seketer to R.I. assembly, June 1832, doc. 86, NRIA; Griffen 1858; Deforest, *Indians of Connecticut,* 489.

36. Adams 1880, 29; Ross, Harry, and Seketer to assembly, June 1832, doc. 86, NRIA; Jedidiah Morse, *A Report to the Secretary of War of the United States on Indian Affairs* (New Haven: Converse, 1822), 74; Holmes, "Additional Memoirs of Mohegans," 90; Fawcett, *Medicine Trail,* 17, 22; Conn., resolve regarding petition of Mohegan and Niantic Indians, May 1819, CAr2, 107.

37. Gary Kulik, "Dams, Fish, and Farmers: Defense of Public Rights in Eighteenth-Century Rhode Island," in *The Countryside in the Age of Capitalist Transformation: Essays in the Social History of Rural America,* ed. Steven Hahn and Jonathan Prude (Chapel Hill: University of North Carolina Press, 1985), 28, 31, 27.

38. Childs 1827, 12; Anonymous, "Description of Mashpee," 5; Ross, Harry, and Seketer to assembly, June 1832, doc. 86, NRIA; Hawley to Jonathan Edwards, June 1802, Hawley Papers, MHS

39. Levi Mie to Mass. legislature, 13 July 1791, MUSL no. 1491.

40. "A Description of Duke's County, Aug. 13th, 1807," *MHSC,* 2nd ser., 3 (1815): 44, 94; Gay Head resolution, 1 April 1815, MGCF, box 22; Gay Head petition to Mass. legislature, 1818, MUHL no. 8029; MGCF, box 21; Ebenezer Skiff to Frederick Baylies, 3 Feb. 1823, Misc. Docs., MHS; Koch, *Journey through a Part of the United States,* 24–25 (quotation). The men digging and loading the clay usually earned three dollars a day, and women and children half that. These were very good wages. By comparison, in 1828, farm laborers in Essex County, Mass., were hired for $13 per month (about $0.50 per day), and wages four years later were about the same; Daniel Vickers, *Farmers and Fishermen: Two Centuries of Work in Essex County, Massachusetts, 1630–1850* (Chapel Hill: University of North Carolina Press, 1994), 306, 308. Black laborers in Philadelphia during the 1840s were paid $1.15 per day, and black women domestics, $0.60 per day; James Oliver Horton and Lois E. Horton, *In Hope of Liberty: Culture, Community and Protest among Northern Free Blacks, 1700–1860* (New York: Oxford University Press, 1997), 114.

41. Narragansetts to R.I. assembly, 1813, doc. 50, NRIA; Tobias Ross to assembly, 15 Oct. 1822, note added by Christopher Harry, unnumbered, NRIA; Eunice Rogers to R.I. assembly, 1822, unnumbered, NRIA; doc. 71, NRIA; R.I. assembly, report of legislative committee on Narragansetts, Jan 1831, doc. 81, NRIA; Seketer, Harry, and Amos to R.I. assembly, June 1832, doc. 86, NRIA. These rivals joined ranks in large part because the 1831 report also recommended that the state should abolish the tribal council and eliminate the tribe's legal disabilities and protections.

42. Hawley to Gov. John Hancock, 8 July 1791, Hawley Papers, MHS; Gay Head petition to Mass. legislature, 13 July 1811, MGCF, box 19; Gay Head resolution, 30 April 1816, MUHL no. 8029; Gay Head petition to Mass. legislature, 1838, in "An Act to Prohibit the

Sale of Ardent Spirits to the Gay Head Indians," *MHR*, no. 48 (Boston, 1838), 3; Bird 1849, 21; Narragansett Council to assembly, petitions to the general assembly, vol. 17, 1778–80, no. 79; Coe, Journal, 7 July–7 Dec. 1810, SPGPE; Tobias Ross and Narragansett Council to R.I. assembly, 30 Oct. 1821, unnumbered, NRIA; Ross, Harry, and Seketer to assembly, June 1832, doc. 86, NRIA; Moses Stanton to legislative committee, 1832, doc. 96, NRIA.

43. Herring Pond Indians to Mass. legislature, 6 Jan. 1762, MA 33: 186; Mashpees to Mass. Commission of Indian Affairs, 4 Aug. 1757, Hawley Letters, MHS; Hawley to Bourne, 15 Dec. 1788, Hawley Letters, MHS; Mie to Mass. legislature, 13 June 1791, MUSL no. 1419a; Hawley to Mass. Senate and House, 1 May 1795, ibid.; act to regulate alewife fishery in brook from Wakepee Pond, 13 June 1801, in *Private and Special Statutes of the Commonwealth of Massachusetts, from the Year 1780, to . . . May, A.D. 1805* (Boston: Manning and Loring, 1805); addition to act to regulate alewife fishery in brook from Wakepee Pond, 22 Feb. 1803, ibid.; Mashpee guardians to Mass. legislature, 1813, MUSL no. 4678; report of legislative commission on the Marshpee and Herring Pond Indians, 18 June 1818, MIGA, box 2, folder 10.

44. Ralph Micah to Mass. legislature, 1799, MUHL no. 4847; *Moses Susonun v. John Packer and Ben Packer*, March 1817, NLCC, box 2; *James Sansamen and the rest of the Pequot tribe v. James Latham, Amos Latham, and Robert Latham, all of Groton*, 25 June 1833, NLCC, box 2; Joseph Charles and Immanuel Simons, Groton Pequots, to assembly, Oct. 1793, CAr2-2, 26–27; Pequot overseers to assembly, May 1800, CAr2-2, 30–31; Chappaquiddicks to Mass. legislature, 1799, in MUSL no. 2532; Chappaquiddicks to governor, ca. 1805, in MIGA, box 3, folder 15.

45. Hawley to Mass. legislature, 1799, MUSL no. 2397; Gay Head to Mass. legislature, 1818, MUHL no. 8029; *MAR* ch. 84, 8 March 1805; MUSL no. 9097 (1830); MUSL no. 9108 (1830); MUSL no. 9243 (1832); Mashpee petitions and legislative reports in MUSL no. 1419 (1791) and MUSL no. 1643 (1792); Mass., legislative committee report on Marshpee and Herring Pond, 1818, MIGA, box 2, folder 10.

46. Mass., legislative committee report on Marshpee and Herring Pond.

47. Child 1827, 12; Earle 1861, 6; Mandell, *Behind the Frontier*, 143–58; Adams 1880, Appendix B, 30–31; Griffin 1858, 7. On shifts in New England farming around 1800, see Carolyn Merchant, *Ecological Revolutions: Nature, Gender, and Science in New England* (Chapel Hill: University of North Carolina Press, 1989), 185–97, 275–76, 282–85; Brian Donahue, *The Great Meadow: Farmers and the Land in Colonial Concord* (New Haven: Yale University Press, 2005), 205–20.

48. "Marshpee Disturbance, 1833–1834," MIGA, box 2, file 1; Mie to Mass. legislature, 13 July 1791, MUSL no. 1419; MUSL no. 1643 (1792); Mashpees to Mass. legislature, 8 Jan. 1796, MUSL no. 2194; Mass., legislative commission, report, 18 June 1818, MIGA, box 2, folder 10. On the effects of the actions of guardians, see Mandell, *Behind the Frontier*, 205–7.

49. Edward Mitchell to Mass. legislature, request for reimbursement of expenses in Dunbar's lawsuit, MPL ch. 130, Resolves of 1815.

50. Mandell, "'To Live More Like My Christian English Neighbors': Natick Indians in the Eighteenth Century," *William and Mary Quarterly*, 3rd ser., 48 (1991): 552–79; Natick Indians to Mass. legislature, in MPL ch. 262, Resolves of 1808; Mandell, *Behind the Fron-*

tier, 90, 98, 101, 122, 134–36, 154–56, 174; Elizabeth Senah to Mass. legislature, MPL ch. 11, Resolves of 1784; Edward Mitchell, Pembroke, to Mass. legislature, MPL ch. 130, Resolves of 1815; various resolves from the Mass. legislature authorizing Hassanamisco land sales, Earle Papers, box 1, folder 5.

51. Dudley Nipmucs to Mass. legislature, 12 Feb. 1796, MUSL no. 2151; Dudley Indian guardian accounts, 1804, MAR ch. 152, and 1805, MAR ch. 167; Yarmouth Indians to Mass. legislature, 1820, MUSL no. 6568; selectmen of Harwich, Orleans, and Brewster to Mass. legislature, MPL ch. 212, Resolves of 1818; MAR ch. 212, 27 Jan. 1819.

52. Thomas Weston, *History of the Town of Middleboro Massachusetts* (Boston: Houghton, Mifflin, 1906), 13; Larned, *History of Windham County,* 2:389–90.

53. L. H. Bradford, South Gardner, to Earle, 30 July 1859, Earle Papers, box 2, folder 5; Harriett Merrifield Forbes, *The Hundredth Town: Glimpses of Life in Westborough, 1717–1817* (Boston: Press of Rockwell and Churchill, 1889), 178.

54. Holly Izard, "Hepsibeth Hemenway's Portrait: A Native American Story," *Old-Time New England* 77, no. 267 (fall/winter 1999), 49–75, www.spnea.org/resources/articles/pdf585.pdf (accessed 6 July 2006).

55. MPL ch. 113, Resolves of 1814; MPL ch. 74, Resolves of 1824; Earle Papers, box 1, folder 5; Jonathan Denny, Leicester town clerk, to Earle, 18 Oct. 1859, in Earle Papers, box 1, folder 1; Mass. resolve allowing Johns to sell land in Grafton, 4 Feb. 1796, in Earle Papers, box 1, folder 5; Earle Papers, bound vol. 2, p. 107 (Johns's date of death); MUSL no. 7153. Another Hassanamisco, Deborah Brown, described by Harriet Forbes as "a celebrated tramp," also moved from Grafton to Worcester, but after bearing eight children (without a legal marriage) died at the city's poor farm; S. W. Griggs, Worcester town clerk, to John Milton Earle, 7 Oct. 1859, in Earle Papers, box 1, folder 1. See generally Doughton, "Unseen Neighbors: Native Americans of Central Massachusetts, A People Who Had 'Vanished,'" in *After King Philip's War: Presence and Persistence in Indian New England,* ed. Colin Calloway (Hanover, N.H.: University Press of New England, 1997), 207–31.

56. Izard, "Hepsibeth Hemenway's Portrait"; Jack Larkin, "Counting People of Color: Worcester County, Massachusetts 1790–1860, a Preliminary Report," presented at the Conference on Reinterpreting New England Indian History and the Colonial Experience, Old Sturbridge Village, April 2001.

57. Leman Stone to assembly, 9 May 1823, CGA1, folder 2; Stone to assembly, 9 May 1825, CGA1, folder 5; Stone to assembly, 7 May 1827, ibid.

58. William Brigham, *An Address Delivered before the Inhabitants of Grafton on the First Centennial Anniversary of that Town, April 29, 1835* (Boston: Light and Horton, 1835), appendix; MIGA, box 3, folders 3–9.

59. G. B. Blachard, South Natick, to Alden Bradford, Boston, 4 Dec. 1835, SPG Papers, box 6, MHS. The SPG paid a small stipend to Blachard to minister to the Indians, who (he noted) rarely attended the church but still expected a right to his services for funerals and other needs. By November 1837, the SPG ended its support for the Indians at Natick because their numbers had dropped so low; SPG Select Committee, report, Nov. 1837, SPG Papers, box 6, MHS.

60. Larned, *History of Windham County,* 2:532, 540; Doughton, "Unseen Neighbors."

61. MUSL no. 319; MUSL no. 1862; Ruth Herndon, *Unwelcome Americans: Living on*

the Margins in Early New England (Philadelphia: University of Pennsylvania Press, 2001); Douglas L. Jones, "The Strolling Poor: Transiency in Eighteenth-Century Massachusetts," *Journal of Social History* (1975): 28–39.

62. Joseph Bates et al., Haddam, May 1789, CAr2-2, 142–49; Guilford selectmen to assembly, May 1789, CAr2-2, 142–49; Canaan and Cornwall selectmen to assembly, Oct. 1802, CAr2-2, 116–17; Norwich to assembly, Oct. 1795, CAr2-2, 155–57; Woodbridge selectmen to assembly, Oct. 1801, CAr2-2, 158–60; Newtown selectmen to assembly, Oct. 1817, CAr2-2, 15–16; various petitions to assembly, CGA1, folder 2, folder 4; Montville selectmen to assembly, Oct. 1818, CAr2, 82–85.

63. Yarmouth Indians to Mass. MUSL no. 6568 (1820); Stephen Badger, "Historical and Characteristic Traits of the American Indians in General," *MHSC*, 1st ser., 5 (1798): 40.

64. T. S. Gold, "Fostering the Habit of Industry," *Connecticut Magazine* 8, no. 3 (March 1904): 452; Frances Manwaring Caulkins, notes of research on Indians, bound volume titled "Indians" Caulkins Collection, CHS.

65. Tudor, *Letters on the Eastern States*, 289, 281.

66. William Williams, Stonington Justice Court Book of Records, 1784, p. 13, CHS, mss. 89762, photocopy in collection of Mashantucket Pequot Research Library; Hawley to Peter Thatcher, 1 Jan. 1794, Hawley Letters, MHS.

67. Stonington, Conn., Selectmen Select Annals, 1723–1781, 108–9, 114, mss., Town Hall, Stonington, Conn.; Barbara W. Brown and James M. Rose, *Black Roots in Southeastern Connecticut, 1650–1900* (Detroit: Gale, 1980), 20, 27, 34, 44; Dwight, *Travels in New England*, 3:14; *On Our Own Ground: The Complete Writings of William Apess, a Pequot,* ed. Barry O'Connell (Amherst: University of Massachusetts Press, 1992), xxx–xxxii, 7–22; Morse, *Report to the Secretary of War*, 71; Conn., assembly committee report, 1 May 1826, CGA1, folder 8. On the decline of indentures among Anglo-Americans, see W. J. Rorabaugh, "'I Thought I Should Liberate Myself from the Thraldom of Others': Apprentices, Masters, and the Revolution," in *Beyond the American Revolution*, ed. Alfred E. Young (DeKalb: Northern Illinois University Press, 1993), 186, 196–208.

68. Hawley to James Freeman, 15 Nov. 1802, Hawley Letters, MHS; Killborn Whitman, report to Mass. legislature, 1818, in MPL ch. 99, Acts of 1817; see also Gay Head letter in "An Act to Prohibit the Sale of Ardent Spirits," 2.

69. Mark A. Nicholas, "Mashpee Wampanoags of Cape Cod, the Whalefishery, and Seafaring's Impact on Community Development," *American Indian Quarterly* 26 (2002): 173, 176; Mary A. Cleggett Vanderhoop, "The Gay Head Indians: Their History and Traditions," series in the *New Bedford Evening Standard* beginning 25 June 1904; *The Uncas Monument, 1492–1842: published once in three hundred and fifty years* (Norwich, Conn.: John G. Cooley, 1842); Charles Marston to John Milton Earle, 14 Feb. 1860, Earle Papers, box 2, folder 2; Barber, *Historical Collections of Massachusetts*, 48; John Avery, *History of the Town of Ledyard, 1650–1900* (Norwich, Conn.: Noyes and Davis, 1901), 261.

70. On the shift in New England agriculture generally, see Merchant, *Ecological Revolutions*, 185–97, 275–76, 282–85; for a detailed study of land use and deforestation in Concord, Massachusetts, and problems with using woodland, see Donahue, *The Great Meadow*, 205–20.

71. Frederick Baylies and Joseph Thaxter to Mass. legislature, 22 Sept. 1818, MIGA, box 3, folder 15; Christiantown to Mass. legislature, 29 Jan. 1805, MPL ch. 84, Acts of 1804; Kendall, *Travels through the Northern Parts*, 2:163–66; Mashpee to Mass. legislature, July 1788, MPL ch. 38, Acts of 1788; MUHL no. 7666 (1814).

72. Hawley, report to Mass. legislature, 2 Sept. 1795, Savage Papers, 2:218; Gay Head letter in "Report on Act to Prohibit the Sale of Ardent Spirits," 2. Hawley's 1795 letter identified Amos as "J. Amos' widow," and the only J. Amos in his 1793 census was Joseph Amos (his wife was not identified); Hawley 1793. See generally Larkin, *Reshaping of Everyday Life*, 172, 175, 284–86; Peter C. Mancall, *Deadly Medicine: Indians and Alcohol in Early America* (Ithaca, N.Y.: Cornell University Press, 1995).

73. Hawley to Thacher, 15 Sept. 1800, box 2, folder 16, SPGPE; C. L Whitemore, Framingham town clerk, to Earle, 24 Dec. 1859, Earle Papers, box 1, folder 1; Avery, *History of the Town of Ledyard*, 260; Hawley to Freeman, 2 Nov. 1802, Hawley Letters, MHS. Few Indian names appeared on the city's "warning out" list published in 1800, which indicates that most lived with white families as domestics, came to get a berth on a ship, or managed to remain "invisible" while residing among blacks; *Massachusetts Mercury*, 16 Sept. 1800.

74. Dwight, *Travels in New England*, 3:14, 18; see also ibid., 2:28, on Mohegans. Dwight did not notice whether those farms were on some of the land leased from the tribe, or perhaps even directly from the individuals who worked on that land. If this happened, one wonders at the dynamics of the relationship that resulted between white farmer-renter and Indian laborer.

75. Forbes, *Hundredth Town*, 170. Various records in the Hassanamisco guardian accounts show Sarah (Philips) Boston as an adult member of the community ca. 1790–1830, and a receipt from 1851 notes that she had recently died; Earle Papers, box 3, folders 1–2, 5.

76. Winifred Rothenberg's survey of farmer's journals in Massachusetts found not one woman listed as a laborer; Rothenberg, *From Market-Places to a Market Economy: The Transformation of Rural Massachusetts, 1750–1850* (Chicago: University of Chicago Press, 1992), 151 n. 6.

77. Anonymous, "Description of Mashpee," 5. This document says that Mashpee women *made* cheese and butter and *traded* baskets and mats in neighboring towns; they may not have traded the milk products. Later documents refer to cranberry bogs being important resources to Indian groups at Punkapoag, Herring Pond, and Gay Head, although only the latter is described as having sold the fruit to outsiders.

78. Lydia Sigourney, *Sketches of Connecticut, Forty Years Since* (Hartford, Conn.: Oliver D. Cooke & Sons, 1824), 34–35; Avery, *History of the Town of Ledyard*, 259–60; Apess, "Experiences of Five Christian Indians," in *On Our Own Ground*, 152.

79. Frank G. Speck, *Eastern Algonkian Block-Stamp Decoration: A New World Original or an Acculturated Art*, Research Series no. 1, Archaeological Society of New Jersey, State Museum (Trenton, 1947); Ann McMullen, "Native Basketry, Basketry Styles, and Changing Group Identity in Southern New England," in *Algonkians of New England, Past and Present*, ed. Peter Benes (Boston: Boston University Press, 1993), 76–88; Samuel Orcutt and Ambrose Beardsley, *History of Derby, Connecticut, 1642–1880* (Springfield, Mass.: Springfield Printing Company, 1880), 50. See also Henry David Thoreau's description of

an Indian basket peddler in Concord in the 1840s; *Walden* (1854; reprint, New York, 1937), 17. In 1839, the Montauks of Long Island were scorned by *Niles' National Register* as "a few basket making miserable half-breeds"; *Niles' National Register*, Dec. 14, 1839, 57, p. 256.

80. Alason Borden, ed., *Our County and Its People: A Descriptive and Biographical Records of Bristol County, Massachusetts* (n.p.: Boston History Company, 1899), 679; Noyes Holmes, *The Life of Major Holmes, Written by His Direction* (Ledyard: A and G. Gray, 1861), 5–6; Samuel Bulfinch Emmons, *'Every Man His Own Physician': The Vegetable Family Physician . . . Embracing Many Valuable Indian Recipes* (Boston: George P. Oakes, 1836), 2. Borden, *Our County and Its People,* 679; Seth Holderwell, *Receipts for the Cure of Most Diseases Incident to the Human Family, by the Celebrated Indian Doctor, John Mackentosh, of the Cherokee Nation* (New York: privately printed, 1827); "Dr. Newall, the Native Indian Doctor" (New Hampshire: n.p., [ca. 1849]), broadside advertisement in AAS collection; Joshua David Bellin, "Taking the Indian Cure: Thoreau, Indian Medicine, and the Performance of American Culture," *New England Quarterly* 79 (2006): 3–36.

81. William Biglow, *History of the Town of Natick, Mass.* (Boston: Marsh, Capen, and Lyon, 1830), 83; "Hannah Dexter," manuscript in files at Natick Historical Society; William S. Simmons, *Spirit of the New England Tribes: Indian History and Folklore, 1620–1984* (Hanover, N.H.: University Press of New England, 1986), 101. An Esther Howwoswee in the 1823 census, born about 1797, was hired by Frederick Baylies to teach school at Gay Head in 1820 and 1821, and I have assumed that she was the doctress remembered generations later; Baylies 1823; Baylies to Holmes, 10 Oct. 1820 and 15 Oct. 1821, box 1, folder 8, SPGPE. Earle 1861, appendix, shows Tameson Weeks born in 1806; Frank G. Speck, *Territorial Subdivisions and Boundaries of the Wampanoag, Massachusett, and Nauset Indians,* Indian Notes and Monographs no. 44 (New York: Museum of the American Indian, Heye Foundation, 1928), 46.

82. Simmons, *Spirit of the New England Tribes,* 93, 107–8. Gershom appeared in Baylies's census, aged 45; Baylies 1823.

83. Daniel Huntoon, *History of the Town of Canton, Norfolk County, Massachusetts* (Cambridge, Mass.: John Wilson and Son, 1893), 39; Earle 1861, xliv.

84. Benson J. Lossing, "The Last of the Pequods," *Scribner's Monthly* 2, no. 6 (Oct. 1871): 577; William Bentley, *The Diary of William Bentley, D.D., Pastor of the East Church, Salem, Massachusetts* (Salem: Essex Institute, 1905–14), 3:41.

85. Hawley to Gov. John Hancock, 8 July 1791, Hawley Letters, MHS; Hawley to SPG or to Genl. Court, 2 Sept. 1795, Savage Papers, 2:218; Tudor, *Letters on the Eastern States,* 289, 281, 287; Badger, "Historical and Characteristic Traits," 42, 44; Jeremy Belknap to Henry Knox, *Columbian Centinel,* 24 Jan. 1795; Dwight, *Travels in New England,* 3:14–15.

86. Avery, *History of the Town of Ledyard,* 39; *Uncas Monument;* Ross, Harry, and Seketer to R.I. assembly, June 1832, doc. 86, NRIA.

87. Sally Law, Norwich, to Conn. assembly, 1823, CGA1, folder 2; Sarah Law, Norwich, to assembly, 13 May 1845, CGA1, folder 17.

88. Badger, "Historical and Characteristic Traits," 39; Tudor, *Letters on the Eastern States,* 280–81; Dwight, *Travels in New England,* 3:14. When Konkepot visited Salem in 1803, his friend, Rev. William Bentley, wrote in his diary, "He is an Indian. He loves to ramble. He is now abroad without a farthing. He goes to the best public houses, puts up, when

pay is asked he has none & then he calls upon the public to pay this tax for him." Bentley, *Diary of William Bentley*, 3:41.

89. Hingham town petition to Mass. legislature, 1796, MUSL no. 2200.

90. Mark S. Schantz, *Piety in Providence: Class Dimensions of Religious Experience in Antebellum Rhode Island* (Ithaca, N.Y.: Cornell University Press, 2000), 71; Christopher Clark, *The Roots of Rural Capitalism: Western Massachusetts, 1780–1860* (Ithaca, N.Y.: Cornell University Press, 1990), 252–61, 306–9; Karen V. Hansen, *A Very Social Time: Crafting Community in Antebellum New England* (Berkeley: University of California Press, 1994); "Report of the House Commissioners on the Pauper System," *MHR* 6 (Boston, 1833): 6.

91. Daniel Mandell, "Shifting Boundaries of Race and Ethnicity: Indian-Black Intermarriage in Southern New England, 1760–1880," *Journal of American History* 85 (1998): 466–501; Edward Countryman, "Indians, the Colonial Order, and the Social Significance of the American Revolution," *William and Mary Quarterly*, 3rd ser., 53 (1996): 355.

92. Hawley to Jedidiah Morse, Boston, 29 Oct. 1800, box 2, folder 16, SPGPE; Child 1827, 5; Sarah Huntington to Lewis Cass, 8 Dec. 1830, reprinted in Edward Hooker, *Memoir of Mrs. Sarah L. Huntington Smith*, 3rd ed. (New York: American Tract Society, 1846), 119; Adams 1880, 6; Adams 1881, 51.

93. Rothenberg, *From Market-Places*; Immanuel Wallerstein, "The Construction of Peoplehood: Racism, Nationalism, Ethnicity," in *Race, Nation, Class: Ambiguous Identities*, ed. Etienne Balibar and Immanuel Wallerstein (1988; trans., New York: Verso, 1991), 78–79; Eric Foner, "Free Labor and Nineteenth-Century Political Ideology," in *The Market Revolution in America: Social, Political, and Religious Expressions, 1800–1880*, ed. Melvyn Stokes and Stephen Conway (Charlottesville: University of Virginia Press, 1996), 112–13.

94. Magistrates and others in Barnstable, Sandwich, and Falmouth, to Mass. legislature, 22 Dec. 1788, MPL ch. 38, Acts of 1788; Coe, Journal, 24 June–7 Oct. 1809; "William Penn," *Boston Advocate*, Dec. 1833, in *On Our Own Ground*, 199; William Morgan to Deforest, 22 Aug. 1849, in Deforest, *Indians of Connecticut*, 445; Earle 1861, 34.

95. Dwight, *Travels in New England*, 3:14–16; Rothenberg, *From Market-Places*, 150, 156, 174.

96. Ibid.; Wallerstein, "The Construction of Peoplehood," in *Race, Nation, Class*, 79, 83–84; Wallerstein, "Class Conflict in the World Economy," in ibid., 117.

97. Wallerstein, "Class Conflict in the World Economy," 117.

98. Balibar, "Preface," in *Race, Nation, Class*, 8.

99. Gregory Dowd, *A Spirited Resistance: The North American Indian Struggle for Unity, 1745–1815* (Baltimore: Johns Hopkins University Press, 1992); Anthony F. C. Wallace, "Revitalization Movements," *American Anthropologist*, n.s., 58 (1956): 264–81.

100. Frederick E. Hoxie, *A Final Promise: The Campaign to Assimilate the Indians, 1880–1920* (Lincoln: University of Nebraska Press, 1984); David Wallace Adams, *Education for Extinction: American Indians and the Boarding School Experience, 1750–1928* (Lawrence: University Press of Kansas, 1995). Americans' concerns in the early twentieth century about changes brought by immigration, urbanization, and industrialization sparked a strong interest in Indians and Indian cultures as an antidote to the perceived problems; Alan

Trachtenberg, *Shades of Hiawatha: Staging Indians, Making Americans, 1880–1930* (New York: Hill and Wang, 2004); Philip Deloria, *Playing Indian* (New Haven: Yale University Press, 1998).

CHAPTER 2: COMMUNITY AND FAMILY

1. William J. Brown, *The Life of William J. Brown* (Providence, R.I.: Angell and Co., Printers, 1883), 10–11.

2. Zaccheus Howwoswee, Gay Head, to John Milton Earle, 27 Jan. 1860, Earle Papers, box 2, folder 3.

3. Marlborough Wood, deposition, 29 Aug. 1859, in John Milton Earle, "Dartmouth Indian Land Claim," *MHR* 216 (Boston, 1861): 6; "Indian" binder, Martha's Vineyard Historical Society; Daniel Mandell, *Behind the Frontier: Indians in Eighteenth-Century Eastern Massachusetts* (Lincoln: University of Nebraska Press, 1996), 106, 128. Amos's gravestone reads "I have fought a good fight/I have finished my course/Kept the faith/I'm forever with the Lord/Its immortality."

4. For example, see the many residences of heirs to an allotment of Gay Head land, in Dukes County Registry of Deeds, Book 22, no. 339, copy in SPM, box 3; Joseph Mingo's account of Christiantown meetings in the 1830s that drew attendees from Gay Head, Mashpee, and Chappaquiddick, and his kinship and marriage connections to Troy, Dartmouth, and Gay Head, in *New Bedford Sunday Standard*, 1909, in SPM; and the marriage on 25 Sept. 1865 of Charles Peters of Christiantown and Cordelia Amos of Mashpee, performed in Sandwich and recorded in Mashpee; Massachusetts certificate of marriage for Charles Peters and Cordelia Amos, "Indian" binder, MVHS.

5. Coe, Journal, 4 June–11 Sept. 1811; *Providence [R.I.] Journal*, 14 Aug. 1843, reprinted as "The Narragansett Indians of R.I.," *Niles' National Register*, 26 Aug. 1843, 45.

6. Mohegan 1861, 9–10.

7. Conn., assembly committee report, 28 April 1823, CGA1, folder 3; Ernest Dodge, "Indians at Salem in the Mid-Nineteenth Century," *Old-Time New England* 42 (1951–52): 93–95; *Sandwich Observer*, 15 Sept. 1849; John W. Johnson, *Life of John W. Johnson*, ts., Maine Historical Society, 11–12.

8. Herring Pond accounts, MIGA, box 3, folder 1; *Massachusetts Mercury*, 16 Sept. 1800, 1 (only two family names from the list of "Indians and Mulattoes" showed up on subsequent surveys of Indians in southern New England: Sprague and Doras [Dorcas], both Nipmuc); William J. Spooner, Attorney of Overseers of Poor of Boston, to Mass. Governor's Council, 17 Oct. 1823, MIGA, box 2, folder 12; Earle 1861, appendix; various accounts in MIGA, box 3, folder 15; "An Act to Prohibit the Sale of Ardent Spirits to the Gay Head Indians," *House Report* no. 48 (1838): 2; Bird 1849, 62–63; *The Uncas Monument, 1492–1842: published once in three hundred and fifty years* (Norwich, Conn.: John G. Cooley, 1842); John Avery, *History of the Town of Ledyard, 1650–1900* (Norwich, Conn.: Noyes and Davis, 1901), 261; New London Crew List database, G. W. Blount White Library, Mystic Seaport, Mystic, Conn. Earle's 1861 survey shows that most Indians in Boston were connected to Punkapoag (28 in 12 households), including two black men and one white woman with Punkapoag spouses. Others came from Hassanamisco, Mashpee, Dartmouth, Natick, and Dudley.

9. Daniel Mandell, "Shifting Boundaries of Race and Ethnicity: Indian-Black Intermarriage in Southern New England, 1760–1880," *Journal of American History* 85 (1998): 466–501.

10. Hawley to James Freeman, 2 Nov. 1802, Hawley Letters, MHS; Earle 1861, 34. Around 1750, an English colonist, Daniel Cyrus, married a Tunxis, Sarah, and their two sons died fighting in the Revolutionary War; Sarah Cyrus, Lyme, to assembly, Oct. 1790, CAr2-2, 150.

11. Mandell, "Shifting Boundaries of Race and Ethnicity"; John W. Sweet, *Bodies Politic: Negotiating Race in the American North, 1730–1830* (Baltimore: Johns Hopkins University Press, 2003). Narragansett tradition explains the Rhode Island figures as a reluctance among their men to be identified by officials because their women moved more easily between Native and European worlds and because a higher rate of female than male babies survived; Ruth Wallis Herndon and Ella Wilcox Sektatau, "The Right to a Name: The Narragansett People and Rhode Island Officials in the Revolutionary Era," in *After King Philip's War: Presence and Persistence in Indian New England*, ed. Colin Calloway (Hanover, N.H.: University Press of New England, 1997), 121. Some Indian men did marry African American women. One of the most infamous cases was the short and controversial marriage of Narragansett sachem Thomas Ninigret and "molatto" Mary Whitfield, 1761–66. Contemporaries were agreed, however, that most mixed marriages involved Indian women and African American men.

12. Frances Green, *Memoirs of Elleanor Eldridge* (Providence: B. T. Albro, 1839), 20; Huntoon, *History of the Town of Canton*, 32, 26–39; Edward Kendall, *Travels through the Northern Parts of the United States in the Years 1807 and 1808* (New York: I. Riley, 1809), 2:179.

13. Conn., legislative committee report on Mohegans, 3 Sept. 1774, CAr1, 315b and 312b; Hawley 1776; Hawley to William Phillips, Boston, 24 June 1776, NEC Records, box 3, folder 53, NEHGS; Hawley to Peter Thacher, Boston, 5 Aug. 1800, box 2, folder 16, SPGPE; E. A. Holyoke, Salem, to Jeremy Belknap, 19 March 1795, in Belknap, "Letters and Documents Relating to Slavery in Massachusetts," *MHSC*, 5th ser., 3 (1877): 400.

14. Testimony in *Westport v. Chilmark*, 1816, Bristol County Superior Court, transcription by Andrew Pierce in Pierce-Segal Collection, MVHS; Revolutionary War Pension Files, case W23726, reel 0425, frames 0283, 0288, National Archives; William C. Nell, *The Colored Patriots of the American Revolution* (1855; reprint, New York: Arno, 1968), 22–23; Hawley 1793.

15. Kenneth L. Feder, *A Village of Outcasts: Historical Archaeology and Documentary Research on the Lighthouse Site* (Mountain View, Calif.: Mayfield, 1994).

16. [Johnson Green], *The Life and Confession of Johnson Green, Who Is to Be Executed This Day, August 17th, 1786, for the Atrocious Crime of Burglary* (Worcester: Isaiah Thomas, 1786); "Introduction," in *On Our Own Ground: The Complete Writings of William Apess, a Pequot*, ed. Barry O'Connell (Amherst: University of Massachusetts Press, 1992), xxvii, lxii–lxiii; Daniel Porter, Sturbridge Town Clerk, to John Milton Earle, 14 July 1859, Earle Papers, box 2, folder 5; Alfred Bingham, "Squatter Settlements of Freed Slaves in New England," *Connecticut Historical Society Bulletin* 41 (July 1976): 65–80; Donna Keith Baron, J. Edward Hood, and Holly V. Izard "They Were Here All Along: The Native American

Presence in Lower-Central New England in the Eighteenth and Nineteenth Centuries," *William and Mary Quarterly*, 3rd ser., 53 (1996): 561–86. The evidence on the Lake of Isles, the two Pequot settlements outside the Mashantucket reserve, and the travels of William Apess has been assembled by Jason Mancini and others at the Mashantucket Pequot Research Library; Mancini, interview with author, 10 Jan. 2006.

17. Eliot to Belknap, "Letters and Documents Relating to Slavery," 383; Jeremy Belknap, Boston, to St. George Tucker, Va., 21 April 1795, in Belknap, "Judge Tucker's Queries Respecting Slavery, with Doctor Belknap's Answers," *MHSC*, 1st ser., 4 (1795): 209; Council order passed 24 June 1822, Providence Town Records, vol. 112, no. 39155, RIHS; *Hard Scrabble Calendar; Report of the Trials of Oliver Cummings, Nathaniel C. Metcalf, Gilbert Humes and Arthur Farrier; Who Were Indicted with Six Others for a Riot* (Providence, 1824); *History of the Providence Riots, from Sept. 21 to Sept. 24, 1831, Printed by order of the Town* (Providence, 1831); Joseph Barnum, "A Riot," *Sunday Journal of Hartford 1883–1884*, in John W. Stedman Scrapbook, CHS, 1:27, 30.

18. Hawley, list of marriages, Sept. 1764, Hawley Papers, vol. 4, Congregational Library, Boston; on trends in informal marriages, see Richard Godbeer, *Sexual Revolution in Early America* (Baltimore: Johns Hopkins University Press, 2002), 181–85, 236, 245–52, 300, 302, 308.

19. *Vital Records of Grafton, Massachusetts, to the End of the Year 1849* (Worcester, Mass.: Franklin Rice, 1906), 178; Earle Papers, box 1, folder 1; Sarah Phillips petition, MPL ch. 14, Resolves of 1821, 13 June 1821.

20. Henry A. Baker, *History of Montville, Connecticut, Formerly the North Parish of New London* (Hartford: Case, Lockwood & Brainerd, 1896), 58–61; Moses Howwoswee, 1792 census, Misc. Docs., MHS; Hawley 1793; Hawley to Thacher, 15 Sept 1800, box 2, folder 16, SPGPE; Conn., assembly committee report, 28 April 1823, CGA1, folder 3.

21. New London Crew Lists Index, 1803–78, database created by Mystic Seaport, provided by Kelly Drake of Mystic Seaport, Jan. 2006, individual records in the database available at www.mysticseaport.org/library/initiative/CrSearch.cfm; Herndon and Sekatau, "Right to a Name," 126–27.

22. Hawley 1776; Hawley to William Phillips, Boston, 24 June 1776, NEC Records, box 3, folder 53, NEHGS; Hawley to Bourne, 15 Dec. 1788, S. P. Savage Papers, MHS; Hawley 1793; Hawley to Thacher, 15 Sept 1800, SPGPE.

23. Howwoswee, 1792 census; Capt. Jerningham and Benjamin Bassett, "Report," *MHSC*, 1st ser., 1 (1790): 206.

24. Baylies 1823; David Silverman, *Faith and Boundaries: Colonists, Christianity, and Community among the Wampanoag Indians of Martha's Vineyard, 1600–1871* (New York: Cambridge University Press, 2005), 229–31. The variants in Gay Head 1792–1823 included Thomas Cooper (1/2 Indian and 1/2 black in 1792, 1/2 Indian, 1/4 black, and 1/4 white in 1823) and Isaac Johnson (1/2 Indian, 1/4 white, and 1/4 black in 1792, 3/4 Indian and 1/4 black in 1823).

25. Stephen Badger, "Historical and Characteristic Traits of the American Indians in General," *MHSC*, 1st ser., 5 (1798): 43; Kendall, *Travels through the Northern Parts*, 47; Child 1827, 11–13; Bird 1849, 7, 19; Timothy Dwight, *Travels in New England and New York* (1821–22; reprint, Cambridge, Mass.: Harvard University Press, 1969), 3:16; John Deforest,

History of the Indians of Connecticut, From the Earliest Known Period to 1850 (Hartford: William Jason Hamersley 1851), 443, 445; Dan King, "Report of Committee on [Narragansett] Indian Tribe," Jan. 1831, doc. 81, NRIA; Griffin 1858, 4.

26. "List of the Pequot tribe which belong and live in Groton, 13 Dec. 1833," Mohegan papers in William S. Johnson Papers, 3:100, CHS; Act of 22 June 1786, *Laws of the Commonwealth of Massachusetts*, 1:324; "An Act to prevent clandestine Marriages," section 5, *The Public Laws of the State of Rhode Island . . . January, 1798* (Providence, 1798); Earle 1861, appendix; Kendall, *Travels through the Northern Parts*, 2:180–81 (on McGregor); Hawley 1793.

27. Hawley to Mass. governor and House, July 1788, in MPL ch. 38, Acts of 1788; Jerningham and Bassett, "Report," 206; Hawley to Peter Thacher, Boston, 5 Aug. 1800, Hawley file, SPGPE. In nine couples, Hawley listed the race of the wife as "unknown." The 1800 census shows little by itself about trends or tendencies in the community, does not necessarily identify the mother of every child (some were indeed identified as the result of a previous marriage), and is unfortunately the only such record. Hawley's other major census (1793) describes various households as "with children" or "with children and grandchildren" but does not list individuals or number of children in those households.

28. Hawley 1793; Jeremy Belknap to Henry Knox, Boston *Columbia Centinel*, 24 Jan. 1795, 1; Isaac Backus, 10 Nov. 1798, in *Diary of Isaac Backus*, ed. William G. McLoughlin (Providence: Brown University Press, 1979), 1437; Hawley to John Davis, 17 Oct. 1794, Savage Papers, 2:214.

29. Hawley to Bourne, 15 Dec. 1788; Hawley to Thacher, 15 Sept. 1800, SPGPE; Hawley to Freeman, March 1803, Hawley Letters, MHS; Hawley to Thacher, Boston, 7 Dec. 1800, SPG, box 2, folder 16.

30. Reginald Horsman, *Race and Manifest Destiny: The Origins of American Racial Anglo-Saxonism* (Cambridge, Mass.: Harvard University Press, 1981), 145; Joseph Thaxter to James Freeman, 1 March 1823, Misc. Bound Docs., 1820–1837, MHS; King, "Report of Committee on [Narragansett] Indian Tribe"; Conn., assembly committee report on the Eastern Pequots, May 1855, CGA1, folder 26 ("disgrace the Saxon race"). On the simultaneous development of these attitudes in Virginia and their effects on the Powhatans, see Helen C. Rountree, *Pocohantas's People: The Powhatan Indians of Virginia through Four Centuries* (Norman: University of Oklahoma Press, 1990), 182–87, 194–95.

31. *Medway v. Natick*, 7 *Mass. Reports* (1810): 88. On Christopher Vickers, see Vickers Family Summary, assembled by the Nipmuc Tribal Acknowledgment Project and the New England Native American Institute.

32. *Andover v. Canton*, 13 *Mass. Reports* (1816): 547, which cited *Dighton v. Freetown*, 4 *Mass Reports* 539, regarding the residence of the son of a slave.

33. Report of *Dunbar v. Mitchell* in MPL ch. 130, Resolves of 1815, 5 Feb. 1816.

34. Mohegan agreement, 12 May 1773, William Samuel Johnson Papers, vol. 3, docs. 72–73, CHS; Zachary Johnson and "principal [Mohegan] Indians" to Conn. assembly, 1774, CAr1, 320a; Johnson to Conn. assembly, undated but ca. 1780, CAr1, 321a–321b; Johnson to Conn. assembly, May 1783, CAr1, 326a; Johnson to Conn. assembly, March 1779, Johnson Papers, vol. 3, no. 75, and undated, CAr1, no. 77; CAr1, 312ab; CAr1, 300; John Uncas et al. to Conn. assembly, 24 April 1820, CGA2; David Conroy, "In 'Times' Turned 'Up-

side Down': Race and Gender Relations in Mohegan, 1760–1860," paper delivered at the Old Sturbridge Village Colloquium on Early New England Society and Culture, 1995; Conroy, "The Defense of Indians Rights: William Bollan and the Mohegan Case in 1743," *Proceedings of the American Antiquarian Society* 103, no. 2 (1993): 395–424.

35. Deake to Joseph Fish, Dec. 1765, in *Old Light on Separate Ways: The Narragansett Diary of Joseph Fish, 1765–1776*, ed. William and Cheryl Simmons (Hanover, N.H.: University Press of New England, 1982), 21–22; "An Act for regulating the Affairs of the *Narragansett* Tribe of *Indians*, in this State," Feb. 1792, *Records of the State of Rhode Island, 1784–92*, vol. 10 (Providence, 1865): 476.

36. Narragansett council to R.I. assembly, 3 May 1815, unnumbered, NRIA; Adams 1881, 60; Coe, Journal, 4 June–11 Sept. 1811, SPGPE. Nor did the 1792 law stop intermarriage: in 1835 the tribal council complained that "there is a Number of Negroes, and others that has come in the town and taken our women to live with, some are Married and Some not." Narragansett council to R.I. assembly, Oct. 1835, doc. 102, NRIA

37. Brown, *Life of William J. Brown*, 10–11; Gay Head petition to Mass. legislature, 1776, Indian Box S, MVHS, quoted in Arthur R. Railton, "The Indians and the English on Martha's Vineyard," *Dukes County Intelligencer* 34, no. 3 (Feb. 1993): 143; Mashpees to Mass. legislature, July 1788, MPL ch. 30, Acts of 1788; William S. Simmons, *Spirit of the New England Tribes: Indian History and Folklore, 1620–1984* (Hanover, N.H.: University Press of New England, 1986), 99–100; Frank G. Speck, "Native Tribes and Dialects of Connecticut, A Mohegan-Pequot Diary," *Bureau of American Ethnology Annual Report, no. 43: 1925–1926* (Washington, D.C.: GPO, 1928), 274.

38. Benjamin Allen to Mass. legislature, 29 Dec. 1845, MUSL no. 12207.

39. Samson Occom to Richard Law, 5 Dec. 1789, Occom Papers, CHS, quoted in Conroy, "In 'Times' Turned 'Upside Down,'" 31, also 9–10, 13–15; William Simmons and Cheryl Simmons, eds., *Old Light on Separate Ways: The Narragansett Diary of Joseph Fish, 1765–1776* (Hanover, N.H.: University Press of New England, 1982), xxxiii–xxxiv, 32–33, 39; James Axtell, "Dr. Wheelock's Little Red School," in *The European and the Indian: Essays in the Ethnohistory of Colonial North America* (New York: Oxford University Press, 1981), 87–109; William DeLoss Love, *Samson Occom and the Christian Indians of New England* (Boston: Pilgrim Press, 1899), 302; Sweet, *Bodies Politic*, 451.

40. Benomi Occom and other Mohegans to assembly, April 1819, CAr2, 86; Benomi George et al. to Conn. assembly, May 1819, CAr2, doc. 86; Uncas et al. to Conn. assembly; Benomi Occom and other Mohegans to New London County Court, 20 Feb 1823, NLCC, box 3; Narragansett council, May 1834, unnumbered, NRIA.

41. Narragansetts to R.I. assembly, 3 Feb. 1821, doc. 67, NRIA; Eunice Rogers to general assembly, Oct. 1822, unnumbered, NRIA; Narragansett council to R.I. assembly, Oct. 1823, unnumbered, NRIA; Narragansett council to R.I. assembly, Oct. 1827, doc. 72, NRIA; R.I. legislative report, Jan. 1831; King, "Report of Committee on [Narragansett] Indian Tribe."

42. Narragansett council remonstrance to King report, June 1832, doc. 86, NRIA; Narragansett council to R.I. assembly, May 1834, doc. 105, NRIA; Narragansett council to R.I. assembly, Oct, 1835, doc. 102, NRIA.

43. Melissa J. Fawcett, *Medicine Trail: The Life and Lessons of Gladys Tantaquidgeon*

(Tucson: University of Arizona Press, 2000), 18; Frances M. Caulkins, notes of research on Indians, four bound books, all with "Indians" as title, plus loose leafs, CHS. Deforest, *Indians of Connecticut*, reprinted a newspaper clipping from an unidentified Norwich newspaper, 12 Sept. 1787: "Lately died at his wigwam in Powachaug (Norwich)," aged 100 years, "old Zachariah, Regent of the Mohegan tribe of Indians" (479).

44. Love, *Samson Occom*, 302.

45. Tom Hatley found similar patterns among Cherokees during the eighteenth century; Hatley, *The Dividing Paths: Cherokees and South Carolinians through the Revolutionary Era* (New York: Oxford University Press, 1995), 60.

46. Frederik Barth, "Introduction," in *Ethnic Groups and Boundaries: The Social of Cultural Difference*, ed. Frederik Barth (Boston: Little, Brown, 1969), 36–37. Helen Rountree found the same trend among the Powhatans of Virginia; Rountree, *Pocahantas's People*, 13.

47. James Clifford, "Identity in Mashpee," in *The Predicament of Culture: Twentieth-Century Ethnography, Literature, and Art* (Cambridge, Mass.: Harvard University Press, 1988), 306–7; Immanuel Wallerstein, "The Construction of Peoplehood: Racism, Nationalism, Ethnicity," in *Race, Nation, Class: Ambiguous Identities*, ed. Etienne Balibar and Immanuel Wallerstein (1988; trans., New York: Verso, 1991), 79, 83–84.

48. Kendall, *Travels through the Northern Parts*, 2:48–51, 179–80, 183; Simmons, *Spirit of the New England Tribes*, vii, 83, 85, 172–234, 97–101, 105–8; Constance Crosby, "The Algonkian Spiritual Landscape," in *Algonkians of New England Past and Present*, ed. Peter Benes (Boston: Boston University Press, 1993), 35–41; Baylies 1823; "Census of the Inhabitants of Gay Head Indians," *MSR* 14 (Boston, 1871), 32–53. By 1849, the Gershum family name disappeared from Vineyard Indian communities; Bird 1849, 60–63. Gay Head oral tradition holds that with Gershum's death "the practice of the black art" in the community ended; Vanderhoop, "Gay Head Indians," 18.

49. Mandell, *Behind the Frontier*, 147, 156–58, 195; Mandell "The Saga of Sara Muckamugg: Indian and African Intermarriage in Colonial New England," in *Sex, Love, Race: Crossing Boundaries in North American History*, ed. Martha Hodes (New York: New York University Press, 1998), 72–90.

50. Howwoswee to Earle, 27 Jan. 1860, Earle Papers; Mashpees to Mass. governor and legislature, July 1788, in MPL ch. 38, Acts of 1788; Mashpee proprietors to Mass. council and House, 28 May 1792, MUSL no. 1643; Mass. legislative committee report, 16 Jan. 1796, in MPL ch. 48, Acts of 1795; Josiah Fiske, "Report on Marshpee Disturbance," MIGA, box 2, file 1, 17–26.

51. Hawley 1776; Kendall, *Travels through the Northern Parts*, 2: 48–51, 179–180; Sweet, *Bodies Politic*, 220.

52. Child 1827, 12; Joseph Thaxter and Frances Peters to Mass. council and House, 26 Dec. 1823, Unpassed House no. 9419; Howwoswee to Earle, 27 Jan. 1860, Earle Papers, box 2, folder 3. The one exception seems to have been among the Narragansetts with their 1792 regulations limiting the vote in annual meetings to men over 21, but even there women could claim and hold communal property.

53. See, for example, Theda Perdue, *Cherokee Women* (Lincoln: University of Nebraska Press, 1998).

54. Mary Cook, Elizabeth Carter, Hannarette Simpson, and Charlotte Matteson, Chappaquiddick, to Massachusetts governor, 1809, Misc. Indian Papers, box 18a, MVHS (thanks to Ann Marie Plane for this reference); Zachariah Mayhew to the Company in England for Propagating the Gospel, April 1791, misc. docs., MHS; John Thaxter, Edgartown, to John Lothrop, Boston, 30 Sept. 1808, misc. bound docs., MHS.

55. Milton Gordon, *Assimilation in American Life: The Role of Race, Religion, and National Origins* (New York, 1964), 80–81; Russell A. Kazal, "Revisiting Assimilation: The Rise, Fall, and Reappraisal of a Concept in American Ethnic History," *American Historical Review,* 100 (1995): 437–71.

56. Herbert Gans, "Symbolic Ethnicity: The Future of Ethnic Groups and Cultures in America" (1979), in *Theories of Ethnicity: A Classical Reader,* ed. Werner Sollers (New York: New York University Press, 1996), 434–44.

57. Lamont D. Thomas, *Rise to Be a People, A Biography of Paul Cuffe* (Urbana: University of Illinois Press, 1986); "Several poor negroes and mulattoes" to the Massachusetts council and House, 10 Feb. 1780, reprinted in Nell, *Colored Patriots,* 87–88; Howwoswee, . 1792 census; Gay Head proprietors to Mass. legislature, 1821, in MPL ch. 46, Resolves of 1820; Paul Cuffee, receipts for supporting Joseph Degrass, a "colored foreigner" [Cape Verdean] living in Gay Head, 16 Feb. 1817, ibid.; Paul Cuffe [Jr.], *Narrative of the Life and Adventures of Paul Cuffe, a Pequot Indian: During Thirty Years Spent at Sea, and in Travelling in Foreign Lands* (Vernon, [N.Y.]: Horace Bill, 1839).

58. Moses and Cesear Gimbee to Mass. council and House, 19 Jan. 1801, MPL ch. 68, Resolves of 1800; records of Hassanamisco Trustees [guardians], 2 vols., Earle Papers; Mandell, *Behind the Frontier,* 88–89, 97, 190–192 (on the creation of the Hassanamisco fund).

59. Notes signed by Cesear and Moses Gimbee in Worcester, 1800 and 1805, Worcester County Probate Records, 1:168, case 23876; Moses Gimbee and Lucy Hector to Mass. council and House, Jan. 1815, in MPL ch. 113, Resolves of 1814; Franklin P. Rice, comp., *Worcester Births, Marriages and Deaths* (Worcester, 1894), 346; Nick Salvatore, *We All Got History: The Memory Books of Amos Webber* (New York: Times Books, 1996), 113; Bird 1849, 69–70; Earle 1861, li–lv.

60. Reports and receipts, Earle Papers, box 1; Hassanamisco trustee accounts, Unpassed Senate, no. 1671; James and Patience Cook to Mass. legislature, 21 Jan. 1793, MUSL, no. 1921; Earle 1861, 88, 100.

61. Legislative committee report, 3 April 1837, Earle Papers, box 1, folder 1; *MAR* ch. 71, 9 April 1839; John Hector to Mass. legislature, 1853, MUSL no. 13811; Hector to Mass. legislature, 1855, MPL ch. 245, Acts of 1855; Earle 1861, li–lv; Salvatore, *We All Got History,* 103–4, 107, 118–19, 209, 218; Mandell, "Shifting Boundaries," 487–88.

62. Abner Cohen, "The Lessons of Ethnicity" (1974), in Sollors, *Theories of Ethnicity,* 375.

63. Salvatore, *We All Got History,* 103, 113; Earle 1861, li–lv; "Dr. [E. A.] Holyoke's Observations" (1795), in Belknap, "Letters and Documents Relating to Slavery," 401; *Laws of the African Society, Instituted at Boston, Anno Domini, 1796* (Boston, 1802); William Robinson, ed., *The Proceedings of the Free African Union Society and the African Benevolent Society; Newport, Rhode Island, 1780–1824* (Providence: Urban League of Rhode Island, 1976); James O. Horton and Lois E. Horton, *Black Bostonians: Family Life and Commu-*

nity Struggle in the Antebellum North (New York: Oxford University Press, 1979), 91; James O. Horton and Lois E. Horton, *In Hope of Liberty: Culture, Community and Protest among Northern Free Blacks, 1700–1860* (New York: Oxford University Press, 1997), 178–79.

64. Essex Boston, Betty Boston, and Jeffrey Summons to SPG, Boston, 17 May 1822, box 1, SPGPE (thanks to Nathaniel Philbrick for sending me a transcript of this document); Baylies, Edgartown, to Alden Bradford, Boston, 14 April 1823, box 1, folder 8, SPGPE.

65. Patrick Rael, *Black Identity and Black Protest in the Antebellum North* (Chapel Hill: University of North Carolina Press, 2002), 82–117; David Waldstreicher, *In the Midst of Perpetual Fetes: The Making of American Nationalism, 1776–1820* (Chapel Hill: University of North Carolina Press, 1997), 327–47; Horton and Horton, *In Hope of Liberty*, 187–88, 200–201; Elizabeth R. Bethel, *The Roots of African-American Identity: Memory and History in Free Antebellum Communities* (New York: St. Martin's, 1997), 131–37; *Minutes of the Boston Baptist Association, 1828* (Boston, 1839), 14, quoted in Horton and Horton, *Black Bostonians*, 91.

66. Rael, *Black Identity and Black Protest*, 118–208; James O. Horton and Lois E. Horton, "Violence, Protest, and Identity: Black Manhood in Antebellum America," in *Free People of Color: Inside the African American Community*, ed. James Horton (Washington, D.C.: Smithsonian Institution Press, 1993), 86, 95; James Horton, "Freedom's Yoke: Gender Conventions among Free Blacks," in ibid., 102, 107–8, 116; Bethel, *Roots of African-American Identity*, 137; Maria Stewart, "Religion and the Pure Principles of Morality," in *Maria Stewart, America's First Black Woman Political Writer: Essays and Speeches*, ed. Marilyn Richardson (Bloomington: Indian University Press, 1987), 38.

67. Horton and Horton, "Violence, Protest, and Identity," 86, 95.

68. Ewa Morawska, "In Defense of the Assimilation Model," *Journal of American Ethnic History* 13 (winter 1994): 76–87; Marshall Sklare, *America's Jews* (New York: Random House, 1971), 202–3; James H. S. Bossard and Eleanor Stoker Boll, "When the Children Come in Interfaith Marriages," in *The Blending American: Patterns of Intermarriage*, ed. Milton L. Barron (Chicago: Quadrangle Books, 1972), 296–308; David M. Heer, "Intermarriage," in *Harvard Encyclopedia of American Ethnic Groups*, ed. Stephen Thernstrom (Cambridge, Mass.: Harvard University Press, 1980), 520.

69. Marcus L. Hanson, "The Problem of the Third Generation Immigrant" (1937), quoted in Kazal, "Revisiting Assimilation," 448–49; Gans, "Symbolic Ethnicity," 425, 436–44; Barth, "Introduction," 36–37. This seems to fit James Clifford's concept that tribal identity should be seen "not as a boundary to be maintained but as a nexus of relations and transactions actively engaging a subject"; Clifford, "Identity in Mashpee," 344. Rountree, in her work on the Powhatans, analyzed intermarriage, ethnic identity, and affiliation in terms of a "recognized" core and a more amorphous fringe; Rountree, *Pocahantas's People*, 13. Such a dichotomy may be misleading in New England, however, for members of Indian communities that lacked reservations, such as the Hassanamisco Nipmucs, sometimes seemed to be "an easily recognized core" and at other times appeared to be "a fringe." In addition, these conflicts over rights to community resources do not show a clear structure of core and fringe.

CHAPTER 3: AUTHORITY AND AUTONOMY

1. L. H. Butterfield, ed. *Adams Family Correspondence* (Cambridge, Mass.: Harvard University Press, 1963–), 1:369–71; Hawley to Mass. legislature, 2 Sept. 1795, S. P. Savage Papers, 2:218, MHS.

2. Daniel Mandell, *Behind the Frontier: Indians in Eighteenth-Century Eastern Massachusetts* (Lincoln: University of Nebraska Press, 1996), 113–14, 143–52; Wendy B. St. Jean, "Inventing Guardianship: The Mohegan Indians and Their 'Protectors,'" *New England Quarterly* 72 (1999): 362–87.

3. Paul R. Campbell and Glenn W. LaFantosie, "Scattered to the Winds of Heaven: Narragansett Indians, 1676–1800," *Rhode Island History* 37 (1978): 72, 73, 74, 76

4. Nathan Hatch, *The Democratization of American Christianity* (New Haven: Yale University Press, 1989); Susan Juster, *Disorderly Women, Sexual Politics, and Evangelism in Revolutionary New England* (Ithaca, N.Y.: Cornell University Press, 1994), 108–44; William Simmons and Cheryl Simmons, eds., *Old Light on Separate Ways: The Narragansett Diary of Joseph Fish, 1765–1776* (Hanover, N.H.: University Press of New England, 1982), xix–xxxvii; "Introduction," in *On Our Own Ground: The Complete Writings of William Apess, a Pequot*, ed. Barry O'Connell (Amherst: University of Massachusetts Press, 1992), lviii; James O. Horton and Lois E. Horton, *In Hope of Liberty: Culture, Community and Protest among Northern Free Blacks, 1700–1860* (New York: Oxford University Press, 1997), 133–36.

5. MAR ch. 1068, 30 April 1778. The Mashpee appointments are mysterious, as that community governed itself until 1788, as discussed below. There were guardians for Herring Pond in January 1783 when they petitioned to sell some of that community's land, Revolutionary Petitions, 188:216–17, Mass. Archives.

6. John S. Whitehead, *The Separation of College and State: Columbia, Dartmouth, Harvard, and Yale, 1776–1876* (New Haven: Yale University Press, 1973); Johann Neem to Daniel Mandell, personal communication, 26 April 2005.

7. Herring Pond Indians to Mass. legislature, 6 Aug. 1783, MUSL no. 353; House bill, 15 Feb. 1785, ibid.; MAR ch. 23, 5 June 1789; CPR 7:261; John Deforest, *History of the Indians of Connecticut, from the Earliest Known Period to 1850* (Hartford: William Jason Hamersley 1851), 356; MPL ch. 13, Resolves of 1829, approved 11 June 1829. For examples of poor children being bound out see Carver selectmen to Mass. legislature, 3 Feb. 1826, MPL ch. 74, Resolves of 1825, approved 24 Feb. 1826; and MPL ch. 54, Resolves of 1826, approved 14 Feb. 1827.

8. CPR 6:57; CPR 6:460; Deforest, *Indians of Connecticut*, 437; CPR 10:38; CPR 2:531; CPR 5:178, 298.

9. Micah to Mass. legislature, 1799, MUHL no. 4847; 13 Middleborough Indians to Mass. legislature, n.d., MUSL no. 3567, 1807 (the legislature did not act on this petition but did not explain why); Mandell, *Behind the Frontier*, 144–49.

10. MA 33:143; Gay Head to Mass. legislature, 19 May 1785, MPL ch. 4, Resolutions of 1785; Resolution of House, 3 June 1785, ibid.; "Act to Set off to the Patentees, and other Pur-

chasers, Certain Lands on the Island of Chappaquiddick," 26 Jan. 1789, in *Private and Special Statutes of the Commonwealth of Massachusetts* (Boston: Manning and Loring, 1805), vol. 1; MAR ch. 164, 8 March 1774; MA 33:615/a.

11. CPR 5:156; Kendall, *Travels through the Northern Parts of the United States in the Years 1807 and 1808* (New York: I. Riley, 1809), 1:308 (description of Mohegan council); CPR 13:355, 133; Samuel Niles, Ephraim Cohis, Jo Cowyons, James Niles, Daniel Shattuck to R.I. assembly, Aug. 1779, in Petitions to the General Assembly 17 (1778–80): 79, RISA; RICR 9:603; RICR 10:476; "Rules & Regulations for Narragansett tribe," 17 Dec. 1792, RIAR, Jan. 1839 (Providence, 1839), 32–33.

12. Peter Linebaugh and Marcus Rediker, *The Many Headed-Hyrda: The Hidden History of the Revolutionary Atlantic* (Boston: Beacon Press, 2000).

13. MAR ch. 3, 17 June 1763, reprinted in Benjamin Hallett, *Rights of the Marshpee Indians* (Boston: J. Howe, 1834), 10–11; Hawley to William Cushing, Boston, 8 May 1788, William Cushing Papers, 1664–1814, MHS; Hawley to Andrew Oliver, Boston, 3 April 1764, 20 May 1765, 7 April 1766, Hawley Papers, MHS; Hawley to William Phillips, 26 Dec. 1776, SPG Papers, mss. B C40, box 3, folder 59, NEHGS; Hawley to Phillips, Boston, 15 July 1776, SPG Papers, box 3, folder 54.

14. Hawley to Isaac Smith, Boston, 14 Dec. 1784, Savage Letters, vol. 3, MHS; "Miscellany," *Massachusetts Centinel*, 2 June 1798, 83; Hawley to Rev. Oaks Shaw, Barnstable, 9 June 1787, Savage Letters, 2:204. On similar controversies in Connecticut, see Christopher Grasso, *A Speaking Aristocracy: Transforming Public Discourse in Eighteenth-Century Connecticut* (Chapel Hill: University of North Carolina Press, 1999), ch. 7–8. On the ecclesiastical and political results from the split between Unitarian and Calvinist Congregationalists at the turn of the century, see Johann Neem, "The Elusive Common Good: Religion and Civil Society in Massachusetts, 1780–1833," *Journal of the Early Republic* 24 (2004): 381–417, and Jonathan D. Sassi, *A Republic of Righteousness: The Public Christianity of Post-Revolutionary New England Clergy* (New York: Oxford University Press, 2003).

15. Hawley to Cushing, Boston, 8 May 1788, Cushing Papers. Strangely, no one discussed the legislature's appointment of three guardians for Mashpee in April 1778: Daniel Davis, Simon Fish, and Thomas Smith—a close friend of Hawley. This act may have been a wartime emergency measure that was temporary and largely ineffective. MAR ch. 1068, 30 April 1778.

16. Mashpee to Mass. legislature, 3 Feb. 1783, MUSL no. 25d, 1783; Barnstable to Mass. legislature, MPL ch. 2, May 1788, Acts of 1788.

17. Mashpee proprietors to Mass. legislature, July 1788, MPL ch. 38, 30 Jan. 1789, Acts of 1788; Hawley to Mass. legislature, 5 Nov. 1788, and Fish to Mass. legislature, MPL ch. 38, 23 Dec. 1788; magistrates and others in Barnstable, Sandwich, and Falmouth to Mass. legislature, MPL ch. 38, 22 Dec. 1788; John Percival, Barnstable, to the Mass. legislature, MPL ch. 38, 19 Nov. 1788; Mashpees to the Mass. legislature, MPL ch. 38, 31 Oct. 1788.

18. An Act for the Better Regulation of the Indian, Mulatto and Negro Proprietors and Inhabitants of the Plantation Called Marshpee, in the County of Barnstable, MPL ch. 38, 30 Jan. 1789; Hawley to James Freeman, Boston, 24 Dec. 1805, Hawley Letters, MHS; Haw-

ley to Mass. legislature, 12 May 1789, MUSL no. 1036. The five overseers included two from Barnstable County and one from each of the adjoining counties: Bristol, Plymouth, and Dukes (Martha's Vineyard).

19. Mashpee Indians to Mashpee Overseers, 24 Nov. 1789, Savage Papers, 2:209 (only a corner of the petition remains, so little of the text can be reconstructed); Mashpees to the Mass. legislature, 13 June 1791, MUSL no. 1419a; deposition by Levi Mie, 13 June 1791, ibid.; Mashpees to Mass. legislature, 28 May 1792, MUSL no. 1643; Hawley mss., 2 Sept. 1795, Savage Papers, 2:218.

20. Hawley to Mass. Gov. John Hancock, 8 July 1791, Hawley Papers, MHS; Hawley to Robert Treat Paine, Boston, 25 Nov. 1791, Robert Treat Paine Papers, vol. 28 (reel 5 of 19), MHS; Hawley to Peter Thacher, 12 Dec. 1791, Hawley Journal and Letters, vol. 2, Congregational Library, Boston. In his 1793 census of Mashpee inhabitants, Hawley referred to Sarah Mie as a "competent Squaw"—the equivalent of a "good wife," skilled in household business—and condemned Hannah Babcock for being a rum seller, which meant that she ran an unlicensed tavern; Hawley 1793.

21. Joyce Appleby, *Capitalism and a New Social Order: The Republican Vision of the 1790s* (New York: New York University Press, 1984), 16–18; Jack Rakove, *Declaring Rights: A Brief History with Documents* (Boston: Bedford Books, 1998), 19–22; Mashpees to Mass. legislature, July 1788, MPL ch. 38, Acts of 1788.

22. Theda Perdue, "The Conflict Within: Cherokees and Removal," in *Cherokee Removal, Before and After*, ed. William L. Anderson (Athens: University of Georgia Press, 1991), 55–74; Claudio Saunt, *A New Order of Things: Property, Power, and the Transformation of the Creek Indians, 1733–1816* (New York: Cambridge University Press, 1999); Melissa L. Meyer, *The White Earth Tragedy: Ethnicity and Dispossession at a Minnesota Anishinaabe Reservation* (Lincoln: University of Nebraska Press, 1994).

23. Depositions by Levi Mie and Ebenezer Crocker, June 1795, Hawley Journal and Letters, vol. 2. Freeman graduated from Harvard in 1787; he was elected twice to Congress before dying of tuberculosis in 1800; R. A. Lovell Jr., *Sandwich: A Cape Cod Town* (Sandwich, MA: Town of Sandwich, 1996), 244. His father had served as head of the Sandwich Committee of Safety during the Revolution and may have wrestled with Hawley's opposition to the war. But there are no extant documents from the Sandwich committee, and no letters or other documents that shed light on that committee's work with regard to Hawley.

24. Hawley to Mass. legislature, 1 May 1795, Hawley Letters; committee appointed by resolve of 11 June 1795, report 16 Jan. 1796, MPL ch. 48, Acts of 1795.

25. Hawley to SPG or to Mass. legislature, 2 Sept. 1795, Savage Papers, 2:218; Hawley, Mashpee, to Jeremy Belknap, 30 Aug. 1796, J. Belknap Papers, P-380, 6:161, B. 160–61, MHS. Jeffers was known as Jeffrey during his time in Mashpee but as Jeffers at Gay Head, where he and his family become an integral part of the Gay Head community. He signed his will "Thomas Jeffer"; docket I/584a, Dukes County Probate Court, Edgartown, Mass. Jeffers probably came from Middleborough, as an 1807 petition from the Indians in that town included a number of Jeffreys, and there were also Jeffers in the area; Middleborough Indians to Mass. legislature, 1807, MUSL no. 3567. Jeffers would die 30 Aug. 1818, aged 75; *New Bedford Mercury*, 2 Oct. 1818, copy in SPM. On the growing alliance between dissi-

dents and Democrat-Republicans in southern New England in the late 1790s, see Sassi, *Republic of Righteousness*, 69–120.

26. Hawley to Peter Thacher, 7 May 1794 and 20 Oct. 1795, box 2, folder 16, SPGPE. Hawley's social and religious prejudices were clearly at work here, as another writer observed, years after Jeffers had moved to Gay Head, that "his abilities were considerable, his deportment Christian-like, and he was of undoubted piety.—He was well-received as a preacher." John Tripp, "Native Church at Gay Head," *Zion's Advocate*, Sept. 1831, reprinted in *Magazine of New England History* 3, no. 4 (Oct. 1893): 250–53. Hawley's colleague on Martha's Vineyard, Zaccheus Mayhew, hired Jeffers's wife a few years after he arrived at Gay Head to teach the Indian school, and noted that she was well qualified and "reputed a person of good morral [*sic*] character"; Mayhew to Peter Thacher, Boston, 28 July 1801, box 3, folder 11, SPGPE. This was about the year that Sandwich received its first itinerant Methodist minister, and saw the "beginning of a Baptist society." Generally, those who joined this church were considered the "lower sorts" in the town. Lovell, *Sandwich*, 275; Isaac Backus, *A History of the New England, with Particular Reference to the Denomination of Christians called Baptists*, 2nd ed. (1871; reprint, New York: Arno, 1969), 2:270.

27. Hawley to Jeremy Belknap, 4 Sept. 1795, Belknap Papers, P-380, 6:161, B. 138, J; Hawley to Mass. legislature committee, 2 Sept. 1795. The minister was compelled to produce his nearly illegible accounts from the past two years, which primarily served to convince the committee that he was incompetent to be the Indians' treasurer. The accounts also show nepotism, as Hawley paid his son to cut and transport timber and provide other services for Mashpee, ibid.

28. Mashpees to Mass. legislature, 8 Jan. 1796, MUSL no. 2194; Mass. legislature, report of committee appointed by resolve of 11 June 1795 "to enquire into circumstances of the Inhabitants of Color" in Marshpee and "to ascertain the Causes of their Uneasiness," and to consider alterations, 16 Jan. 1796, MPL ch. 48, 22 Feb. 1796, Acts of 1795. Fifty-five Mashpees signed this petition, compared to the second-highest count of 29 in July 1788. Even more remarkable, among the 55 were 22 women, compared to the next highest count of only three in the 1792 petition.

29. "An Act especially providing for the Removal of poor Persons from the District of Marshpee, who have no legal Settlement there," MPL ch. 23, 17 June 1796, Acts of 1796; Hawley to Belknap, 27 July and 30 Aug. 1796, Belknap Papers, P-380, 6:161, B. 157, B. 160–61; Gay Head Indians to the Gospel Society of Boston, 14 May 1798, with list of children under 18 yrs of age, including heads of household, Misc. Docs., MHS; Tripp, "Native Church at Gay Head"; *Diary of Isaac Backus*, 3:1431–32; Mashpees to Mass. legislature, n.d., MUSL, no. 2525, Feb 1799. In October 1801, Hawley referred to a petition carried to Boston by party from Mashpee "in the year 1799 with the baptist minister at their head." Hawley to "Gentlemen" [SPG?], 6 Oct. 1801, Savage Papers, 2:220.

30. Mashpees to the Mass. legislature, Dec. 1807, MPL ch. 109, Acts of 1807.

31. Ibid.; Mark A. Nicholas, "Mashpee Wampanoags of Cape Cod, the Whalefishery, and Seafaring's Impact on Community Development," *American Indian Quarterly* 26 (2002): 174–79.

32. Mashpees to Mass. legislature, Dec. 1807, and Sandwich town meeting to Mass. leg-

islature, 9 Dec. 1807, both in MPL ch. 109, Acts of 1807. The Sandwich letter was also signed by the Barnstable selectmen. James Freeman served as state representative and senator and as Barnstable County High Sheriff before drowning in January 1816 during a trip to Martha's Vineyard; Lovell, *Sandwich*, 265.

33. Mashpees to Mass. legislature, Jan. 1808, and Herring Pond and Black Ground Tribe to Mass. legislature, Jan. 1808; Zaccheus Pognit deposition, 2 Jan. 1808; John Fish, Sandwich, deposition, 2 Jan. 1808; Lemuel Ewer, Sandwich, deposition, 2 Jan. 1808; Benjamin Burgess, deposition, 7 Jan. 1808; Mass., legislature, committee report, draft act, and final act, all in MPL ch. 109, Acts of 1807.

34. Mashpees to Mass. legislature, undated, in MPL ch. 109, Acts of 1807; Elisha Clapp, Sandwich, to Harvard College, 20 April 1809, Doc. 33, Letters, Harvard Grants for Work Among the Indians, Harvard University Archives, Cambridge, Mass.; Solomon Francis et al. to John Davis, Boston, 15 Aug 1808, Misc. Bound Docs., MHS. See also Fish and Ewer depositions, 2 Jan. 1808. Both Fish and Ewer called Francis a "lazy, idle, mischief-making, lying fellow"—a mantra that seems suspicious because both men used precisely the same words in their separate dispositions. Two decades, later, when Francis died at the age of 58, the neighboring *Barnstable Patriot* saluted him as "much respected for his moral worth . . . always watchful and anxious for the proper management of its affairs, jealous of any encroachment upon, and tenacious of all the rights of the TRIBE. In his life, he was exemplary for sobriety, benevolence and all of the Christian virtues." *Barnstable Patriot and Commercial Advertiser*, 16 March 1831.

35. Hawley, Mashpee, to Jeremy Belknap, 25 Aug. 1796 and 13 Sept. 1796, Belknap Papers, P-380, 6:161, B. 159; Hawley to James Freeman, 3 April 1801, Hawley Letters, MHS; Hawley to Jedidah Morse, 22 July 1807, box 2, folder 16, SPGPE; Hawley to Rev. D. Strong, Aug. 1802, Savage Papers, 2:222.

36. Grasso, *Speaking Aristocracy*, 4; Sassi, *Republic of Righteousness*, 11, 19–51; Peter S. Field, *The Crisis of the Standing Order: Clerical Intellectuals and Cultural Authority in Massachusetts, 1780–1833* (Amherst: University of Massachusetts Press, 1998); *SPG petition to the Legislature requesting support from Governor John Hancock . . . 20 June 1788* (Boston: Adams and Norse, 1788); "Petition of the Society for Propagating the Gospel among the Indians and others," *American Magazine* 4 (1789): 430–31; Massachusetts, *Act to Incorporate Certain Persons, By the name of the Society, for Propagating the Gospel among the Indians and Others, in North America* (Boston: Adams and Nourse, 1787).

37. SPG, *A Brief Account of the Present State of the Society for Propagating the Gospel . . . [a] Supplement to the Independent Chronicle, Thursday, February 3, 1791* (Boston: Thomas Adams, 1791), 1; Alan Taylor, *Liberty Men and Great Proprietors: The Revolutionary Settlement on the Maine Frontier, 1760–1880* (Chapel Hill: University of North Carolina Press, 1990); Philip Deloria, *Playing Indian* (New Haven: Yale University Press, 1998), 25–45.

38. Daniel Little to Richard Cary, Aug. 1786, in Cary, *To the Members of the Society for Propagating the Gospel among the Indians. . . . Charlestown, Mass., May 27, 1789* (Boston: S. Hall, 1789); Little to Thacher, 24 Nov. 1790, in *Brief Account of the Present State of the Society . . . 1791*, 2–3; SPG, *A Brief of the Account of the Present State, . . . of the Society* (Boston, 1795), 1–2; Appendix in Joseph Eckley, *A Discourse before the Society for Propa-*

gating the Gospel (Boston: E. Lincoln, 1806), 32–34; Appendix in Joshua Bates, *A Sermon Delivered before the Society for Propagating the Gospel* (Boston: Cummings and Hilliard, 1813), 29–41.

39. Timothy Dwight, *Travels in New England and New York* (1821–22; reprint, Cambridge, Mass.: Harvard University Press, 1969), 3:14–16. On Dwight, see Grasso, *Speaking Aristocracy*, 329, 338; on the ideas and significance of William Godwin (1756–1836), see John Passmore, "Perfectibility of Man," in *The Dictionary of the History of Ideas*, ed. Philip P. Wiener (New York: Charles Scriber's Sons, 1973), 3:470–71.

40. Coe was born in Middletown, Conn., in 1750, two years before Dwight, and graduated from Brown in 1776. He was invited to preach in Durham, N.H., in 1779, and was ordained one year later. Coe left that post in 1806, and began working as an itinerate missionary in the area. In 1809, he traveled south to preach to the Narragansetts and whites in the area. Coe died in South Newmarket, N.H., 7 June 1829. Roland Goodbody, University of New Hampshire Library Special Collections, personal communication, 14 June 2001.

41. Curtis Coe, appendix to journal 24 June–17 Oct. 1809, box 1, folder 21, SPGPE; Coe, journal entry, 28 Oct. 1810, ms. journal, 7 July–7 Dec. 1810, ibid.

42. Simmons and Simmons, *Old Light on Separate Ways*. Toward the end of Fish's efforts among the Narragansett, an Indian woman told him that Niles warned them not to come hear "Any of Our Ministers, that wore great White wigs"; ibid., 105.

43. Coe, journal, 28 Oct. 1810.

44. Coe, journal, 22 June–14 July 1811, 21 July 1811.

45. On 25 July 1817, Daniel Waldo, a textile mill owner and Congregationalist lay leader, wrote in his diary that Charlestown was "still groaning under the [seed?] of ignorance which Mr. James David poured upon them. He *encouraged* the disorderly conduct of the Indians in their meeting. For instance-the whole meeting praying out loud at the same time." Daniel Waldo diary, 25 July 1817, John Carter Brown Library, Providence, R.I., emphasis in original. My thanks to Richard Ring at the Brown Library for his assistance in obtaining a copy of this page from Waldo's diary. See generally Mark S. Schantz, *Piety in Providence: Class Dimensions of Religious Experience in Antebellum Rhode Island* (Ithaca, N.Y.: Cornell University Press, 2000), 45–77.

46. Frederick Baylies, Edgartown, to Abiel Holmes, Cambridge, 28 Sept. 1819, box 1, folder 8, SPGPE.

47. Elisha Clapp, Sandwich, to Jedidiah Morse, Charlestown, 22 July 1808, Misc. Bound Docs, MHS.

48. Mandell, *Behind the Frontier*, 114–15; David Silverman, *Faith and Boundaries: Colonists, Christianity, and Community among the Wampanoag Indians of Martha's Vineyard, 1600–1871* (New York: Cambridge University Press, 2005), 181; Zachariah Mayhew to Richard Jackson, 26 Dec. 1786, NEC, ms. 7956, Guildhall Library, London (my thanks to Constance Crosby for her transcripts of these records).

49. Minutes of Gay Head proprietors' meeting, 16 April 1784, Zach Howwoswee Papers, ms. 1784, John Carter Brown Library, Brown University, Providence; MPL ch. 4, Resolves of 1785, approved 3 June 1785; Silverman, *Faith and Boundaries*, 181; John Thaxter, Edgartown, to John Lothrop, Boston, 30 Sept. 1808, Misc. Bound Docs, MHS.

50. Thaxter to Lothrop, 30 Sept. 1808; Goddard and Bragdon, *Native Writings in Mass-*

achusett, 1:73, 361; Clapp to Morse, 22 July 1808, Misc. Bound Docs, MHS; Silverman, *Faith and Boundaries*, 181–82.

51. Gay Head to Mass. governor, 1 April 1815, MGCF box 22; *New Bedford Gazette*, 21 Nov. 1811, SPM. This petition supported a request by Chilmark men to finish draining a marsh shared with Gay Head; they told the legislature that the Indians had initially supported the project but now were refusing to let them finish.

52. Kendall, *Travels through the Northern Parts*, 2:196; Gay Head to Mass. governor, 23 July 1811, MGSF box 19; Gay Head to Mass. governor, 1 April 1815, MGCF box 22.

53. Gay Head to Mass. legislature, 18 May 1816; MUHL no. 8029.

54. Joel Rogers to Paul Cuffee, 24 Oct. 1816, Cuffee Collection, New Bedford Free Public Library, copy in SPM.

55. Indeed, the three guardians had recently submitted their resignations to the governor, though they were not granted until after the Indians sent their petition to Boston; Simon Mayhew and Tristram Allen to Governor's Council, 4 March 1816, accepted 8 and 7 June, MGCF box 23. John Milton Earle found no evidence that Gay Head guardians had been appointed since 1814; Earle 1861, 38–39.

56. Wright to Walker and Parkman, 9 April 1839, SPG Papers, box 7, MHS.

57. Jack Campisi, "Emergence of the Mashantucket Pequot Tribe, 1637–1975," in *The Pequots in Southern New England: The Rise and Fall of an American Indian Nation*, ed. Laurence M. Hauptman and James D. Wherry (Norman: University of Oklahoma Press, 1990), 126; Sassi, *Republic of Righteousness*, 84–120; Neem, "The Elusive Common Good."

58. Christiantown to Mass. legislature, read 29 Jan. 1805, MPL ch. 84, approved 8 March 1805, Acts of 1804; Christiantown petition to Mass. legislature, 24 April 1817, MPL ch. 20, approved 11 June 1817, Resolves of 1817; MPL ch. 99, approved 12 Feb. 1818, Acts of 1817; MPL ch. 123, approved 16 Feb. 1818, Resolves of 1817.

59. Chappaquiddicks to Mass. legislature, 1 June 1805, MGCF, box 14 (the first signature on this petition was that of Simon Porridge, who had taken the community's 1772 plea for relief from trespass and tyranny to London); Mass., legislative committee report, 13 Oct. 1818, MIGA box 3, folder 15; Chappaquiddick petition, 18 May 1807, MGCF box 15; report on petition, 8 June 1807, ibid.; order of 10 July 1807, ibid.; Mass. legislative committee report on Chappaquiddick complaints, 10 June 1811, MGCF box 19; Committee report on Gay Head, 10 June 1815, MGCF box 23; Chappaquiddicks to Mass. governor, 8 Sept. 1818, MGCF box 26.

60. Chappaquiddicks (10 women and 7 men) to Mass. legislature, n.d. but received 28 Jan. 1808, reprinted in *New Bedford Gazette*, in SPM, box 3, "Sanchekantackett/Farm Neck" folder; Report of committee, 7 June 1809, MGCF box 17; Chappaquiddick petition to Mass. governor, 28 Oct. 1811, MIGA, box 3, folder 15; Chappaquiddick petition to Mass. governor, 14 Jan. 1824, and council committee report, 12 Feb. 1824, MGCF, box 33.

61. Mashpees to Mass. legislature, 13 June 1817, MPL ch. 89, Resolves of 1817; Mashpees to Mass. legislature, undated, ibid. Several signatories appear on both petitions.

62. Report of Legislative Commission on the Marshpee and Herring Pond Indians, 18 June 1818, MIGA, box 2, folder 10; ch. 105, passed 18 Feb. 1819, reprinted in Hallett, *Rights of the Marshpee Indians*, 14–15. Lemuel Ewers, for a time a Mashpee overseer and trea-

surer, testified in 1834 that this committee never actually visited Mashpee. They spent two days in the area: one day meeting over five miles from the village and the next day meeting at the Crocker residence or tavern in Cotuit, on Mashpee's southwest border—and the home of a man disliked and perhaps feared by many Mashpees. Ewer testimony in "Minutes of the Legislative Committee Appointed to Inquire into the Complaints of the Mashpee Indians," 5 Feb.–8 March 1834, Ira Moore Barton Papers, box 1, folder 1, AAS.

63. Mohegans to Conn. assembly, 30 April 1819, CAr2 doc. 86a–c; John Uncas and other Mohegans to Conn. assembly, 24 April 1820, General Assembly Rejected Bills, box 5 (1820–1824), folder 1, CSA; Report of Conn. assembly committee on Mohegan petition, 25 May 1820, CAr2 doc. 87. The overseers were required to help those descendants under a new state law passed after the town of Montville complained of vagrants who were of partial Mohegan ancestry and needed public support.

64. Title 50, "An Act for the Protection of Indians, and Preservation of their Property," CPL (Hartford, 1821), 278–87.

65. Conn. assembly committee report, 28 April 1823, CGA1, folder 3.

66. Benomi Occom and other Mohegans to NLCC, 20 Feb 1823, NLCC, box 3. This petition also shows the continued or increased significance of women in the tribe, for the only individual whose position or status in the tribe was shown on the petition was Lucy Tantiquigeon, identified as "eldest woman."

67. Benoni Occom and other Mohegans to New London County Court, 14 June 1823, NLCC, box 3; Samson Occom et al. to New London County Court, 17 June 1823, ibid.

68. Nathaniel Bradford to Conn. assembly, May 1825, CGA1, folder 5; various men, Montville, to NLCC, June 1834, NLCC, box 3; Mohegans to NLCC, 12 June 1834, ibid.; Mohegans to NLCC, 20 June 1836, NLCC, box 3; Mohegan petition to NLCC, 16 Feb. 1838; ibid.

69. Campisi, "Emergence of the Mashantucket Pequot Tribe," 126–31; Benjamin George et al. to assembly, May 1804, CAr2-2, 35; Mashantucket Pequots to assembly, April 1819, CAr2, 21; Pequots to New London County Court, Feb. 1848, 26 June 1848, and 3 Feb. 1849 (quotation), NLCC, box 2.

70. Pequots to New London County Court, 30 Jan. 1855, NLCC, box 2; Mashantucket Pequots petition to New London County Superior Court, 18 April 1856, NLCSC, box 5.

71. Deforest, Indians of Connecticut, 426–27, 445; John Cottle to Mass. legislature, ca. 1819, MUSL no. 6314; B. C. Merchant to John Milton Earle, 17 Sept. 1859, Earle Papers, box 2, folder 3; Chappaquiddicks to Mass. legislature, ca. 1805, MIGA, box 3, folder 15; Charles Endicott to John M. Earle, 6 Aug. 1859, Earle Papers, box 2, folder 1; Leavitt Thaxter to Earle, 28 Jan. 1860, Earle Papers, box 2, folder 3; Dan Fellows to Mass. governor, 18 Dec. 1836, MIGA, box 3, folder 15. Compensation for some Massachusetts guardians began in 1836; Holder Wordwell, 12 March 1843, MIGA, box 3, folder 11; Nathaniel Hunt, Dudley guardian, 18 Feb. 1843, MIGA, box 3, folder 12.

72. Chappaquiddicks to Mass. governor, 28 Oct. 1811, MIGA, box 3, folder 15; Campisi, "Emergence of the Mashantucket Pequot Tribe," 129, 131; Mandell, Behind the Frontier, 115–16, 118, 146, 148–150, 152–53, 158; Deforest, Indians of Connecticut, 429–30; Dudley Indians to Mass. legislature, 11 Jan. 1816, MPL ch. 118, Resolves of 1815; Christiantown Indi-

ans to Mass. legislature, 25 April 1817, MPL ch. 20, Resolves of 1817; Chappaquiddick Indians to Mass. legislature, 24 May 1810, MUSL no. 4093; Child 1827; Christiantown and Chappaquiddick "Real and Personal Estate Inventory," MIGA, box 3, folder 15; Bird 1849.

73. Docs. 51, 50, 54, NRIA.

74. Narragansett council to R.I. assembly, 3 May 1815, unnumbered, NRIA; *RIAR*, June 1816 (Providence, 1816), 24–25.

75. Report of assembly committee on Indian affairs, Feb. 1818, doc. 60, NRIA; Narragansetts to R.I. assembly, 14 Oct. 1823, unnumbered, NRIA; petition from physicians and surgeons of Charlestown and Westerly, 24 Oct. 1823, unnumbered, NRIA; Indian Council to general assembly, Oct. 1827, doc. 71, NRIA

76. Report of committee on Indian Tribe, Jan 1830, doc. 80, NRIA; King report, Jan 1831, doc. 81, NRIA; Narragansett objection to King report, Jan. 1832, doc. 89, NRIA; Narragansett remonstrance to King report, June 1832, doc. 86, NRIA

77. Neem, "The Elusive Common Good."

78. Child 1827.

79. Ibid.

80. Daniel Fellows Jr., accounts from guardianship of Chappaquiddick and Christiantown Indians, 1828–1835, MIGA, boxes 38–41, and MGCF, boxes 43–46; Levitt Thaxter, accounts from guardianship of Chappaquiddick and Christiantown Indians, 1836–1851, MIGA box 3, folder 15; Thaxter to Earle, 3 Sept. 1859 and 3 Feb. 1860, Earle Papers, box 2, folder 3; Isaiah Belain and Abrahm Brown, overseers, and Lawrence Prince, constable, Chappaquiddick, to Mass. legislature, 9 March 1840, MUHL no. 746; 16 Edgartown whites to Mass. legislature, 29 Feb. 1840, ibid.

81. E. B. [Elizabeth Browning] Chace, "The Narragansett Tribe.—A Lesson from Marshpee," *Providence Journal*, ca. 1880, NRIA; Daniel Amos, testimony in "Minutes of the Legislative Committee Appointed to Inquire into the Complaints of the Mashpee Indians."

82. Joseph Amos, testimony in "Minutes of the Legislative Committee Appointed to Inquire into the Complaints of the Mashpee Indians"; Chace, "A Lesson from Marshpee."

83. Karim Tiro, "Denominated 'SAVAGE': Methodism, Writing, and Identity in the Works of William Apess, A Pequot," *American Quarterly* 48 (1996): 661–62; Apess, "Indian Nullification," in *On Our Own Ground*, 169–72. For Apess's life through 1829, see generally Apess, "A Son of the Forest," in ibid., 3–52. On the gentry's monopoly of public discourse, see Grasso, *Speaking Aristocracy*, 2, 4.

84. Apess, "Indian Nullification," 173–77; Josiah Fiske, report to Governor Levi Lincoln, n.d. [but probably 6 July 1832], MIGA box 2, file 1; Apess, "Indian Nullification," 173–86; Mashpees to Fish, 26 June 1833, MIGA box 1, file 1.

85. Fiske to governor, 4 July 1832, MIGA box 2, file 1.

86. Ibid. Elders did play an important role in the Mashpee uprising: the two men who signed the initial petition and headed the 21 May meeting, Ebenezer Attaquin and Israel Amos, were born in 1782 and 1786 respectively. But the three men who clearly spearheaded the revolt and then led the community were all born between 1795 and 1810: William Apess (1798); Daniel Amos (ca. 1804); and Joseph Amos (1806). This was the generation that among African Americans became increasingly unwilling to accept political and social subordination, and also included Anglo-Americans who would drive the reform ferment in the

North such as Charles Finney (b. 1792), Henry David Thoreau (b. 1817), and William Lloyd Garrison (b. 1805). For birthdates of the Mashpees, see "Minutes of the Legislative Committee Appointed to Inquire into the Complaints of the Mashpee Indians"; list of Mashpee proprietors taken November 1832, MIGA, box 2, folder 15; and U.S. Department of Commerce, Federal Census of 1860, Mashpee schedule.

87. Apess, "Indian Nullification," 196–98; Jill Lepore, *The Name of War: King Philip's War and the Origins of American Identity* (New York: Knopf, 1998), 210–16 (on *Metamora*); William Apes, Daniel B. Amos, and Isaac Coombs to Speaker of the House, 21 Jan. 1834, MUSL no. 12843; Apess, "Indian Nullification," 206–27 (quoting Boston newspapers quoting their speeches). On Hallett, see *Barnstable Patriot*, 11 Sept. 1833; *Narragansett Weekly*, 9 Oct. 1862.

88. Apess, "Indian Nullification," 177, 239; *Old Colony Democrat*, 6 July 1833, 13 July 1833.

89. Apess, "Indian Nullification," 205–42; "Minutes of the Legislative Committee"; Cornelius Dalton et al., *Leading the Way: A History of the Massachusetts Legislature, 1629-1980* (Boston: Commonwealth of Massachusetts, 1984), 126, 135. For a description of the first district meeting on 5 May 1834, see MUHL no. 13838.

90. Mass. legislative commission, report on Mashpee Meetinghouse, *MHR* 72 (Boston, 1839): 7; Mashpee petition to Mass. Senate, 1838, MUSL no. 10417.

91. Various documents in MUSL no. 111612, 1842; Fish, Cotuit, to L. K. Lathrop, 13 Oct. 1853, box 2, folder 8, SPGPE. Fish was actually buried in the Mashpee church burial ground, and his son George (who became a highly regarded artist in Boston and Philadelphia) led an (unsuccessful) effort to get a seven-foot-tall granite marker that looked remarkably like the Washington Monument for the gravesite; George Fish to Lathrop, 29 July 1854, ibid.

92. Christopher Tomlinson, comments on Mandell, "New England Indians, Guardians, and Developing Notions of Authority in the Early Republic," presented at the Seventh Annual Conference of the Omohundro Institute of Early American History and Culture, Glasgow, Scotland, July 2001.

93. Simmons, *Spirit of the New England Tribes*, 96–97, 116–117, 165–171.

94. These were the arguments that the Mashpees and Narragansetts raised against detribalization and the gaining of full citizenship in (respectively) 1869 and 1879; see chap. 6.

CHAPTER 4: REFORM AND RENASCENCE

1. Baylies, Edgartown, to Rev. Abiel Holmes, secretary of SPG, 28 Sept. 1819, SPGPE; Bird 1849, 7, 12.

2. Grindal Rawson and Samuel Danforth, "Account of an Indian Visitation, A.D. 1698," *MHSC*, 1st ser., 10 (1809): 129–34; E. Jennifer Monaghan, "'She loved to read in good Books': Literacy and the Indians of Martha's Vineyard, 1643–1725," *History of Education Quarterly* 30 (1990): 502–3 n.38; David Silverman, "The Impact of Indentured Servitude on the Society and Culture of Southern New England Indians," *New England Quarterly* 74 (2001): 656–60; Kathleen Bragdon, "'Another Tongue Brought In': An Ethnohistorical Study of Native Writings in Massachusett" (Ph.D. diss., Brown University, 1981), 55.

3. William Kellaway, *The New England Company, 1649–1776: Missionary Society to the American Indians* (New York: Barnes and Noble, 1962), 277–81; "Account of the Certificates Granted by the SPG for Service 1778–1780," SPG Records, NEHGS, Boston; *RIAR*, Oct. 1843, (Providence, 1843), 75–76; Kevin McBride, "Historical Archaeology of the Mashantaucket Pequots, 1637–1900, a Preliminary Analysis," in *The Pequots in Southern New England: The Rise and Fall of an American Indian Nation*, ed. Laurence M. Hauptman and James D. Wherry (Norman: University of Oklahoma Press, 1990), 111–14.

4. William Rorabaugh, *The Alcoholic Republic: An American Tradition* (New York: Oxford University Press, 1979); Jack Larkin, *The Reshaping of Everyday Life, 1790–1840* (New York: Harper and Row, 1988), 172, 175, 284–86; Peter C. Mancall, *Deadly Medicine: Indians and Alcohol in Early America* (Ithaca, N.Y.: Cornell University Press, 1995); Hawley, report to Mass. legislature, 2 Sept. 1795, S. P. Savage Papers, 2:218, MHS.

5. Apess, "Indian Nullification," in *On Our Own Ground: The Complete Writings of William Apess, A Pequot*, ed. Barry O'Connell (Amherst: University of Massachusetts Press, 1992), 186; Hawley to Thacher, 8 Nov. 1792 and 25 Dec. 1793, box 2, folder 16, SPGPE; Hawley to Thacher, 14 Nov. 1800, ibid.; Hawley to Walley, 28 Oct. 1806, ibid.; William Davis, Sandwich, [to James Freeman?], 19 Jan. 1808, Misc. Bound Docs., MHS; Joel Perlmann, Silvana R. Siddali, and Keith Whitescarver, "Literacy, Schooling, and Teaching among New England Women, 1730–1820," *History of Education Quarterly* 37 (1997): 127–31.

6. Elisha Clapp, Sandwich, to Jedidiah Morse, Charlestown, 22 July 1808, Misc. Bound Docs., MHS; Fish, in Morse, *A Report to the Secretary of War of the United States on Indian Affairs* (New Haven, 1822), 70.

7. Zechariah Mayhew to Thacher, 22 May 1792, 15 June 1793, 28 July 1801, box 3, folder 11, SPGPE; Perlmann, Siddali, and Whitescarver, "Literacy, Schooling, and Teaching"; Edward Kendall, *Travels through the Northern Parts of the United States in the Years 1807 and 1808* (New York: I. Riley, 1809), 2:197; Gay Head to Mass. legislature, 13 July 1811, box 19, MGCF.

8. Frederick Baylies to Abiel Holmes, 28 Sept. 1819, box 1, folder 8, SPGPE; Chappaquiddick petition to SPG, 1809, in envelope 32, box 174a, Indians, Prehistory to 1799, MVHS; Abiel Holmes, "Additional Memoirs of Mohegans," *MHSC* 9 (1804): 79; John W. Barber, *Connecticut Historical Collections* (New Haven: Durrie and Peck and J. W. Barber, 1849), 338; Conn. assembly committee report, 1 May 1826, CGA1, folder 8; Curtis Coe, journal with unnumbered and generally undated pages, 24 June–17 Oct. 1809, and 7 July–7 Dec. 1810, box 1, folder 21, SPGPE; various letters from Baylies to the SPG, box 1, folder 8, SPGPE; Baylies, journal, 10 Jan. 1827, "a retrospect of the year past," folder: 1827–24 January 1827, box 3, SPG Papers, MHS.

9. Apess, "Indian Nullification," 187; Silverman, "Indians and Indentured Servitude"; Stephen Badger, "Historical and Characteristic Traits of the American Indians in General," *MHSC*, 1st ser., 5 (1798): 44; Joshua Bates, *A Sermon Delivered before the Society for Propagating the Gospel* (Boston: Cummings and Hilliard, 1813), 31; John Thaxter, Edgartown, to John Lothrop, Boston, 30 Sept. 1808, Misc. Bound Docs, MHS; Timothy Dwight, *Travels in New England and New York* (1821–22; reprint, Cambridge, Mass.: Harvard University Press, 1969), 3:14–15; Morse, *A Report to the Secretary of War*, 71, 75; Narragansett letter to SPG, Sept. 1827, folder: Sept. 1827–17 Sept.1827, SPG Papers, MHS; Coe, journal, 4 June–

11 Sept.1811, SPGPE; Francis Atwater, *History of Kent, Connecticut* (Meriden, Conn.: Journal Publishing Company, 1897), 78–79; T. S. Gold, "Fostering the Habit of Industry," *Connecticut Magazine* 8, no. 3 (March 1904): 452–53; Samuel Orcutt and Ambrose Beardsley, *History of Derby, Connecticut, 1642–1880* (Springfield, Mass.: Springfield Printing Company, 1880), xxxiv.

10. Coe, journal, 4 June–11 Sept. 1811, box 1, folder 21, SPGPE; Narragansett letter to SPG, Sept. 1827; Clapp to Morse, 22 July 1808; Abisha Samson, Tisbury, to Joseph Grafton, Newton, 3 Feb. 1810, in *Massachusetts Baptist Missionary Magazine* 2 (1810): 300–301; "Description of Dukes County, Aug. 13, 1807," *MHSC*, 2nd ser., 3 (1815): 93. On the increasing authoritarianism of mainstream Baptist churches in southern New England, see Susan Juster, *Disorderly Women, Sexual Politics, and Evangelism in Revolutionary New England* (Ithaca, N.Y.: Cornell University Press, 1994). Supposedly in the 1790s, Chappaquiddick men killed the first Methodist preacher on the Vineyard, John Saunders, at least in part because he condemned "their many vicious habits"; Richard Pease "Sketches of Edgartown, Tisbury and Chilmark: Martha's Vineyard," ts. by Thomas Minns, Aug. 1877, MHS; "Old, Forgotten Indian Meeting House on Martha's Vineyard about Which Center Some of the Most Interesting Traditions of the Island," *New Bedford Sunday Standard*, 1909, clipping in SPM, from New Bedford Free Public Library.

11. William Simmons and Cheryl Simmons, eds., *Old Light on Separate Ways: The Narragansett Diary of Joseph Fish, 1765–1776* (Hanover, N.H.: University Press of New England, 1982), 93; Curtis Coe, journal, 4 June–11 Sept. 1811, SPGPE; Apess, "Son of the Forest" and "Experiences of Five Christian Indians," in *On Our Own Ground*, 40, 150. On the visionary culture in eighteenth-century America and Europe, see Douglas Winiarski, "Souls Filled with Ravishing Transport: Heavenly Visions and the Radical Awakening in New England," *William and Mary Quarterly* 3rd ser., 56 (2004): 41–42; Mark S. Schantz, *Piety in Providence: Class Dimensions of Religious Experience in Antebellum Rhode Island* (Ithaca, N.Y.: Cornell University Press, 2000), 47.

12. Kendall, *Travels through the Northern Parts*, 2:49–50, 183; Melissa J. Fawcett, *Medicine Trail: The Life and Lessons of Gladys Tantaquidgeon* (Tucson: University of Arizona Press, 2000), 23–27, 31–36; William S. Simmons, *Spirit of the New England Tribes: Indian History and Folklore, 1620–1984* (Hanover, N.H.: University Press of New England, 1986); Frank G. Speck, "Native Tribes and Dialects of Connecticut, A Mohegan-Pequot Diary," *Bureau of American Ethnology Annual Report, no. 43: 1925–1926* (Washington, D.C.: GPO, 1928), 224, 245, 254, 273–76; Alan Taylor, "The Early Republic's Supernatural Economy: Treasure Seeking in the American North-East," *American Quarterly* 38 (1986): 8; Simmons, *Spirit of the New England Tribes*, 162–71.

13. John Lathrop, *A Discourse before the Society for Propagating the Gospel* (Boston: Manning and Loring, 1804), 17; Thaxter to Lathrop, 30 Sept. 1808, Misc. Bound Docs., MHS.

14. Bates, *A Sermon Delivered before the Society*, 29–30; "Domestic Missions, Narragansett Indians," *Religious Intelligencer* [New Haven, Conn.] 1, no. 42 (15 March 1817): 662–63.

15. Jonathan D. Sassi, *A Republic of Righteousness: The Public Christianity of Post-Revolutionary New England Clergy* (New York: Oxford University Press, 2003); Johann Neem, "The Elusive Common Good: Religion and Civil Society in Massachusetts, 1780–1833,"

Journal of the Early Republic 24 (2004): 381–417; Daniel Walker Howe, *The Political Culture of the American Whigs* (Chicago: University of Chicago Press, 1979), 9–21, 36–38.

16. Morse, *Report to the Secretary of War*; Fawcett, *Medicine Trail*, 12.

17. Thaxter to Lothrop, 30 Sept. 1808. Baylies's first child, Frederick (who would become a famous architect), was born in Windham, Conn., in 1797, and his second child, Sally, was born in Edgartown in 1799; Bob Juch, "Bob Juch's Kin [Frederick Baylies/Sally Lee]," http://freepages.genealogy.rootsweb.com/~bobjuch/fam/fam01231.htm (updated 5 June 2002, accessed 1 July 2004).

18. Chappaquiddicks to SPG, 12 Feb. 1810, doc. 32, Letters, Harvard Grants for Work among the Indians, Harvard University Archives; Thaxter to SPG, 15 Jan. 1810, 13 June 1810, 29 Nov. 1810, all doc. 34, ibid.; Baylies to Harvard College, 11 June 1810, unnumbered, ibid.

19. Baylies to Abiel Holmes, 5 and 16 May 1819 (same letter), box 1, folder 8, SPGPE; Baylies, Taunton, to Abiel Holmes, SPG Secretary, 25 May 1819, ibid.

20. Baylies to Holmes, 28 Sept. 1819; MPL ch. 89, Resolves of 1826 (Gay Head schoolhouse); MPL ch. 43, Resolves of 1828 (Christiantown schoolhouse).

21. Baylies to Alden Bradford, 8 April 1835, SPG Papers, box 6, MHS; Baylies to Holmes, 28 Sept. 1819; Baylies Edgartown, to Abiel Holmes, Cambridge, 15 March 1824, ibid.; Baylies to Alden Bradford, 8 April 1835, SPG Papers, box 6, MHS; Baylies to Holmes, 13 Sept. 1825, box 3, folder 16, SPG Papers, MHS.

22. Baylies to SPG, 20 March 1820, box 1, folder 8, SPGPE; R.I., report of legislative committee on Narragansetts, Jan. 1830, doc. 80, NRIA; MPL ch. 7, Acts of 1820; accounts of Chappaquiddick church, box 30, MGCR; Morse, *Report to the Secretary of War*, 71–72. While about 40 Narragansett students attended Baylies' school during the late 1820s, when the Narragansett tribal council asked for a share of the Rhode Island school fund in 1828 they noted that they had more than 100 children under the age of 16; Tobias Ross and Narragansett tribal council to assembly, Oct. 1828, doc. 73, NRIA.

23. Baylies to Holmes, 28 Sept. 1819; Peter Thacher reporting for SPG committee, 22 May 1835, SPG Papers, box 6, MHS. The number of students in each of Baylies's schools fluctuated widely during the 1820s, although he provided figures only for the one to four weeks that he personally taught at each community. Every year or two Baylies reported on the total number of students during his sessions and who could write and could read from the Bible, a spelling book, or the alphabet.

24. Baylies to Holmes, 15 March 1824, SPGPE, box 1, folder 8; Wright to Walker and Parkman, Boston, 9 April 1839, SPG Papers, box 7, MHS.

25. Baylies to Holmes, 28 Sept. 1819; Mary A. Cleggett Vanderhoop, "The Gay Head Indians: Their History and Traditions," series in the *New Bedford Evening Standard* beginning 25 June 1904; "Forgotten Indian Meeting House on Martha's Vineyard."

26. Peter Thacher, SPG committee report, 22 May 1835, SPG Papers, box 6, MHS; Francis Parkman, "Report of a Visit of Inquiry at Nantucket, Martha's Vineyard, & to the Narragansett Indians [27 Oct. 1835]," ibid.

27. Baylies to Bradford and SPG, 2 April 1836, SPG Papers, box 6, MHS; SPG committee, report, 3 Nov. 1836, ibid.

28. Thacher, report, 22 May 1835.

29. Solomon Francis et al., Mashpee, to Mass. legislature, n.d., and Phineas Fish, Mashpee, to Mass. legislature, 30 Jan. 1830, MPL ch. 53, Resolves of 1829.

30. Neem, "The Elusive Common Good."

31. "The Narragansett Indians of Rhode Island," *Providence Journal*, reprinted in *Niles' National Register* 64 (1843): 415. The Narragansett meetinghouse was the only church in the area and drew blacks and whites from surrounding areas; a meeting in August 1859 attracted nearly 2,000 people; "The Indian Meeting," *Narragansett Weekly* [Westerly, R.I.], 6 Aug. 1859.

32. Thomas Cooper and Simon Johnson, Gay Head, to Alden Bradford, New Bedford, 12 Nov. 1831, box 5, folder 1, SPG Papers, MHS; Edward S. Burgess, "The Old South Road of Gay Head," [1926] reprint, *Dukes County Intelligencer* 12 (Aug. 1970), 19–20; "Forgotten Indian Meeting House on Martha's Vineyard"; Report on Herring Pond, 1850, MUSL no. 13098; unsigned report, 30 April 1859, Earle Papers, box 2, folder 3; Bird 1849, 33. The 1848 commission reported that Chappaquiddick and Christiantown "have no preaching or religious teaching," but they overlooked Amos and the services that he led at their meetinghouses; ibid., 10, 14.

33. Apess, "Indian Nullification"; Mashpee commissioner and tribal council to Mass. legislature, 15 Dec. 1834, MUHL no. 13838; Mashpee commissioner to Mass. legislature, 30 Dec. 1836, MUSL no. 9795; Bird 1849, 37; E. B. [Elizabeth Browning] Chace, "The Narragansett Tribe.—A Lesson from Marshpee," *Providence Journal*, ca. 1880, NRIA.

34. John Deforest, *History of the Indians of Connecticut, From the Earliest Known Period to 1850* (Hartford: William Jason Hamersley 1851), 482–86; Edward Hooker, *Memoirs of Mrs. Sarah L. Huntington Smith*, 3rd ed. (New York: American Tract Society, 1846), 110–11, 120–21; Fawcett, *Medicine Trail*, 12, 53; Speck, "Native Tribes and Dialects," 255; Trudie Lamb Richmond and Amy E. Den Ouden, "Recovering Gendered Political Histories: Local Struggles and Native Women's Resistance in Colonial Southern New England," in *Reinterpreting New England Indians and the Colonial Experience*, ed. Colin G. Calloway and Neal Salisbury (Boston: Colonial Society of Massachusetts, 2003), 187–88; "Disposition of the Mohegan Tribe Lands," *Norwich Daily Courier*, 7 June 1859.

35. Neem, "The Elusive Common Good."

36. In addition to the reports cited below, see Conn. assembly committee report on the Golden Hill Paugussetts, 1823, CGA1, folder 3, Mohegans, 1830, folder 8, and Mashantucket Pequots, 1855, folder 26.

37. Earle 1861.

38. Apess, "Indian Nullification."

39. Childs 1827, 9–10; Mashpee commissioner and council to Mass. legislature, 15 Dec. 1834, MUHL no. 13838, Mass. Archives; Mashpee Commissioner to Mass. legislature, 30 Dec. 1836, MUSL no. 178; Bird 1849, 37; various documents in box 52, MGCF; *CRPA*, May 1839 (Hartford, 1839), 103–4; legislative committee report, Jan. 1843, unnumbered, NRIA; Section 22, *Rhode Island Institute of Instruction* 7 (1845): 146.

40. *Gideon Ammons, Jr., v. School District no. 5, in the Town of Charlestown*, and *Joshua H. Nokake v. same*, Jan. 1864, *Rhode Island Reports* 7 (Providence, 1896): 596–600.

41. Accounts submitted by Smith Mayhew for Gay Head, 24 April 1850, box 62, MGCF.

In Mashpee in 1839, Rev. E. G. Perry received $30 a month to teach at one school, and "Miss Winslow" received only $16; both were boarded as part of their salary; Perry probably received a higher salary because of his pastoral position and duties and because he was male. Mashpee commissioner and selectmen to Mass. legislature, 1839, MUSL no. 10422.

42. Herring Pond to Mass. legislature, March 1838, ch. 64, 17 April 1838, MPL; Mass. commission's report on building the Herring Pond school house, 20 March 1839, box 49, MGCF; box 53, MGCF; Thaxter, report to governor, 31 Dec. 1850, box 63, MGCF; MAR ch. 35, 26 April 1855.

43. Apess, "Indian Nullification"; Gay Head petition in "Report on Act to Prohibit the Sale of Ardent Spirits" MHR 48 (Boston, 1838), 2.

44. Gay Head petition, 13 July 1811, box 19, MGCF; King report, Jan 1831, doc. 81, NRIA; Narragansett objection to King report, Jan. 1832, doc. 89, NRIA; Narragansett remonstrance to King report, June 1832, doc. 86, NRIA; Moses Stanton to R.I. assembly, not dated, doc. 96, NRIA. For a biography of Dan King, see "Dr. Dan King," Representative Men and Old Families of Rhode Island (Chicago: J. H. Beers and Co., 1908), 2272.

45. Mashpee petition to Mass. legislature, 28 Jan. 1837, MUSL no. 10176; MUSL no. 10416. According to a note in this file, of 66 qualified voters in Mashpee in 1837, 11 or 12 signed this petition, nine of whom opposed the 1833–34 revolt and reforms.

46. "Report of the House Commissioners on the Pauper System," MHR 6 (Boston, 1833): 23–25 and passim; MAR ch. 159, 17 April 1863.

47. Morton J. Horwitz, The Transformation of American Law, 1780–1860 (Cambridge, Mass.: Harvard University Press, 1977), 130–39 and passim; James Willard Hurst, Law and the Conditions of Freedom in the Nineteenth Century United States (Madison: University of Wisconsin Press, 1956); Gary Kulik, "Dams, Fish, and Farmers: Defense of Public Rights in Eighteenth-Century Rhode Island," in The Countryside in the Age of Capitalist Transformation: Essays in the Social History of Rural America, ed. Steven Hahn and Jonathan Prude (Chapel Hill: University of North Carolina Press, 1985). At midcentury, Mohegans and Niantics were forced to be part of this process, as the Conn. legislature directed their overseers to sell reservation land to railroads; CPRA, May 1848 (New Haven, 1848): 104–5; CPRA, May 1851 (Hartford, 1851): 125–26.

48. Chappaquiddicks to Joseph Thaxter, April 1826, envelope 22, box 141.1, MVHS; documents Hannah Pocknett and Bathsheba Wickett, petitions to sell Christiantown land, 1824, MUHL no. 9419; Chappaquiddicks to Mass. legislature, 24 May 1810, MUSL no. 4093; Christiantown to Mass. legislature, 25 Dec. 1824, MUHL no. 9419.

49. Child 1827.

50. Chappaquiddick and Christiantown inventories, 1828, folder 15, box 3, MIGA; Bird 1849; Earle 1861.

51. Charles Marston, Mashpee commissioner, to Mass. legislature, 1840, MUSL no. 10618; Solomon Attaquin, testimony in "[Report to the] House of Representatives, June 3, 1869 [on Marshpee hearings]," MHR 502 (Boston, 1869): 31; Marston to Mass. legislature, MUHL no. 13838; MPL ch. 61, 4 March 1845, Resolves of 1845. Solomon Attaquin's gravestone shows that he died on 16 March 1895, aged 87 years; Robert Paine Carlson, "Mashpee Attaquin Cemetery up to 1895," 17th, 18th & 19th Century Cape Cod Gravestones, www.capecodgravestones.com/mashatt.html (updated July 2005, accessed 20 Aug. 2005).

52. *MAR* ch. 168, 6 April 1850; MUSL no. 13098, 1851. The legislature decided that eligible individuals would be those who, "according to the customs, usages, descent, inhabitancy, or general acquiescence," were Herring Pond proprietors, or those of "of Indian descent born in Plymouth or Barnstable counties" married to a Herring Pond proprietor and a permanent resident of the reserve on 1 Jan. 1850—except for individuals granted land in Mashpee in 1842. The 1848 commission reported that only around 100 of 2,500 acres in the reserve were divided among members of the tribe; Bird 1849, 38.

53. Simeon L. Deyo, ed., *History of Barnstable County, Massachusetts* (New York: H. W. Blake and Company, 1890), 715–16; B. C. Merchant to Earle, 27 Aug. 1859, Earle Papers, box 2, folder 3.

54. Solomon Weeks et al. to Mass. legislature, n.d., MUHL no. 10112, June 1827; Solomon Weeks et al. to Mass. legislature, 30 Dec. 1828, box 3, folder 15, MIGA. Two of the five complainants in 1828, Solomon Weeks and Thomas James, had received sizeable allotments, with Weeks getting the largest area of cropland of any proprietor, and the elderly Recall Degrass was given 47 acres of cropland and 6 acres of woodland. All of the signatories had high percentages of Native ancestry, from five-eighths to "full blood"; Baylies 1823. James W. Degrass, who signed the 1827 petition, returned from fairly lucrative whaling voyages in 1837, 1847, and 1850; Christiantown guardian accounts, box 3, folder 15, MIGA.

55. Charles Marston, "Report," 1837, MUSL no. 10212; 1838, MUSL no. 10422; Bird 1849, 7, 21, 23, 26–27; Earle 1861, 32, 49–50, 68–69; Chappaquiddick to Mass. legislature, 24 May 1810, MUSL no. 4093; [Report] June 3, 1869 [on Marshpee hearings]," 15, 31.

56. Conn. assembly committee report, 1 May 1826, CGA1, folder 8; Lucy Tantaquigeon, Lucy Comewawas, John Uncas, and Benomi Occum to assembly, 30 April 1827, ibid.; Mohegans to assembly, 30 April 1827, ibid.

57. U.S. Department of the Interior, Office of Federal Acknowledgment, "Summary under the Criteria and Evidence for Proposed Finding Eastern Pequot Indians of Connecticut" (24 March 2000), 109; Conn. assembly, special committee report, May 1855, CGA1, folder 26; ch. 66, June 1855, *CAR*, May 1855 (Hartford, 1855): 80–82; Brothertown Pequots to Conn. assembly, May 1850, CGA2; William Morgan to Deforest, 22 Aug. 1849, in Deforest, *Indians of Connecticut*, 444–45; ch. 60, 3 July 1868, *CRPA* 1868, 249.

58. Puolly Mossock et al. to assembly, 4 May 1844, CGA1, folder 16; *CRPA*, May 1844 (New Haven, 1844), 30–31; Puolly Mossock et al. to New London County Court, Nov. 1845, NLCC, box 3; Puolly Mossock to assembly, 20 April 1848, CGA1, folder 19; William Crosby et al. to assembly, 23 April 1849, CGA1, folder 20; Solomon Paul to New London County Court, 12 Aug. 1851, NLCC, box 3; Puolly Mossock et al. to assembly, April 1850, CGA2, folder 15; Henry Mathews et al. to assembly, 22 April 1850, ibid.; Moses Samson et al. to assembly, May 1850, ibid.

59. Mohegans to Conn. assembly, 13 May 1850, CGA2, folder 15; ch. 51, 19 June 1850, *CPA*, May 1850 (New Haven, 1850): 37–38; ch. 55, 17 June 1852, *CPA*, May 1852 (New Haven, 1852): 66. There was also at least one land sale request from a Niantic, Martha Paul, daughter of David Walkut and Anna Occuish, who had lived with the tribe until age 17 and then had moved to Brothertown; Martha and Solomon Paul, Wisconsin, to New London County Court, 30 Sept. 1851, NLCC, box 4.

60. Solomon Weeks et al. to Mass. legislature, n.d., MUHL no. 10112, 1 June 1827; Bird 1849, 4, 6–8, 13–15.

61. Bird 1849, 19–22, 24–25.

62. Gay Head, Chappaquiddick, and Christiantown to James Walker, Boston, 19 Nov., 2 Dec., and 16 Dec. 1838, SPG Papers, box 6, MHS; Wright to Walker and Parkman, Boston, 9 April 1839, SPG Papers, box 7, MHS; Bird 1849.

63. Wright to Walker and Parkman, 9 April 1839, SPG Papers, box 7, MHS; Parkman, "Report of a Visit of Inquiry [27 Oct. 1835]," SPG Papers, box 6, MHS.

64. Legislative committee report, Jan. 1830, doc. 80, NRIA; legislative committee report, Jan. 1831, doc. 81, NRIA; Narragansett council to R.I. assembly, June 1832, doc. 86, NRIA; Narragansett commissioner's report, *RIAR*, May 1862 (Providence, 1862), 67–69; see also Griffin 1858, 6.

65. Esther and Ezekiel Cooper to assembly, 20 April 1848, CGA1, folder 20; *CRPA*, May 1849, 90–91; *CRPA*, May 1852, 122; Superior Court decree on petition of William Wallace et al, 25 April 1857, box 133, Mohegans, overseers reports, 1846–64, RG3, NLCSC, CSA; Deforest, *Indians of Connecticut*, 489.

66. Herring Pond treasurer, 1844 report, MUHL no. 1698; Josiah Fiske, 1833 report on Mashpee, box 2, folder 1, MIGA; Earle 1861, 49, 68, 26.

67. John Brooke to H-SHEAR, 1 July 2004, archived at www.h-net.org/~shear/; Jack Larkin, "Sustainable Lives Part II: How the Rural Landscape Changed," *Visitor* (2000), 4–5; Andrew Baker, "Notes on Sheep Raising in Early 19th-Century New England," Old Sturbridge Village Online Resource Library, 1989 (my thanks to Jack Larkin for these sources).

68. Bird 1849, 13–15; Chace, "A Lesson from Marshpee."

69. Zaccheus Howwoswee to Earle, 25 Aug. 1859, 27 Jan. 1860, Sept. 1860, Earle Papers, box 2, folder 3; Earle 1861, 31, 44, generally 31–45. Similarly, Earle found that 14 Mashpees had not been assigned rights in the reserve and had been gone for so long they were no longer recognized by the tribe as members; ibid., 47.

70. *CRPA* 1835, 315–17; *CRPA* 1838, 358–59. In 1834, just the Mohegans were protected, but in 1835 the law as extended to the Mashantuckets and in 1836 to the Niantics and all other Indians; CGA1, folders 10, 11, 12. In 1855, this was changed so that violators would also lose all of their tools, carts, and animals; ch. 65, 12 June 1855, *CPA*, May 1855, 79–80. Seven years later, the fine was raised to $7 per load; ch. 34, 2 July 1862, *CPA Special Session, October 1861, and May session 1862*, 31–32.

71. Barber, *Historical Collections of Massachusetts*, 47–48; Nymphas Marston and Kilburn Whitman to Mass. legislature, 31 Jan. 1822, ch. 75, Resolves of 1822, MPL; MUHL no. 2091, 1846; Bird 1848, 39.

72. Narragansetts to assembly, June 1832, doc. 86, NRIA; docs. 102 and 105, NRIA; assembly committee report, 1839, doc. 100, NRIA (the race-based 1792 state laws governing Narragansett membership were apparently rarely enforced, and nothing had taken their place); *RIAR*, Oct. 1849 (Providence, 1849), 3; Narragansett constitution of 1850, in Charlestown, R.I., town records.

73. Griffin 1858, 4–5, 7; Narragansett tribal records, in Charlestown records. On tavern permits as welfare, see David Conroy, *In Public Houses: Drink and the Revolution of*

Authority in Colonial Massachusetts (Chapel Hill: University of North Carolina Press, 1995), 101–8.

74. Apess, "An Indian's Looking-Glass for the White Man" (1833), in *On Our Own Ground*, 155. William Lloyd Garrison wrote that Mashpees were bound by "the chains of a servile dependence," which removed "all motives for superior exertions"; *The Liberator*, 25 Jan. 1834, reprinted in Apess, "Indian Nullification," 220–23.

75. "Indian Enterprise," *New Bedford Mercury*, 13 Oct. 1837; Marston, report on Mashpee, 1835, MUSL no. 9795; MUSL no. 10212, 1837; Barber, *Historical Collections of Massachusetts*, 48; Marston, Report on Mashpee, MUHL no. 13838; MUSL, no. 10618 (1840); Deyo, *History of Barnstable County*, 715–16; Matthias Amos and Solomon Attaquin in "[Report] 1869 [on Marshpee hearings]," 15, 31.

76. Deyo, *History of Barnstable County*, 715–16; Russell M. Peters, *The Wampanoags of Mashpee* (Massachusetts: Indian Spiritual and Cultural Training Council, 1987), 40–41; Bird 1849, 21; *Sandwich Observer*, 17 Feb. 1849, and 24 Feb. 1849. The newspaper also called for a law protecting "the noble deer in our forests which have been hunted the past season by every loafer from abroad who could command any kind of firearms, accompanied by hounds, mongrels, and curs of low degree"; ibid.

77. MAR ch. 36, 16 March 1849 (violators were fined $5 plus $0.50 per trout found in their possession, and guardians were penalized for the offenses of minors); MAR ch. 94, 26 March 1858; MAR ch. 105, 17 March 1859; MAR ch. 46, 24 Feb. 1860; MAR ch. 150, 13 April 1864; Mashpee District Meeting Book (district fishing regulations and appointment of agents), Mashpee Archives, Town Hall, Mashpee, Mass.; Earle 1861, 51; N. J. Holden et al., "Report on Indians of the Commonwealth [1869]," MHR 483 (Boston, 1869): 5; Deyo, *Barnstable County*, 715–16. One writer called Mashpee River the finest trout stream in the state, and Mashpee Pond one of the finest fishing ponds in the region; Charles F. Danforth, "Trout Fishing in New England," *New England Magazine* 14, no. 4 (June 1893): 500. I deeply appreciate Rosemary Burns's generous sharing of her notes of the District Meeting Book and other Mashpee records, and for supplying photocopies of many of the documents.

78. Ephraim Spooner and Joshua Thomas to Mass. legislature, 1813, MUSL no. 4678; MAR ch. 285, 12 April 1854; MAR ch. 96, 23 March 1867; Holden, "Report [1869]," 5.

79. Bird 1849, 7, 19, 25; Earle 1861, 26; Griffin 1858, 6; Deforest, *Indians of Connecticut*, 489. The 1861 census of Indians in Massachusetts shows a noticeable decrease since 1792 in women-headed households in Gay Head: 10 of 69, 14.5 percent. The other two Indian communities on the Vineyard show similar percentages: 4 of 19 (21 percent) in Chappaquiddick and 2 of 16 (12.5 percent) in Christiantown; ibid., appendix.

80. Morse, *Report to the Secretary of War*, 24, 70, 74; Adams 1880, 32–34; Bird 1849, 12, 14, 23; Earle 1861, 65–66 and passim. On the issue in another region, see William G. McLoughlin, *Cherokee Renascence in the New Republic* (Princeton, N.J.: Princeton University Press, 1986).

81. MHR 72 (Boston, 1839).

82. Yarmouth Indians to Mass. governor, 14 Jan. 1819, MUSL no. 6568. In 1713, the town had set aside a tract of land "for the native Indians of this town to live upon . . . forever";

the natives were denied the right "to sell or dispose of any part of said land"; ibid. Bird 1849, 46; Earle 1861, 108–10.

83. Charles Endicott to Earle, 19 March 1860, Earle Papers, box 2, folder 1; Punkapoags to Mass. legislature, n.d. [but probably early 1854 (the committee was created April 1854)], MUSL no. 18442; Earle 1861, 76. On the many leases signed by English settlers on the Punkapoag reserve ca. 1703–06, averaging 153 years, and on subsequent controversial land deals involving Punkapoag, see Daniel Mandell, *Behind the Frontier: Indians in Eighteenth-Century Eastern Massachusetts* (Lincoln: University of Nebraska Press, 1996), 77–78.

84. *MAR* ch. 69, 17 May 1855; *MAR* ch. 206, 28 May 1856; Earle 1861, 115–16.

85. Mass., governor's special committee report, 11 Jan. 1860, box 74, MGCF; council report, 10 Feb. 1860, ibid. The committee left any substantive decisions to the Governor's Council, who in turn authorized the state attorney general and district attorney "to adjust or compromise" the claims.

86. Earle 1861, 112; Earle, "Dartmouth Case," *MHR* 216 (Boston, 1861), 4–14; Asa F. Wainer, South Westport, to Earle, 2 Feb. 1861, Earle Papers, box 2, folder 5; *MAR* ch. 40, 28 March 1863; *MAR* ch. 93, 14 May 1864; "Amounts Paid to Indians [1861–1866]," *MHR* 73 (Boston, 1867), 1–4.

87. B. F. Winslow to Earle, 29 Aug. 1859, Earle Papers, box 2, folder 5, various letters from Mitchell and others in 1859, ibid.; Earle 1861, 86; Mitchell to Mass. Governor's Council, 7 Jan. 1860, box 74, MGCF; Ebenezer W. Pierce, *Indian History, Biography, and Genealogy* (North Abington, Mass.: Zerviah Gould Mitchell, 1878); "A Princess' Death," *Abington Times*, March 1898.

88. B. F. Winslow to Earle, 29 Aug. 1859, Earle Papers, box 2, folder 5, and various letters from Mitchell and others in 1859, ibid.; Mitchell to Mass. Governor's Council, 7 Jan. 1860, MGCF box 74; Pierce, *Indian History, Biography, and Genealogy*; Zaccheus Howwoswee to Earle, 25 Aug. 1859, Earle Papers, box 2, folder 3.

89. Bird 1849, 23. The one extant documentation of an effort by Anglo-Americans to gain control of Gay Head clay is a January 1832 petition to the state legislature from Frederic and Henry Tudor of Boston—who became famous for shipping ice to Calcutta—asking for the right to make a contract with Vineyard Indians for rights to "clays, fossils, and mineral substances"; MUHL no. 11818.

90. Holden, "Report [1869]," 5; Moses Brown, Vineyard Haven, to Rufus Ellis, Boston, 23 Sept. 1876, SPG Papers, box 8, MHS; Earle 1861, 33, generally 32–33.

91. Koch, *Journey Through a Part of the United States*, 15–24; "A Visit to Gay Head," *Vineyard Gazette*, 8 June 1848. The 1848 visitor also complained that he was fed leftover turkey for lunch, to which a "friend of Cooper" replied (in the *Vineyard Gazette* on 22 June) that "we don't think it's best to be cooking great dinners on Lord's day, no matter who comes." This hurtful response boasted of how Indians were more devout than whites who broke the Sabbath. The 1848 commission also stayed at "old uncle Cooper's"; F. W. Bird, "Cotuit Port (Cape Cod), Sept. 10," *Norfolk Democrat*, 22 Sept. 1848. See also "Correspondence of the *Vineyard Gazette*," Gay Head, 19 Aug. 1847, in SPM.

92. "A Visit to Martha's Vineyard," *Atlantic Monthly* 4 (Sept. 1859): 281–94; Francis En-

dicott, "Striped Bass," *Scribner's Monthly*, vol. 21, issue 5 (March 1881): 704–5; Elias Nason, *A Gazatteer of the State of Massachusetts* (Boston: B. B. Russell, 1874), 325–26.

93. Barber, *Historical Collections of Massachusetts*, 48; Charles Marston to Earle, 14 Feb. 1860, Earle Papers, box 2, folder 2; *The Uncas Monument, 1492–1842: published once in three hundred and fifty years* (Norwich, Conn.: John G. Cooley, 1842); John Avery, *History of the Town of Ledyard, 1650–1900* (Norwich, Conn.: Noyes and Davis, 1901), 260; Isaiah Belain and Abrahm Brown to Mass. legislature, 9 March 1840, MUHL no. 746; Thacher, SPG committee report, 22 May 1835, SPG Papers, box 6, MHS; Wright to Walker and Parkman, Boston, 9 April 1839, SPG Papers, box 7, MHS; Nathaniel Philbrick, *Abram's Eyes: The Native American Legacy of Nantucket Island* (Nantucket: Mill Hill Press, 1998), 225; Jeffrey Bolster, "'To Feel Like a Man': Black Seamen in the Northern States, 1800–1860," *Journal of American History* 76 (1990): 1173–99.

94. Frank G. Speck, *Eastern Algonkian Block-Stamp Decoration: A New World Original or an Acculturated Art*, Research Series no. 1, Archaeological Society of New Jersey, State Museum (Trenton, 1947), 5; Eva Butler, "Addendum," ibid., 40–54; Ann McMullen, "Native Basketry, Basketry Styles, and Changing Group Identity in Southern New England," in *Algonkians of New England, Past and Present*, ed. Peter Benes (Boston: Boston University Press, 1993), 76–88; John W. Johnson, *Life of John W. Johnson*, ts., Maine Historical Society, 11–12; *Uncas Monument*; MAR ch. 41, 19 Feb. 1867, and ch. 207, 4 May 1867; MAR ch. 120, 13 April 1868; Deyo, *History of Barnstable County*, 715–16.

95. Johnson, *Life of John W. Johnson*, 19, 27, 32, 36, 43.

96. Harald Prins, "Chief Big Thunder (1827–1906): The Life History of a Penobscot Trickster," *Maine History* 37 (1998): 140–158; Bunny McBride, *Molly Spotted Elk: A Penobscot in Paris* (Norman: University of Oklahoma Press, 1995), 45–46; Harald Prins, personal communication, 22 July 1998; Harvey W. Root, *The Unknown Barnum* (New York: Harper and Brothers, 1927), 92; Larkin, *Reshaping of Everyday Life*, 209; Johnson, *Life of John Johnson*, 13–16, 36, 41–42;"Last of Massasoit's Line Lived in Abington," ts., collections of Dyer Library (Abington, Mass.), 219. Although the dates of the Mitchells's work with the circus are not recorded in this article, Delores was born in 1834, Melinda in 1836, and Charlotte in 1848. I assume that they were still young women during their stints with the circus.

97. McMullen, "Native Basketry," 76–88; Ann McMullen and Russell G. Handsman, "Introduction," in *A Key into the Language of Woodsplint Baskets*, ed. Ann McMullen, Russell G. Handsman, and Joan Lester (Washington, Conn.: American Indian Archaeological Institute, 1987), 21–40; Sarah Peabody Turnbaugh and William A. Turnbaugh, "Weaving the Woods," in ibid., 78–90.

98. See, for example, Joan Lester, "We Didn't Make Fancy Baskets until We Were Discovered," in McMullen, Handsman, and Lester, *A Key into the Language of Woodsplint Baskets*, 42–53; Gary W. Hume, "Joseph Laurent's Intervale Camp: Post-Colonial Abenaki Adaptation and Revitalization in New Hampshire," in Benes, *Algonkians of New England*, 101–13; Ernest Dodge, "Indians at Salem in the Mid-Nineteenth Century," *Old-Time New England* 42 (1951–52): 93–95; "Penobscot Indians," *Sandwich Observer*, 15 Sept. 1849; Johnson, *Life of John Johnson*.

99. Interview with Matthias Amos in Chace, "A Lesson from Marshpee."

100. Eric Lott, *Love and Theft: Black-face Minstrelsy and the American Working Class* (New York: Oxford University Press, 1993), 63–88; Stephen Thernstrom, *The Battle for Christmas* (New York: Random House, 1996), 251–56.

101. Koch, *Journey through a Part of the United States,* 23; Herring Pond overseers to Mass. legislature, 25 Jan. 1814, MUHL no. 7666; Marston and Whitman to Mass. legislature, 31 Jan. 1822, ch. 75, MPL; Bird 1849, 18–20, 39, and passim; Earle 1861; Barber, *Connecticut Historical Collections,* 338; Mohegan 1861, 7; Simmons, *Spirit of the New England Tribes,* esp. 175–256.

102. Bird 1849, 41–43; Earle 1861, 84, 103; William Morgan to Deforest, 22 Aug. 1849, in Deforest, *Indians of Connecticut,* 445.

103. *MSR* 10 (Boston, 1857), 2–3; Earle 1861, 10; *MAR* ch. 80, 29 May 1857; Earle 1861, 103–104, 84; PF Webster 64–65.

CHAPTER 5: REALITY AND IMAGERY

1. Mrs. Charles H. Smith, "The Last of the Niantics," *Connecticut Magazine* 8 (1903–4): 455–56; Melissa J. Fawcett, *Medicine Trail: The Life and Lessons of Gladys Tantaquidgeon* (Tucson: University of Arizona Press, 2000), 37–41, 57–58; J. Dyneley Prince and Frank G. Speck, "The Modern Pequots and Their Language," *American Anthropologist,* n.s., 5 (1903): 197–98.

2. Narragansett tribal council to Conn. assembly, June 1832, no. 86, NIRA.

3. Griffin 1858, 6; Earle 1861, 6, 10–11.

4. F. W. Bird, untitled, *Norfolk Democrat,* 22 Sept. 1848; Smith, "Last of the Niantics."

5. Baylies 1823; Bird 1849; Wright to Walker and Parkman, 9 April 1839, SPG Papers, box 7, MHS; U.S. Chamber of Commerce, 1850 census schedule for Edgartown, Mass., transcribed in Chris Baer, "Historical Records of Dukes County, Massachusetts," http://history.vineyard.net/edgcen50.htm (accessed 13 May 2005); Earle 1861, appendix; U.S. Department of Commerce, 1860 census schedules for Sandwich; Earle 1861, 6–7. Wright also noted that "many of the unmarried females are employed in housework at Edgartown, Holmes Hole, New Bedford, &c. and obtain good wages. Their manners are hereby improved and their minds informed, especially when they are in respectable, intelligent, and benevolent families"; Wright to Walker and Parkman, 9 April 1839, SPG Papers, box 7, MHS.

6. Griffin 1858, 4, 7; George N. Greene, Charlestown, to Rufus Ellis, 22 May 1877, SPG Papers, box 8, MHS; Adams 1881, 44–84; Ledyard (Mashantucket) Pequot overseer's report, 1857, CSA; U.S. Department of the Interior, Office of Federal Acknowledgment, "Summary under the Criteria and Evidence for Proposed Finding Paucatuck Eastern Pequot Indians of Connecticut" (24 March 2000), 76; William Morgan to John Deforest, 22 Aug. 1849, in John Deforest, *History of the Indians of Connecticut, from the Earliest Known Period to 1850* (Hartford: William Jason Hamersley 1851), 445; Samuel Maynard testimony at legislative hearing, transcript in *Norwich Daily Courier,* 7 June 1859; Mohegan 1861, 4, 9–10; PF Mohegan, 169–70.

7. "List of the Pequot tribe which belong and live in Groton, Dec. 13, 1833," William

S. Johnson Papers 3:100, CHS; Ledyard Pequot overseer's report, 1857, CSA; Narragansett commissioner, "Report [of 27 Dec. 1858]," *RIAR*, Jan. 1859 (Providence, 1859), 94. U.S. Department of Commerce, 1860 census schedule from Charlestown, R.I.; Addams 1881, 51 and passim. The 1859 report showed the average age and total number in each household, which I used to calculate the average age within the community as a whole. Unfortunately, the ages of only a few Mohegans are provided in the 1861 report.

8. Bird 1849, 43; Earle 1861, 104, appendix, 75, 77, 83; Ledyard Pequot overseer's report, 1857; U.S. Department of the Interior, Office of Federal Acknowledgment, "Summary under the Criteria and Evidence for Proposed Finding Eastern Pequot Indians of Connecticut" (24 March 2000), 59–78; PF Schaghticoke, 82–84. Between 1848 and 1860 the average and median ages of men increased and those of women decreased, although this may be because Earle found and recorded many more families and individuals than did the Bird commission.

9. Earle 1861, 111–14, quote on 114.

10. Sarah Peabody Turnbaugh and William A. Turnbaugh, "Weaving the Woods," in *A Key into the Language of Woodsplint Baskets*, ed. Ann McMullen, Russell G. Handsman, and Joan Lester (Washington, Conn.: American Indian Archaeological Institute, 1987), 78, 81; "Report on Household Manufactures," *Pittsfield Sun*, 14 Oct. 1858; Lucius E. Ammidown, "The Southbridge of Our Ancestors, Its Homes and Its People," *Quinabaug Historical Society, Leaflets*, 1, no. 2–4 (1902): 13–57; Trudie Lamb Richmond, "Spirituality and Survival in Schaghticoke Basket-Making," in McMullen, Handsman, and Lester, *A Key into the Language of Woodsplint Baskets*, 133–39; PF Schaghticoke, 106–7, n.131 and 132. In 1831, a band of 30 Indians from the Lake Champlain area camped for two weeks at a site in Milford, Conn. They told a local that their ancestors had come from that point and that this would be their final visit; Edward R. Lambert, *History of the Colony of New Haven Before and after the Union with Connecticut* (New Haven: Hitchcock and Stafford, 1838), 130–31.

11. Earle, 1861, 15–17; Morgan to Deforest, 22 Aug. 1849, in Deforest, *Indians of Connecticut*, 445; George Stanton, "Report of Narragansett Commissioner," *RIAR*, May 1862 (Providence, 1862), 67.

12. Earle 1861, 12, appendix (female-headed household percentages ranged from 12.5 percent in Christiantown to 14.5 percent in Gay Head to 21 percent in Chappaquiddick); Morgan to Deforest, 22 Aug. 1849, in Deforest, *Indians of Connecticut*, 445; Isaac Wilmer, 9 Sept. 1857, box 3: Niantics, 1855–1877, NLCSC; Earle 1861, 11, 84.

13. Earle 1861, appendix; Jack Larkin, "Counting People of Color: Worcester County, Massachusetts 1790–1860: A Preliminary Report," presented at the Conference on Reinterpreting New England Indian History and the Colonial Experience, Sturbridge, Mass., April 2001; PF Schaghticoke, 82.

14. Samuel E. Blair, Warren, to Earle, 29 July 1859, Earle Papers, box 2, folder 5.

15. Earle 1861, appendix. While many young women also left to work as domestics, they were more seemingly more likely to return after a relatively short period. The percentage of Indian men whose occupations were shown by Earle ranged from about a quarter (Gay Head and Troy) to slightly more than half (Chappaquiddick, Christiantown, Herring Pond, and Dudley). Jack Larkin found that, of all people of color listed in the 1850 federal cen-

sus for Worcester County, 35 percent can be linked to Indian family names in the region; Larkin, "Counting People of Color," chart 3.

16. Earle 1861, 20, 27, 34–36, appendices; D. H. Strother "A Summer in New England," *Harper's New Monthly Magazine* 124 (Sept. 1860): 452; G. C. Marchant to Earle, 15 Feb. 1860, Earle Papers, box 2, folder 3.

17. Christopher Simons, testimony in "Disposition of the Mohegan Tribe Lands," *Norwich Daily Courier*, 7 June 1859; Dept. of Interior, "Proposed Finding Paucatuck Eastern Pequot Indians," 77; Narragansett Commissioner, "Report [of 27 Dec. 1858]," *RIAR*, appendix, 6; Narragansett Commissioner, "Report [of May 1862]," *RIAR*, May 1862 (Providence, 1862), 67–69.

18. Wright to Walker and Parkman, 9 April 1839, SPG Papers, box 7; T. S. Gold, "Fostering the Habit of Industry," *Connecticut Magazine* 8, no. 3 (March 1904): 452–54; PF Schaghticoke 97–100, 108; Trudie Lamb Richmond, "Spirituality and Survival in Schaghticoke Basket-Making," in McMullen, Handsman, and Lester, *A Key into the Language of Woodsplint Baskets*, 133–39; Narragansett commissioner, "Report [of 27 Dec. 1858]," 6; Narragansett commissioner, "Report [of May 1862]," 67–69.

19. Kathleen J. Bragdon, *Native People of Southern New England, 1500–1650* (Norman: University of Oklahoma Press, 1996).

20. U.S. Department of Commerce, 1860 census schedules for Charlestown, North Stonington, and Montville; "Disposition of the Mohegan Tribe Lands," *Norwich Daily Courier*, 7 June 1859; Griffin 1858, 6; 1850 Edgartown census schedule; U.S. Department of Commerce, 1850 census schedules for Tisbury, Mass., transcribed in Chris Baer, "Historical Records of Dukes County, Massachusetts," http://history.vineyard.net/tiscen50.htm (accessed 13 May 2005).

21. On the relationship between age and status in colonial New England, see Robert Gross, *The Minutemen and Their World* (New York: Hill and Wang, 1975), chaps. 2 and 4.

22. Bird 1849, 14–15; Earle 1861, appendix; Edgartown and Tisbury 1850 censuses; F. W. Bird, untitled, *Norfolk Democrat*, 22 Sept. 1848.

23. "Supposed Loss of Life," *Vineyard Gazette*, 15 July 1847; Nathaniel Philbrick, *Abram's Eyes: The Native American Legacy of Nantucket Island* (Nantucket: Mill Hill Press, 1998), 225.

24. Bird 1849; Earle 1861; Griffin 1858; Russ Handsman, "Wisdom Sits in Pequot Gardens," [Mashantucket Pequot] *Tribal Nation*, Feb. 2005, p. 3; Gary Kulik, "Dams, Fish, and Farmers: Defense of Public Rights in Eighteenth-Century Rhode Island," in *The Countryside in the Age of Capitalist Transformation: Essays in the Social History of Rural America*, ed. Steven Hahn and Jonathan Prude (Chapel Hill: University of North Carolina Press, 1985).

25. 1870 census in Richard L. Pease, *Report on Gay Head* (Boston: Wright and Potter, 1871), 32–53; 1861 Earle appendix; Wright to Parkman, 9 April 1839, SPG Papers, box 7, MHS; Mary A. Cleggett Vanderhoop, "The Gay Head Indians: Their History and Traditions," series in the *New Bedford Evening Standard* beginning 25 June 1904; Earle 1861, 32.

26. Karen V. Hansen, *A Very Social Time: Crafting Community in Antebellum New England* (Berkeley: University of California Press, 1994), 30–32; Simeon L. Deyo, ed., *History of Barnstable County, Massachusetts* (New York: H. W. Blake and Company, 1890), 714, 151.

27. Ch. 83, *CPA* (Hartford, 1872), 79; ch. 79, ibid., 43–44.

28. Earle 1861, appendix; Adams 1881, appendix C.

29. Benjamin Winslow, Fall River, to Earle, 18 July 1859, Earl Papers, box 2, folder 5, AAS; Earle 1861, appendix; Winslow to Earle, 2 April 1860, box 2, folder 5, AAS.

30. Adams 1880; Adams 1881.

31. Earle 1861, 6; testimony by Edward S. Cone, in Adams 1880, 71; *The Uncas Monument, 1492–1842: published once in three hundred and fifty years* (Norwich, Conn.: John G. Cooley, 1842); Fawcett, *Medicine Trail*; PF Mohegan; PF Narragansett; "The Indian Meeting," *Narragansett Weekly*, 16 Aug. 1859; Adams 1881.

32. Earle 1861, 86; various letters in Earle Papers, box 2, folder 5; Ebenezer W. Pierce, *Indian History, Biography, and Genealogy* (North Abington, Mass.: Zerviah Gould Mitchell, 1878); Adams 1881; Celia Watson, Griswold, Conn., to New London County Superior Court, Aug. 1856, NLCSC, box 2; *Town of Ledyard v. William Morgan*, 11 March 1857, ibid. (thanks to Bruce Stark, Connecticut State Library, for showing me this case).

33. R.I., Charlestown, Narragansett council records, 30 March 1858, 93.

34. For example, in October 1827, the tribal council asked the assembly to ignore a petition that they heard Lodowick Paul was going to present "to have the Indian Council put down or Dismisst, and a white man put over us"; doc. no. 72, NIRA. See additional examples in the Narragansett council records, Charlestown, R.I.

35. Ibid.; Dan King, "Report of Committee on [Narragansett] Indian Tribe," Jan. 1831, doc. 81, NRIA; Narragansett tribal council to R.I. assembly, June 1851, NRIA.

36. Mashpee District Meeting Book, Mashpee Archives, Town Hall, Mashpee, Mass., notes by Rosemary Burns.

37. MUHL no. 13838, 15 Dec. 1834; Mashpee District Meeting Book; MUHL no. 178, 31 Dec. 1836; MUSL no. 10422, 31 Dec. 1839; MUHL no. 1698, 31 Dec. 1844; MUHL no. 2091, 31 Dec. 1846; MUHL no. 2685, 1 Jan. 1850; MUSL no. 13098, 31 Dec. 1850.

38. Nathan Pocknett and 19 other Mashpee proprietors to Mass. legislature, 28 Jan. 1837, MUSL no. 10176; Pocknett and 15 other Mashpee proprietors to Mass. legislature, 1838, MUSL no. 10416; Earle 1861, 49; Mashpee District Meeting Book; N. J. Holden, "Report on [Mashpee hearings] Indians of the Commonwealth, June 1869," *MHR* 502 (Boston, 1869): 15, 31.

39. Solomon Attaquin and 36 other Mashpee proprietors to Mass. legislature, 22 Jan. 1840, in MUHL no. 714, March 1840; Mashpee District Meeting Book; Bird 1849, 29–30; Earle 1861, 49–53.

40. Earle 1861, 40; Gay Head records excerpted by Richard Pease, Edgartown, in letter to Everett Davis, Boston, 10 Feb. 1885, E2, box 174b, MVHS; Zaccheus Howwoswee to Earle, 25 Aug. 1859, box 2, folder 3, Earle Papers.

41. John Brown, Narragansett Indian Tribal Historic Preservation Officer, interview with author, 16 April 2007; Child 1827; Bird 1849, 16–17; Jack Campisi, "Emergence of the Mashantucket Pequot Tribe, 1637–1975," in *The Pequots in Southern New England: The Rise and Fall of an American Indian Nation*, ed. Laurence M. Hauptman and James D. Wherry (Norman: University of Oklahoma Press, 1990), 127–31.

42. Jason Mancini, "Creating a Baseline and Establishing Continuity at Mashantucket," in personal communication to author, 27 May 2005; resolve of 29 May 1857; Nar-

278 NOTES TO PAGES 173–175

ragansetts to R.I. assembly, June 1851, NRIA; various letters to Earle, Earle Papers, box 2, folders 4–5.

43. Mancini, "Creating a Baseline"; PF Webster, 60 n. 94, 63; William Brigham, *An Address Delivered before the Inhabitants of Grafton on the First Centennial Anniversary of that Town, April 29, 1835* (Boston: Light and Horton, 1835), appendix; Bird 1849, 44; Earle 1861, 100. All 24 Nipmucs were shown in one household, with Luke Jaha listed as its head; PF Webster, 60 n. 94. By 1860, only the Ciscos were left in Grafton: eleven (40 percent) lived in Worcester, six (22 percent) were more than two towns away from Grafton, four (15 percent) lived in Boston, and one had moved to Iowa. Only 3 of 22 married Hassanamiscos had a spouse from within the tribe.

44. George B. Kirsch, "Belknap, Jeremy," *American National Biography* (New York: Oxford University Press, 1991), 2:439–94; "About the Society," www.masshist.org/about/ (accessed 17 Jan. 2007); Frederick Weis, *The Society for Propagating the Gospel among the Indians and Others in North America* (Dublin, N.H.: n.p., 1953), 15, 7; Louis Leonard Tucker, *Clio's Consort: Jeremy Belknap and the Founding of the Massachusetts Historical Society* (Boston: MHS, 1990), 88–97; Alfred Young, *The Shoemaker and the Tea Party* (Boston: Beacon, 1999), 123. The SPG was limited by its bylaws to 50 members, while the MHS was limited to 30 local and 30 corresponding members.

45. Daniel Gookin, "Historical Collections of the Indians in New England," *MHSC*, ser. 1, 1 (1792): 181–95. Examples of important articles published during the next decade include [Benjamin?] Lincoln to MHS, 29 Oct. 1795, "Observations on the Indians of North America," [in response to David Ramsay's remarks published in the *MHSC*, 1795], *MHSC*, ser. 1, 5 (1798): 6–12; Jeremy Belknap and Jedidiah Morse, "Report of the Committee . . . Who Visited the Oneida and Mohekunuh Indians in General," ibid., 12–32; Stephen Badger, "Historical and Characteristic Traits of the American Indians in General," ibid., 32–45; and other publications cited in the Essay on Sources.

46. William Tudor, *Letters on the Eastern States*, 2nd ed. (Boston: Wells and Lilly, 1821), 279. Tudor (1749–1830) had an astonishingly varied career. He graduated from Harvard, trained as a lawyer in John Adams's law office, served as judge advocate with the Continental Army during the Revolutionary War, established the *North American Review* in 1815, as a merchant developed the ice trade, worked in the Republican and Federalist parties, and was an important figure in the Massachusetts movement to bar slavery from Missouri, 1819–21. Tucker, *Clio's Consort*, 88; Robert Forbes to H-SHEAR, 3 Sept. 1998; David B. Mattern to H-SHEAR, 3 Sept. 1998, archived at www.h-net.org/~shear/.

47. Hawley wrote that "the nearer [white people] are, the worse for the Indians, for they will live on the vices and the follies of the latter"; Hawley to Rev. James Freeman, 15 Nov. 1802, Hawley Papers, MHS. Badger noted that Indians "are generally considered by white people, and placed, as if by common consent, in an inferior and degraded condition, and treated accordingly," which encouraged the settlers to take "every advantage of [the Indians] that they could, under colour of legal authority, and without incurring its censure, to dishearten and depress them"; Badger, "Historical and Characteristic Traits," 38.

48. Ibid., 42, 44.

49. Joseph Thaxter to Mass. legislature, 22 Sept. 1818, MIGA, box 3, folder 15; Hawley to Gov. John Hancock, 8 July 1791, Hawley Papers, MHS.

50. Belknap and Tudor felt that blacks were superior to Indians, and they, along with other MHS members like Timothy Dwight and correspondents like Hawley, thought the growing rate of intermarriage was "improving" the "mixed" race. Tudor, *Letters on the Eastern States*, 301; Dwight, *Travels in New England*, 16; Hawley to Hancock, 8 July 1791; Capt. Jerningham and Benjamin Bassett, Esq., "Report," *MHSC*, 1st ser., 1 (1790): 206.

51. Jeremy Belknap to Henry Knox, *Columbian Centinel*, 24 Jan. 1795; Gideon Hawley to Freeman, March 1803, Hawley Letters, MHS; Hawley to Peter Thacher, Boston, 7 Dec. 1800, box 2, folder 16, SPGPE.

52. Jeremy Belknap to Henry Knox, *Columbian Centinel*, 24 Jan. 1795, p. 1; Gideon Hawley to Freeman, March 1803, Hawley Letters, MHS; Hawley to Peter Thacher, Boston, 7 Dec. 1800, box 2, folder 16, SPGPE.

53. Hansen, *A Very Social Time*; Stephen Nissenbaum, *The Battle for Christmas* (New York: Knopf, 1996), 49–257. By contrast, Richard L. Bushman, *The Refinement of America: Persons, Houses, Cities* (New York: Knopf, 1992), sees an eighteenth-century material culture of gentility creating a clear line between "cultivated and coarse" (183), with that line shifting during the early republic to include the new American middle class—but still "exclud[ing] those who clung to rude ways" (424).

54. Joel Munsell, *Reminiscences of Men and Things in Northfield as I Knew Them from 1812 to 1825* (Albany, 1876), 20; Jill Lepore, *The Name of War: King Philip's War and the Origins of American Identity* (New York: Knopf, 1998), 186–90; Edward R. Lambert, *History of the Colony of New Haven before and after the Union with Connecticut* (New Haven: Hitchcock and Stafford, 1838), 132; Daniel R. Mandell, "The Indian's Pedigree (1794): Indians, Folklore, and Race in Southern New England," *William and Mary Quarterly*, 3rd ser., 61 (2004): 519–36.

55. *The Trial of Alpheus Livermore and Samuel Angier before the Supreme Judicial Court of the Commonwealth of Massachusetts upon an Indictment for the Murder of Nicholas John Crevay [also Creway], an Indian, Committed November 23, 1813. From Minutes Taken at the Trial* (Boston: Watson and Bangs, 1813), 10–13, 47–49; various petitions and reports in MGCF, boxes 21 and 22; Governor's Council Pardon Files, GC3/328, 313/B/15/4–6, 1817–19. My thanks to David Silverman for bringing this trial transcript to my attention and to Richard Brown for additional references to the petitions and reports that resulted in pardons for Livermore and Angier. The trial received considerable publicity; William Bentley, commented on it in his diary; *The Diary of William Bentley, D.D., Pastor of the East Church, Salem, Massachusetts* (Salem: Essex Institute, 1905–14), 4:221.

56. Frances Caulkins, Norwich, to Sylvester Judd, 2 Nov. 1849 and [no day] May 1851, Sylvester Judd Collection, folders of letters from Frances Caulkins, CSA; my thanks to Nancy Steenberg for her transcriptions and notations. For examples of descriptions of western Indians, see "Characteristics of the American Indians (1753)," reprinted in *Universal Asylum and Columbian Magazine* 6 (1791): 18–20, and "Instance of Indian Fidelity," *Massachusetts Magazine* 3 (1791): 230.

57. Perry Miller, *Errand into the Wilderness* (Cambridge, Mass.: Harvard University Press, 1956), 1–15; David Waldstreicher, *In the Midst of Perpetual Fetes: The Making of American Nationalism, 1776–1820* (Chapel Hill: University of North Carolina Press, 1997), 251–62.

58. William Tudor, *Letters on the Eastern States*, 2nd ed. (Boston: Wells and Lilly, 1821), 118, 373. On Tudor, see Robert Forbes to H-SHEAR, 3 Sept. 1998, archived at www.h-net .org/~shear/; David McCullough, *John Adams* (New York: Simon Schuster, 2001), 63.

59. Tudor, *Letters on the Eastern States*, 281–89; on blacks, ibid., 298–99.

60. "[Review of] *An Account of the History, Manners and Customs of the Indian Nations who once inhabited Pennsylvania and the neighbouring States*, by Rev. John Heckwelder," *North American Review* 9 (June 1819): 167, 168, 169.

61. Irving, "Philip of Pokanoket," in *The Sketch Book of Geoffrey Crayon, Gent.* (1819–20), in *The Complete Works of Washington Irving*, ed. Haskell Springer, vol. 8 (Boston: Twayne, 1978): 240, 246, 235.

62. *Yamoyden*, quoted in John Gorham Palfrey, "Review of *Yamoyden*," *North American Review* 12 (1820): 485; Carolyn L. Karcher, "Introduction," in Lydia Marie Child, *Hobomok and Other Writings on Indians*, ed. Karcher (New Brunswick, N.J.: Rutgers University Press, 1986), xvii–xxxv; Daniel Walker Howe, *The Political Culture of the American Whigs* (Chicago: University of Chicago Press, 1979), 38–39. As an adolescent, Child was sent by her father to Norridgewock, Maine, where she spent eight years and often met Penobscot Indians; Karcher, "Introduction," xviii.

63. Charles Sprague, *An Oration: Pronounced before the Inhabitants of Boston, July the Fourth, 1825, in Commemoration of American Independence* (Boston: John H. Eastburn, City Printer, 1825), 8.

64. Catherine Maria Sedwick, *Hope Leslie: or, Early Times in the Massachusetts*, 2 vols. (New York: White, Gallaher, and White, 1827).

65. Sarah Savage, *Life of Philip, the Indian Chief* (Salem: Whipple and Lawrence, 1827), 7–8, 16, 24–25, 29, 32, 51.

66. Huntington journal, 17 Dec. 1830, in *Memoir of Mrs. Sarah L. Huntington Smith*, ed. Edward Hooker, 3rd ed. (New York: American Tract Society, 1846), 115–16, and 121 (referring to Ezekiel, 37, and Amos, 9); Apess, "Son of the Forest," 1829 and 1831, in *On Our Own Ground*, 53, 74–94, 114. This concept was also embraced by Indians in other parts of North America. On 5 March 1858, Thoreau went to a Concord lecture by "a Chippeway Indian, a Doctor Mung-somebody," who, after discussing the probable Asian origins of his people, "thought Indians might be Jews, because of a similarity of customs." *The Journal of Henry D. Thoreau*, ed. Bradford Torrey and Francis H. Allen (Boston: Houghton Mifflin, 1949), 10:292.

67. Samuel Goodrich, *The Tales of Peter Palfrey about America* (Boston, 1827), 8, 14, 19.

68. Jeffrey D. Mason, "The Politics of *Metamora*," in *The Performance of Power: Theatrical Discourse and Politics*, ed. Sue-Ellen Case and Janelle Reinelt (Iowa City: University of Iowa Press, 1991), 99–110; Lepore, *Name of War*, 191–92 (quotation on weeping audiences).

69. Lydia Marie Child, *The First Settlers of New England; or, Conquest of the Pequods, Narragansetts and Pokanokets, as Related by a Mother to her Children, by a Lady of Massachusetts* (Boston 1829), 13, 65, 272.

70. Ibid., iii–iv.

71. *Barnstable Patriot*, 26 June 1833. On the interest of abolitionists (including William

Lloyd Garrison) in Indians, see Linda K. Kerber, "The Abolitionist Perception of the Indian," *Journal of American History* 62 (1975): 271–95.

72. *Barnstable Patriot*, 24 July 1833, 18 Sept 1833, 2 April 1834.

73. *The Old Colony Democrat*, 6 July 1833; 13 July 1833.

74. *Barnstable Patriot*, 16 May 1832; (the jury awarded Smith $176 in damages).

75. "Trouble in the Wigwam," *Barnstable Patriot*, 10 July 1833; "Letter to the Editor," *Barnstable Patriot*, 5 Feb. 1834.

76. "Trouble in the Wigwam"; "Letter to the Editor."

77. "Indian Anecdote," *Barnstable Patriot*, 21 Aug. 1833.

78. "Character of Philip the Indian King," *Old Colony Democrat*, 3 Aug. 1833.

79. Howe, *Political Culture of American Whigs*, 40. Michael Holt's recent magisterial examination of *The Rise and Fall of the American Whig Party* (New York: Oxford University Press, 1999) ignored the Removal issue as a factor in the formation of the Whig Party, as did Ronald Formisano's earlier *The Transformation of Political Culture: Massachusetts Parties, 1790s-1840s* (New York: Oxford University Press, 1983).

80. Deforest, *Indians of Connecticut*; Robert F. Berkhofer Jr., *The White Man's Indian: Images of the American Indian from Columbus to the Present* (New York: Knopf, 1978), 28.

81. Peter Whitney, *The History of the County of Worcester in the Commonwealth of Massachusetts* (Worcester: Isaiah Thomas, 1793); Charles Bickford, ed., *Voices of the New Republic: Connecticut Towns, 1830–1832* (Hartford: Connecticut Academy of Arts and Sciences, 2004); John C. Pease and John M. Niles, *A Gazetteer of the States of Connecticut and Rhode Island* (Hartford: William S. Marsh, 1819); Jeremy Belknap, *History of New Hampshire* (Philadelphia and Boston, 1784–1792). Neither Pease nor Niles was among the men who wrote responses to the questions sent by the Connecticut Academy, and their *Gazetteer* contained descriptions of every town in the state (and Rhode Island) whereas a noticeable number of towns did not respond to the Academy.

82. Sigourney, *Sketchs of Connecticut*, 31, 33, 34–36, 54–55. The historical sketch of tribal leaders is on 38–61. Johnson, who died in 1787, is described in Deforest, *Indians of Connecticut*, 472–79. When Edward Kendall visited the Mohegans in 1807, Cooper was apparently the tribe's leader; *Travels through the Northern Parts of the United States in the Years 1807 and 1808* (New York: I. Riley, 1809), 1:308. For a similar fictionalized account of the Natick Indians in the early republic, see Harriet Beecher Stowe, *Oldtown Folks* [1869], ed. Henry May (Cambridge, Mass.: Harvard University Press, 1966), 89.

83. John W. Barber, *Historical Collections of Massachusetts* (Worcester: Dorr, Howland, and Co., 1839), 150; idem., *Historical Collections of Connecticut*, 2nd ed. (New Haven, Conn.: Durrie and Peck, 1842), 338; Joseph A. Conforti, *Imagining New England: Explorations of Regional Identity from the Pilgrims to the Mid-Twentieth Century* (Chapel Hill: University of North Carolina Press, 2001), 131–32; Sarah S. Jacobs, *Nonantum and Natick* (Boston: Massachusetts Sabbath School Society, 1853).

84. Joseph Allen, "Historical Account of Northborough," *Worcester Magazine and Historical Journal*, 2 (1826): 148–49; William Biglow, *History of the Town of Natick, Mass.* (Boston: Marsh, Capen, and Lyon, 1830), 83–84; *Niles' National Register* 57 (14 Dec. 1839): 256; Frances Caulkins, Norwich, to Sylvester Judd, 2 Nov. 1849 and [no day] May 1851.

85. Charles Brooks, *History of the Town of Medford* (Boston: James M. Usher, 1855), 80–81; George Cooke, "Our Aborigines," *Winchester Record* 1, no. 4 (Oct. 1885), 274.

86. Deloriane Pendre Corey, *The History of Malden Massachusetts, 1633–1785* (Malden: published by author, 1899), 412–14.

87. Harriet Merrifield Forbes, *The Hundredth Town: Glimpses of Life in Westborough, 1717–1818* (Boston, 1889), 174. Forbes described Gigger's hut as built in a swamp, which is typical in narratives of a town's "last Indian" (173).

88. Alice Morse Earle, *Stage-coach and Tavern Days* (New York, 1900), 94. The only documentary record of Deborah Brown is in the Hassanamisco guardians' accounts between 1828 to 1841; accounts of Hassanamisco Indian Trustees, 2:133, 138, Earle Papers; MIGA, box 3, folders 8 and 9, Mass. Archives. By 1841, Brown was living in Westborough, apparently in the town's poor house, and she died by 1859; ibid.; S. W. Griggs, Worcester clerk, to Earle, 7 Oct. 1859, Earle Papers, box 1, folder 1.

89. William Brigham, *An Address Delivered before the Inhabitants of Grafton on the First Centennial Anniversary of that Town, April 29, 1835* (Boston: Light and Horton, 1835), Appendix; Ledyard Bill, *The History of Paxton, Massachusetts* (Worcester: Putnam, Davis and Co., 1889), 45; Samuel Orcutt and Ambrose Beardsley, *History of Derby, Connecticut, 1642–1880* (Springfield, Mass.: Springfield Printing Company, 1880), l–li; Samuel Hosmer, "Indian Churches on Nantucket," *Congregational Quarterly* 7 (1865): 31–34 (quotation). On Quary, see also Thoreau, *Journal*, 7:96; Nathaniel Philbrick, *Abram's Eyes* (Nantucket, Mass.: Mill Hill Press, 1998), 1–9; Elizabeth Little, "Abram Quary of Abram's Point, Nantucket Island," Nantucket Algonquian Studies, no. 16 (Nantucket: Nantucket Historical Association, 1994).

90. David Willard, *Willard's History of Greenfield* (Greenfield: Kneeland and Eastman, 1838), 12.

91. Jacobs, *Nonantum and Natick*, 320–21.

92. See "Essay on Sources" for a full discussion of these local histories.

93. Mohegans to assembly, 30 April 1827, CGA1, folder 8; Conn. assembly committee report, May 1855, folder 26.

94. *Newark Daily Advertiser* reprinted in *Niles' National Register* 63 (31 Dec. 1842): 280; Edward Everett, *Dorchester in 1630, 1776, and 1855, an Oration Delivered on the Fourth of July, 1855* (Boston: David Clapp, 1855), 39.

95. Samuel Deane, *History of Scituate, Massachusetts, from Its First Settlement to 1831* (Boston: J. Loring, 1831), 144–45; William Tilden, "Indians in Medfield," *Dedham Historical Register* 10 (1899): 53; Charles Endicott to John Milton Earle (on the Punkapoag Indians), 6 Aug. 1859, Earle Papers, box 2, folder 1; Doughton, "Unseen Neighbors: Native Americans of Central Massachusetts, A People Who Had 'Vanished,'" in *After King Philip's War: Presence and Persistence in Indian New England*, ed. Colin Calloway (Hanover, N.H.: University Press of New England, 1997), 207–30.

96. Thoreau, *Journal* 2:42, 83. Dan Ricketson, *The History of New Bedford, Bristol County, Massachusetts* (New Bedford: privately published, 1858), 95 (on Simon as "the solitary specimen"); Thoreau, *Journal* (26 June 1856), 8:390–91; (23 Jan. 1858), 10:251–52.

97. George F. Clark, *A History of the Town of Norton, Bristol County, Mass., from 1669 to 1850* (Boston, 1859), 56; Willard, *Willard's History of Greenfield*, 12; Deane, *History of Sc-*

ituate, 145–46; Francis M. Caulkins, *History of Norwich, Connecticut* (1866; Chester, Conn.: Pequot Press, 1976), 104; Corey, *History of Malden*, 52.

98. Barbara E. Lacey, "Women of Connecticut," in www.ctheritage.org/encyclopedia/topicalsurveys/women.htm (accessed 7 Feb. 2006); Hooker, *Memoir of Mrs. Sarah L. Huntington*, 113 and passim; Nina Baym, "Reinventing Lydia Sigourney," *American Literature* 62 (1990): 394 n. 19; Daniel Buchanan, "Tares in the Wheat: Puritan Violence and Puritan Families in the Nineteenth Century Liberal Imagination," *Religion and American Culture* 8 (1998): 205–36; Carolyn L. Karcher, *The First Woman in the Republic: A Cultural Biography of Lydia Maria Child* (Durham, N.C.: Duke University Press, 1994), 66–67.

99. N. J. Holden et al., "Report [on the portion of the Governor's Address that concerns the Indians of the Commonwealth]," *MHR* 483 (Boston, 1869): 1–2; Vanderhoop, "Gay Head Indians," 25 June 1904.

CHAPTER 6: CITIZENSHIP AND TERMINATION

1. Frederic Denison, *Westerly and Its Witnesses, for Two Hundred and Fifty Years. 1626–1876* (Providence: J. A. and R. A. Reid, 1878), 82–84, quoting the *Providence Journal*, 17 Oct. 1866. The article noted that, after the committee asked to hear the tribe's view on the proposal, "the tribe made a reply, which we give in a connected form" instead of quoting individuals; ibid., 83. The Ocean House still exists, but is now in Westerly.

2. On this process in Massachusetts, and how it developed from changing social and political structures during Reconstruction and struggles over race and gender, see Ann Marie Plane and Gregory Button, "The Massachusetts Indian Enfranchisement Act: Ethnic Contest in Historical Context, 1849–1869," *Ethnohistory* 40 (1993): 594–606.

3. U.S. Department of Commerce, Bureau of the Census, *Twenty Censuses: Population and Housing Questions, 1790–1980* (Washington, D.C.: GPO, 1979), 19.

4. Colin Calloway, *First Peoples: A Documentary Survey of American Indian History*, 2nd ed. (Boston: Bedford–St. Martin's, 2004), 335–43, 367–73, 404–13. No evidence exists of a direct connection between the efforts of New England states to terminate Indian tribes and the Dawes Act, although the reform agenda of the mid- to late nineteenth century drove and shaped both developments, and the chief sponsor of the Dawes Act, Senator Henry Dawes, represented Massachusetts.

5. *North American Review*, 2 (Nov. 1815): 113–14, 118–19; Jedidiah Morse, *A Report to the Secretary of War of the United States on Indian Affairs* (New Haven: Converse, 1822), 70, 74, 24; Baylies to Holmes, 18 May 1821, box 1, folder 8, SPGPE; Dan King, "Report of Committee on [Narragansett] Indian Tribe," Jan. 1831, doc. 81, NRIA.

6. *Clark v. Williams et al.*, Octavius Pickering, *Reports of Cases Argued in the Supreme Judicial Court of Massachusetts* (Boston: Wells and Lilly, 1824–42), 19:499. The decision concerned the claim of an Indian family to land in Middleborough, and the court based its decision on the erroneous impression that a recognizable native community no longer existed in the town. The Childs commission, just ten years before, reported that at least five Indians still held land in Middleborough; Child 1827, 5.

7. Howwoswee to Earle, 25 Aug. 1859, 27 Jan. 1860, John Milton Earle Papers, box 2, folder 3, AAS.

8. John W. Sweet, *Bodies Politic: Negotiating Race in the American North, 1730–1830* (Baltimore: Johns Hopkins University Press, 2003), 354–95; Joanne Melish, *Disowning Slavery: Gradual Emancipation and "Race" in New England, 1780–1860* (Ithaca, N.Y.: Cornell University Press, 1998), 201–8; *History of the Providence Riots from Sept. 21 to Sept. 24, 1831* (Providence, R.I., 1931); Louis Richames, "Race, Marriage, and Abolition in Massachusetts," *Journal of Negro History* 40 (1955): 251 and passim; James O. Horton and Lois E. Horton, *In Hope of Liberty: Culture, Community and Protest among Northern Free Blacks, 1700–1860* (New York: Oxford University Press, 1997), 213–220; Hanover Barney and 59 others to Conn. assembly, May 1834, in Conn. Assembly Rejected Bills, box 10 (1834–35), folder 54 (Judiciary), CSA; additional petitions regarding Crandall's school in Conn., RG 2, box 18, docs. 158–77, CSA.

9. Jesse Chickering, *A Statistical View of the Population of Massachusetts, from 1765 to 1840* (Boston: Charles C. Little and James Brown, 1846), 111–12, 157; Theresa S. Gaul, *To Marry an Indian: The Marriage of Harriet Gold and Elias Boudinot in Letters, 1823–1839* (Chapel Hill: University of North Carolina Press, 2005), 4–15; *Barnstable Patriot*, 16 May 1832; "The Massachusetts Indians," *Boston Daily Courier*, 15 March 1849; MUHL no. 11938, 20 June 1832; Mass. House Judiciary Committee, "Report on sundry petitions respecting distinctions of color," 25 Feb. 1839, *MHR* 28 (Boston, 1839): 8; B. Maxim, Carver, to Earle, 28 Dec. 1859, Earle Papers, box 2, folder 5.

10. William C. Nell, *The Colored Patriots of the American Revolution* (1855; reprint, New York: Arno, 1968), 17, 112–13, 117, 144; Richames, "Race, Marriage, and Abolition"; Robert J. Cottrol, *The Afro-Yankees: Providence's Black Community in the Antebellum Era* (Westport, Conn.: Greenwood, 1982), 74–101; James O. Horton and Lois E. Horton, *Black Bostonians: Family Life and Community Struggle in the Antebellum North* (New York: Oxford University Press, 1979), 42–74, 92–95, 118–27; Kazuteru Omori, "Race-Neutral Individualism and Resurgence of the Color Line: Massachusetts Civil Rights Legislation, 1855–1895," *Journal of American Ethnic History* 21 (2002): 32–51; Scott Hancock, "The Elusive Boundaries of Blackness: Identity Formation in Antebellum Boston," *Journal of Negro History* 84 (1999): 115–29; Mass. House Judiciary Committee, "Report on sundry petitions"; Mass. Joint Committee, "Report [on intermarriage], Jan. 1841, *MHR* 7 (Boston, 1841); *MAR* ch. 4, 25 Feb. 1843; *MAR* ch. 5, 25 Feb. 1843; various petitions in MUSL no. 1286, 1843; *MSR* 10 (Boston, 1843); *MAR* ch. 5, 25 Feb. 1843; Charles Slack et al., "Report on Public or District Schools," 17 March 1855, *MHR* 167 (Boston, 1855); *MAR* ch. 277, 16 May 1865; *MSR* 242, 281 (Boston, 1865); *MHR* 256 (Boston, 1866); *MSR* 264 (Boston, 1866). The Rhode Island ban on intermarriage was not repealed until 1881, supposedly because it was "so easily circumvented" by marrying elsewhere (like Connecticut or Massachusetts); William Robinson, "Blacks in Nineteenth-Century Rhode Island, an Overview," unpublished ms. in R.I. Historical Society.

11. Laurence M. Hauptman, *Between Two Fires: American Indians in the Civil War* (New York: Free Press, 1995), 146–48, 229 n. 1; PF Webster, 74; Thomas Minns, presented to MHS on Aug. 1877, Richard Pease "Sketches of Edgartown, Tisbury and Chilmark: Martha's Vineyard," ts. MHS; Simeon L. Deyo, ed., *History of Barnstable County, Massachusetts* (New York: H. W. Blake and Company, 1890), 715.

12. *The War of the Rebellion: Official Records . . .*, 3rd ser. (Washington, D.C.: GPO,

1880–1901), 3:567–68; Frederick Denison, *Westerly and Its Witnesses, for Two Hundred and Fifty Years. 1626–1876* (Providence: J. A. and R. A. Reid, 1878), 84.

13. Garrison, *The Liberator*, 25 Jan. 1834, reprinted in Apess, "Indian Nullification," in *On Our Own Ground: The Complete Writings of William Apess, A Pequot*, ed. Barry O'Connell (Amherst: University of Massachusetts Press, 1992), 220–23; N. J. Holden et al., "Report [on the portion of the Governor's Address that concerns the Indians of the Commonwealth]," *MHR* 483 (Boston, 1869): 8; idem., "Report on [Mashpee hearings] Indians of the Commonwealth, June 1869," *MHR* 502 (Boston, 1869): 6.

14. Earle 1861, 6, appendix. The law fulfilled the desire of Gay Head proprietors by making the reserve into a district with legal powers of self-government, with the right to bar foreigners and emigrants from voting in district affairs unless two-thirds of the voters agreed to extend the right to particular individuals. Finally, Mashpee, Gay Head, and the guardians of other tribes were to keep vital records and a registry of lands held in common or severalty on the plantation; *MAR* ch. 184, 30 April 1862. Apparently some Indians made citizens by this act complained that they were being dunned for back taxes; ten months later, the Judiciary Committee held hearings, and while it proposed no bills it did emphasize that local assessments prior to the 1862 act were illegal; *MHR* 78 (Boston, 1863)

15. Plane and Button, "Indian Enfranchisement Act," 600–605; N. J. Holden et al., "Report [on the portion of the Governor's Address that concerns the Indians of the Commonwealth]," *MHR* 483 (Boston, 1869): 1–2; *Worcester Daily Spy*, 11 Jan. 1869.

16. Griffin 1858, 7.

17. Denison, *Westerly and Its Witnesses*, 82–84.

18. John Brown, Narragansett Indian Tribal Historic Preservation Officer, interview with author, 25 May 2005.

19. Rhode Island, *Fourth Annual Report of Commission on the Affairs of the Narragansett Indians* (Providence, 1884), 35.

20. Adams 1881, 25.

21. Adams 1880, 24. Neither the Ammons nor the Thomas petition is extant.

22. *CRPA*, May 1848; *CRPA*, May 1851, 125–26; [House Bill 82] ch. 19, 14 June 1876, *CPA*, May 1876 (Hartford, 1876), 93.

23. "Disposition of the Mohegan Tribe Lands," *Norwich Daily Courier*, 7 June 1859.

24. Ch. 58, 22 June 1860, *CPA*, May 1860 (New Haven, 1860), 46; no. 87, 3 July 1861, *CPRA*, May 1861 (Hartford, 1861), 74.

25. Mohegans to New London County Court, 26 Oct. 1852, NLCC, box 3.

26. Denison, *Westerly and Its Witnesses*, 82–84. The grave-robbing incident was first reported in the *Narragansett Weekly*, 28 April 1859. The men were indicted for trespass; for the transcript of their trial (*State v. Asa Noyes, J. P. Card, J. Congdon, Geo Madison, Oliver Fiske, George Babcock, Christopher Card, Samuel Nocake, and Chas. Cross*) see ibid., 16 June 1859. At this trial the judge refused to dismiss the charges and declared that all of the accused were probably guilty and that each had to post a $200 bond and to appear at the next term of the Supreme Court.

27. "The Narragansett Indians of Rhode Island," *Providence Journal*, reprinted in *Niles' National Register* 64 (1843): 415; *RIAR*, Oct. 1843 (Providence, 1843), 75–76.

28. Earle, 1861, 24–25, 41–43, 64; Leavitt Thaxter to Earle, 29 Jan. 1860, file 2, box 2, Earle Papers; Earle, Mashpees to Earle, 19 Oct. 1859, folder 2, box 2, Earle Papers.

29. "Disposition of the Mohegan Tribe Lands," *Norwich Daily Courier*, 7 June 1859. As in Mashpee, the men represented the tribe, but here as many "chief women" spoke (9) as men (11).

30. Mohegan 1861, 3–4, 6–7; Fawcett, *Medicine Trail*, 38 (on Baker).

31. Denison, *Westerly and Its Witnesses*, 82–84.

32. *CPRA*, May 1859 (Hartford, 1859), 223; "Disposition of the Mohegan Tribe Lands," *Norwich Daily Courier*, 7 June 1859; *Narragansett Weekly*, 16 June 1859.

33. Holden, "Report [Mashpee hearings]," 10–12, 15–18, 21–23.

34. Adams 1880, 52–53, 44–46, 47–48, 49, 64–66.

35. Ibid., 25–29, 32–33, 35, 38, 41, 43–44.

36. Ibid., 68, 76–78.

37. "A Summer in New England: Second Paper," *Harper's New Monthly Magazine* 124 (Sept. 1860): 452, 454; *Vineyard Gazette*, 4 June 1869; David Silverman, *Faith and Boundaries: Colonists, Christianity, and Community among the Wampanoag Indians of Martha's Vineyard, 1600–1871* (New York: Cambridge University Press, 2005), 246, 259–60, 264.

38. Act Relating to the Ledyard Pequot Indians, and the Preservation of their Property, 16 June 1855, CGA1, folder 25; Sept. 1855–Aug. 1856 accounts, C. S. Manwaring, overseer, box 3: Niantic, 1855–1877, NLCSC; John Deforest, *History of the Indians of Connecticut, from the Earliest Known Period to 1850* (Hartford: William Jason Hamersley, 1851), 386–87; *Zacheus Nonsuch v. F. W. Bolles*, Sept. 1865, NLCSC, box 4; Bolles, overseer's report, 13 Sept. 1866, NLCSC, box 4; no. 131, 30 June 1866, *CRPA*, May 1866 (New Haven, 1866), 135; New London County Superior Court decision, 4 Jan. 1867, NLCSC, box 4; no. 60, 3 July 1868, *CRPA*, May 1868 (New Haven, 1868), 249; 1870, L. Hebard Committee, Report on Niantic Indian Burying Ground, Box 3: Niantic, 1855–1877, NLCSC; ch. 62 [Senate Joint resolution no. 24], 25 June 1873, *CRPA May* 1873 (Hartford, 1873), 76.

39. Holden, "Report [Mashpee hearings]," 32–33; *Vineyard Gazette*, 4 June 1869; Bird 1880, 52–53.

40. Holden, "Report [Mashpee hearings]," 3–9.

41. Ibid.

42. *Vineyard Gazette*, 4 June 1869; Silverman, *Faith and Boundaries*, 264–65.

43. Holden, "Report [Mashpee hearings]," 6, 16, 22; *Worcester Daily Spy*, 15 Feb. 1869.

44. Adams 1881, 53, 57, 58–59. While Edward Cone was a member of the tribal council in 1851, that may have been the father of the one at these hearings (who would have been 28 years old in 1851, young for a tribal leader); Narragansett Council to R.I. assembly, June 1851, NRIA, unnumbered. Regardless, the younger Cone had played a leadership role in the tribe after midcentury and helped organize opposition to state termination before the 1879 hearings.

45. Mohegan 1861, 7, appendix; Frank G. Speck, "Native Tribes and Dialects of Connecticut, A Mohegan-Pequot Diary," *Bureau of American Ethnology Annual Report, no. 43: 1925–1926* (Washington, D.C.: GPO, 1928), 274, 208.

46. Benson J. Lossing, "The Last of the Pequods," *Scribner's Monthly* 2, no. 6 (Oct. 1871): 577.

47. *Vineyard Gazette*, 26 Aug 1870, in SPM.

48. Holden, "Report [Governor's Hearings]," 2, 6–8, 14–16; *Worcester Daily Spy*, 15 Feb. 1869.

49. *Worcester Daily Spy*, 3 June 1869, 23 June 1869, 24 June 1869; Mass., ch. 463, Acts of 1869; N. J. Holden et al., "Report on Gay Head Indians," *MSR* 14 (Boston, 1870). The joint legislative committee had, in their 3 June report, also proposed sending another joint committee to Gay Head during the legislative recess to get that community's reactions to the proposal. But this proposal was never passed by the House, largely because that body refused to fund the committee and no doubt expected that the enfranchisement bill would pass regardless.

50. THC Kingsbury, New Haven, to Learned Hebard, Lebanon, 20 May 1872, Learned Hebard Papers relating to the Mohegan Indians, 1699–1861, Connecticut State Library, Hartford.

51. *The Daily Star* [New London, Conn.], 24 July 1872; ch. 67, 31 July 1872, *CPA*, May 1872 (Hartford, 1872), 36–38.

52. Ansom Cooper, Mary Tantigeon, Henry Bake, Emma Baker, Jerome Bahome, Sarah Bahoma, Stephen Congdon to Conn. assembly, 1 May 1873, doc. 96, General Assembly Rejected Bills, box 47 (1872–73), folder 319, CSA.

53. *CPR*, May 1802– Oct. 1803 (Hartford, 1967), 11:177; PF Golden Hill, 29–30; ch. 35 [Senate Bill 50], 19 June 1876, *CPA*, May 1876 (Hartford, 1876), 102; ch. 8 [House Bill 11], 7 June 1876, *CPA*, May 1876, 88. Unfortunately, the resolve did not detail how many remained in the tribe or what property they held.

54. Hurd 1882, 35; PF Pautucket 109–10; ch. 31, 17 June 1873, *CRPA*, May 1873 (Hartford, 1873), 53–54; Richard A. Wheeler, *The Pequot Indians, an Historical Sketch* (Westerly, R.I.: G. B. and J. H. Utter, 187-?), 23; Charles Chipman, Accounts, 1878–79, NLCSC, box 5.

55. Ch. 66, *CPA*, May 1855 (Hartford, 1855), 82; Deforest, *Indians of Connecticut*, 445; May 1873–74, Pequot Indian account, Ledyard Pequots, overseers accounts etc., 1824–88, RG 3, NLCSC, box 133: Indians 1711–1867, CSA; Jack Campisi, "Emergence of the Mashantucket Pequot Tribe, 1637–1975," in *The Pequots in Southern New England: The Rise and Fall of an American Indian Nation*, ed. Laurence M. Hauptman and James D. Wherry (Norman: University of Oklahoma Press, 1990), 130–33.

56. Lossing, "The Last of the Pequods," 573–75; Indian overseers reports, 1881–84; Francis Atwater, *History of Kent, Connecticut* (Meriden, Conn.: Journal Publishing Company, 1897), 71–80.

57. Nathan B. Lewis, "The Last of the Narragansetts," *Proceedings of the Worcester Society of Antiquities* 16 (1898): 47.

58. Adams 1880, 7–8; Adams 1881, 3, 23.

59. Adams 1881, 26–42; Ethel Boissevain, "The Detribalization of the Narragansett Indians: A Case Study," *Ethnohistory* 3 (1956): 236.

60. Adams 1881, 5–6, 11; Boissevain, "Detribalization of the Narragansett Indians," 236.

61. Meunomennie L. Maimi to T. A. Maimi, March 1863, in *Black Abolitionist Papers*, vol. 5: 1859–1865, ed. C. Peter Ripley et al. (Chapel Hill: University of North Carolina Press, 1992), 188, 192. See also *The Life of William J. Brown* (Providence, R.I.: Angell and Co., Printers, 1883), 10–11

62. "Last of the Mohegans," *Niles' National Register* 63 (1842): 280. See generally Melish, *Disowning Slavery*, 210–25; Peter Novick, *That Noble Dream: The "Objectivity Question" and the American Historical Profession* (New York: Cambridge University Press, 1988), 61–84; David Morgan, *Protestants and Pictures: Religion, Visual Culture, and the Age of American Mass Production* (New York: Oxford University Press, 1999), 87.

63. Julius Gay, *The Tunxis Indians; An Historical Address Delivered at the Annual Meeting of the Village Library Company of Farmington, Conn., September 11, 1901* (Hartford: Case, Lockwood and Brainard, 1901), 19–20; Lillian Baynes Griffin, "The Record of the Red Man," *Farmington Magazine* 1 (Nov. 1902): 2; L. Hebard Committee, Report on Niantic Indian Burying Ground, 1870, box 4: Niantic, 1855–1877, NLCSC.

64. R.I., *Fourth Annual Report . . . Narragansett Indians; Canonicus Memorial, Services of Dedication, under the Auspices of the Rhode Island Historical Society, September 21, 1883* (Providence: Providence Press, 1883), 27. See also "Native Indians," *Barnstable Patriot*, 5 April 1915, for a picture of the monument erected at Long Pond, South Yarmouth, with the inscription "On this site lie buried the last native Indians of Yarmouth."

EPILOGUE

1. J. Dyneley Prince and Frank G. Speck, "The Modern Pequots and Their Language," *American Anthropologist*, n.s., 5 (1903): 193.

2. Fidelia Fielding, diary, published and translated by Speck in "Native Tribes and Dialects of Connecticut, A Mohegan-Pequot Diary," *Bureau of American Ethnology Annual Report, no. 43: 1925–1926* (Washington, D.C.: GPO, 1928), 247.

3. Alan Trachtenberg, *Shades of Hiawatha: Staging Indians, Making Americans, 1880–1930* (New York: Hill and Wang, 2004); Philip Deloria, *Playing Indian* (New Haven: Yale University Press, 1998); Joseph A. Conforti, *Imagining New England: Explorations of Regional Identity from the Pilgrims to the Mid-Twentieth Century* (Chapel Hill: University of North Carolina Press, 2001), 203–63.

4. Ethel Boissevain, "The Detribalization of the Narragansett Indians: A Case Study," *Ethnohistory* 3 (1956): 234–35; Adams 1880, 24; "The Narragansetts," *Newport Herald*, 28 Feb. 1896; PF Narragansett, 5–6, 13–15.

5. Speck, "Native Tribes and Dialects," 211–55; PF Mohegan, 71–78; Melissa J. Fawcett, *Medicine Trail: The Life and Lessons of Gladys Tantaquidgeon* (Tucson: University of Arizona Press, 2000), 9–51.

6. Fawcett, *Medicine Trail*, 52–59; Prince and Speck, "Modern Pequots and Their Language," 196–97; Speck, "Native Tribes and Dialects."

7. Description of 250th anniversary ceremonies, *Records and Papers of the New London County Historical Society*, part 3, vol. 2 (New London, Conn., 1897): 321; Arthur L. Peale, *Memorials and Pilgrimages in the Mohegan Country* (Norwich, Conn.: The Bulletin Company, 1930), 28, 31, 33, 37, 43.

8. Issac Rose et al. to Dukes County judge of probate, 1 Sept. 1860; Alexander Nevers et al. to Dukes County judge of probate, n.d.; Zaccheus Cooper et al. to Dukes County judge of probate; all unnumbered in Dukes County Probate Records, Edgartown, Mass.; Moses Brown, Vineyard Haven, to Rufus Ellis, 30 March 1876 and 23 Sept. 1876, SPG Pa-

pers, box 8, MHS. See also David Silverman, *Faith and Boundaries: Colonists, Christianity, and Community among the Wampanoag Indians of Martha's Vineyard, 1600–1871* (New York: Cambridge University Press, 2005), 269–72.

9. Mashpee, Indian mortgage records, 1834–1862, transcribed by Rosemary Burns, Mashpee Archives, Town Hall, Mashpee, Mass.; Russell M. Peters, *The Wampanoags of Mashpee* (Massachusetts: Indian Spiritual and Cultural Training Council, 1987), 37–39; Simeon L. Deyo, ed., *History of Barnstable County, Massachusetts* (New York: H. W. Blake and Company, 1890), 714, 716.

10. Edward S. Burgess, "The Old South Road of Gay Head" (1926), *Dukes County Intelligencer* (Aug. 1970), 30–31, 26–27; *Vineyard Gazette*, 27 Oct. 1871 (thanks to David Silverman for his transcript of this article); Indian binder, MVHS (on death and age of Thomas Jeffers).

11. Simeon L. Deyo, ed., *History of Barnstable County, Massachusetts* (New York: H. W. Blake and Company, 1890), 715–16.

12. Mary A. Cleggett Vanderhoop, "The Gay Head Indians: Their History and Traditions," series in the *New Bedford Evening Standard* beginning 25 June 1904; E. B. [Elizabeth Browning] Chace, "The Narragansett Tribe.—A Lesson from Marshpee," *Providence Journal*, ca. 1880, NRIA; G. W. Soper, "Among the Friendly Indians of Mashpee," *New England Magazine*, n.s., 2 (1890): 277–79; *Martha's Vineyard Directory . . . 1907* (Boston: Boston Suburban Book Co., 1907), 207, transcribed by Chris Baer, "Historical Records of Dukes County, Mass.," http://history.vineyard.net/dukes/chilgh1907.htm (accessed 30 June 2005).

13. Sarah Peabody Turnbaugh and William A. Turnbaugh, "Weaving the Woods," in *A Key into the Language of Woodsplint Baskets*, ed. Ann McMullen, Russell G. Handsman, and Joan Lester (Washington, Conn.: American Indian Archaeological Institute, 1987), 79, 92; Eva L. Butler, "Some Early Indian Basket Makers of Southern New England," in *Eastern Algonkian Block-Stamp Decoration: A New World Original or an Acculturated Art*, ed. Frank Speck, Research Series no. 1, Archaeological Society of New Jersey, State Museum (Trenton, 1947); Chace, "A Lesson from Marshpee"; Soper, "Among the Friendly Indians."

14. Tamara Race, "Indian Descendants Rekindle Culture," *Bourne Courier*, 20 July 1996; Hugo A. Dubuque, *Fall River Indian Reservation* (Fall River, Mass., 1907), i–iii, 6–7; PF Wampanoag, 96; D.W. Stevens, to Rufus Ellis, Boston, 29 March 1876, 31 Oct. 1876, 27 April 1877, 31 Oct. 1877, March or April 1880, SPG Papers, box 8, MHS; Moses Brown to Ellis, 3 April 1880, ibid.; Chappaquiddick gravestones, photos in MVHS; *New Bedford Evening Standard*, 4 April 1913, clipping in Indian binder, MVHS; notation on death of Lydia Mingo, ibid.; transcription of Samuel C. Mingo headstone in Oak Bluffs cemetery, ibid.

15. Campisi, "Mashantucket Pequot Tribe," 133–34; Calista Potter Thresher, "Homes and Haunts of the Pequots," *New England Magazine* 25, no. 6 (Feb. 1902): 753–54; PF Eastern Pequot, 88; Speck, *Eastern Algonkian Block Stamp Decoration*, 40–41; PF Schaghticoke 98–126; Russell G. Handsman and Ann McMullen, "An Introduction to Woodsplint Basketry and its Interpretation," in McMullen, Handsman, and Lester, *A Key into the Language of Woodsplint Baskets*, 33; Trudie Lamb Richmond, "Spirituality and Survival in Schaghticoke Basket-Making," in ibid., 140–43; T. S. Gold, "Fostering the Habit of Industry," *Connecticut Magazine* 8, no. 3 (March 1904): 454; Russell G. Handsman and Trudie

Lamb Richmond, "Confronting Colonialism: The Mahican and Scahaghticoke Peoples and Us," essay prepared for "Making Alternative Histories," School of American Research, Santa Fe, New Mexico, April 1992.

16. In 1899, Medfield residents remembered Natick Indians traveling through town and staying in barns; William Tilden, "Indians in Medfield," *Dedham Historical Register* 10 (1899): 53.

17. PF Nipmuc 102–5, 143–44; Frank G. Speck, "A Note on the Hassanamisco Band of Nipmuc," *Massachusetts Archaeological Society Bulletin* 4 (1943): 53; Zara Cisco Brough (Princess White Flower), "Days of Hassanamesit," *Nipmuc Nation Newsletter*, 1, no. 4 (July 2004): 5.

18. Mass., "Report of the Commissioners to determine the Title of Certain Lands Claimed by Indians," 11 Jan. 1860, MGCF, box 74; Mass., "Dartmouth Case," 22 March 1861, *MHR* 216 (Boston, 1861): 5–15; Earle 1861, 76; Daniel Huntoon, *History of the Town of Canton, Norfolk County, Massachusetts* (Cambridge, Mass.: John Wilson and Son, 1893), 28.

19. PF Webster 72–76, see 73 for Daily quotation, from Charles Leavens, Leavens Papers, n.d., 163; PF Nipmuc, 143–44; Speck, "A Note on the Hassanamisco Band," 53.

20. PF Webster 72–76; Frank G. Speck, *Territorial Subdivisions and Boundaries of the Wampanoag, Massachusett, and Nauset Indians*, Indian Notes and Monographs no. 44 (New York: Museum of the American Indian, Heye Foundation, 1928), 141–42; Rochester (Mass.), *Rochester's Official Bi-Centennial Record, Tuesday, July 22, 1879* (New Bedford: Mercury Publishing Company, 1879), 121; Z. W. Pease, "Fighting for Royal Domain," *Boston Daily Globe*, 26 April 1903.

21. Elroy S. Thompson, *History of Plymouth, Norfolk, and Barnstable Counties, Massachusetts* (New York: Lewis Historical Publishing Company, 1928), 1:80.

22. Butler, "Some Early Indian Basket Makers," 51–52; Speck, "Note on the Hassanamisco Band," 55; Speck, *Territorial Subdivisions*, 141–142; Turnbaugh and Turnbaugh, "Weaving the Woods," 92; "Fighting for Royal Domain"; Thresher, "Homes and Haunts of the Pequots," 753–54; PF Eastern Pequot 88.

23. Daniel Mandell, *Behind the Frontier: Indians in Eighteenth-Century Eastern Massachusetts* (Lincoln: University of Nebraska Press, 1996); Ann McMullen, "What's Wrong with This Picture? Context, Conversion, Survival, and the Development of Regional Native Cultures and Pan-Indianism in Southeastern New England," in *Enduring Traditions: The Native Peoples of New England*, ed. Laurie Weinstein (Westport, Conn.: Bergin and Garvey, 1994), 125, 140; Peale, *Memorials and Pilgrimages*, 27; Laura E. Conkey, Ethel Boissevain, and Ives Goddard, "Indians of Southern New England and Long Island: Late Period," in *Smithsonian Handbook of North American Indians*, ed. William C. Sturtevant, vol. 15: *Northeast*, ed. Bruce G. Trigger (Washington, D.C.: Smithsonian Institution, 1978), 185. The council brought together activists from the Wampanoag, Mohegan, Narragansett, Dudley Nipmuc, Pequot, Massachusett, Penobscot, Passamaquoddy, Niantic, Hassanamisco, and Wabenaki tribes; McMullen, "What's Wrong with This Picture," 147 n. 13. In 1939, the "affairs" of the Eastern and Mashantucket Pequots were managed by the Connecticut State Park and Forest Commission; the latter tribe had an organization and a chief

recognized by outsiders; Arthur L. Peale, *Uncas and the Mohegan Pequot* (Boston: Meador, 1939), 45–46.

24. Speck, "Native Tribes and Dialects"; Carolyn Battista, "A Museum's Many Miles: Tiny Connecticut Museum Chronicles Indian History," 21 June 2002, *Online Magazine of the National Trust for Historic Preservation*, www.nationaltrust.org/magazine/archives/arch_story/062102p.htm (accessed 20 June 2005); Turnbaugh and Turnbaugh, "Weaving the Woods," 79, 92; Butler, "Some Early Indian Basket Makers," 43; Means, *Wampanoags of Mashpee*, 46; Anne McMullen, "Talking through Baskets: Meaning, Production, and Identity in the Northern Woodlands," in *Basketmakers: Meaning and Form in Native American Baskets*, ed. Linda Mowat, Howard Murphy, and Penny Dransalt (Oxford: P. H. Rivers Museum, University of Oxford, 1992), 25; Richmond, "Spirituality and Survival," 140–43; Thompson, *History of Plymouth, Norfolk, and Barnstable Counties*, 2:813–14; PF Narragansett, 5–6, 13–15; Boissevain, "Detribalization of the Narragansett Indians," 239; Mandell, "Shifting Boundaries of Race and Ethnicity."

25. Peters, *Wampanoags of Mashpee*, 50–52; Fawcett, *Medicine Trail*, 143–44; Cheryll Holley, "Schaghticoke Tribal Nation Still Battling for Recognition," *Nipmuc Nation* 1, no. 4 (July 2004): 4; Rae Gould, "Nipmuc Nation Receives Final Determination from BIA," ibid., 1; "History and Culture," *Wampanoag Tribe of Gay Head*, www.wampanoagtribe.net/Pages/Wampanoag_WebDocs/history_culture (accessed 7 July 2005); PF Mohegan; PF Nipmuc.

Essay on Sources

The richest sources of documents on Indians in southern New England are the three state archives. Indian individuals, factions, and tribes sent many letters and petitions to state, county, and local officials. These contain descriptions of their communities, economic and social condition, and relations with neighboring whites. Occasionally, other individuals and groups within the community and white neighbors, including selectmen and justices of the peace, would write with dissenting views. Sometimes the legislature or governor would respond by appointing committees that reported on what they found, as well as what they recommended; a few, but not the majority, of these reports were published. Many of these documents were generated in the hope of achieving or opposing government actions, and (particularly in Massachusetts) notes by committee chairs and drafts of bills—many not passed—provide an intimate view of legislative opinion. Guardian accounts and reports vary in detail and regularity but generally provide bits of information that illuminate conditions of Indian groups and individuals. As Indians "not taxed" were rarely counted in the federal census, these records are the only sources of demographic data on Native tribes and communities.

Manuscript collections in the CSA include letters and petitions to the general assembly from various tribes before 1820 in CAr2. Those after 1820 are in General Assembly, Special Papers, Indians, box 1 and box 2—Rejected Bills. The annual reports by each tribe's guardian after 1820, as well as some petitions by or about Indians, were made to the county courts. This material dated 1820 to 1854 from the Eastern Pequots, Mashantucket Pequots, Mohegans, and Niantics is in NLCC, and material from 1855 to the 1900s is in NLCSC. In both collections, box 1 contains petitions from and reports on the Eastern Pequots, box 2 concerns the Mashantucket Pequots, box 3 concerns the Mohegans, box 4 concerns the Niantics, and box 5 contains assorted documents. Finding aids are available online at the State Library web site. State laws and resolves were published in CPA, CPL, CPR, and CPRA, various volumes, all from the state printers in Hartford. There were far fewer reports on Indians by state commissions because county courts were given administrative oversight of Indians beginning in 1822.

The Massachusetts Archives is a particularly rich lode. Particularly fruitful are manuscripts filed in shoestring-tied packets in MPL, MUHL, and MUSL. Many of these packets had not been opened since their original filing, and all three sets have excellent indices by subject. The governor and his council were also involved on various levels with Indians in the state, and the MGCF is a collection of manuscripts very much like the legislature's but without an index. Finally, MIGA contains letters and the reports and accounts submitted by the guardians for Chappaquiddick, Christiantown, Dudley Nipmucs, Gay Head, Herring Pond, Mashpee, Natick, and Watuppa-Troy. The Mashpee collection includes nearly all of the significant documents on that tribe's revolt in 1833–34.

Many of the guardians' accounts and some of the most important legislative committee reports were published by the state in *MHR* and *MSR*. Particularly significant are Child 1827, Bird 1849, and Earle 1861. Other notable reports on specific tribes, most commonly Mashpee and Gay Head, include "Legislative Commissioners' Report on Mashpee Meetinghouse," *MHR* 72 (Boston, 1839); "An Act to Prohibit the Sale of Ardent Spirits to the Gay Head Indians," *MHR* 48 (Boston, 1838); the transcript of the 3 June 1869 Mashpee hearings is in *MHR* 502 (Boston, 1869); and "Census of the Inhabitants of Gay Head Indians," *MSR* 14 (Boston, 1871). In 1992, during an Old Sturbridge Village (OSV) research fellowship, I put together an index to all of the published reports dealing with Indian tribes; that index is available at OSV, the Massachusetts State House Library, and the Massachusetts Archives. Also significant were acts and resolves published in *Laws of the Commonwealth of Massachusetts, from November 28, 1780 . . . to February 28, 1807*, 3 vols. (Boston, 1807); and *Acts and Resolves Passed by the General Court of Massachusetts, 1782–1870* (Boston, 1784–1922). The decisions of the Massachusetts Superior Court were published in *Massachusetts Reports*; several involved Indians, including *Medway v. Natick*, 7, *Mass. Reports* 88; *Dighton v. Freetown*, 4, *Mass Reports* 539; and *Andover v. Canton*, 13, *Mass. Reports* 547.

Almost all of the manuscripts connected with Rhode Island's only recognized tribe, the Narragansetts, are in NRIA, assembled during the battle over federal recognition of the tribe. This collection includes letters and petitions from the council and members of the tribe, plus reports from state officials and commissions on the tribe, 1770–1880. Most of the manuscripts are numbered, but many are not. The manuscript collections, Petitions to the General Assembly, vols. 1–36, 1725–1806; and Letters to the Governor, 1731–1871, have few relevant documents. The judicial hearings on the 1824 (Hardscrabble) and 1831 (Snowtown) race riots in Providence are interesting and reveal a great deal about urban development and shifting attitudes toward race and class in the region but unfortunately contain no hint that Narragansetts or other Indians were living in the area at the time; see documents relating to *State v. Cummings, et al.* (1824) and *State v. John Gardner* (1831), Judicial Records Center, Rhode Island Supreme Court, Pawtucket. Two reports of the Commissioner for the Narragansetts were published, Griffin 1858 and *Communication from Governor Dyer Accompanying the Report of the Commissioner of the Narragansett Tribe of Indians* (Providence, 1859). But the most extensive depictions of the tribe appeared in the legislative committee minutes from the tribal termination hearings, Adams 1880 and Adams 1881. An additional and final report in the termination process was Dwight R. Adams, George Carmichael Jr., and William P. Sheffield Jr., *Third Annual Report of Commission on the Affairs of the Narragansett Indians* (Providence, 1883).

Other public records provide a scattering of information. There were few county court cases involving Indians or Indian rights. In 1822, Connecticut gave county courts charge of Indian tribes, but those records are now in CSA and only occasionally involve lawsuits. County probate and court records in Massachusetts varied in their usefulness. Of particular use were the many wills and probate records deposited with the Dukes County Probate

Court, Edgartown, Mass. Only a few relevant cases were found in the *Plymouth County Court Records, 1686–1859*, ed. David Thomas Konig; the Plymouth County Court of Common Pleas; Bristol County Supreme Judicial Court; and Barnstable County Court of Common Pleas (the last three sets microfilmed by the Church of Latter Day Saints); and Worcester County Probate Records, Worcester, Mass. The Nantucket County probate, deeds, and court records were of little use since the 1763 epidemic that killed most of the Natives and the concomittant rise in the African American population on the island meant that after the Revolutionary War the documents provide no more than an occasional glimpse of an individual of Indian descent. My student assistants also searched the index to the Bristol County Court of Common Pleas (also an LDS microfilm) but found no names that matched lists from Indian communities in the county. One court case that revealed movement and connections between Indian communities in coastal Massachusetts was *Westport v. Chilmark*, 1816, Bristol County Superior Court, transcribed by Andrew Pierce, in SPM.

Some families and individuals can be traced through scattered regional and local public records. Maritime records, including lists of ship's crews kept at New Bedford Library, and seamen's papers (particularly important for mariners of color who were voyaging into Southern ports) provide details on particular men. Federal law required lists of ship crews to be filed with the nearest customs house, and Mystic Seaport has assembled the useful database New London Crew Lists Index, 1803–1878, provided by Kelly Drake of Mystic Seaport, January 2006, individual records in the database available at www.mysticseaport .org/library/initiative/CrSearch.cfm. A few bits of data come from Boston and Providence "warning out" committees, who filed reports on individuals—including Indian women and men working as domestics or whalers—believed to lack sufficient residency to be given public support. Some town records, particularly those from Stonington, Connecticut, between 1780 and 1816, show individual Indians bound over by the board of selectmen to white families. Finally, vital records from a few towns provide information on births, marriages, and deaths among some Indians and Indian descendants. Various vital and other records relating to people of color (including Indians) in southeastern Connecticut have been assembled and published in Barbara W. Brown and James M. Rose, *Black Roots in Southeastern Connecticut, 1650–1900* (Detroit: Gale, 1980). County, town, and ship records have the best potential for information about Indians living outside tribal reserves, but unfortunately contemporary paradigms of class and race means that these records rarely identify Indians and generally provide insufficient details on particular individuals for researchers to connect them with Native families or communities.

The public library in New Bedford, which was the whaling capital of New England, has an archive with a wide range of documents that provide a few glimpses into Indian life in the city and region and offers opportunities for future research. The New Bedford Seamen's Register shows the crew lists of ships leaving that port, with the crew member's name, hometown, height, and skin color or ethnicity, and the dates that the ship left and returned. The lists from 1840 to 1880 include individuals identified as from Gay Head or Mashpee, or with family names that were common in the coastal tribes by the nineteenth century. But these names, such as Belain, DeGrasse, and Anthony, were also common among non-Indians in the region, which makes a large-scale analysis of these records problematic. The James Bunker Congdon Papers includes in folder 18 a report on the "Colored Population of New Bedford," which noted that many in the city were part Indian. The City Watch Reports, 1 June 1848–24 March 1850, includes incidents involving "people of color," including Benjamin Paul, who was destitute and seeking lodging in September and October, and may have been a member of the Paul family of Gay Head. The daybooks and other records of the New Bedford Overseers of the Poor sometimes include personal and family histories of those applying for assistance, describing birthplaces, birthdates, marriages, and other details; although only a few such detailed records are about Indians, they confirm kinship connections and social networks among Indians in Gay Head, Fall River, and New Bedford.

There are also Mashpee and Narragansett records. The annual financial reports submitted by Mashpee when it was a district, from 1834 to 1870, along with its 1834 and 1842 censuses, are now in various files in MGCF, MIGA, and MPL. The town of Mashpee still retains district and town meeting minutes for most of the years between 1834 and 1890, including records of the elections of town officers, fishing licensing and regulations, and spending for roads and other community concerns; records of mortgages (mostly of personal property rather than land), beginning in 1834; and land deeds and allotments under the 1834 law creating the district of Mashpee. Rosemary Burns with the Mashpee Historical Society was kind enough to send me notes, transcripts, and photocopies of these records. The Narragansetts constitution of 1850 and minutes of tribal council meetings (1850–62 and 1865) are in the Charlestown Town Council and Town Meetings records, 1787–1889, available on microfilm through the library of the Church of Latter Day Saints, though many pages are illegible. The constitution put into print many of their political customs, and the council minutes detail land allotments to members of the tribe, reviews of boundaries of lands already held, the lease of lands and sale of timber-cutting licenses, and reviews of the tribe's accounts and settlement of debts.

Indian ministers and their people wrote many petitions and letters, which are in the files of particular laws and resolves or rejected bills, described above. A few are deposited in private libraries, particularly the MHS, including Moses Howwoswee's 1792 census of Gay Head (in Misc. Bound Docs.) and another census from Gay Head sent to the Gospel Society of Boston, 14 May 1798. But the only collection of papers from an individual is the small and eclectic set of Zach Howwoswee Papers, 1792–1826, in the John Carter Brown Library, Mss. 1784, Brown University. John W. Johnson, who became Mi'kmaq and Wabonaki after being taken as a boy in Maine, left his "Life of John W. Johnson," typescript, in the Maine Historical Society.

The most important source of correspondence between white men about New England Indian communities was the SPG, which had two incarnations: first as a London-financed and Boston-administered missionary organization during the colonial period, and then as the missionary society organized by Boston ministers and intellectuals in 1795 and chartered by Massachusetts. Most of the papers from the London-based Society for the Propagation of the Gospel in Foreign Parts are in NEHGS, Mss. C40, 3 boxes; this correspondence, mostly between the Boston-based secretary for the organization and ministers receiving SPG salaries, ends in the 1780s as some of the American ministers tried to obtain funds due them during the Revolution. The later incarnation of the society left records and correspondence in many places. One of the largest is SPGPE, Ms. 48, 3 boxes, which contains letters from Zachariah Mayhew on Martha's Vineyard (1793–1801); Leavitt Thaxter, an Edgartown attorney who worked for Gay Head, Christiantown, and Chappaquiddick (1849–63); a particularly rich lode from Gideon Hawley (1792–1807); one of the few sets from Phineas Fish (1817–53); and Frederick Baylies, including his lists of students in Indian schools (1819–33). Most unique are the journals kept by Curtis Coe (1809–21), a retired minister who recorded his experiences preaching on summer trips through the Narragansett Bay area. His diary describes traveling among poor isolated white communities but also focuses on the Narragansetts during a period generally undocumented for the tribe. There is also a set of SPG correspondence in the MHS, which makes perfect sense, as the two organizations were established at about the same time, in the same place, by many of the same men who served as officers in both societies. The MHS collection has many of the reports from Frederick Baylies and others on the Vineyard in the second quarter of the nineteenth century. The MHS has photocopied many of the letters and put them in their Misc. Bound Docs., which are kept in chronological order, and have published many in *MHSC*. The SPG published annual reports that often included excerpts of letters from ministers working with Indians, as well as financial reports showed the stipends paid those ministers.

The largest set of letters from a white minister were left by Gideon Hawley, whose correspondence between 1753 and 1807 sits in many collections, including the Massachusetts Archives (MGCF, MIGA, MPL, MUHL, and MUSL); the SPGPE (which includes a very detailed 1800 census of Mashpee); Hawley's Papers in the Congregational Library, Boston; his letters, in the MHS (to whose collections he frequently contributed); a 1793 census of Mashpee in the Autograph File, Houghton Library, Harvard University (thanks to Andrew Pierce); the SPG Papers in the MHS; and various letters in the S. P. Savage Papers, 3 vols., MHS. Unfortunately, only a few letters *to* Hawley have been preserved. Frederick Baylies, who worked in a different manner with many coastal Indian tribes a generation after Hawley died, left extensive correspondence in the SPGPE and the SPG Papers, MHS (including his journal from 1827); in Harvard Grants for Work among the Indians, Harvard University Archives, UAI 20.720, Houghton Library; and Baylies 1823.

Most of the many state and private historical societies in southern New England own a smattering of Indian documents. The MHS has the richest collection of Indian-related materials in the region. In addition to the Hawley letters, SPG papers, S. P. Savage Papers, and Misc. Bound Docs., the MHS has a particularly impressive range of letters, diaries, and other documents. The Jeremy Belknap Papers and William Cushing Papers contain letters and other documents relating to Indians in southern New England. Charles Banks, who published a three-volume history of Martha's Vineyard in 1911, left to the MHS twenty-three volumes of papers, including many maps and documents. Society members and correspondents wrote about Indians or Indian towns for the *MHSC*; some of the more significant are Captain Jerningham and Benjamin Bassett, "Report [on Indians on Martha's Vineyard]," *MHSC*, 1st ser., 1 (1790): 206; Stephen Badger, "Historical and Characteristic Traits of the American Indians in General," *MHSC*, 1st ser., 5 (1798): 32–45; Timothy Alden Jr., "Memorabilia of Yarmouth," *MHSC*, 1st ser., 5 (1798): 55; Abiel Holmes, "Additional Memoirs of the Mohegans," *MHSC*, 1st ser., 9 (1804): 75–99; Anonymous (possibly Gideon Hawley), "A Description of Mashpee, in the County of Barnstable, September 18th, 1802,"

MHSC, 2nd ser., 3 (1815): 1–12; Anonymous, "Report of a Committee on the State of the In-dians in Mashpee and Parts Adjacent [in 1767]," MHSC, 2nd ser., 3 (1815): 13–17; Anonymous, "A Description of Duke's County, Aug. 13th, 1807," MHSC, 2nd ser., 3 (1815): 44, 93–94.

The CHS owns the William Samuel Johnson Papers in three volumes, including a vol-ume of Mohegan Papers, with tribal petitions and letters to the Connecticut assembly through 1789, and an 1833 census of the Mashantucket Pequots. The CHS also holds the Ernest Law Papers, with letters from Mohegan council chairman Zachary Johnson written during the 1780s, and the Samson Occom Papers, with correspondence in the 1780s from the famed Mohegan preacher and Brothertown organizer. The AAS holds the John Milton Earle Papers in two boxes and two bound volumes, which includes the accounts and vital records kept by the Hassanamisco guardians, 1727–1860; the contract, deeds, and other doc-uments from the 1727 purchase of Hassanamisco and the Indian allotments that followed; and Earle's correspondence with Indians and town officials in his 1859–61 investigation. The AAS also owns the "Minutes of the Legislative Committee Appointed to Inquire into the Complaints of the Mashpee Indians, Feb. 5–March 8, 1834," in the Ira Moore Barton Papers, box 1, folder 1. The Rhode Island Historical Society does not have an Indian col-lection with nineteenth-century materials, although individuals of Narragansett and Ni-antic descent are among those listed in the Providence Town Papers and other documents in their library.

The MVHS holds various letters, records, photographs, and other documents from In-dian communities on the Vineyard and is also the repository for the SPM, an outstanding collection of photocopies and transcripts of documents gathered by Jerome Segel, R. An-drew Pierce, and Ronald Monterosso from many libraries and archives for the multivolume The Wampanoag Geneaological History of Martha's Vineyard, Massachusetts. The Nan-tucket Historical Society contains many outstanding collections on the island's Indian and African American communities, but unfortunately I found that these documents suffer the same blurring of Indian and "colored" as the Nantucket County records. Also, since I be-gan this work, the Mashantucket Pequot Museum and Research Center has been gather-ing copies or originals of many local, county, and tribal documents. Most of these libraries now have Internet-based catalogues, which often provide details of the files in their col-lections.

There are many published primary sources on Indians in southern New England be-tween 1780 and 1880 in addition to the state and historical society publications described above. The few documents in Native languages written after the middle of the eighteenth century have been collected and translated in Ives Goddard and Kathleen Bragdon, Na-tive Writings in Massachusett, 2 vols. (Philadelphia: American Philosophical Society, 1988). William Apess published a number of pieces between 1827 and 1834, including his autobi-ography The Son of the Forest (1829); Experiences of Five Christian Indians (1831), which in-cludes short biographies of his wife and the famous Pequot basketmaker Ann Wampy; and Indian Nullification (1834), which presents his view of his involvement in the Mashpee re-volt and its aftermath, and catalogues public reaction to the events. These can be found in On Our Own Ground: The Complete Writings of William Apess, a Pequot, ed. Barry O'Con-nell (Amherst: University of Massachusetts Press, 1992). Paul Cuffe [Jr.], Narrative of the Life and Adventures of Paul Cuffe, a Pequot Indian: During Thirty Years Spent at Sea, and in *Travelling in Foreign Lands* (Vernon, N.Y., 1839), has little to say about his people in New England, although his experiences at sea no doubt resembled those of other Indian men from the region. How this son of a Pequot woman and an African American leader identified himself highlights the issues of exogamous marriages, ethnicity, and race in the early Republic.

Some useful and fairly balanced accounts of Indians were left by whites during this period. When Jedidiah Morse traversed the United States and its territories in 1819 to compile *A Report to the Secretary of War of the United States on Indian Affairs* (New Haven: Converse, 1822), he asked ministers and lawyers who worked with New England Indians to comment on conditions within the tribes and how they felt about removing west of the Mississippi River; the results are unique glimpses of Indians' attitudes towards their homelands. William Tudor's *Letters on the Eastern States* (1819), 2nd ed. (Boston: Wells and Lilly, 1821) paints southern New England Indian life (and white stereotypes) in fairly broad and evocative brushstrokes and provides some details on specific tribes. The single-issue newspaper, *The Uncas Monument, 1492–1842* (Norwich, Conn.: John G. Cooley, 1842) contains an exceptional description of the Mohegan's wigwam festival in 1842—perhaps their first. While John Deforest viewed Indians as a dwindling, pitiful race, his *History of the Indians of Connecticut, from the Earliest Known Period to 1850* (Hartford: William Jason Hamersley 1851), contains excerpts from colonial and state documents, and letters from Indian overseers in Connecticut describing their charges in 1849 and 1850. William Bentley, a Salem minister and community leader at the turn of the century, was an acute and fairly balanced observer of people and events, although unfortunately his only Indian acquaintance was from New Stockbridge, not Massachusetts; see *The Diary of William Bentley, D.D., Pastor of the East Church, Salem, Massachusetts*, 4 vols. (Salem: Essex Institute, 1905–14).

The few published accounts by travelers who visited Indian communities are particularly useful. Yale president Timothy Dwight commented on the Mohegans and Niantics and visited Brothertown, New York, in 1799 and the Eastern Pequots in 1807; *Travels in New England and New York*, 4 vols. (New Haven, Conn.: S. Converse, 1821–22; reprint, Cambridge, Mass.: Harvard University Press, 1969). Englishman Edward Kendall left unmatched descriptions of Mohegan, Mashpee, and Gay Head in 1807, with surprisingly similar accounts of some neighboring white communities, in *Travels through the Northern Parts of the United States in the Years 1807 and 1808*, 2 vols. (New York: I. Riley, 1809). In 1844, German scientist Albert C. Koch came to Gay Head at the start of his trip through America and stayed for several days; *Journey through a Part of the United States of North America in the Years 1844–1846* (Carbondale: Southern Illinois University Press, 1972). When the Boston engineer James Winthrop came to Cape Cod in 1791 to survey the area for a ship canal, he kept a journal that included an account of his visit to Mashpee; "Journal of a Survey in 1791, For a Canal Across Cape Cod," *Monthly Bulletin of Books Added to the Public Library of the City of Boston* 6 (1901): 125–26. There are some revealing articles written by fisherman and tourists to Gay Head, including "A Visit to Martha's Vineyard," *Atlantic Monthly* 4 (September 1859): 281–94; D. H. Strother, "A Summer in New England," *Harper's New Monthly Magazine* 124 (Sept. 1860): 447–56; Francis Endicott, "Striped Bass," *Scribner's Monthly* 21, no. 5 (March 1881): 704–5; and Charles F. Danforth, "Trout Fishing in New England," *New England Magazine* 14, no. 4 (June 1893): 500.

Whether published by Democrats or Whigs, newspapers rarely commented on local issues; rather, they focused on international and national news and politics (usually in an extremely partisan manner), and provided a forum for local advertisers and affairs of the editor's political party. As a result, few ran articles on local Indians except during extraordinary
events, although there were exceptions. The AAS holds the premier collection of nineteenth-
century New England newspapers; during my fellowship in 2002, I focused on newspapers
published in towns near Indian tribes or in Boston during important events such as the
Mashpee revolt or state investigative commissions. Boston newspapers (and years of publication) that I examined included the *Columbia Centinel*, 1795; the *Massachusetts Centinel*,
1798–1800; the *Liberator*, 1831–44; *Mirror of Liberty*, 1838; and the *Boston Courier*, 1827,
1849. Other Massachusetts newspapers were the *Barnstable Patriot and Commercial Advertiser*, 1830–34, 1868–70; the *Barnstable Journal*, 1832 and 1834; the *Sandwich Observer*,
1849; the *Old Colony Democrat* (Plymouth), 1833–34; the *Worcester Daily Spy*, 1848, 1869;
the *Fall River Weekly News*, 1845; the *Norfolk Democrat* (Dedham), 1848–49; the *Webster
Weekly Times*, 1859–62, scattered issues. Connecticut newspapers included the *Connecticut Gazette* (New London), 1796; the *Connecticut Centinel* (Norwich), scattered issues,
1802–7; the *Windham Register*, 1817 (three issues in the AAS); the *Yankee* (Stonington),
1825; the *Stonington Telegraph* (two issues at AAS, Sept. 1827 and Oct. 1828); the *Courier*
(Norwich), 1825–35; and the *Religious Messenger* (Norwich), 1831–32. The newspapers
nearest Charlestown were in Westerly, Rhode Island: the *Narragansett Weekly*, 1858–81,
with some years missing and others incomplete, and the *Literary Echo and Pawcatuck Advertiser*, with a scattered run, 1852–53.

Another source of newspaper articles was the digitized, online version of *Early American Newspapers*, which I searched using the names of Native communities and "Indian"
as keywords. I found relevant articles in the *Newburyport Herald* (1811), *Columbian Centi-
nal* (1811, 1818), *New Bedford Mercury* (various articles 1821–38), *Independent Chronicle and
Boston Patriot* (1823), *American Mercury* (1823), *The Boston Journal* (1834), *The Newport
Mercury* (1842), *Pittsfield Sun* (various articles 1845–59); and the *Farmer's Cabinet* (1859).
Most contained reports on legislative committees or actions concerning Indians, particularly the findings of the Bird commission in 1849; reports on the Mashpee revolt and its aftermath; or notes from SPG reports on Indian schools. Two articles were on "last Indians":
the *Newport Mercury* briefly noted the death of John Uncas, "last male of the royal line" of
the Mohegans, and the *Farmers Cabinet* reprinted a report from the *Hampshire Gazette*
on the death of Sally Maminash, an Occom descendant and supposedly the "last Indian"
in Northampton. I also had David Silverman's notes on and photocopies from SPM of the
Vineyard Gazette (1846–71). Additional references to specific newspaper articles that
proved very useful, especially those published in the late nineteenth and early twentieth
centuries, came from various secondary sources, particularly the various proposed findings
issued by the Bureau of Indian Affairs Office of Federal Acknowledgment.

The first half of the nineteenth century saw the emergence of major American periodicals, such as the *North American Review*, which were aimed at the new middle class and
the intellectual elites, and were more likely than newspapers to run longer articles on "human interest" (cultural and social) concerns, including the surviving Indian communities
in southern New England. All of the major periodicals are reproduced in the *American Pe-*

riodical Series (APS), a microfilm set that has recently been digitized for online use; I used both forms. The two forms use different indices: the microfilm has a printed subject index, and the digitized index is searchable by keywords as well as by title or author of individual articles. All the articles I used from national periodicals, such as *Harper's* and *Scribner's Monthly*, were found using these two indices. The AAS also catalogued many nineteenth-century articles contained in more local and regional periodicals in their collection, including *New England Magazine, The Bostonian, Congregational Quarterly, Connecticut Magazine.* I also found some in the files of the MVHS. In addition, in the nineteenth century states and even towns began establishing historical societies, some of which published papers presented by their members, transcriptions of local records, and other materials; particularly noteworthy for articles on New England Indians were the *Dedham Historical Register, Medford Historical Register, MHSC, Winchester Records, Proceedings of the Worcester Society of Antiquities, Quinabaug Historical Society Leaflets; The Farmington Magazine,* and *Collections of the Rhode Island Historical Society.* Particularly important articles are listed below, with books on similar topics.

The antebellum interest in local history continued to grow during the nineteenth century, generating a growing body of town and county histories that often included descriptions of Indians and Indian communities, past and present. Such books are particularly important for understanding how Anglo-Americans in nineteenth century viewed the Indians in their midst; this aspect is analyzed in chapter 5. These works also provide evocative portrayals and important information on individuals barely glimpsed in other records, or details on the past and present of Indian communities within the town or county which are unavailable from any other source. Many contain descriptions of "the last Indian" in town, reprint sections of state reports on Indian groups, or quote long sections from recent speeches that include descriptions of Indians. The AAS holds one of the best collections of these New England town and county histories, particularly those published between 1820 and 1930. While the majority do not contain any information on Indians after King Philip's War, a large number are useful sources of information on Native individuals, families, and communities.

Particularly significant local histories in Massachusetts (in order by date of publication) were William Biglow, *History of the Town of Natick, Mass.* (Boston: Marsh, Capen, and Lyon, 1830); William Brigham, *An Address Delivered before the Inhabitants of Grafton on the First Centennial Anniversary of that Town, April 29, 1835* (Boston: Light and Horton, 1835); John W. Barber, *Historical Collections of Massachusetts* (Worcester: Dorr, Howland, and Co., 1839); Nahum Mitchell, *History of the Early Settlement of Bridgewater* (Boston: Kidder and Wright, 1840); Sarah S. Jacobs, *Nonantum and Natick* (Boston: Massachusetts Sabbath School Society, 1853); Charles Brooks, *History of the Town of Medford* (Boston: James M. Usher, 1855); Dan Ricketson, *The History of New Bedford, Bristol County, Massachusetts* (New Bedford: n.p., 1858); *The Plymouth County Directory and Historical Register of the Old Colony* (Middleboro, Mass.: Stillman B. Pratt and Co., 1867); Frederick Clifton Pierce, *History of Grafton, Worcester County, Massachusetts, from its early settlement by the Indians in 1647 to the Present Time, 1879* (Worcester: C. Hamilton, 1879); Frederick Denison, *Illustrated New Bedford, Martha's Vineyard and Nantucket* (1879, 2nd and rev. ed., Providence, Rhode Island: J. A. and R. A. Reid, 1880); Charles Brooks, *History of the Town of Medford, Middlesex County, Massachusetts, from Its First Settlement in 1630–1855* (Boston: Rand, Avery, 1886); Harriett Merrifield Forbes, *The Hundredth Town: Glimpses of Life in Westborough, 1717–1817* (Westborough, Mass., 1889); Simeon L. Deyo, ed., *History of Barnstable County, Massachusetts* (New York: H. W. Blake and Company, 1890); Daniel Huntoon, *History of the Town of Canton, Norfolk County, Massachusetts* (Cambridge: John Wilson and Son, 1893); Deloriane P. Corey, *The History of Malden, Massachusetts, 1633–1785* (Malden: n.p, 1899); Alason Borden, ed., *Our County and Its People: A Descriptive and Biographical Records of Bristol County, Massachusetts* (n.p.: Boston History Company, 1899); Alice Morse Earle, *Stage-coach and Tavern Days* (New York: MacMillan Company, 1900); Thomas Weston, *History of the Town of Middleboro Massachusetts* (Boston: Houghton, Mifflin, 1906); Henry Litchfield, *Ancient Landmarks of Pembroke* (Pembroke, Mass.: G.E. Lewis, 1909); Elroy S. Thompson, *History of Plymouth, Norfolk, and Barnstable Counties, Massachusetts*, 3 vols. (New York: Lewis Historical Publishing Company, 1928).

Significant articles with descriptions of recent and contemporary Indians in Massachusetts include John Tripp, "Native Church at Gay Head," *Zion's Advocate*, Sept. 1831, reprinted in *Magazine of New England History* 3, no. 4 (Oct. 1893): 250–53; Samuel Hosmer, "Indian Churches on Nantucket," *Congregational Quarterly* 7 (1865): 31–34 (with description of Abram Quary, the "last Indian" of Nantucket, who died in 1854); George Cooke, "Our Aborigines," *Winchester Record* 1, no. 4 (October 1885): 274; G. W. Soper, "Among the Friendly Indians of Mashpee," *New England Magazine*, N.S., 2 (1890): 277–79; Nathan B. Lewis, "The Last of the Narragansetts," *Proceedings of the Worcester Society of Antiquities* 16 (1898): 27–51; William Tilden, "Indians in Medfield," *Dedham Historical Register* 10 (1899): 51–53; and Ruth Coolidge, "Indians of Medford," *Medford Historical Register* 33 (1930): 28.

Some local histories contained one or two references about or documents from Indians in the eighteenth and/or nineteenth centuries. See Peter Whitney, *The History of the County of Worcester* (Worcester: Isaiah Thomas, 1793); Samuel Deane, *History of Scituate, Massachusetts, from Its First Settlement to 1831* (Boston: J. Loring, 1831); James Thacher, *History of the Town of Plymouth*, 2nd ed. (1832; Boston: Marsh, Capen and Lyon, 1835; reprint, Yarmouthport, ME: Parnassus, 1972), 398; George Faber Clark, *A History of the Town of Norton, Bristol County, Mass., from 1669 to 1850* (Boston: Crosby, Nichols, and Co., 1859), 56; Josiah Temple and George Sheldon, *A History of the Town of Northfield, Massachusetts* (Albany, N.Y.: Joel Munsell, 1875); Samuel Hopkins Emery, *History of the Church of North Middleborough, Massachusetts, in Six Discourses* (Middleborough: Harlow and Thatcher, 1876), 8; Adin Ballou, *History of the Town of Milford, Worcester County, Massachusetts, from Its First Settlement to 1881* (Boston: Rand, Avery, 1882), 395; Albert Kendall Teele, ed., *The History of Milton, Mass., 1640–1887* (Boston: Rockwell and Churchill, 1887), 10; Ledyard Bill, *The History of Paxton, Massachusetts* (Worcester: Putnam, Davis, and Co., 1889), 45; Henry Stedman Nourse, *History of the Town of Harvard, Massachusetts, 1732–1893* (Harvard: W. Hapgood, 1894); Frank Smith, *Narrative History: A History of Dover, Massachusetts* (Dover: n.p., 1897); *A History of the Town of Freetown, Massachusetts, with an Account of the Old Home Festival, July 30th, 1902* (Fall River, Mass.: J. H. Franklin, 1902); Henry S. Griffith, *History of Carver, Massachusetts* (New Bedford: E. Anthony and Sons, 1913). Two described Indian tribes from Maine and Canada visiting and camping in the town in the mid-nineteenth century: Edward R. Lambert, *History of the Colony of New Haven* (New Haven: Hitchcock & Stafford, 1838), 130–31, and Alonzo Lewis and James R. Newall, *History of Lynn, Essex County, Massachusetts, including Lynnfield, Saugus, Swampscott, and Nahant, 1629–1864* (Lynn: George C. Herbert, 1890).

There were fewer Connecticut town histories published at this time. The following have fairly extended descriptions of contemporary Indians: John C. Pease and John M. Niles, *A Gazetteer of the States of Connecticut and Rhode Island* (Hartford: William S. Marsh, 1819); W. C. Sharpe, *History of Seymour, Connecticut* (Seymour, Conn.: Record Print, 1879); Samuel Orcutt and Ambrose Beardsley, *The History of the Old Town of Derby, Connecticut, 1642–1880* (Springfield, Mass.: Springfield Printing Company, 1880); Henry A. Baker, *History of Montville, Connecticut, Formerly the North Parish of New London* (Hartford: Case, Lockwood and Brainerd, 1896); Francis Atwater, *History of Kent, Connecticut* (Meriden, Conn.: Journal Publishing Company, 1897); Julius Gay, *The Tunxis Indians; An Historical Address Delivered at the Annual Meeting of the Village Library Company of Farmington, Conn., September 11, 1901* (Hartford: Case, Lockwood & Brainard, 1901); John Avery, *History of the Town of Ledyard, 1650–1900* (Norwich, Conn.: Noyes and Davis, 1901). Relatively short descriptions of local Indians are in Charles Bickford, ed., *Voices of the New Republic: Connecticut Towns, 1800–1932*, vol. 1 (Hartford: Conn. Academy of Arts and Sciences, 2004); Alfred Lee, "The Discourse Delivered at the Bi-Centennial Celebration, Norwich, on Wednesday Evening, Sept. 7th, 1859," in *The Norwich Jubilee: A Report of the Celebration at Norwich, Connecticut, on the Two Hundredth Anniversary of the Settlement of the Town, September 7th and 8th, 1859*, comp. John W. Stedman (Norwich: John W. Stedman, 1859), 135; Ellen Douglas Larned, *History of Windham County, Connecticut*, 2 vols. (Worcester: C. Hamilton, 1874 and 1880); Richard Wheeler, *History of the Town of Stonington, County of New London, Connecticut, from Its First Settlement in 1649 to 1900* (New London, 1900; reprint, Baltimore: Genealogical Publishing Co., 1977), 195; *Two Centuries of New Milford, Connecticut: An Account of the Bi-Centennial Celebration of the Founding of the Town Held June 15, 16, 17 and 18, 1907* (New York: Grafton Press, 1907); George C. Waldo Jr., *History of Bridgeport and Vicinity*, 2 vols. (New York: S. J. Clarke Publishing Company, 1917); Charles R. Stark, *Groton, Conn, 1705–1905* (Stonington, Conn.: Palmer Press, 1922).

Significant articles on contemporary Connecticut Indians are Benson J. Lossing, "The Last of the Pequods," *Scribner's Monthly* 2, no. 6 (October 1871): 573–77, which contains an extensive interview with the Schaghticoke elder Eunice Mawee in 1859; Henry Baker, "The Mohegans: An Historical Sketch of this Famous Tribe," *The Bostonian*, 1 (Jan.–March 1895): 370; Calista Potter Thresher, "Homes and Haunts of the Pequots," *New England Magazine* 25, no. 6 (February 1902): 742–54; T. S. Gold, "Fostering the Habit of Industry, *Connecticut Magazine* 8, no. 3 (March 1904): 452–54; and Mrs. Charles H. Smith, "The Last of the Niantics," *Connecticut Magazine* 8, no. 3 (March 1904): 455–56, with a biography and extensive interview with Mercy Ann Nonesuch.

Only three books on Rhode Island town histories were found to contain sections on the Narragansetts in Charlestown: Pease and Niles, *Gazetteer*; William Tucker, ed., *Historical Sketch of the Town of Charlestown, in Rhode Island, from 1636 to 1876* (Westerly, R.I.: G. B.

and J. H. Utter, 1877); and Frederic Denison, *Westerly and Its Witnesses, for Two Hundred and Fifty Years, 1626–1876* (Providence: J. A. and R. A. Reid, 1878)

Many of these local histories also addressed the question of whether the early English settlers had abused Natives in the region. Additional books with sentimentalist declamations about vanishing Indians include David Willard, *Willard's History of Greenfield* (Greenfield: Kneeland and Eastman, 1838), 12; Charles Hyde, *Historical Celebration of the Town of Brimfield, Hampden County, Massachusetts, Wednesday, October 11, 1876* (Springfield: Clark W. Bryan Company, 1879); Alfred Sereno Hudson, *The History of Sudbury, Massachusetts 1638–1889* (Sudbury: Town of Sudbury, 1889), 23–24; and Thomas B. Wellman, *History of the town of Lynnfield, Mass., 1635–1895* (Boston: Blanchard and Watts, 1895), 52. Books that attacked the tendency to romanticize Indians include Francis Manwaring Caulkins, *History of Norwich, Connecticut* (1866; Chester, Conn.: Pequot Press, 1976); Henry C. Dorr, "The Narragansetts," *Collections of the Rhode Island Historical Society* 7 (1885), 135–237; and James R. Newall, *History of Lynn, Essex County, Massachusetts, Including Lynnfield, Saugus, Swampscott, and Nahant, 1864–1893* (Lynn: Nichols Press, 1897), 14. Less passionate, but still useful, glimpses of how New Englanders viewed Indians can be found in Samuel Hopkins Emery, *History of the Church of North Middleborough, Massachusetts, in Six Discourses* (Middleborough: Harlow and Thatcher, 1876).

Some of the sources listed are speeches that included detailed descriptions on Indians in the town. Public oratory as an art form flourished in the mid-nineteenth century, and the motif of the vanishing Indian, often with a local reference, could play an important role. Two of the most famous New England orators were Charles Sprague and Edward Everett, and their speeches that featured odes to vanishing Indians included Sprague, *An Oration: Pronounced before the Inhabitants of Boston, July the Fourth, 1825, in Commemoration of American Independence* (Boston: John H. Eastburn, City Printer, 1825); Sprague, *An Ode: Pronounced before the Inhabitants of Boston, September the Seventeenth, 1830, at the Centennial Celebration of the Settlement of the City* (Boston: John H. Eastburn, City Printer, 1830); Everett, *Remarks at the Plymouth Festival, on the First of August, 1853, in Commemoration of the Embarkation of the Pilgrims* (Boston: Crosby, Nichols, and Company, 1853); and Everett, *Dorchester in 1630, 1776, and 1855, an Oration Delivered on the Fourth of July, 1855* (Boston: David Clapp, 1855).

By the late nineteenth century, New England towns were staging elaborate pageants to celebrate bicentennials of their founding and other significant public events, generally built around a parade with important groups or personas from the town's history, or reenactments of significant events. These pageants involved Indians (frequently as representatives of the barbaric past inevitably replaced by the promise of a future America), often played by schoolchildren in costume but sometimes by individuals or delegations from nearby Native groups. Such events sometimes included the unveiling of monuments to celebrated seventeenth-century Native leaders such as Uncas. The pageant organizers would then publish souvenir booklets, featuring detailed descriptions of the events and their participants, transcripts of important speeches, and photographs. Booklets that provided useful descriptions of and even speeches by Natives after termination include *Rochester's Official Bi-Centennial Record* (New Bedford: Mercury Publishing, 1879); *Canonicus Memorial, Services of Dedication, under the Auspices of the Rhode Island Historical Society, Septem-*

ber 21, 1883 (Providence: Providence Press, 1883); description of 250th anniversary cere-
monies in *Records and Papers of the New London County Historical Society*, part 3, vol. 2
(New London, Conn.: The Society, 1897), 321; Lillian Baynes Griffin, "The Record of the
Red Man," *Farmington Magazine* 1 (November 1902): 2; Arthur L. Peale, *Memorials and
Pilgrimages in the Mohegan Country* (Norwich, Conn.: The Bulletin Company, 1930).

Although most local histories that included discussions of Indians were nonfiction, a
few significant works of fiction with extensive and useful descriptions of Natives in south-
ern New England were published in the second quarter of the nineteenth century. The
strongest examples of revisionist views of King Philip's War and New England Natives were
Lydia Marie Child, *Hobomok and Other Writings on Indians*, ed. Carolyn L. Karcher (New
Brunswick, N.J.: Rutgers University Press, 1986); Sarah Savage, *Life of Philip, the Indian
Chief* (Salem: Whipple and Lawrence, 1827); and Lydia Marie Child, *The First Settlers of
New England; or, Conquest of the Pequods, Narragansetts and Pokanokets, as Related by a
Mother to Her Children, by a Lady of Massachusetts* (Boston 1829). Fictional descriptions
of Indians at the end of the eighteenth century, which contain include significant details
that reflect local oral traditions, include Lydia Sigourney, *Sketches of Connecticut, Forty
Years Since* (Hartford: Oliver D. Cooke and Sons, 1824), set in Norwich in 1784; and Har-
riet Beecher Stowe, *Oldtown Folks* (1869), ed. Henry May (Cambridge, Mass.: Harvard
University Press, 1966), set in Natick between 1787 and 1800.

Finally the growing market for children's textbooks and giftbooks inspired a number of
publications that included sections on Indians in southern New England. Samuel Goodrich's schoolbooks for children depicted Indians as abused and exterminated by hostile settlers, while maintaining view that the Natives were ignorant if noble barbarians. His *The
Tales of Peter Parley about America* (Boston: S. G. Goodrich, 1827), a fictionalized account
of an elderly man's stories of his youth in the Boston area, includes adventures with Indians in western and northern New England. Goodrich's works of nonfiction include *The
First Book of History* (Boston: Richardson, Lord, and Holbrook, 1831) and *History of the Indians of North and South America* (Boston: Bradbury, Soden, and Co., 1844). His *Lives of
Celebrated American Indians: by the Author of Peter Parley's Tales* (Boston: Bradbury, Soden, and Co., 1843), contains a biography of King Philip, calling him "a savage indeed, and
a ruthless enemy, yet a patriot and statesman." Additional children's books that discussed
Indians in southern New England are Lambert Lilly [Francis Lister Hawks], *The History of
New England* (1831); and *The Child's Picture Book of Indians . . . to Which Is Added a Col-
lection of Indian Antecdotes, Original and Select. By a Citizen of New England* (Boston:
Carter, Hendee, and Co., 1833).

SECONDARY SOURCES

While the scholarship on Indians in southern New England in the seventeenth and
eighteenth century is very large and growing, there are very few works that deal with Indians between the Revolution and termination. Most cover this period as part of a more general study of a particular tribe or community and emphasize developments before 1750 and
after 1900 due to the lack of information on and apparently few changes during the nineteenth century. The most recent study, David Silverman's *Faith and Boundaries: Colonists,*

Christianity, and Community among the Wampanoag Indians of Martha's Vineyard, 1600–1871 (New York: Cambridge University Press, 2005), does pay considerable attention to the nineteenth century and to regional networks, but primarily focuses on the Vineyard, with some attention to related tribes like Mashpee and Herring Pond. Barry O'Connell's introduction to *On Our Own Ground: The Complete Writings of William Apess, A Pequot* (Amherst: University of Massachusetts Press, 1992), contains an excellent analysis of how Apess and other New England Indians were affected by race, class, and politics during the antebellum period but is very narrowly focused.

The most general study that provides very little detail but a useful overview of the entire region from King Philip's War to 1985 is Laura E. Conkey, Ethel Boissevain, and Ives Goddard, "Indians of Southern New England and Long Island: Late Period," in *Smithsonian Handbook of North American Indians*, ed. William C. Sturtevant, vol. 15: *Northeast*, ed. Bruce G. Trigger (Washington, D.C.: Smithsonian Institution, 1978), 177–89. Another very general piece that passes lightly through the nineteenth century is Constance Crosby, "The Algonkian Spiritual Landscape," in *Algonkians of New England: Past and Present*, ed. Peter Benes (Boston: Boston University Press, 1993), 35–41. Ironically, the oldest study of more than one tribe within a large area is also the most detailed: John Deforest, *History of the Indians of Connecticut, from the Earliest Known Period to 1850* (Hartford: William Jason Hamersley 1851). But Deforest's study is limited by his nineteenth-century assumptions and prejudices, and he did not consider the issues that interest modern scholars—including this work.

A few studies of individual tribes or communities include developments during the nineteenth century. Mashpee is particularly well studied: Mark A. Nicholas, "Mashpee Wampanoags of Cape Cod, the Whalefishery, and Seafaring's Impact on Community Development," *American Indian Quarterly* 26 (2002): 165–97; Jack Campisi, *The Mashpee Indians: Tribe on Trial* (Syracuse, N.Y.: Syracuse University Press, 1991), Francis G. Hutchins, *Mashpee: The Story of Cape Cod's Indian Town* (West Franklin, N.H.: Amarta Press, 1979); Russell M. Peters, *The Wampanoags of Mashpee* (Somerville, Mass.: Indian Spiritual and Cultural Training Council, 1987). Nicholas's study of the effects of the whaling trade on Mashpee is particularly noteworthy. In addition to O'Connell's work on Apess, there are a number of studies of the Mashpee revolt of 1833–1834: my "'We, as a tribe, will rule ourselves': Mashpee's Struggle for Autonomy, 1745–1840," in *Reinterpreting New England Indians and the Colonial Experience*, eds. Colin Calloway and Neal Salisbury (Boston: Colonial Society of Massachusetts, 2003), 299–340; Karim Tiro, "Denominated 'SAVAGE': Methodism, Writing, and Identity in the Works of William Apess, A Pequot," *American Quarterly* 48 (1996): 653–79; Kim McQuaid, "William Apes, Pequot: An Indian Reformer in the Jackson Era," *New England Quarterly* 50 (1977): 605–25; and Donald M. Nielsen, "The Mashpee Indian Revolt of 1833," *New England Quarterly* 58 (1985): 400–20.

During the early seventeenth century, the Wampanoag tribe linked many Native communities on Martha's Vineyard and Cape Cod and along Buzzard's Bay (modern southeastern Massachusetts). Those social and cultural links continued among the surviving villages after King Philip's War, including the larger communities of Mashpee and Gay Head on the Vineyard, even as the villages became more like independent tribes. Four studies examine the Wampanoags in the context of individual communities as well as a regional culture and kinship network. Silverman's *Faith and Boundaries* is the most recent, detailed, and original, and it focuses on the Vineyard. Laurie Weinstein, *The Wampanoag Indians* (New York: Chelsea House, 1989), is a broadly focused work meant for the general public rather than the specialist, beginning before European contact and ending with revitalization in the 1980s. Somewhat similar is Nathaniel Philbrick's *Abram's Eyes: The Native American Legacy of Nantucket Island* (Nantucket: Mill Hill Press, 1998), which focuses on Nantucket (and contains more details on Indians on the island) but also covers links with groups on the Vineyard and Cape Cod. Philbrick's book includes a wonderful collection of nineteenth-century photographs of Indians, some of which I also reproduce in this book. Quite different is the multivolume genealogical study by Jerome Segel and R. Andrew Pierce, *The Wampanoag Genealogical History of Martha's Vineyard, Massachusetts*. Volume 1 (Baltimore: Genealogical Publishing, 2003) provides an excellent historical overview and genealogical details of individuals and families into the early eighteenth century.

The Mashantucket Pequot tribe was the first to establish a casino in the region and has used part of the proceeds to establish a historical library and museum, which has hosted a series of conferences and various works on the tribe (and Indians in the region generally). Most notable is Laurence M. Hauptman and James D. Wherry, eds., *The Pequots in Southern New England: The Rise and Fall of an American Indian Nation* (Norman: University of Oklahoma Press, 1990), containing Kevin McBride, "Historical Archaeology of the Mashantucket Pequots, 1637–1900: A Preliminary Analysis," 96–116; and Jack Campisi, "Emergence of the Mashantucket Pequot Tribe, 1637–1975," 117–40. Campisi's article provides extensive details from petitions during this period. McBride has a slightly updated piece, "'Ancient and Crazie': Pequot Lifeways during the Historic Period," in Benes, *Algonkians of New England*, 63–75. The Schaghticoke in western Connecticut has not been as successful or lucky, but Trudie Lamb Richmond has begun revitalizing the history of her tribe; see "A Native Perspective of History: The Schaghticoke Nation, Resistance and Survival," in *Enduring Traditions: The Native Peoples of New England*, ed. Laurie Weinstein (Westport, Conn.: Bergin and Garvey, 1994), 103–22.

There are three surveys of Narragansett history that include brief overviews of the nineteenth century: Paul A. Robinson, "A Narragansett History from 1000 B.P. to the Present," in Weinstein, *Enduring Traditions*, 79–91; Paul R. Campbell and Glenn W. LaFantosie, "Scattered to the Winds of Heaven: Narragansett Indians 1676–1880," *Rhode Island History* 37, no. 3 (1978): 66–83; and William S. Simmons, "Narragansett," in *Smithsonian Handbook of North American Indians*, vol. 15: *Northeast*, 190–97 (which includes only about 120 words on the nineteenth century).

Two short studies have examined Nipmuc communities and families, focusing on kinship connections and persistence despite many generations of intermarriage and assimilation: Donna Keith Baron, J. Edward Hood, and Holly V. Izard, "They Were Here All Along: The Native American Presence in Lower-Central New England in the Eighteenth and Nineteenth Centuries," *William and Mary Quarterly*, 3rd ser., 53 (1996): 561–86; and Thomas Doughton, "Unseen Neighbors: Native Americans of Central Massachusetts, A People Who Had 'Vanished'," in *After King Philip's War: Presence and Persistence in Indian New England*, ed. Colin Calloway (Hanover, N.H.: University Press of New England, 1997), 207–31. Holly Izard has also written an outstanding biography of a Nipmuc descendant, "Hepsibeth Hemenway's Portrait: A Native American Story," *Old-Time New England* (1999): 49–75, connecting Hepsibeth—who lived in the growing city of Worcester, Massachusetts, and gained local fame as a wedding-cake maker—to the larger picture of Nipmuc history and life in the area.

The Bureau of Indian Affairs has issued a series of reports, generally titled "Evidence for Proposed Finding," for tribes that have applied for federal recognition; in southern New England, this has included the Narragansetts, Mohegans, Golden Hill Paugussetts, Eastern Pequots (two different groups both claiming rights to that tribal identity), Schaghticoke, [Hassanamisco] Nipmuc Nation, and Webster/Dudley Band of Chaubunagungamaug Nipmuck. The more recent proposed findings tend to be more thorough, but they were produced as part of a political process and not meant as scholarly works; they contain little to no analysis of the significance of these tribes, changes and developments within the communities, or their relationships with other tribes or the larger region.

A few studies focus on particular aspects of Indian life in southern New England. In the mid-eighteenth century, New Englanders became more interested in the remnants of Native tribes in the region, and began recording their folklore and mythology; these stories provide important revelations about Indian culture and values in the period. The best collection and analysis of this material is William S. Simmons, *Spirit of the New England Tribes: Indian History and Folklore, 1620–1984* (Hanover, N.H.: University Press of New England, 1986). Jane Van Norman Turano, "Taken from Life: Early Photographic Portraits of New England Algonkians, ca. 1845–1865" in Benes, *Algonkians of New England*, 121–43, includes various photos and the painting of Martha Simon I used in this book. Indian slavery and servitude has also attracted considerable interest lately. Other recent studies of southern New England that carry the story into the early republic are Ruth Wallis Herndon and Ella Wilcox Sekatau, "Colonizing the Children: Indian Youngsters in Servitude in Early Rhode Island," in Calloway and Salisbury, *Reinterpreting New England Indians*, 137–73; Nicholas, "Mashpee Wampanoags"; David Silverman, "The Impact of Indentured Servitude on the Society and Culture of Southern New England Indians," *New England Quarterly* 74 (2001): 622–66. Both studies carefully analyze the effects of servitude on individuals, families, and communities; they also connect Indians to English traditions of indentured labor, the development of slavery in the colonies and its form in New England, and concerns of race and emancipation after the Revolution.

Recent scholarship on racial perceptions and prejudice has included a particular interest in the effects of emancipation in the North, most notably John W. Sweet, *Bodies Politic: Negotiating Race in the American North, 1730–1830* (Baltimore: Johns Hopkins University Press, 2003); and Joanne Melish, *Disowning Slavery: Gradual Emancipation and "Race" in New England, 1780–1860* (Ithaca, N.Y.: Cornell University Press, 1998). Sweet also examines how Indians and blacks viewed their racial identities and characteristics during this period, and relationships between members of the two groups and whites. Because both Indians and Africans were a small minority in the region, often intermarried, and were both singled out in law and custom, a few studies have analyzed perceptions of Indians as well as blacks, and the frequent confusion among whites regarding racial identification and treatment of individuals. See my articles "The Indian's Pedigree (1794): Indians, Folklore, and Race in Southern New England," *William and Mary Quarterly*, 3d ser., 61 (July 2004):

519–36, and "Shifting Boundaries of Race and Ethnicity: Indian-Black Intermarriage in Southern New England, 1760–1880," *Journal of American History* 85 (1998): 466–501; Ruth Wallis Herndon and Ella Wilcox Sekatau, "The Right to a Name: The Narragansett People and Rhode Island Officials in the Revolutionary Era," in Calloway, *After King Philip's War*, 114–43; and George B. Kirsch, "Jeremy Belknap and the Problem of Blacks and Indians in Early America," *Historical New Hampshire* 34 (1979): 202–22. Other significant studies of the shifts in how whites viewed Indians during the colonial period and nineteenth century include Alden Vaughan, "From White Man to Redskin: Changing Anglo-American Perceptions of the American Indian, *American Historical Review* 87 (October 1982): 842–43, 949; Reginald Horsman, *Race and Manifest Destiny: The Origins of American Racial Anglo-Saxonism* (Cambridge, Mass.: Harvard University Press, 1981); and Robert F. Berkhofer Jr., *The White Man's Indian: Images of the American Indian from Columbus to the Present* (New York: Knopf, 1978).

Although relatively little has been published on Indians in nineteenth-century New England, the scholarship on the development of the African American community in the region is substantial and expanding. James O. Horton and Lois E. Horton have together published a number of significant books, including *In Hope of Liberty: Culture, Community and Protest Among Northern Free Blacks, 1700–1860* (New York: Oxford University Press, 1997); and *Black Bostonians: Family Life and Community Struggle in the Antebellum North* (New York: Oxford University Press, 1979). Other recent studies include Nick Salvatore, *We All Got History: The Memory Books of Amos Webber* (New York: Times Books, 1996); W. Jeffrey Bolster, *Black Jacks: African American Seamen in the Age of Sail* (Cambridge, Mass.: Harvard University Press, 1996); and Robert J. Cottrol, *The Afro-Yankees: Providence's Black Community in the Antebellum Era* (Westport, Conn.: Greenwood, 1982). Lamont D. Thomas, *Rise to Be a People: A Biography of Paul Cuffe* (Urbana: University of Illinois Press, 1986), presents the African American side of the Cuffe family; my article "Shifting Boundaries" looks at how that family represents the shifting boundary between blacks and Indians in the region.

I found recent studies on the development of African American identity particularly useful, including Sweet, *Bodies Politic*; Kazuteru Omori, "Race-Neutral Individualism and Resurgence of the Color Line: Massachusetts Civil Rights Legislation, 1855–1895," *Journal of American Ethnic History* 21 (2002): 32–51; Patrick Rael, *Black Identity and Black Protest in the Antebellum North* (Chapel Hill: University of North Carolina Press, 2002); Scott Hancock, "The Elusive Boundaries of Blackness: Identity Formation in Antebellum Boston," *Journal of Negro History* 84 (1999): 115–129; and Elizabeth R. Bethel, *The Roots of African-American Identity: Memory and History in Free Antebellum Communities* (New York: St. Martin's, 1997).

A focus of this book is the intersection of race and class, and a number of studies have looked at these issues in southern New England: Sweet, *Bodies Politic*; Lois E. Hornon, "From Class to Race in Early America: Northern Post-Emancipation Racial Reconstruction," in *Race and the Early Republic: Racial Consciousness and Nation-Building in the Early Republic*, ed. Michael A. Morrison and James Brewer Stewart (Lanham, Md.: Rowman and Littlefield, 2002), 55–74; Ruth Herndon, *Unwelcome Americans: Living on the Margins in Early New England* (Philadelphia: University of Pennsylvania Press, 2001);

James Brewer Stewart, "The Emergence of Racial Modernity and the Rise of the White North, 1790–1840," *Journal of the Early Republic* 18 (1998): 181–217; and Melish, *Disowning Slavery*. Two studies that are more theoretical are Eric Lott, *Love and Theft: Black-face Minstrelsy and the American Working Class* (New York: Oxford University Press, 1993); and David Roediger, *The Wages of Whiteness: Race and the Making of the American Working Class* (New York: Verso, 1991). Of these works, only Sweet considers Indians. There are hints in various documents of racially mixed communities that existed in the nineteenth century on the geographic, social, and economic margins of New England towns. The best study is of the Lighthouse in northwest Connecticut, whose inhabitants considered themselves Narragansetts: Kenneth Feder, *A Village of Outcasts: Historical Archaeology and Documentary Research on the Lighthouse Site* (Mountain View, Calif.: Mayfield, 1994).

A larger concern to historians is how the rise of industry and new developments in commerce and agriculture reshaped society, culture, and the class structure in America. The best general work is Jack Larkin, *The Reshaping of Everyday Life, 1790–1840* (New York: Harper and Row, 1988). A recent debate has been whether an identifiable "market revolution" took place in the nineteenth century; see in particular Charles Sellers, *The Market Revolution: Jacksonian America, 1815–1846* (New York: Oxford University Press, 1991), and Melvyn Stokes and Stephen Conway, eds. *The Market Revolution in America: Social, Political, and Religious Expressions, 1800–1880* (Charlottesville: University of Virginia Press, 1996). Works that focus on the socioeconomic and cultural shifts in southern New England include Winifred B. Rothenberg, *From Market-Places to a Market Economy: The Transformation of Rural Massachusetts, 1750–1850* (Chicago: University of Chicago Press, 1992); Christopher Clark, *The Roots of Rural Capitalism: Western Massachusetts, 1780–1860* (Ithaca, N.Y.: Cornell University Press, 1990). One of the most intriguing studies is Karen V. Hansen, *A Very Social Time: Crafting Community in Antebellum New England* (Berkeley: University of California Press, 1994), which sees commonalities among working-class people that transcended racial differences. All these studies have helped me to understand and interpret the lives and experiences of Indians in the region between 1780 and 1880.

Religious-based social-reform movements, often with political overtones, were an important part of American society and culture in the early nineteenth century. This was particularly true in southern New England, where the ties between state, society, and church remained stronger than elsewhere in the country. This study includes a close look at the links between Indians and radical evangelical movements, and an examination of the relationships between tribes and white reformers in the second quarter of the century. Most historians of religion avoid issues of class, but one work explicitly examines how the fault lines between the "lower" and "better" sorts were reflected and influenced by religious differences: Mark S. Schantz, *Piety in Providence: Class Dimensions of Religious Experience in Antebellum Rhode Island* (Ithaca, N.Y.: Cornell University Press, 2000). An opposing study that is also useful is Jonathan D. Sassi, *A Republic of Righteousness: The Public Christianity of Post-Revolutionary New England Clergy* (New York: Oxford University Press, 2003), which sees unity of purpose among the clergy in their reform efforts, despite widening divisions between orthodox, liberals, and evangelicals. Neither book gives much attention to racial or ethnic minorities, although Schantz does note that blacks overwhelmingly favored radical evangelical congregations.

Toward midcentury, as Indians in southern New England became more "amalgamated" (due to exogamous marriages) and assimilated (due to the reform movements), politicians began to discuss terminating the laws that separated tribal reserves and communities in each of the states. Such a change was viewed as ending crippling handicaps and bringing equality and opportunity to a backward people, and served as a prelude to shifts in federal Indian policy after 1880. Only two articles have been published on termination and Native responses: Ann Marie Plane and Gregory Button, "The Massachusetts Indian Enfranchisement Act: Ethnic Contest in Historical Context, 1849–1869," *Ethnohistory* 40 (1993): 594–606, which focuses on tensions between Natives and African American men in Mashpee; and Ethel Boissevant, "The Detribalization of the Narragansett Indians: A Case Study," *Ethnohistory* 3 (1956): 225–45.

Little has been written on the decades following termination in these Indian communities. Melissa J. Fawcett, *Medicine Trail: The Life and Lessons of Gladys Tantaquidgeon* (Tucson: University of Arizona Press, 2000), uses interviews with the Mohegan elder to sketch her biography and the story of the tribe from the 1890s to the present. Earl Mills has published his memoirs of Mashpee, which includes many photographs of people and places in the community from the late nineteenth century through the present; Earl Mills Sr. and Alicja Mann, *Son of Mashpee: Reflections of Chief Flying Eagle, a Wampanoag* (North Falmouth, Mass.: Word Studio, 1996). James Clifford, "Identity in Mashpee," in *The Predicament of Culture: Twentieth-Century Ethnography, Literature, and Art*, (Cambridge, Mass.: Harvard University Press, 1988), 277–346, is an "upstream" piece that uses testimony by Mashpees and whites in a trial in the 1970s to examine questions of exogamous marriages, assimilation, and identity in the tribe in the twentieth century. The emergence of the pan-Indian movement and tribal revitalization in the 1920s and 1930s is the subject of Ann McMullen, "What's Wrong with This Picture? Context, Conversion, Survival, and the Development of Regional Native Cultures and Pan-Indianism in Southeastern New England," in Weinstein, *Enduring Traditions*, 123–150.

In some ways, the most useful scholarship on this period has been studies of baskets and other crafts made by Indians in southern New England. The first, and still outstanding, work is Frank G. Speck's *Eastern Algonkian Block-Stamp Decoration: A New World Original or an Acculturated Art*, Research Series no. 1, Archaeological Society of New Jersey, State Museum (Trenton, 1947), which included Eva L. Butler's historical study "Some Early Indian Basket Makers of Southern New England." Speck was the first anthropologist to take New England Indians seriously as surviving Native communities, beginning fieldwork among the Mohegans around 1900 and expanding his studies to the entire region. His other important works include *Territorial Subdivisions and Boundaries of the Wampanoag, Massachusett, and Nauset Indians*, Indian Notes and Monographs, no. 44 (New York: Museum of the American Indian, Heye Foundation, 1928); "Native Tribes and Dialects of Connecticut, A Mohegan-Pequot Diary," *Bureau of American Ethnology Annual Report, no. 43: 1925–1926* (Washington, D.C.: GPO, 1928), 205–282; J. Dynley Prince and Frank G. Speck, "The Modern Pequots and Their Language," *American Anthropologist*, n.s., 5, no. 2 (1903): 193–212.

Ann McMullen, an anthropologist at the National Museum of the American Indian, has continued this research into Indian basket making, finding more baskets and more information about who made each, and connecting that information with patterns in the baskets to reveal aspects of Native history often not visible in written documents. Her publications include "Native Basketry, Basketry Styles, and Changing Group Identity in Southern New England," in Benes, *Algonkians of New England*, 76–88; "Talking Through Baskets: Meaning, Production, and Identity in the Northern Woodlands," in *Basketmakers: Meaning and Form in Native American Baskets*, ed. Linda Mowat, Howard Murphy, and Penny Dransalt (Oxford: P. H. Rivers Museum, University of Oxford, 1992), 18–35; and editing, with Russell G. Handsman and Joan Lester, *A Key into the Language of Woodsplint Baskets* (Washington, Conn.: American Indian Archaeological Institute, 1987). *A Key into the Language* includes an outstanding introduction by McMullen and Handsman; Sarah P. Turnbaugh and William A. Turnbaugh, "Weaving the Woods: Tradition and Response in Southern New England Splint Basketry"; Trudie Lamb Richmond, "Spirituality and Survival in Schaghticoke Basket-Making"; Gladys Tantaquidgeon and Jayne G. Fawcett, "Symbolic Motifs on Painted Baskets of the Mohegan-Pequot"; and McMullen's own "Looking for People in Woodsplint Basketry Decoration." All focus on the nineteenth century and contain a wealth of information on individuals, families, communities, including photographs of people and their baskets. Within the narrow context of Indian basket makers, they analyze connections with the larger society and culture, relations among tribes, communities, and families, and shifts (both local and regional) over time.

Index

Numbers in **boldface** denote illustrations.

DATE DUE

Demco, Inc. 38-293